ACCURSED
VOLUME 4

WRITTEN BY:
PHIL HESTER

THE DARKNESS CREATED BY:
MARC SILVESTRI, GARTH ENNIS
AND DAVID WOHL

published by
Top Cow Productions, Inc.
Los Angeles

THE DARKNESS
ACCURSED VOLUME 4

written by: **Phil Hester**

"**Bog:** part 1 & 2" issue #80-81

pencils by: **Phil Hester**

inks by: **Ande Parks**

colors by: **Sakti Yumono, Arif Prianto**
& **Admira Wijaya** of IFS

"**The Hunting Party** part 1 & 2" issue #82-83

pencils by: **Michael Broussard**

inks by: **Rick Basaldua**

colors by: **Arif Prianto** of IFS

"**The Three Deaths of Jackie Estacado**" issue #84

line art by: **Whilce Portacio**

colors by: **Arif Prianto** of IFS

"**Shadows and Flame**" issue #1

written by: **Rob Levin**

line art by: **Jorge Lucas**

colors by: **Felix Serrano**

letters: **Troy Peteri**

Jackie's caption font by: **Dave Lanphear**

MATURE AUDIENCE
GRAPHIC CONTENT
SOME MATERIAL MAY NOT
BE SUITABLE FOR CHILDREN

For Top Cow Productions, Inc.:
Marc Silvestri - Chief Executive Officer
Matt Hawkins - President and Chief Operating Officer
Filip Sablik - Publisher
Phil Smith - Managing Editor
Atom Freeman - Director of Sales & Marketing
Bryan Rountree - Assistant to the Publisher
Christine Dinh - Marketing Assistant
Mark Haynes - Webmaster
Kyle Economou - Intern

for **image** comics
publisher:
Eric Stephenson

888-COMIC-BOOK

to find the comic shop
nearest you call:
1-888-COMICBOOK

Want more info? check out:
www.topcow.com and **www.thetopcowstore.com**
for news and exclusive Top Cow merchandise!

For this edition Cover art by:
Michael Broussard,
Sunny Gho & Eko Puteh of IFS

For this edition
Book Design and Layout by:
Phil Smith

Original Series Editors:
Filip Sablik & Phil Smith

The Darkness: Accursed volume 4 Trade Paperback
December 2010. FIRST PRINTING. ISBN: 978-1-60706-194-6
Published by Image Comics Inc. Office of Publication: 2134 Allston Way, Second Floor Berkeley,
CA 94704. $14.99 U.S.D. Originally published in single magazine form as The Darkness volume
3 issues #80-84 and The Darkness: Shadows and Flame #1. © 2010 Top Cow Productions, Inc.

editor's note: Starting with *The Darkne*
volume 3 issue #11 *The Darkness* seri
issues are numbered in a "Lega[c]
numbering system. The Legacy numb
denotes the total number of issu
published regardless of volume numbe

TABLE OF CONTENTS

IN✛R⊕DUC✛I⊕N

I grew up going to Freedonia Funnies on Tustin Ave, in the city of Orange. My Dad would take me there once a week. I'd rifle through the older bins...*Batman, Superboy* (needed to relate to the teen version first), *Wild Dog, Submariner, Spiderman, The Punisher, Green Lantern, Dare Devil, Ronin*... I bought more for the story-telling in pictures than the words when I was a kid. Being drawn to the Jim Aparo cover of *Batman: a Death in the Family. Green Lantern* number 85 with *Green Arrow*, the "Ward is a JUNKIE!" issue. Frank Miller's *Ronin*, violence and sex, all Frank Miller style. Comic books had taken over my third birthday. A *Hulk* T-shirt for my 3rd birthday cake photo, a *Superman* cake at 6 and a *Batman* birthday party at 12. I dreamed about what it would be like to be an alien here on earth that was "fast as a speeding bullet", or a young man who could walk on walls and swing around a major city on a web. I never dreamed about being Jackie Estacado. Even with its release in 1996, I didn't come across *The Darkness* until I was in my late twenties. And even in my late twenties, knowing everything I do about capes and masks and the allure/greatness/curse of the superhero/comic hero, I still have no interest in being Jackie Estacado. But I will take reading about his life and business over any of my boyhood heroes.

Who wants to carry all that Jackie is on their shoulders? To understand the power and strength Jackie wields is only to understand the desires and wants Jackie can never achieve (children, love with a woman not created by him, peace). Sure, he is a son of a bitch that kills and feeds off his power, but can he really have all that AND a code of morality? Yes, he has a code, and a curse, and he is as complex, if not more than the classic heroes or villains in all of literature.

A better version of the Green Lantern. More vengeful than the Dark Knight. And the only man able to find solace and power in the depths of a turkey shit well (*The Darkness: Accursed* Volume 2), Phil Hester and the all star art team (Hester with Ande Parks passing the torch to Mike Broussard who hands it over to Whilce Portacio) continue to take Jackie on a journey of dark enlightenment, having him embrace who he is and what he is capable of doing. And all with some sense of morality in his assassin's creed. Yes, Jackie Estacado is a good guy. Maybe not a good guy but we are rooting for him. A wolf in sheep's clothing? Better a Devil in a wolves coat.

The following volume in the story of Jackie Estacado finds him teaming up with an unsavory bunch, rediscovering his power in the dark, repeatedly destroying that multiplying motherfuckin' Sovereign, and in the end reconnecting with an old "friend", and has become one of my favorite so far.

--Milo Ventimiglia
August 2010

Milo Ventimiglia is best know for his television and film roles including *Heroes, Gilmore Girls, Rocky Balboa,* and *Armored.* With producing partner Russ Cundiff, Ventimiglia co-founded DiVide Pictures. Since 2007, DiVide Pictures has produced a number of projects including *It's a Mall World* and *Ultradome.* DiVide Pictures as also co-produced two comic series in conjunction with Top Cow Productions in *Rest* and *Berserker.*

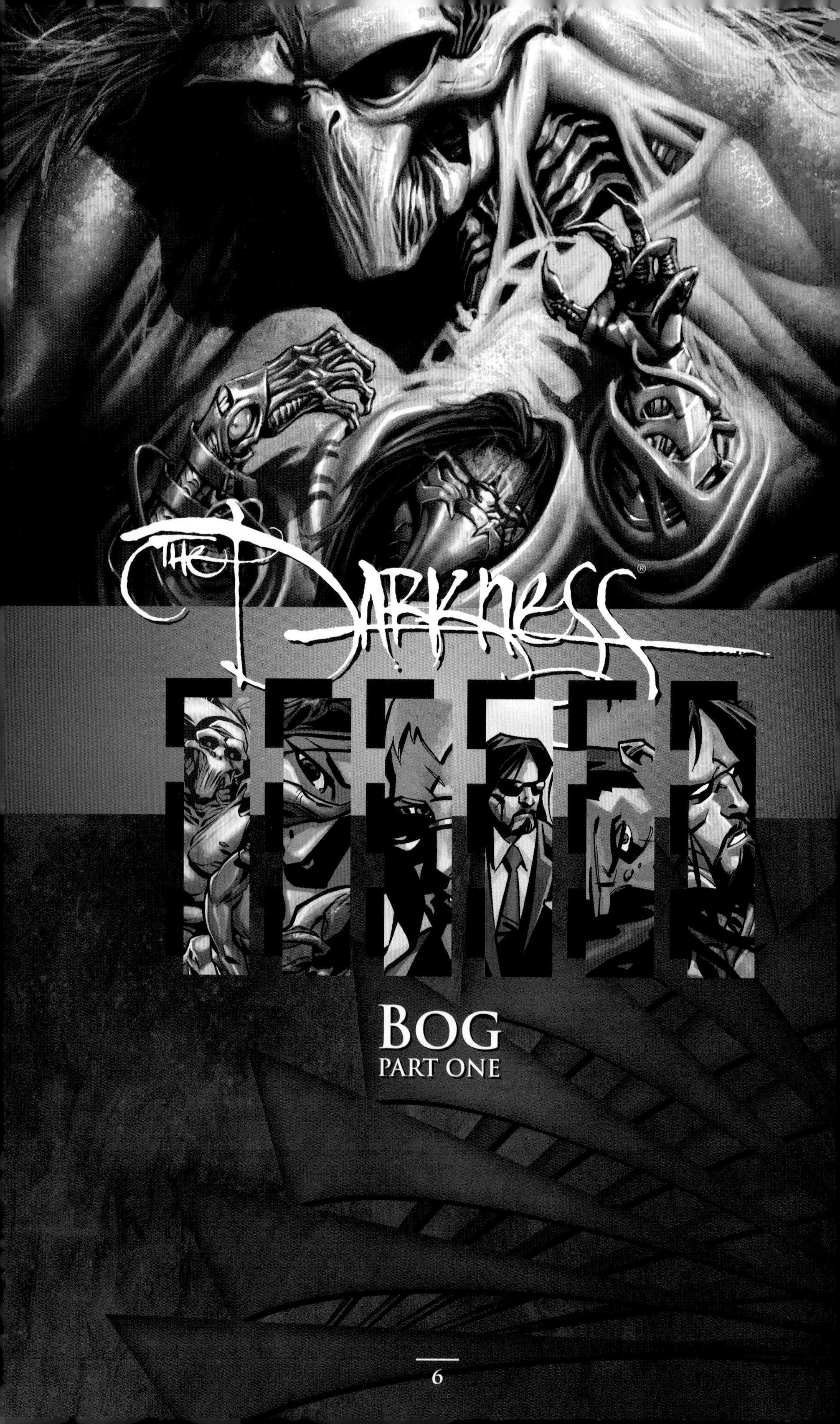
THE DARKNESS®

BOG
PART ONE

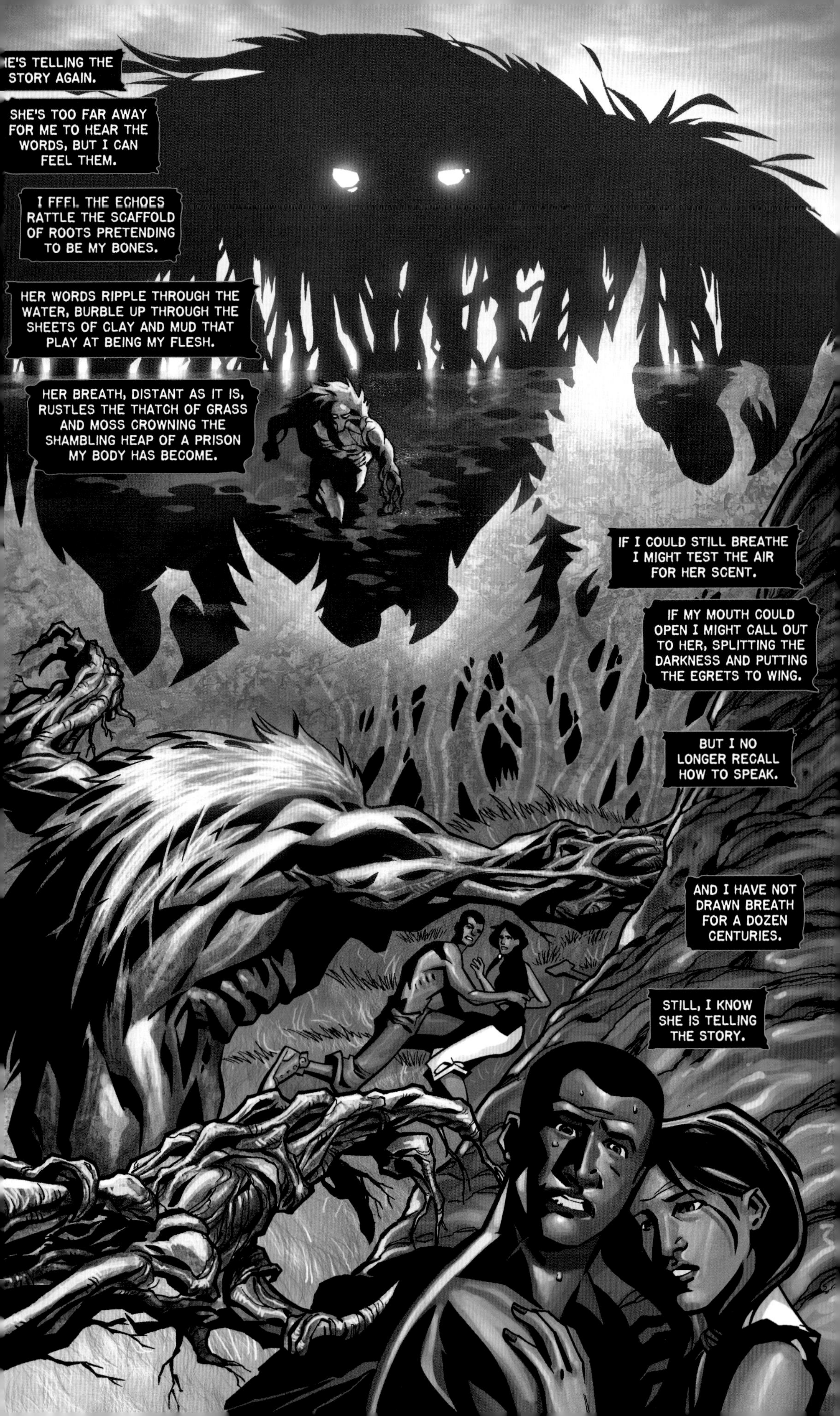
E'S TELLING THE STORY AGAIN.
SHE'S TOO FAR AWAY FOR ME TO HEAR THE WORDS, BUT I CAN FEEL THEM.
I FEEL THE ECHOES RATTLE THE SCAFFOLD OF ROOTS PRETENDING TO BE MY BONES.
HER WORDS RIPPLE THROUGH THE WATER, BURBLE UP THROUGH THE SHEETS OF CLAY AND MUD THAT PLAY AT BEING MY FLESH.
HER BREATH, DISTANT AS IT IS, RUSTLES THE THATCH OF GRASS AND MOSS CROWNING THE SHAMBLING HEAP OF A PRISON MY BODY HAS BECOME.
IF I COULD STILL BREATHE I MIGHT TEST THE AIR FOR HER SCENT.
IF MY MOUTH COULD OPEN I MIGHT CALL OUT TO HER, SPLITTING THE DARKNESS AND PUTTING THE EGRETS TO WING.
BUT I NO LONGER RECALL HOW TO SPEAK.
AND I HAVE NOT DRAWN BREATH FOR A DOZEN CENTURIES.
STILL, I KNOW SHE IS TELLING THE STORY.

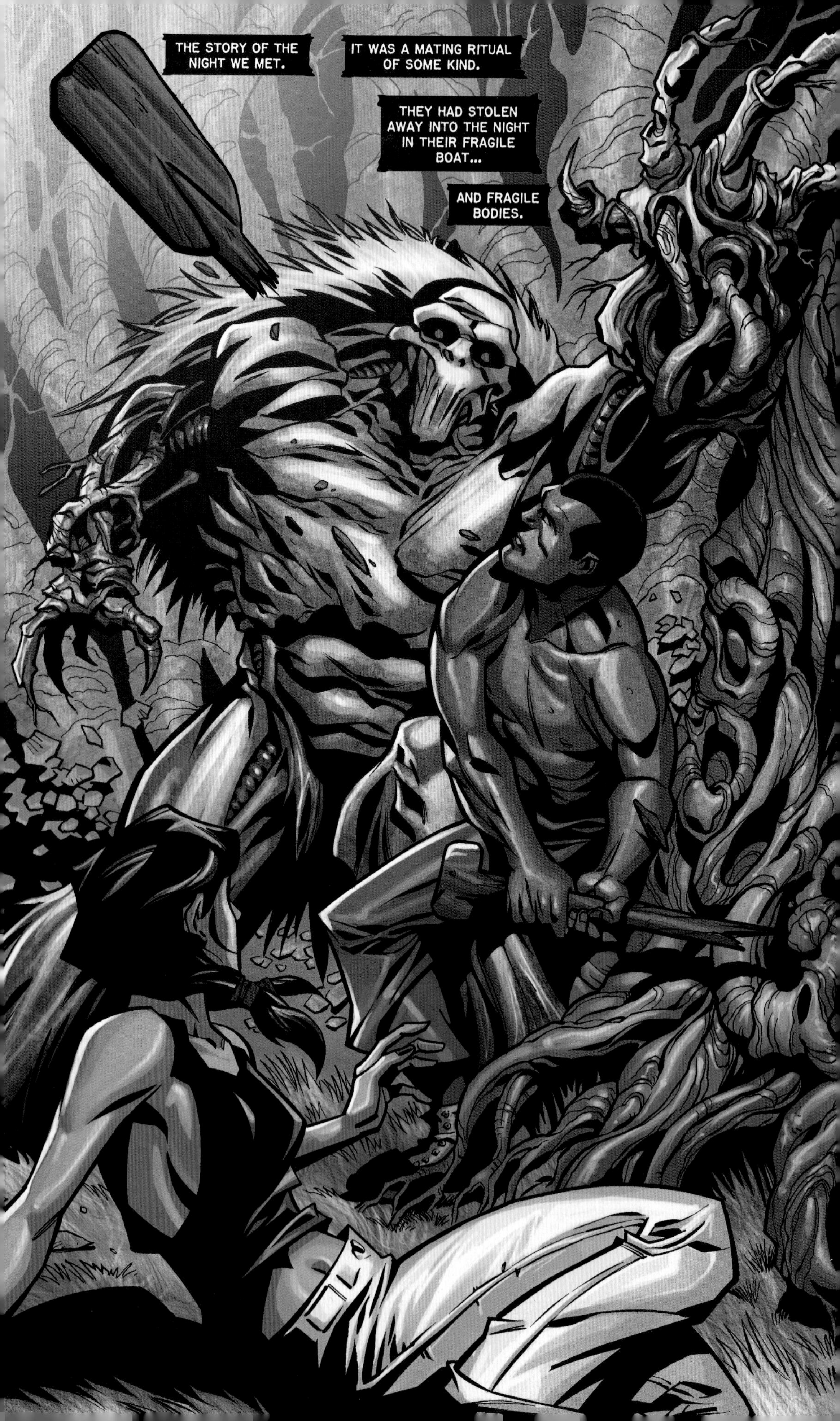
THE STORY OF THE NIGHT WE MET.
IT WAS A MATING RITUAL OF SOME KIND.
THEY HAD STOLEN AWAY INTO THE NIGHT IN THEIR FRAGILE BOAT...
AND FRAGILE BODIES.

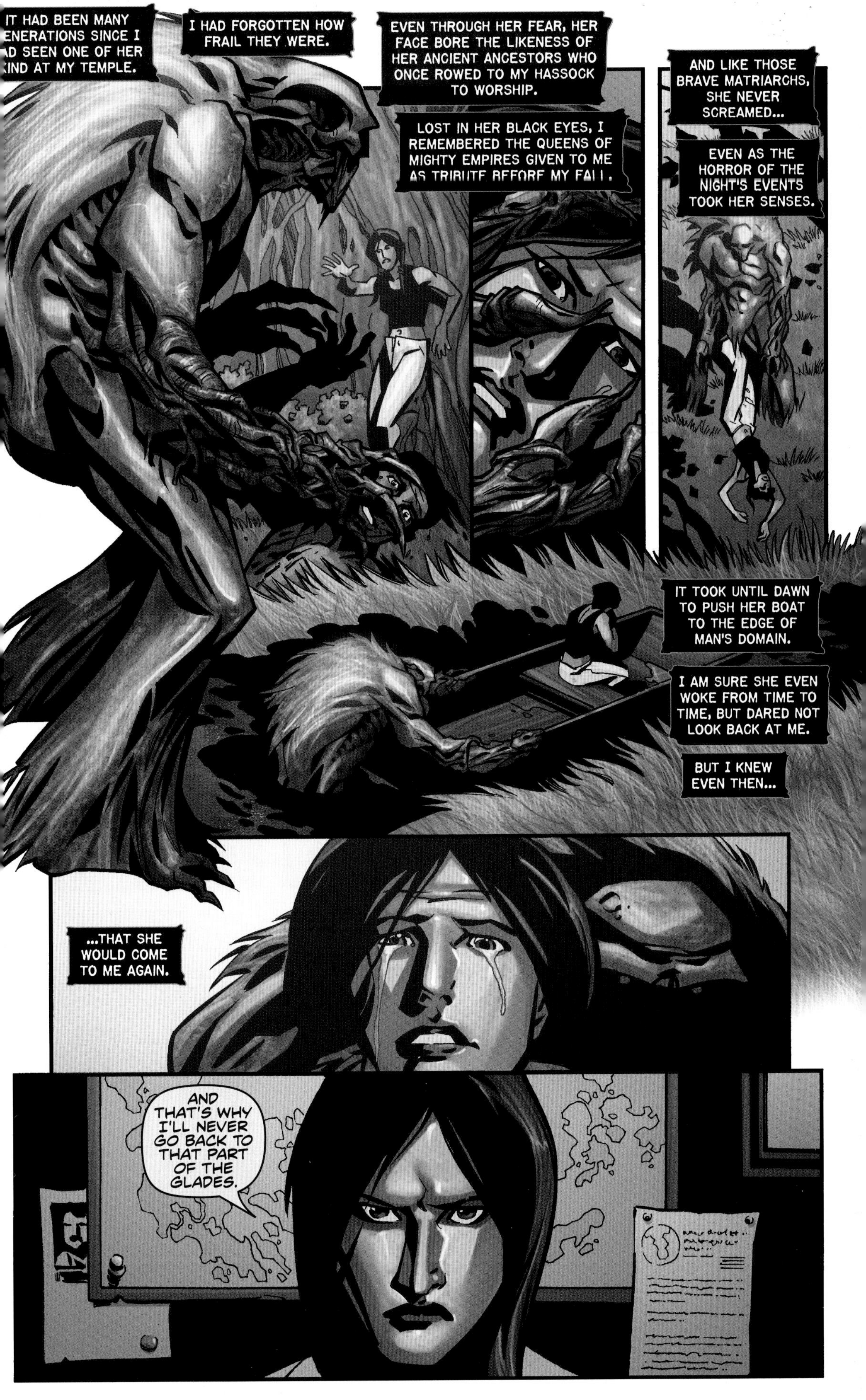
IT HAD BEEN MANY ENERATIONS SINCE I AD SEEN ONE OF HER IND AT MY TEMPLE.
I HAD FORGOTTEN HOW FRAIL THEY WERE.
EVEN THROUGH HER FEAR, HER FACE BORE THE LIKENESS OF HER ANCIENT ANCESTORS WHO ONCE ROWED TO MY HASSOCK TO WORSHIP.
LOST IN HER BLACK EYES, I REMEMBERED THE QUEENS OF MIGHTY EMPIRES GIVEN TO ME AS TRIBUTE BEFORE MY FALL.
AND LIKE THOSE BRAVE MATRIARCHS, SHE NEVER SCREAMED...
EVEN AS THE HORROR OF THE NIGHT'S EVENTS TOOK HER SENSES.
IT TOOK UNTIL DAWN TO PUSH HER BOAT TO THE EDGE OF MAN'S DOMAIN.
I AM SURE SHE EVEN WOKE FROM TIME TO TIME, BUT DARED NOT LOOK BACK AT ME.
BUT I KNEW EVEN THEN...
...THAT SHE WOULD COME TO ME AGAIN.
AND THAT'S WHY I'LL NEVER GO BACK TO THAT PART OF THE GLADES.

TOWNSFOLK CLAIM TO CATCH A GLIMPSE OF HIM FROM TIME TO TIME, CALL HIM "BOG".

BUT I'M THE ONLY WHO'S SEEN HIM FACE TO FACE. TRUST ME, YOU DON'T WANT THAT EXPERIENCE.

A SIMPLE "NO" WOULD SUFFICE.

I FAIL TO SEE THE NEED TO INVENT A GHOST STORY TO REFUSE OUR BUSINESS.

YOUR KIND ARE PERSISTENT. I WANT THERE TO BE NO QUESTION.

OUR KIND?

OIL MEN. WHO ELSE WEARS FOUR HUNDRED DOLLAR SHOES TO A SWAMP?

YOUNG LADY, WE'RE ARCHEOLOGISTS.

RIGHT. ARCHEOLOGISTS WHO JUST HAPPEN TO HAVE THEIR EYES ON THE LAST BIT OF TRIBAL LAND STILL UNCLAIMED BY PETROLEUM COMPANIES.

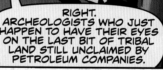

CYPRESS ECOTOURS
FANBOAT RENTAL
CANDACE CYPRESS, PROPRIETOR

TELL YOUR BOSSES TO SPACE THESE TRIPS OUT A LITTLE. ONE OF YOUR THUGS WAS HERE JUST LAST WEEK.

ONE MORE TIME -- WE'RE A PRIVATE ARCHEOLOGY TEAM WORKING ON BEHALF OF A EUROPEAN COLLECTOR WHO BELIEVES HE HAS DOCUMENTATION OF A PRE-COLUMBIAN PERSIAN EXPEDITION TO THE AMERICAS.

HIS DISCOVERY HINTS AT THE POSSIBLE RUINS OF A TEMPLE JUST MILES FROM HERE.

MIGHT AS WELL BE A MILLION MILES FROM HERE.

I'M THE ONLY FANBOAT COMPANY THE TRIBE ALLOWS, AND MY TOURS DON'T GO ANYWHERE NEAR THAT AREA.

AND IF WE WERE TO GO OUT ON OUR OWN?

KNOCK YOURSELVES OUT. I'M SURE YOU KNOW TWO OF YOUR FIELD GEOLOGISTS TRIED THAT LAST YEAR. FAR AS WE KNOW THEY'VE NEVER BEEN FOUND.

SO, YOU KNOW -- PACK A LUNCH.

LEAVE ASIDE YOUR ASSUMPTIONS ABOUT OUR INTENTIONS. WE COULD MAKE THE TRIP WORTHWHILE FOR YOU.

VERY WORTHWHILE.

MONEY WON'T WORK. THREATS EITHER. DIDN'T THE LAST TEAM TELL YOU?

MS. CYPRESS--

CALL HIM OFF.

ME?

I'M NOT DUMB. I CAN TELL WHO'S REALLY CALLING THE SHOTS IN THIS ROOM.

TELL HIM, AND ALL YOUR GOONS THAT THEY'RE NEVER GETTING THEIR HANDS ON THAT LAND. BUYING ME OFF, OR EVEN KILLING ME WON'T CHANGE THAT.

THE TRIBAL COUNCIL WILL TURN ON YOU IN A SECOND, EVEN THE ONES ALREADY IN YOUR POCKET.

WE'RE NOT FROM ANY OIL COMPANY. NO ONE'S GOING TO HURT YOU.

DOESN'T MEAN YOU WON'T TRY.

I DON'T WANT TO BE RESPONSIBLE FOR WHAT HAPPENS TO YOU IF YOU DO.

WE JUST WANT TO SEE THE TEMPLE, CANDACE.

HOW--

I-I'M CLOSED. Y'ALL HAVE TO GO NOW.

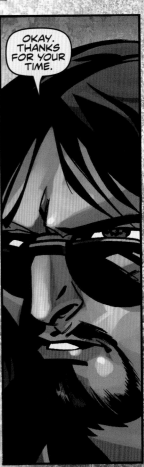

OKAY. THANKS FOR YOUR TIME.

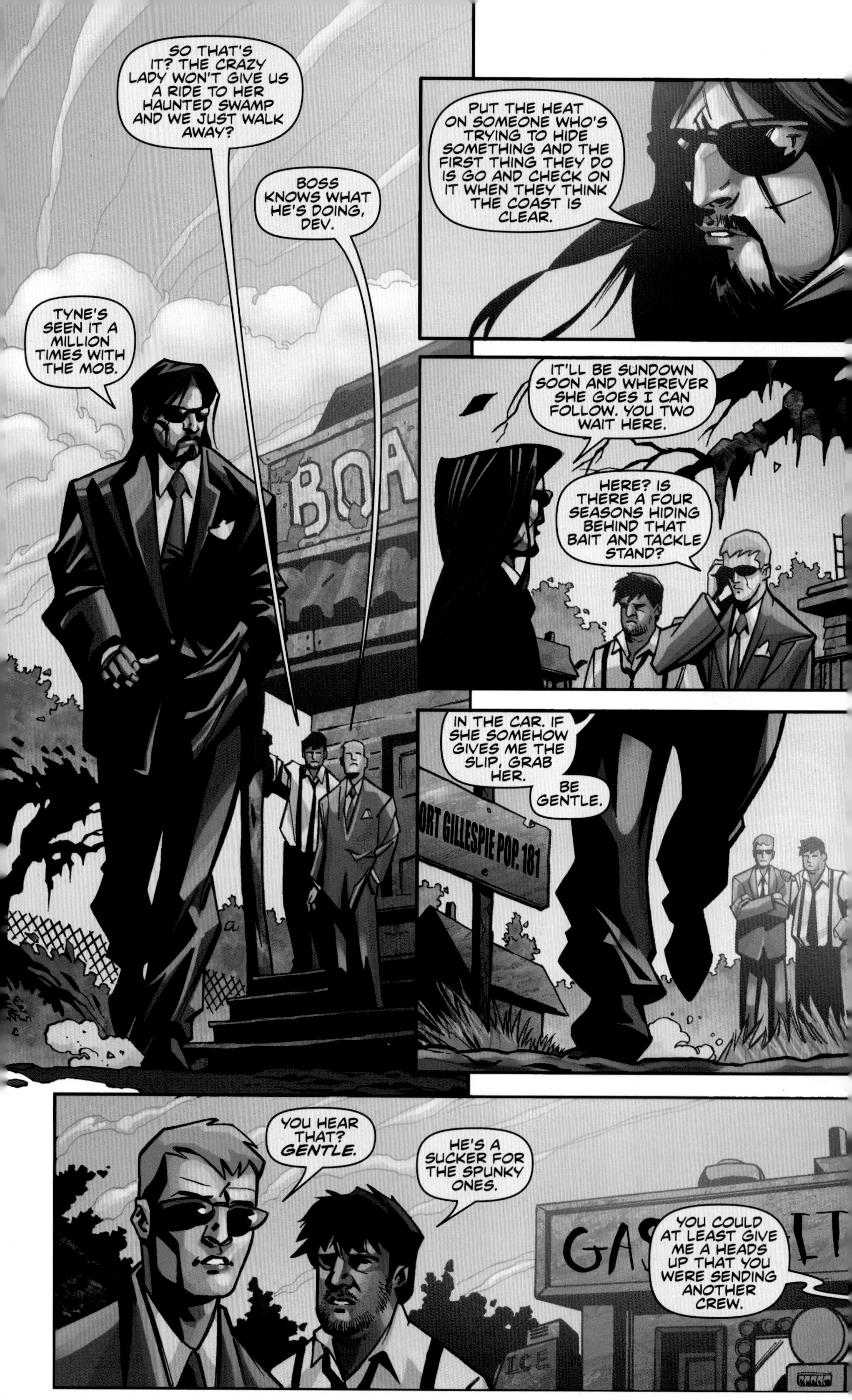
SO THAT'S IT? THE CRAZY LADY WON'T GIVE US A RIDE TO HER HAUNTED SWAMP AND WE JUST WALK AWAY?
BOSS KNOWS WHAT HE'S DOING, DEV.
TYNE'S SEEN IT A MILLION TIMES WITH THE MOB.
BOA
PUT THE HEAT ON SOMEONE WHO'S TRYING TO HIDE SOMETHING AND THE FIRST THING THEY DO IS GO AND CHECK ON IT WHEN THEY THINK THE COAST IS CLEAR.
IT'LL BE SUNDOWN SOON AND WHEREVER SHE GOES I CAN FOLLOW. YOU TWO WAIT HERE.
HERE? IS THERE A FOUR SEASONS HIDING BEHIND THAT BAIT AND TACKLE STAND?
IN THE CAR. IF SHE SOMEHOW GIVES ME THE SLIP, GRAB HER.
BE GENTLE.
ORT GILLESPIE POP. 181
YOU HEAR THAT? *GENTLE*.
HE'S A SUCKER FOR THE SPUNKY ONES.
YOU COULD AT LEAST GIVE ME A HEADS UP THAT YOU WERE SENDING ANOTHER CREW.
ICE

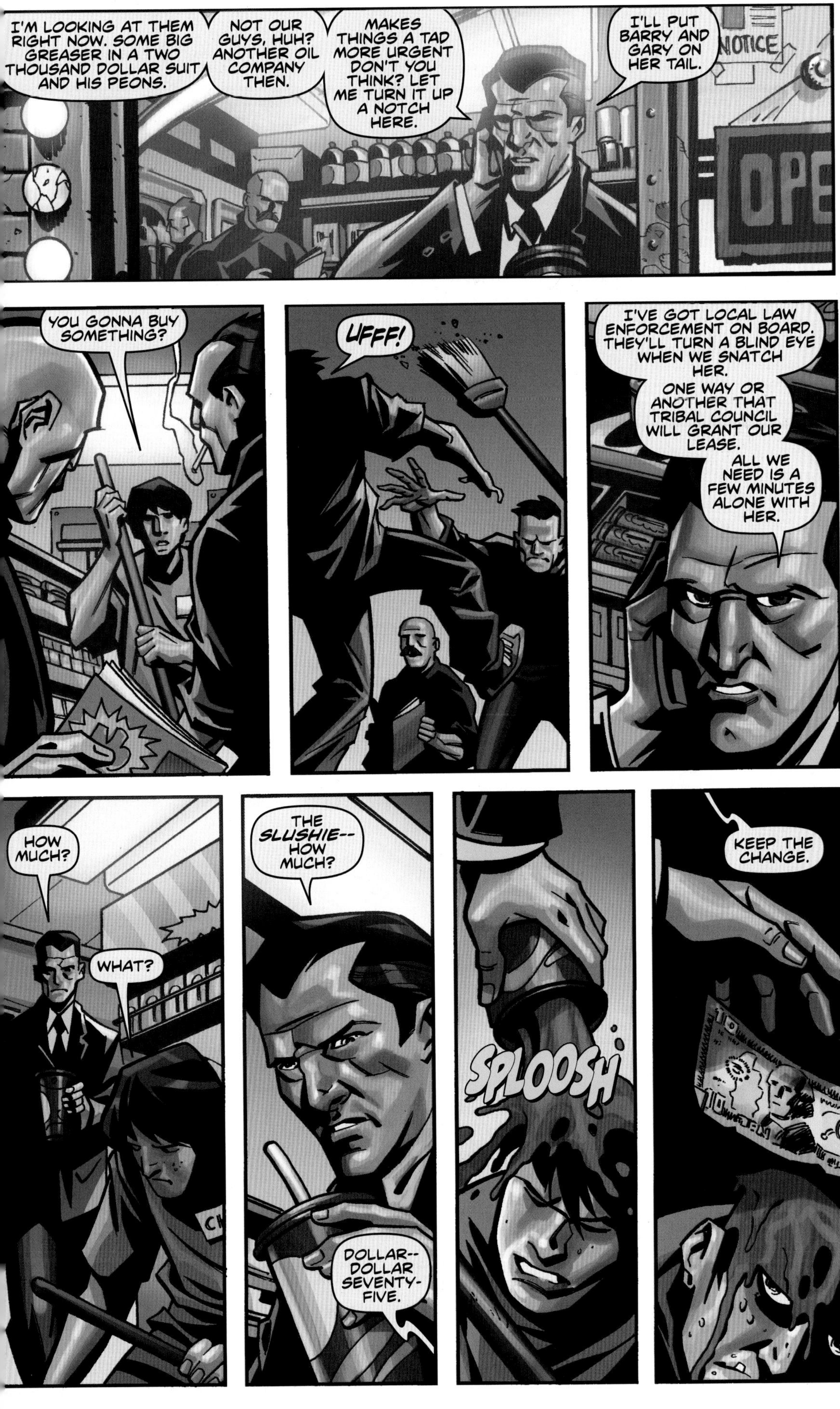
I'M LOOKING AT THEM RIGHT NOW. SOME BIG GREASER IN A TWO THOUSAND DOLLAR SUIT AND HIS PEONS.
NOT OUR GUYS, HUH? ANOTHER OIL COMPANY THEN.
MAKES THINGS A TAD MORE URGENT DON'T YOU THINK? LET ME TURN IT UP A NOTCH HERE.
I'LL PUT BARRY AND GARY ON HER TAIL.
NOTICE
OPE
YOU GONNA BUY SOMETHING?
UFFF!
I'VE GOT LOCAL LAW ENFORCEMENT ON BOARD. THEY'LL TURN A BLIND EYE WHEN WE SNATCH HER.
ONE WAY OR ANOTHER THAT TRIBAL COUNCIL WILL GRANT OUR LEASE.
ALL WE NEED IS A FEW MINUTES ALONE WITH HER.
HOW MUCH?
WHAT?
THE SLUSHIE-- HOW MUCH?
DOLLAR-- DOLLAR SEVENTY-FIVE.
SPLOOSH
KEEP THE CHANGE.

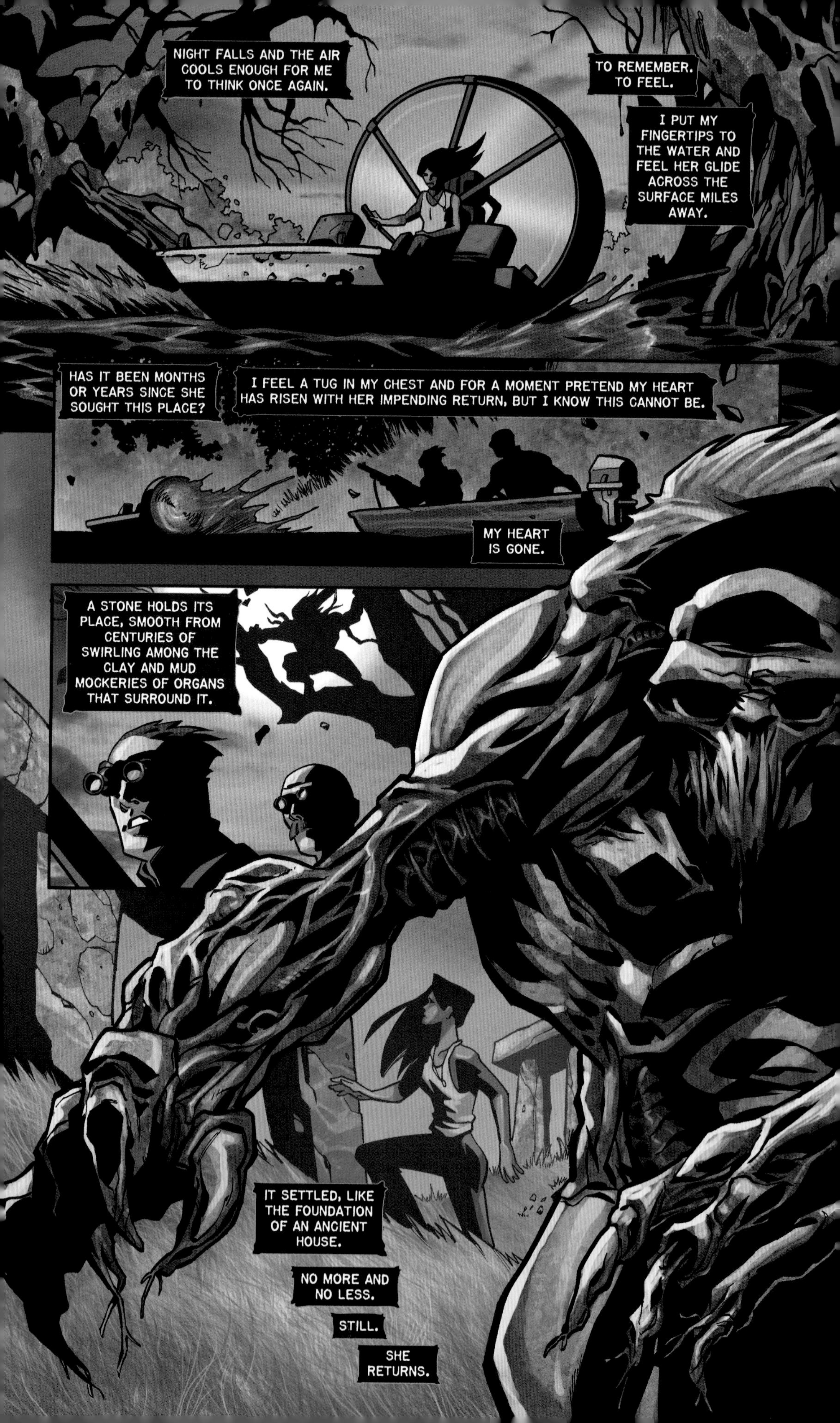
NIGHT FALLS AND THE AIR COOLS ENOUGH FOR ME TO THINK ONCE AGAIN.
TO REMEMBER. TO FEEL.
I PUT MY FINGERTIPS TO THE WATER AND FEEL HER GLIDE ACROSS THE SURFACE MILES AWAY.
HAS IT BEEN MONTHS OR YEARS SINCE SHE SOUGHT THIS PLACE?
I FEEL A TUG IN MY CHEST AND FOR A MOMENT PRETEND MY HEART HAS RISEN WITH HER IMPENDING RETURN, BUT I KNOW THIS CANNOT BE.
MY HEART IS GONE.
A STONE HOLDS ITS PLACE, SMOOTH FROM CENTURIES OF SWIRLING AMONG THE CLAY AND MUD MOCKERIES OF ORGANS THAT SURROUND IT.
IT SETTLED, LIKE THE FOUNDATION OF AN ANCIENT HOUSE.
NO MORE AND NO LESS.
STILL.
SHE RETURNS.

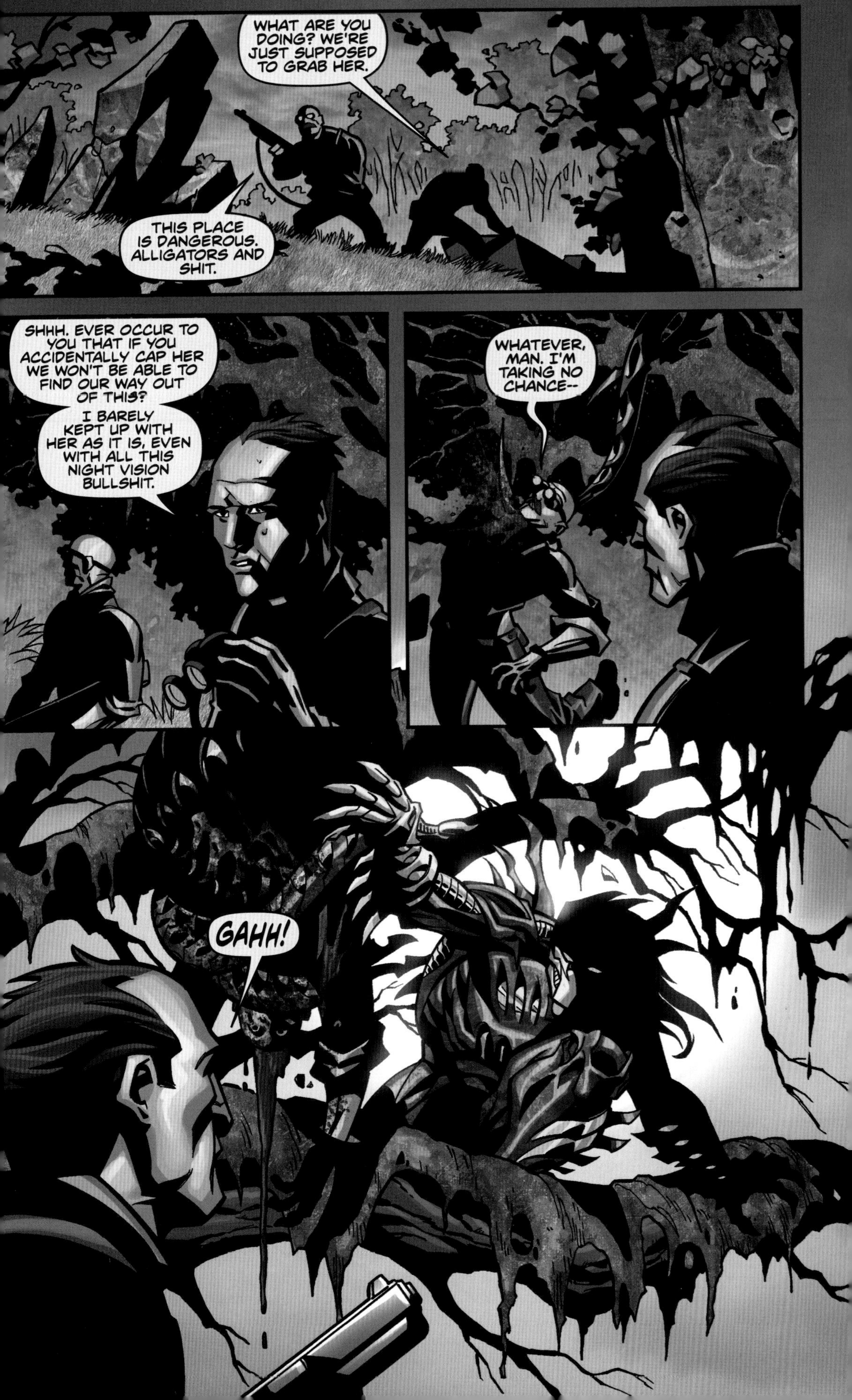
WHAT ARE YOU DOING? WE'RE JUST SUPPOSED TO GRAB HER.
THIS PLACE IS DANGEROUS. ALLIGATORS AND SHIT.
SHHH. EVER OCCUR TO YOU THAT IF YOU ACCIDENTALLY CAP HER WE WON'T BE ABLE TO FIND OUR WAY OUT OF THIS?
I BARELY KEPT UP WITH HER AS IT IS, EVEN WITH ALL THIS NIGHT VISION BULLSHIT.
WHATEVER, MAN. I'M TAKING NO CHANCE--
GAHH!

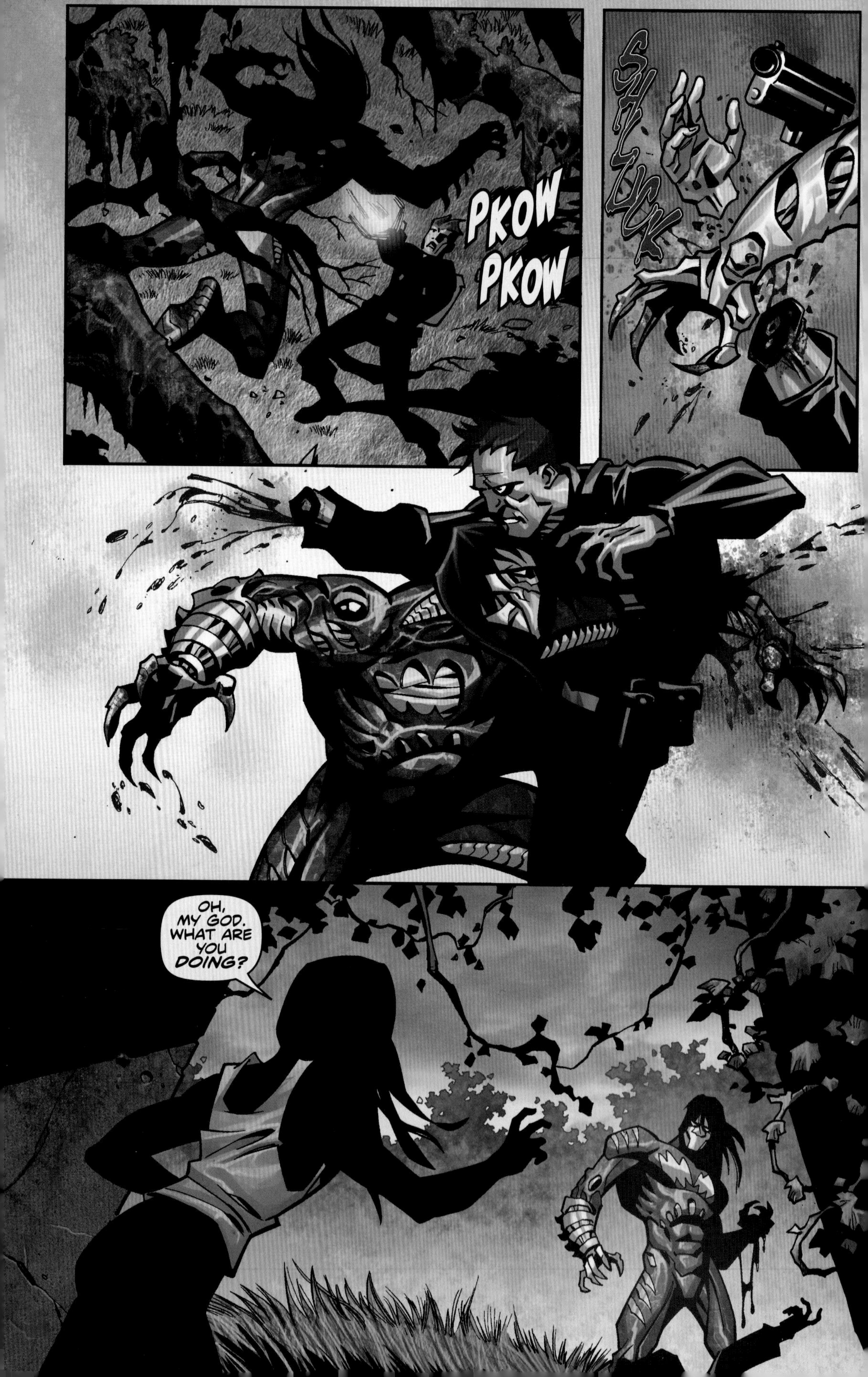
PKOW
PKOW
SHLUCK
OH, MY GOD. WHAT ARE YOU DOING?

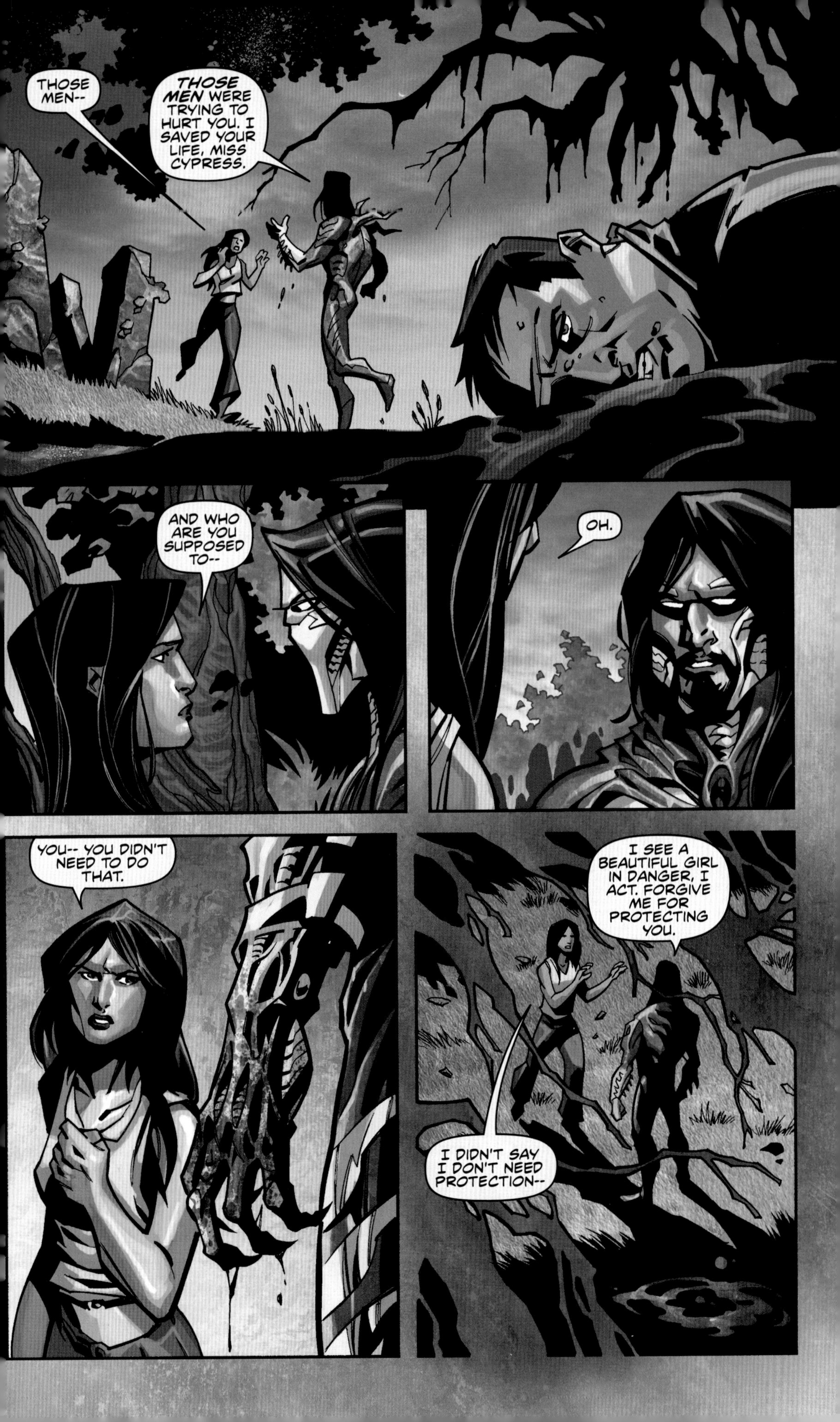
THOSE MEN--
THOSE MEN WERE TRYING TO HURT YOU. I SAVED YOUR LIFE, MISS CYPRESS.
AND WHO ARE YOU SUPPOSED TO--
OH.
YOU-- YOU DIDN'T NEED TO DO THAT.
I SEE A BEAUTIFUL GIRL IN DANGER, I ACT. FORGIVE ME FOR PROTECTING YOU.
I DIDN'T SAY I DON'T NEED PROTECTION--

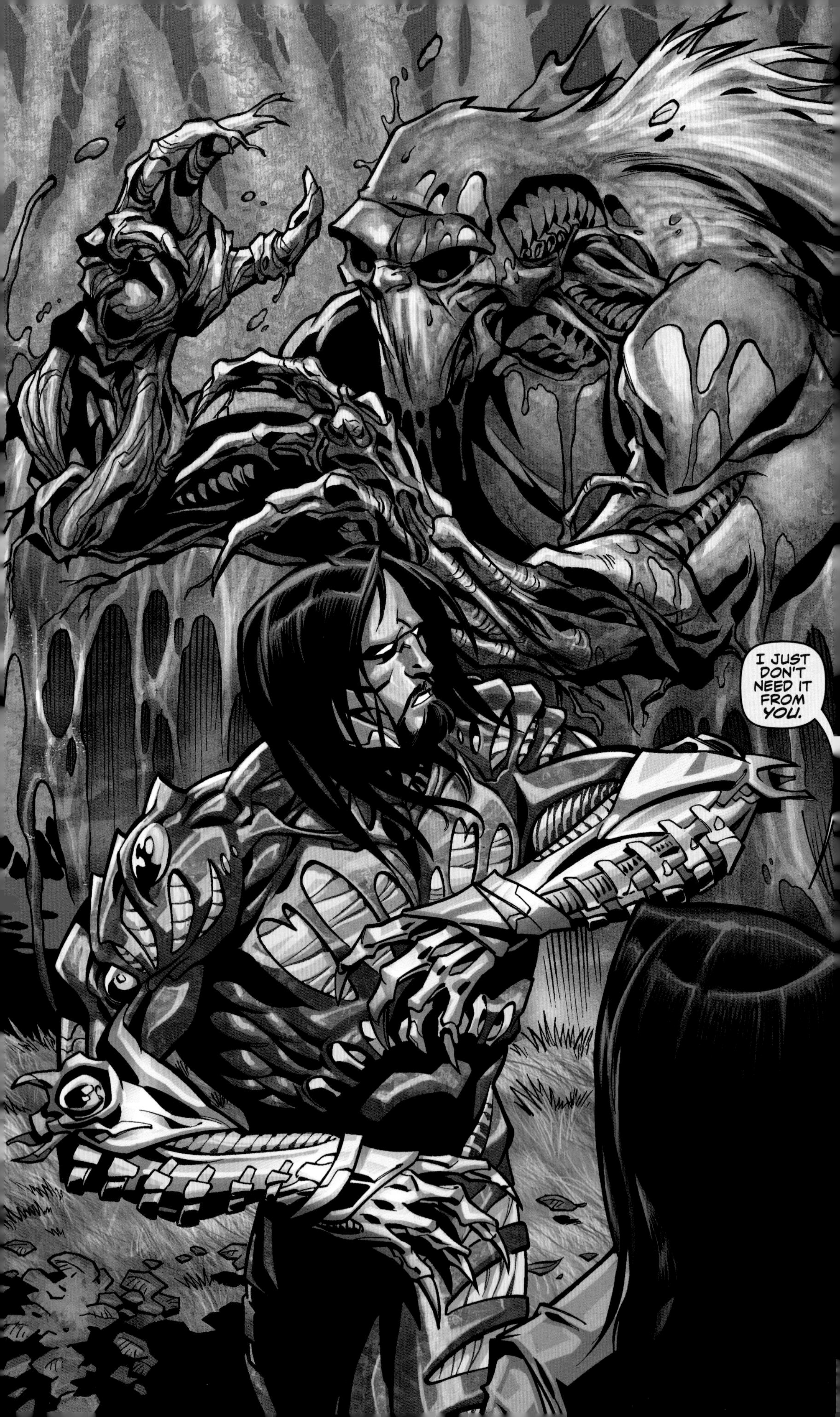
I JUST DON'T NEED IT FROM YOU.

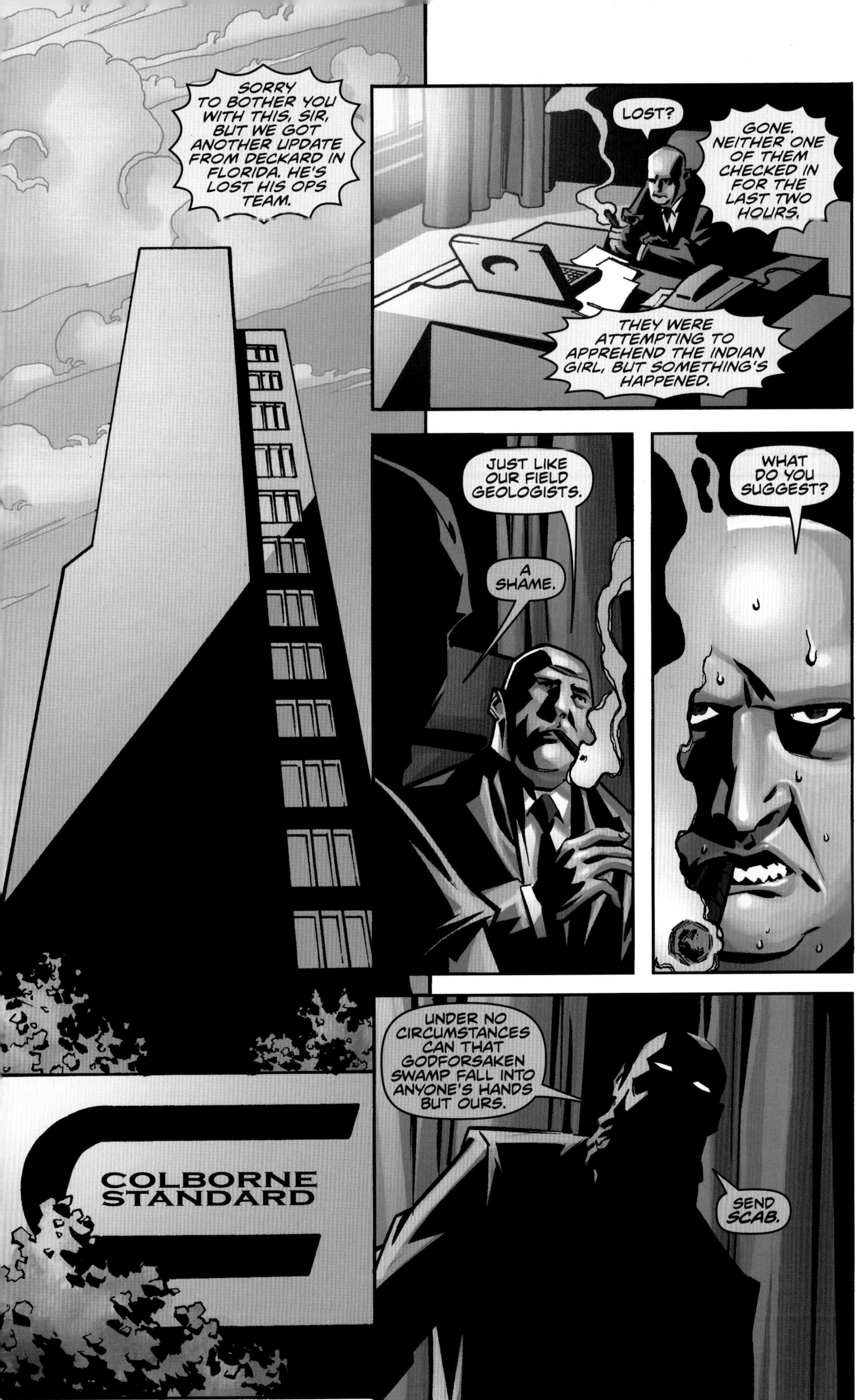
SORRY TO BOTHER YOU WITH THIS, SIR, BUT WE GOT ANOTHER UPDATE FROM DECKARD IN FLORIDA. HE'S LOST HIS OPS TEAM.
LOST?
GONE. NEITHER ONE OF THEM CHECKED IN FOR THE LAST TWO HOURS.
THEY WERE ATTEMPTING TO APPREHEND THE INDIAN GIRL, BUT SOMETHING'S HAPPENED.
JUST LIKE OUR FIELD GEOLOGISTS.
A SHAME.
WHAT DO YOU SUGGEST?
COLBORNE STANDARD
UNDER NO CIRCUMSTANCES CAN THAT GODFORSAKEN SWAMP FALL INTO ANYONE'S HANDS BUT OURS.
SEND SCAB.

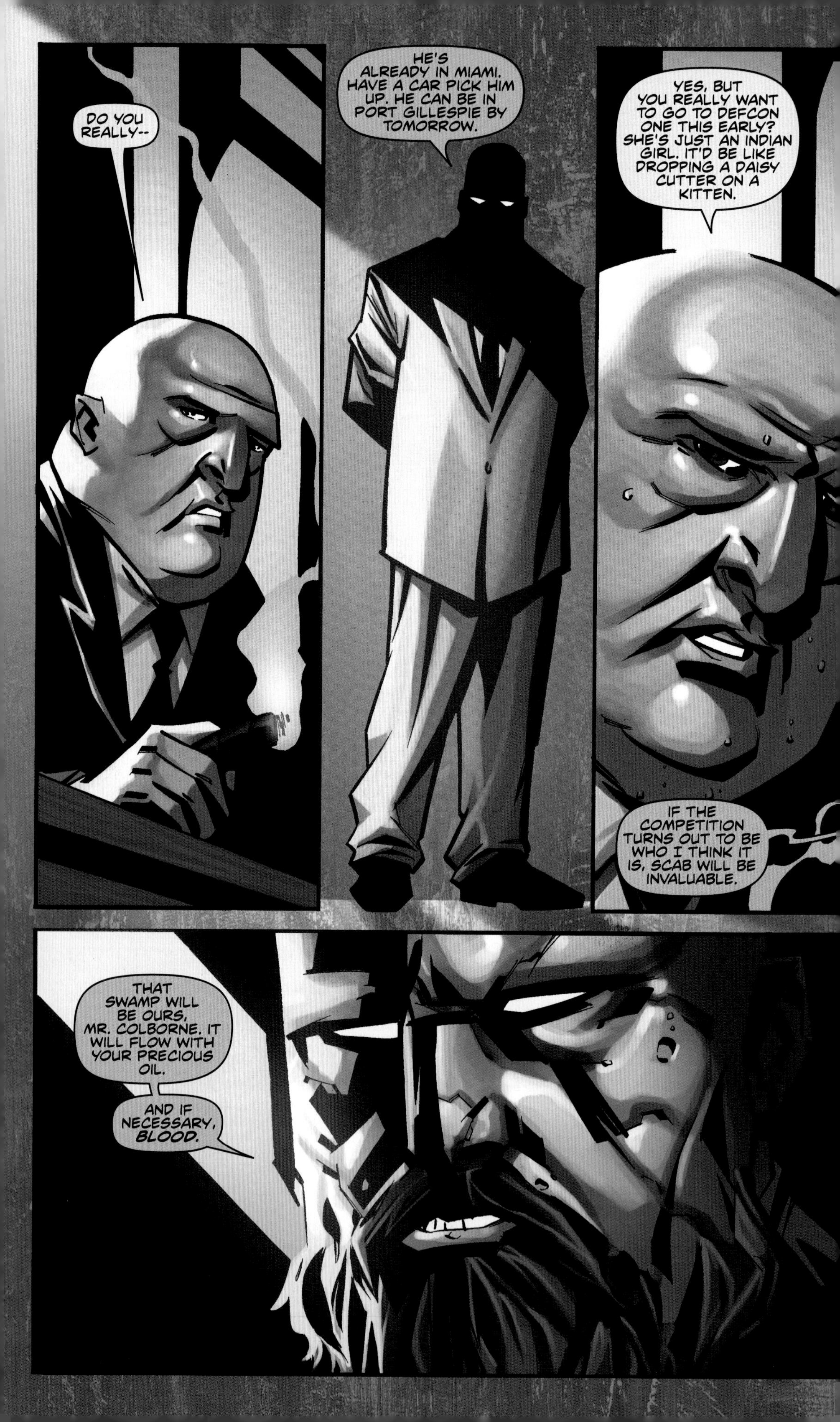
DO YOU REALLY--
HE'S ALREADY IN MIAMI. HAVE A CAR PICK HIM UP. HE CAN BE IN PORT GILLESPIE BY TOMORROW.
YES, BUT YOU REALLY WANT TO GO TO DEFCON ONE THIS EARLY? SHE'S JUST AN INDIAN GIRL. IT'D BE LIKE DROPPING A DAISY CUTTER ON A KITTEN.
IF THE COMPETITION TURNS OUT TO BE WHO I THINK IT IS, SCAB WILL BE INVALUABLE.
THAT SWAMP WILL BE OURS, MR. COLBORNE. IT WILL FLOW WITH YOUR PRECIOUS OIL.
AND IF NECESSARY, BLOOD.

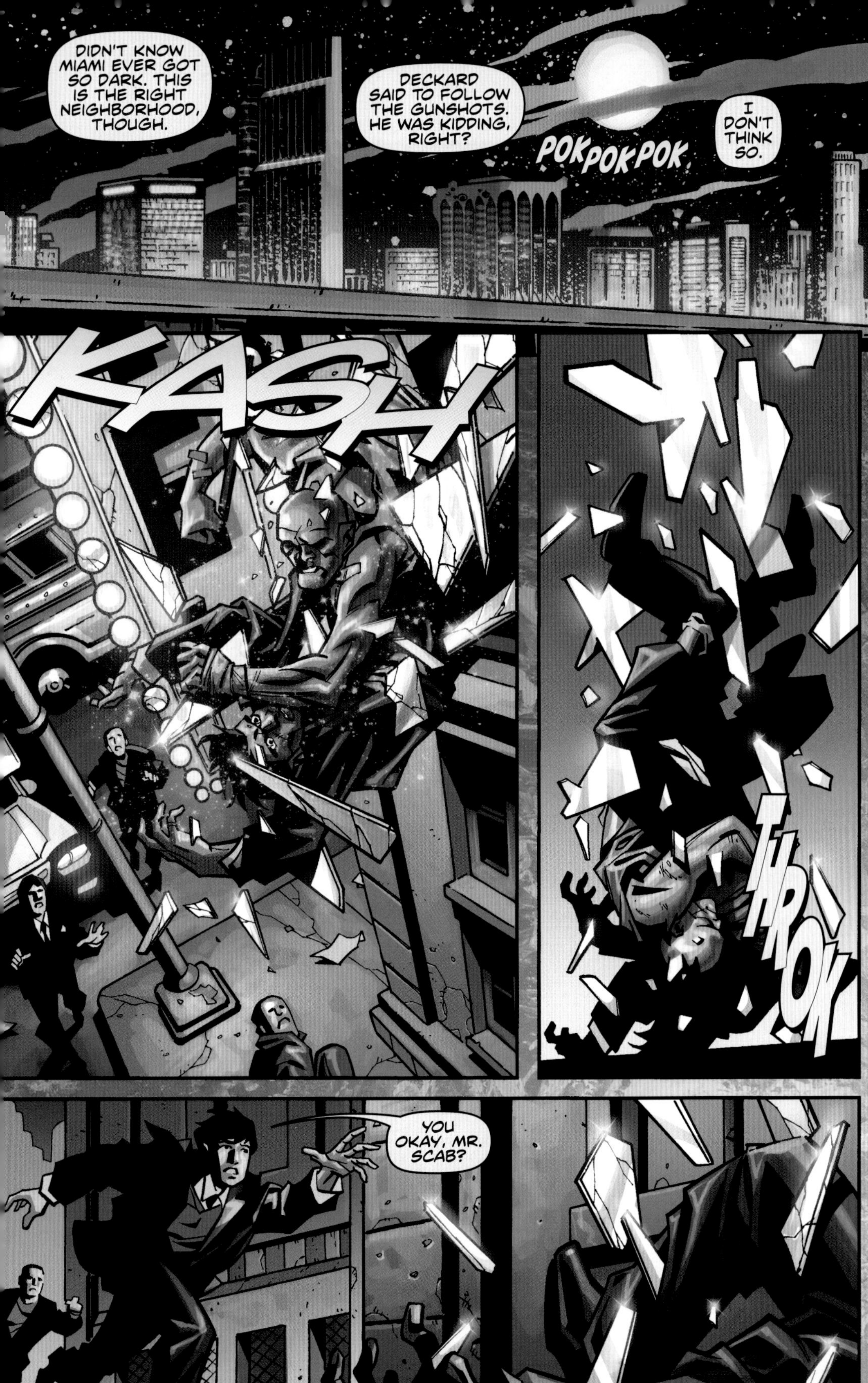
DIDN'T KNOW MIAMI EVER GOT SO DARK. THIS IS THE RIGHT NEIGHBORHOOD, THOUGH.
DECKARD SAID TO FOLLOW THE GUNSHOTS. HE WAS KIDDING, RIGHT?
POKPOKPOK
I DON'T THINK SO.
KASH
THROK
YOU OKAY, MR. SCAB?

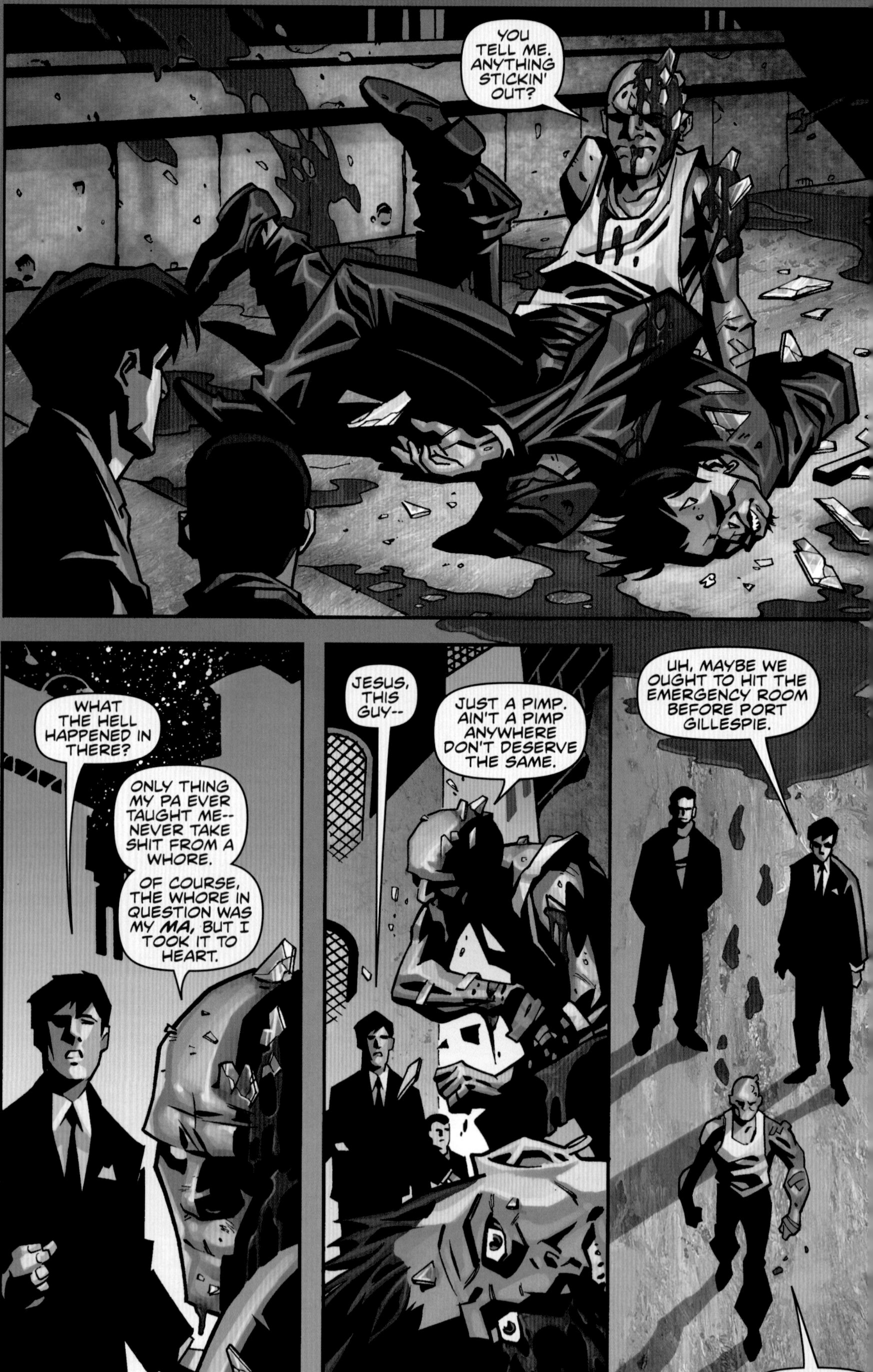
YOU TELL ME. ANYTHING STICKIN' OUT?
WHAT THE HELL HAPPENED IN THERE?
ONLY THING MY PA EVER TAUGHT ME-- NEVER TAKE SHIT FROM A WHORE.
OF COURSE, THE WHORE IN QUESTION WAS MY *MA,* BUT I TOOK IT TO HEART.
JESUS, THIS GUY--
JUST A PIMP. AIN'T A PIMP ANYWHERE DON'T DESERVE THE SAME.
UH, MAYBE WE OUGHT TO HIT THE EMERGENCY ROOM BEFORE PORT GILLESPIE.
FUCK THAT. EITHER YOU GUYS GOT AN LIQUOR?

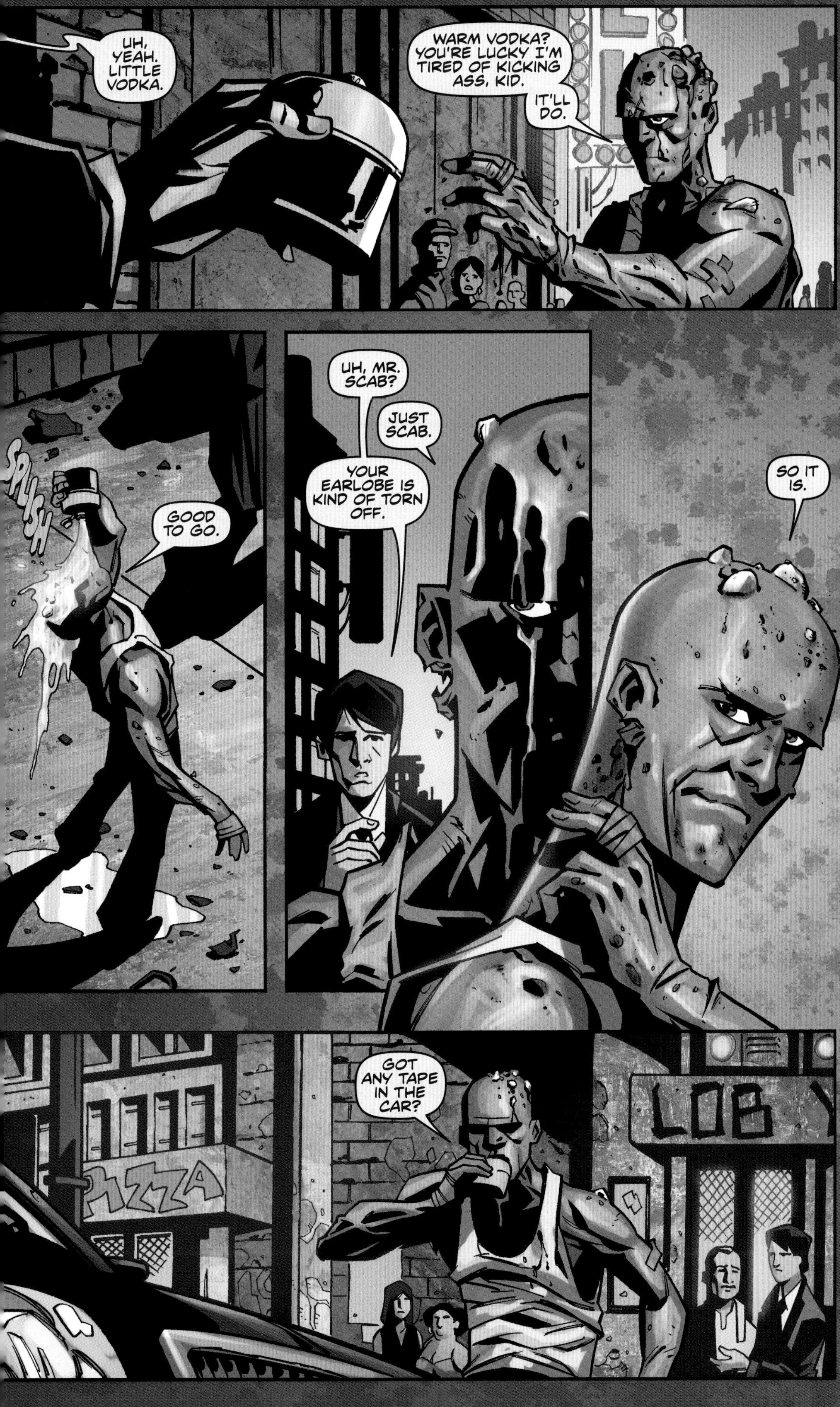
UH, YEAH. LITTLE VODKA.
WARM VODKA? YOU'RE LUCKY I'M TIRED OF KICKING ASS, KID.
IT'LL DO.
SPLISH
GOOD TO GO.
UH, MR. SCAB?
JUST SCAB.
YOUR EARLOBE IS KIND OF TORN OFF.
SO IT IS.
GOT ANY TAPE IN THE CAR?
PIZZA
LOB Y

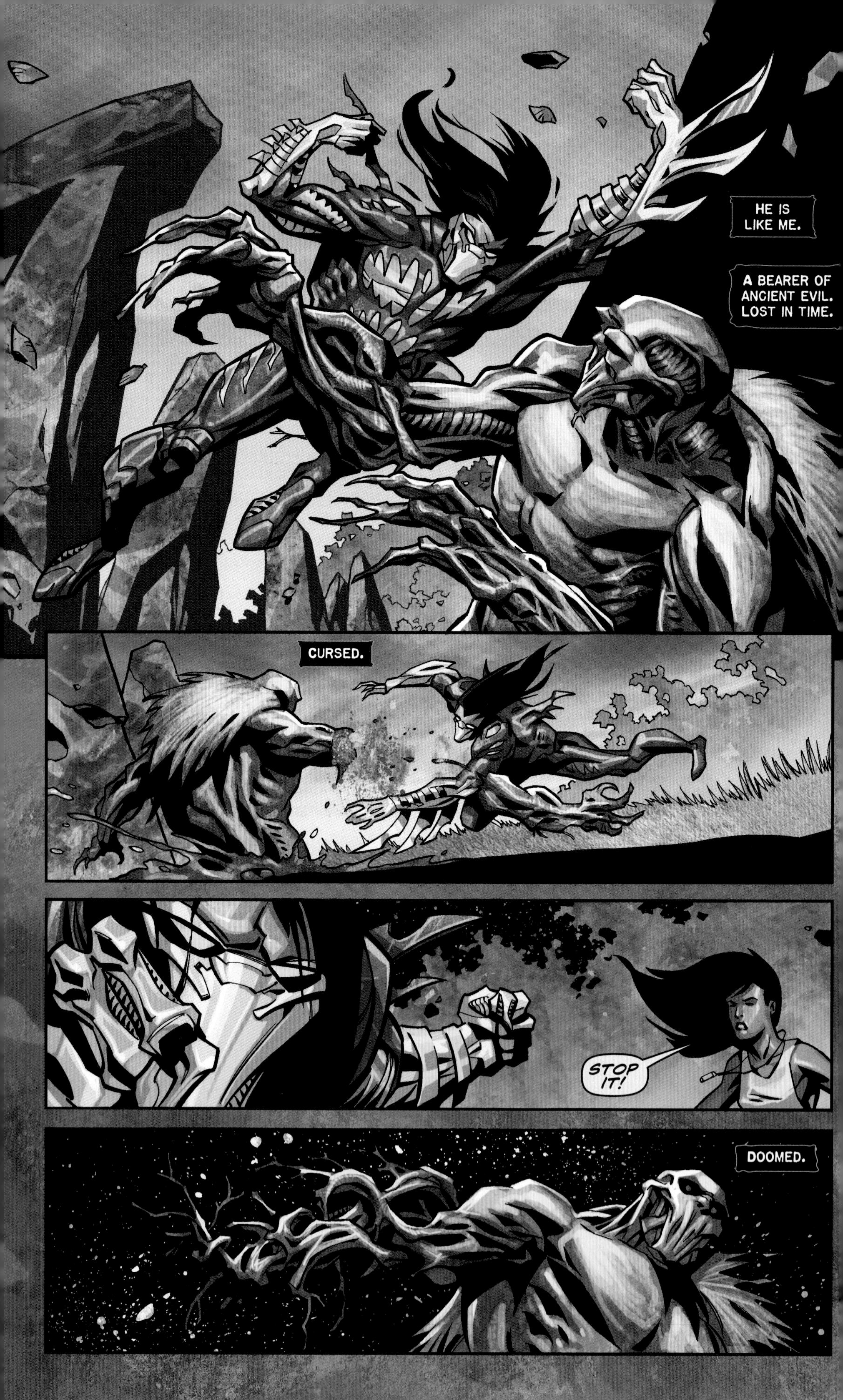
HE IS LIKE ME.
A BEARER OF ANCIENT EVIL. LOST IN TIME.
CURSED.
STOP IT!
DOOMED.

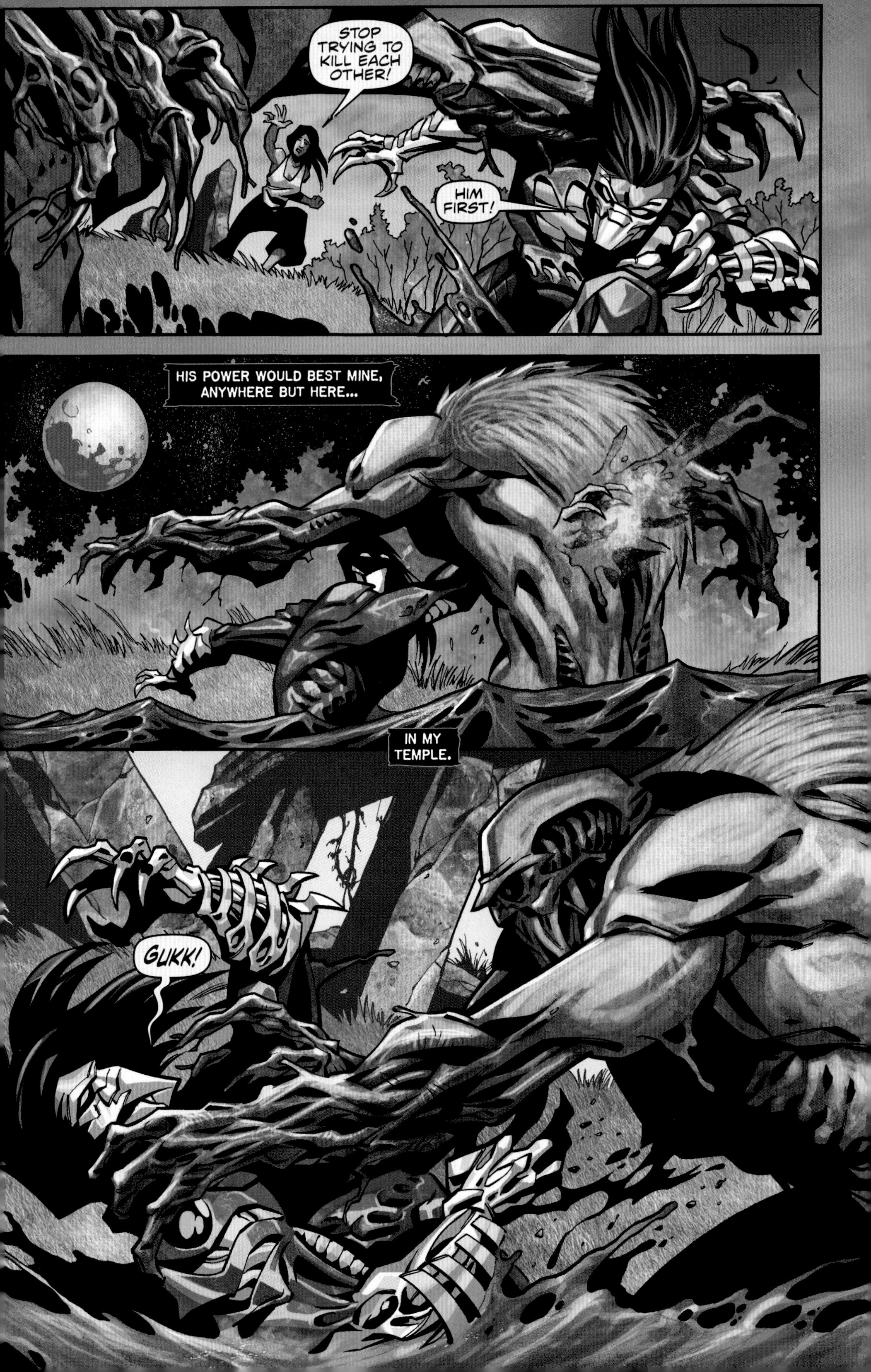
STOP TRYING TO KILL EACH OTHER!
HIM FIRST!
HIS POWER WOULD BEST MINE, ANYWHERE BUT HERE...
IN MY TEMPLE.
GUKK!

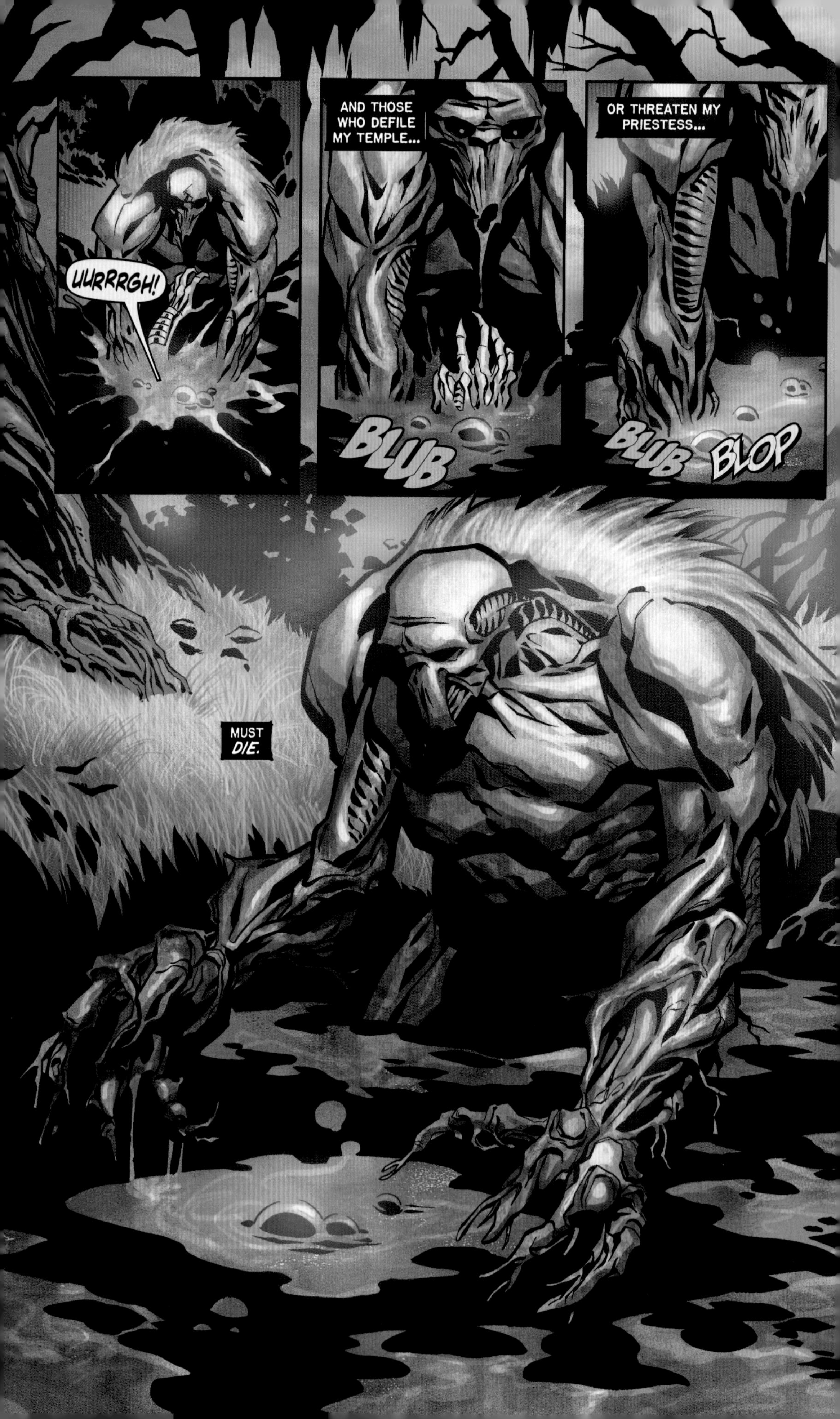
UURRRGH!
AND THOSE WHO DEFILE MY TEMPLE...
BLUB
OR THREATEN MY PRIESTESS...
BLUB
BLOP
MUST DIE.

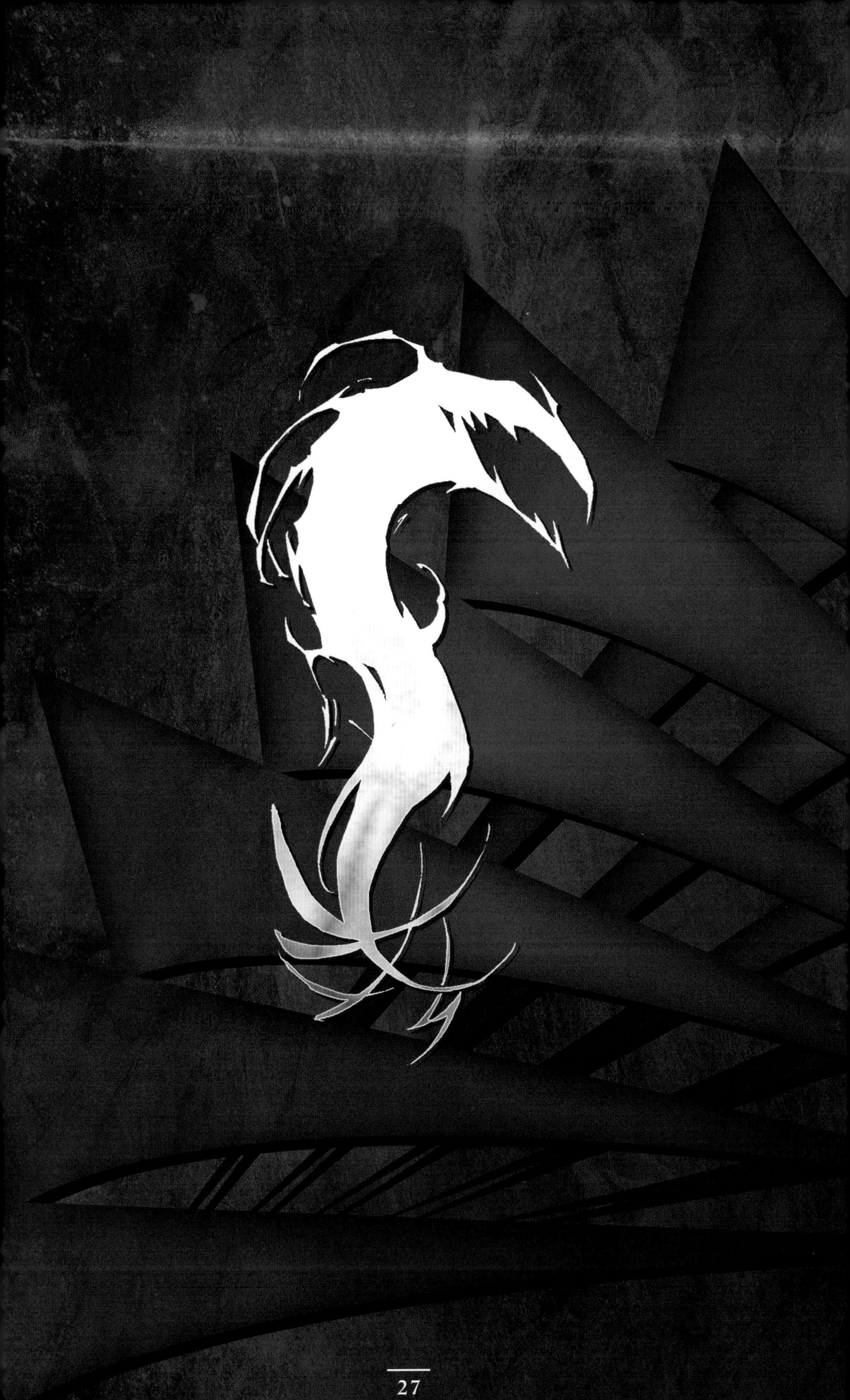

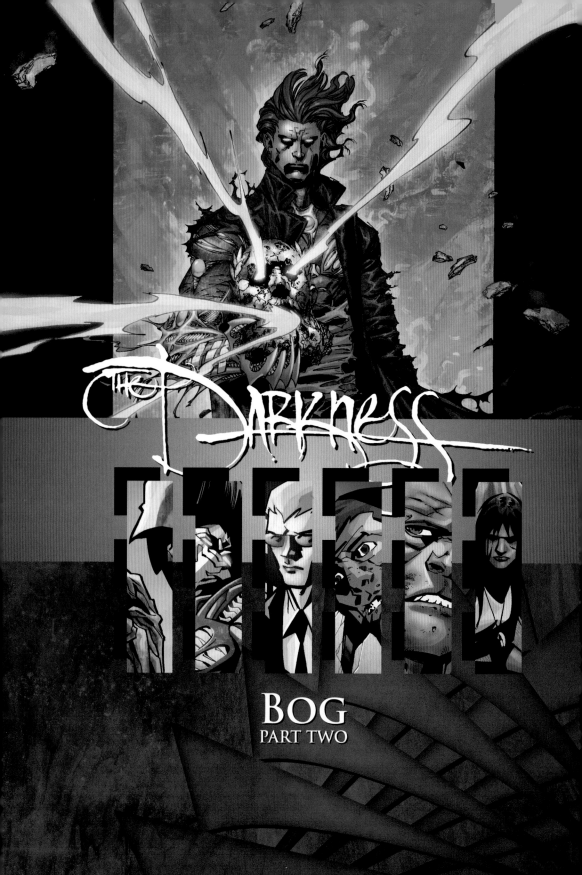

THE DARKNESS

BOG
PART TWO

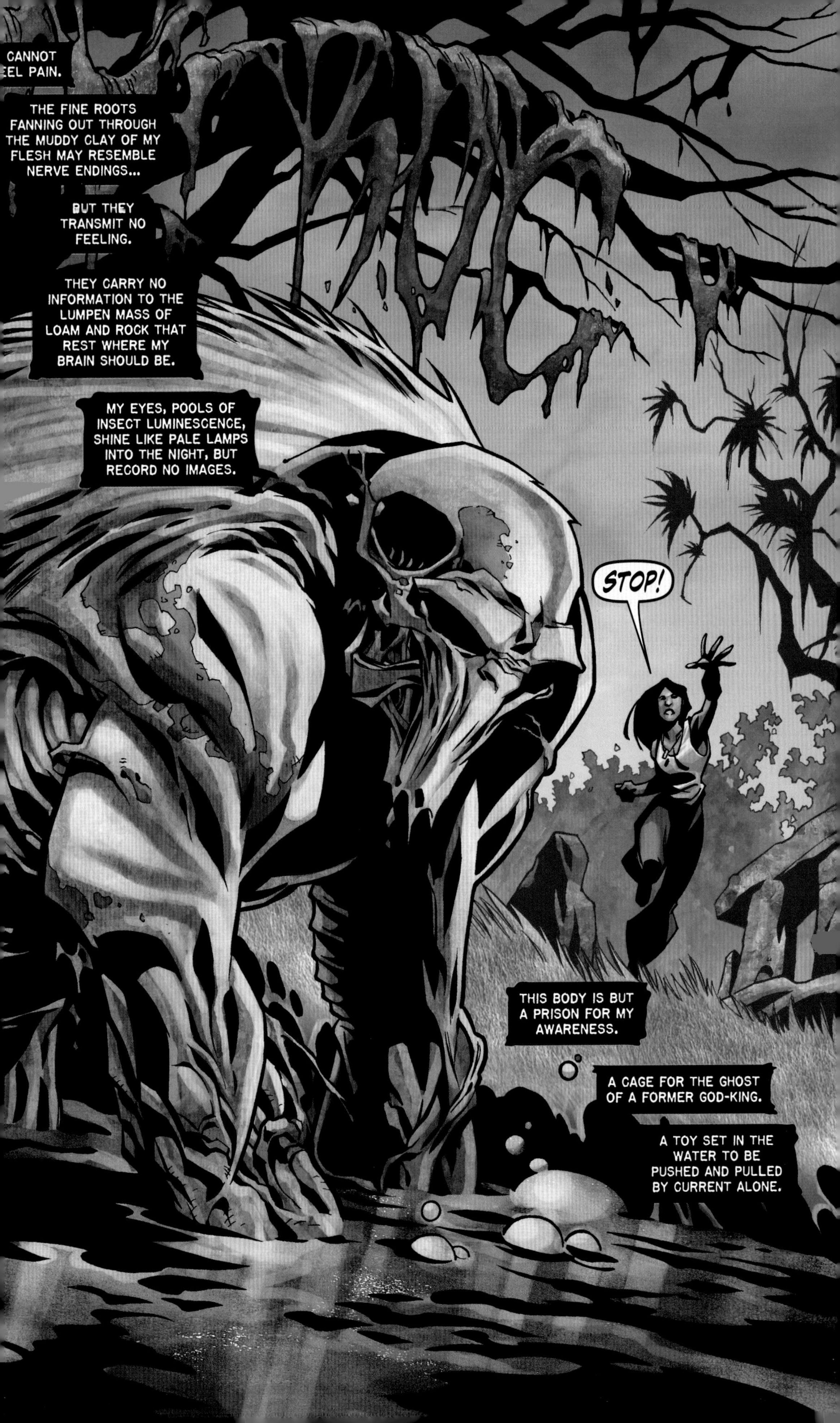
CANNOT
EEL PAIN.
THE FINE ROOTS FANNING OUT THROUGH THE MUDDY CLAY OF MY FLESH MAY RESEMBLE NERVE ENDINGS...
BUT THEY TRANSMIT NO FEELING.
THEY CARRY NO INFORMATION TO THE LUMPEN MASS OF LOAM AND ROCK THAT REST WHERE MY BRAIN SHOULD BE.
MY EYES, POOLS OF INSECT LUMINESCENCE, SHINE LIKE PALE LAMPS INTO THE NIGHT, BUT RECORD NO IMAGES.
STOP!
THIS BODY IS BUT A PRISON FOR MY AWARENESS.
A CAGE FOR THE GHOST OF A FORMER GOD-KING.
A TOY SET IN THE WATER TO BE PUSHED AND PULLED BY CURRENT ALONE.

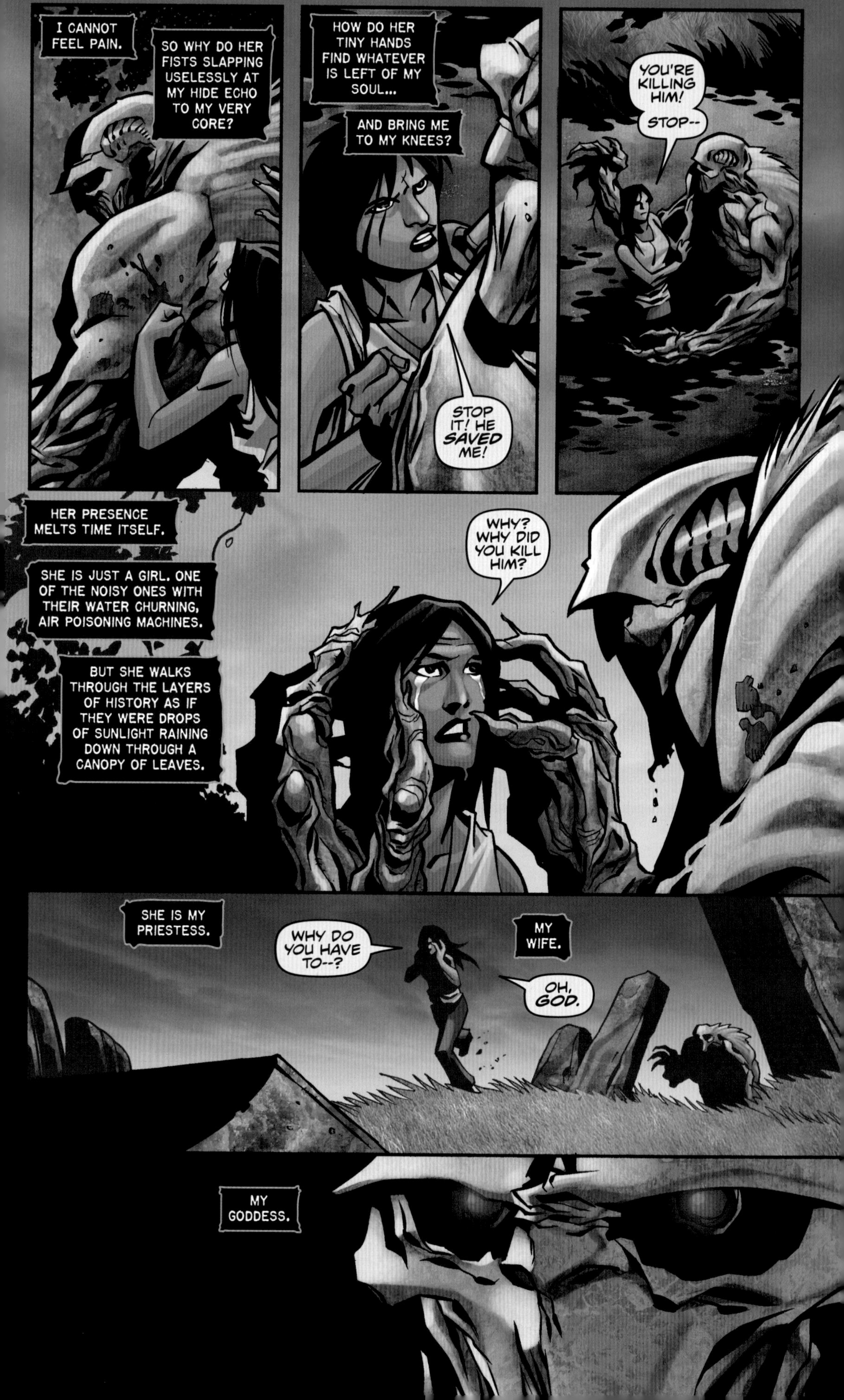
I CANNOT FEEL PAIN.
SO WHY DO HER FISTS SLAPPING USELESSLY AT MY HIDE ECHO TO MY VERY CORE?
HOW DO HER TINY HANDS FIND WHATEVER IS LEFT OF MY SOUL...
AND BRING ME TO MY KNEES?
STOP IT! HE SAVED ME!
YOU'RE KILLING HIM!
STOP--
HER PRESENCE MELTS TIME ITSELF.
SHE IS JUST A GIRL. ONE OF THE NOISY ONES WITH THEIR WATER CHURNING, AIR POISONING MACHINES.
BUT SHE WALKS THROUGH THE LAYERS OF HISTORY AS IF THEY WERE DROPS OF SUNLIGHT RAINING DOWN THROUGH A CANOPY OF LEAVES.
WHY? WHY DID YOU KILL HIM?
SHE IS MY PRIESTESS.
WHY DO YOU HAVE TO--?
MY WIFE.
OH, GOD.
MY GODDESS.

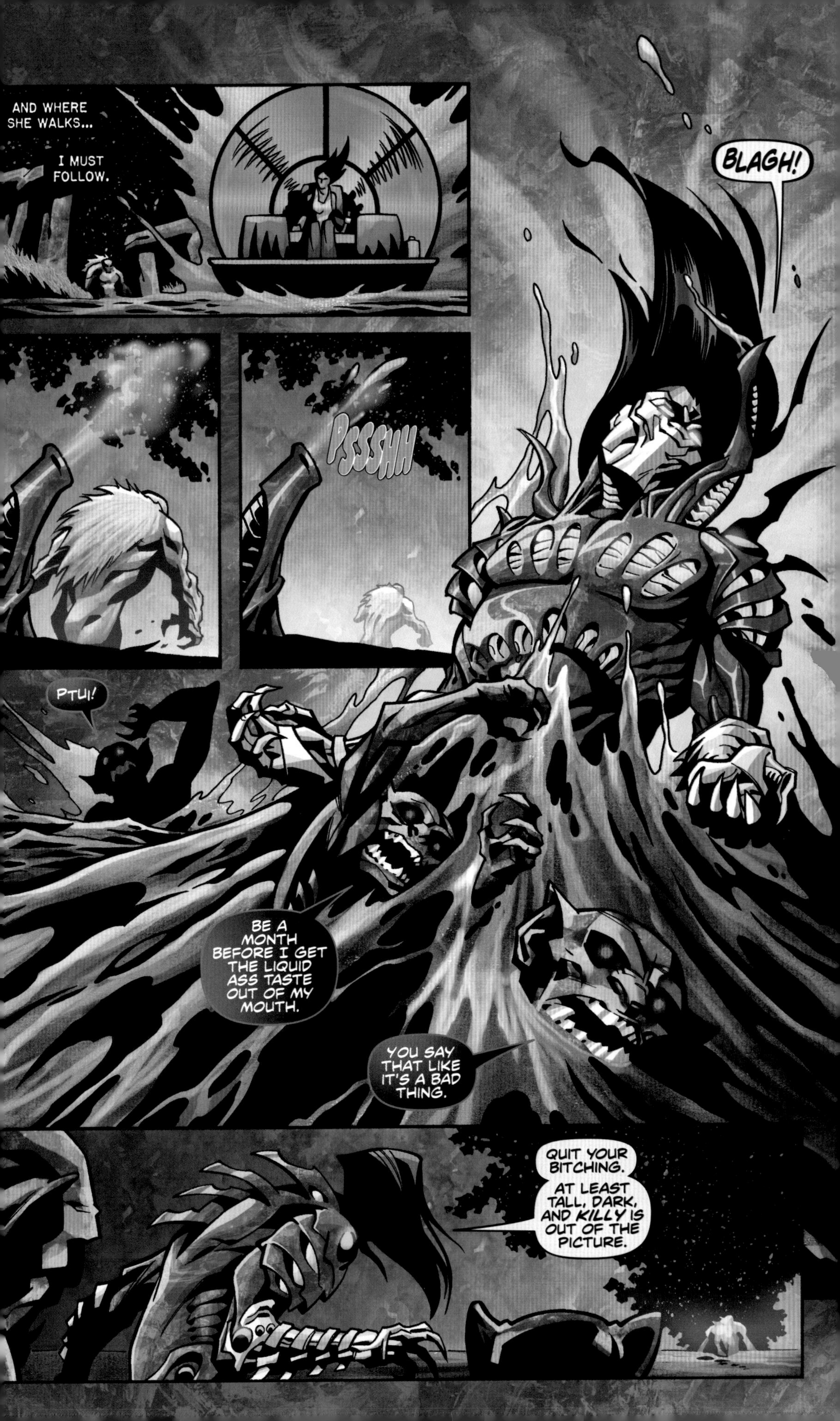
AND WHERE SHE WALKS...
I MUST FOLLOW.
BLAGH!
PSSSHH
PTUI!
BE A MONTH BEFORE I GET THE LIQUID ASS TASTE OUT OF MY MOUTH.
YOU SAY THAT LIKE IT'S A BAD THING.
QUIT YOUR BITCHING.
AT LEAST TALL, DARK, AND KILLY IS OUT OF THE PICTURE.

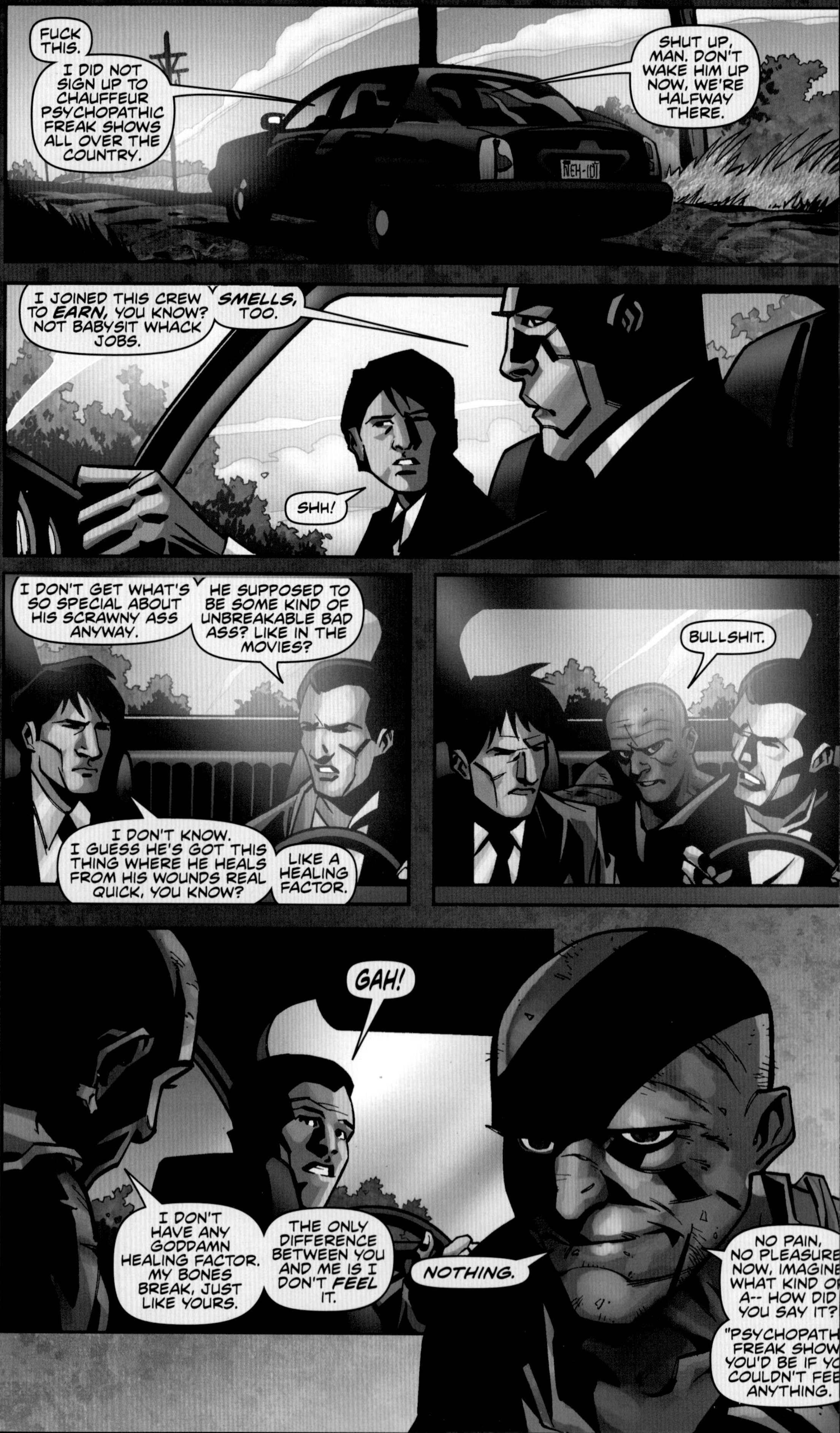
FUCK THIS.
I DID NOT SIGN UP TO CHAUFFEUR PSYCHOPATHIC FREAK SHOWS ALL OVER THE COUNTRY.
SHUT UP, MAN. DON'T WAKE HIM UP NOW, WE'RE HALFWAY THERE.
I JOINED THIS CREW TO EARN, YOU KNOW? NOT BABYSIT WHACK JOBS.
SMELLS, TOO.
SHH!
I DON'T GET WHAT'S SO SPECIAL ABOUT HIS SCRAWNY ASS ANYWAY.
HE SUPPOSED TO BE SOME KIND OF UNBREAKABLE BAD ASS? LIKE IN THE MOVIES?
I DON'T KNOW. I GUESS HE'S GOT THIS THING WHERE HE HEALS FROM HIS WOUNDS REAL QUICK, YOU KNOW?
LIKE A HEALING FACTOR.
BULLSHIT.
GAH!
I DON'T HAVE ANY GODDAMN HEALING FACTOR. MY BONES BREAK, JUST LIKE YOURS.
THE ONLY DIFFERENCE BETWEEN YOU AND ME IS I DON'T FEEL IT.
NOTHING.
NO PAIN, NO PLEASURE NOW, IMAGINE WHAT KIND OF A-- HOW DID YOU SAY IT?
"PSYCHOPATH FREAK SHOW YOU'D BE IF YO COULDN'T FEE ANYTHING.

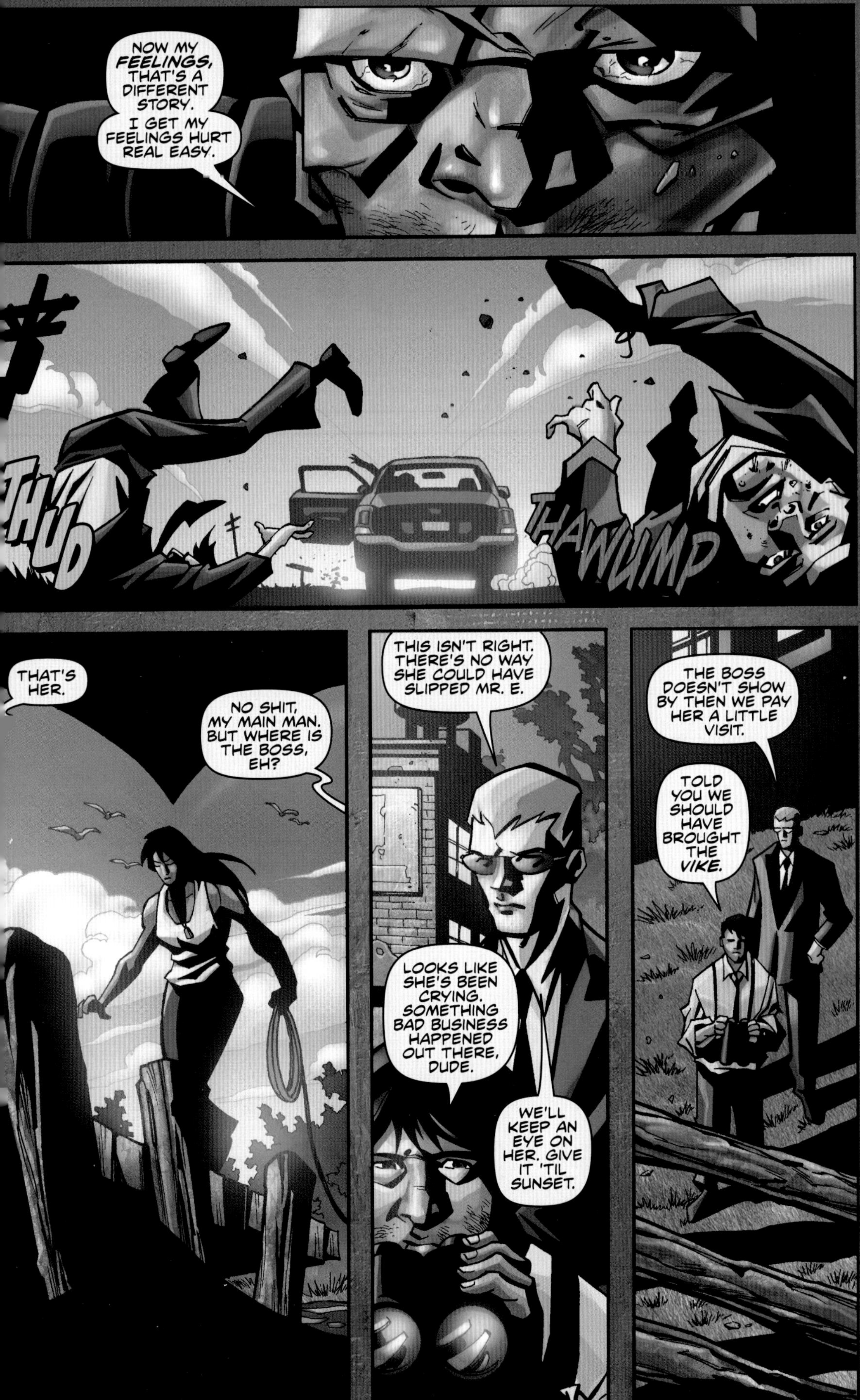
NOW MY FEELINGS, THAT'S A DIFFERENT STORY.
I GET MY FEELINGS HURT REAL EASY.
THUD
THAWUMP
THAT'S HER.
NO SHIT, MY MAIN MAN. BUT WHERE IS THE BOSS, EH?
THIS ISN'T RIGHT. THERE'S NO WAY SHE COULD HAVE SLIPPED MR. E.
LOOKS LIKE SHE'S BEEN CRYING. SOMETHING BAD BUSINESS HAPPENED OUT THERE, DUDE.
WE'LL KEEP AN EYE ON HER. GIVE IT 'TIL SUNSET.
THE BOSS DOESN'T SHOW BY THEN WE PAY HER A LITTLE VISIT.
TOLD YOU WE SHOULD HAVE BROUGHT THE VIKE.

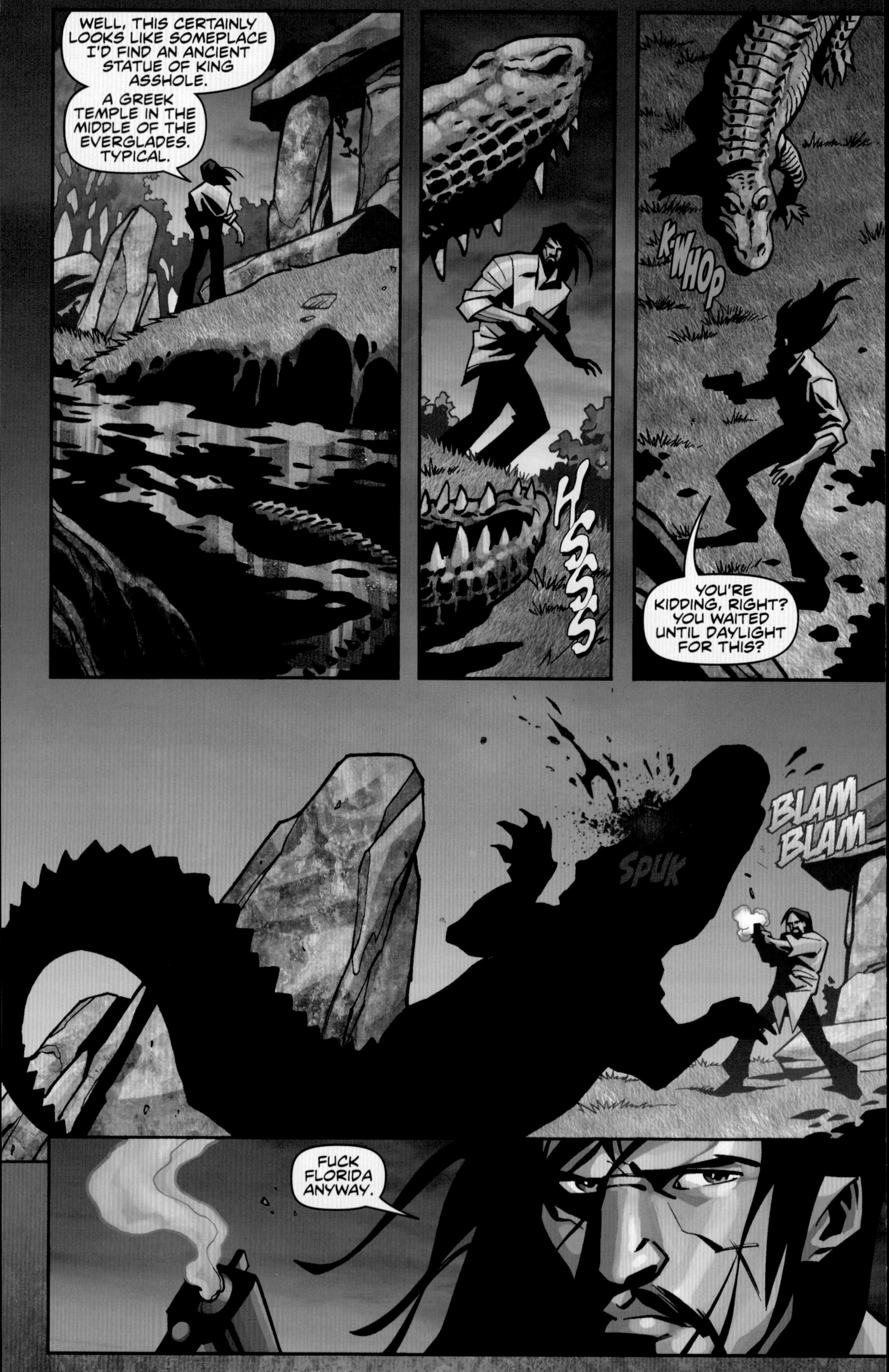
WELL, THIS CERTAINLY LOOKS LIKE SOMEPLACE I'D FIND AN ANCIENT STATUE OF KING ASSHOLE.
A GREEK TEMPLE IN THE MIDDLE OF THE EVERGLADES. TYPICAL.
HSSSS
K-WHOP
YOU'RE KIDDING, RIGHT? YOU WAITED UNTIL DAYLIGHT FOR THIS?
BLAM BLAM
SPUK
FUCK FLORIDA ANYWAY.

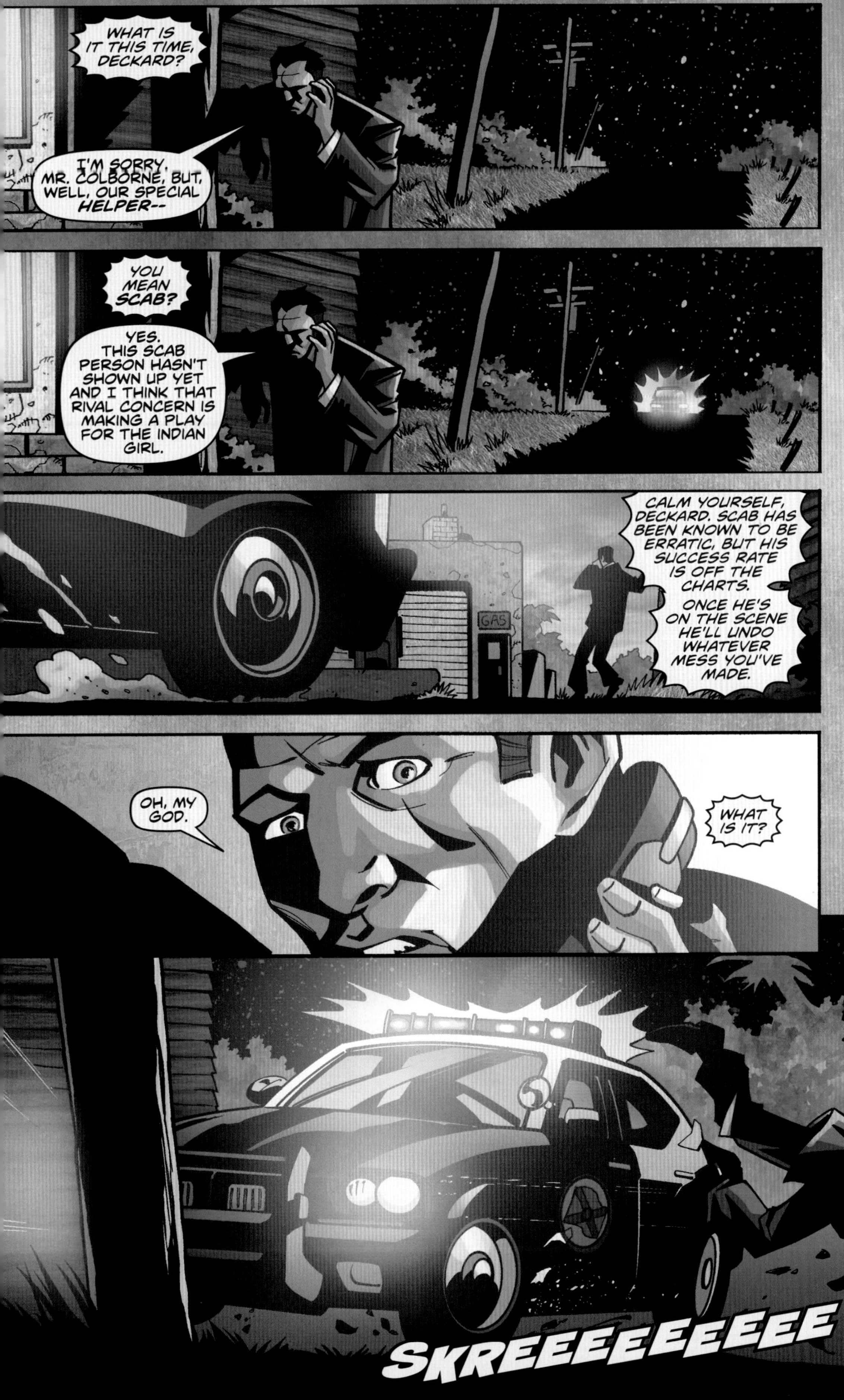
WHAT IS IT THIS TIME, DECKARD?
I'M SORRY, MR. COLBORNE, BUT, WELL, OUR SPECIAL HELPER--
YOU MEAN SCAB?
YES. THIS SCAB PERSON HASN'T SHOWN UP YET AND I THINK THAT RIVAL CONCERN IS MAKING A PLAY FOR THE INDIAN GIRL.
CALM YOURSELF, DECKARD. SCAB HAS BEEN KNOWN TO BE ERRATIC, BUT HIS SUCCESS RATE IS OFF THE CHARTS.
ONCE HE'S ON THE SCENE HE'LL UNDO WHATEVER MESS YOU'VE MADE.
GAS
OH, MY GOD.
WHAT IS IT?
SKREEEEEEEEEE

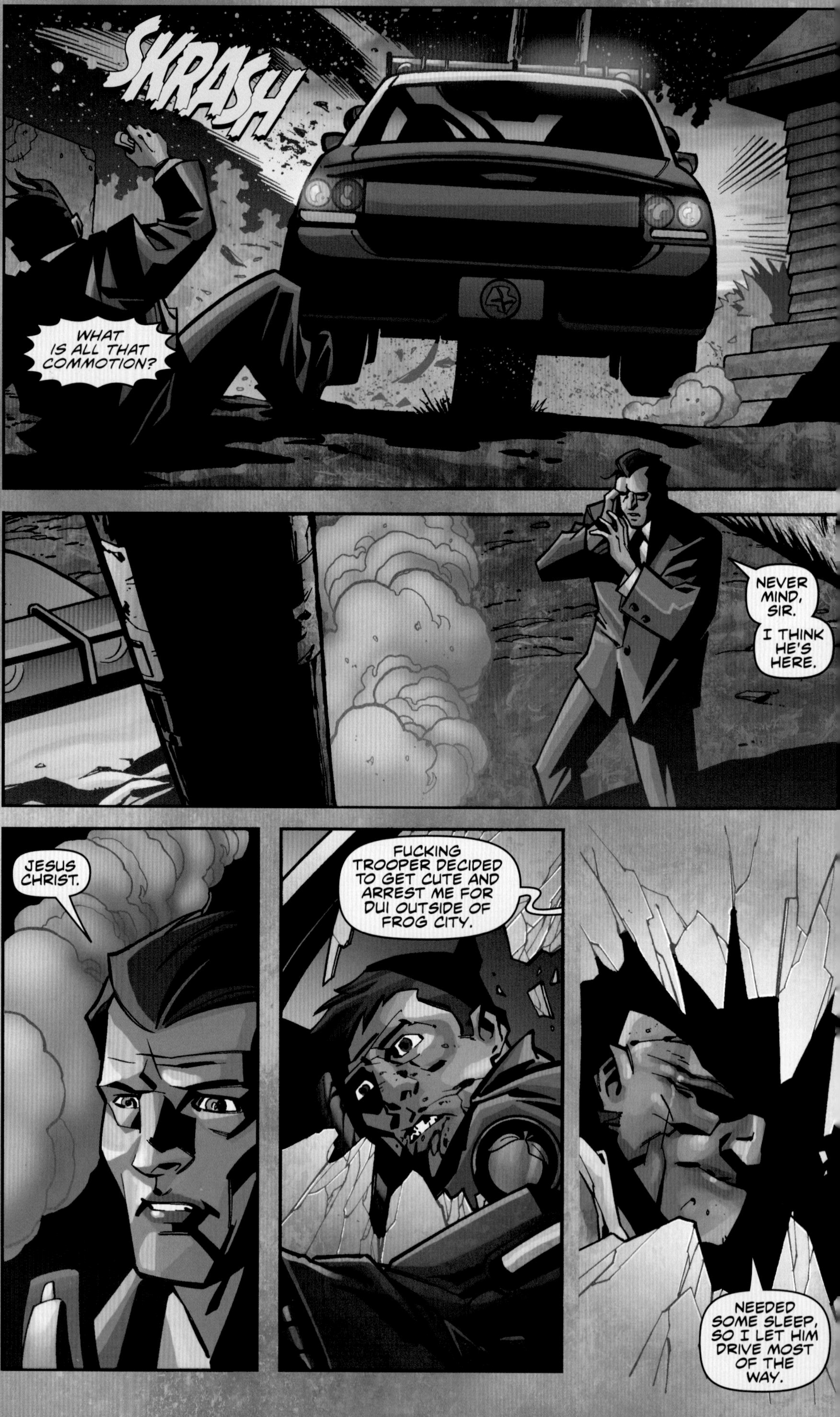
SKRASH
WHAT IS ALL THAT COMMOTION?
NEVER MIND, SIR.
I THINK HE'S HERE.
JESUS CHRIST.
FUCKING TROOPER DECIDED TO GET CUTE AND ARREST ME FOR DUI OUTSIDE OF FROG CITY.
NEEDED SOME SLEEP, SO I LET HIM DRIVE MOST OF THE WAY.

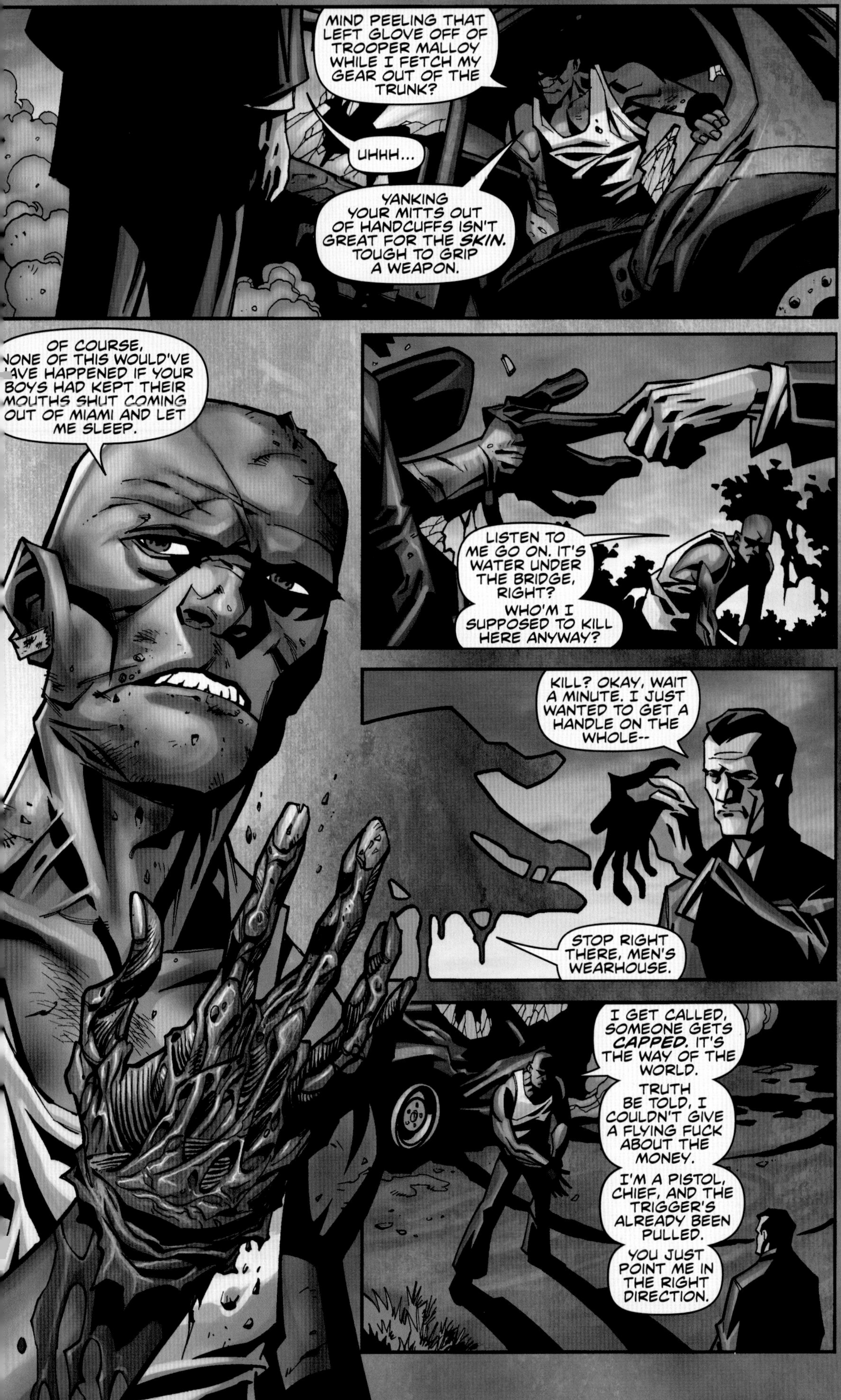
MIND PEELING THAT LEFT GLOVE OFF OF TROOPER MALLOY WHILE I FETCH MY GEAR OUT OF THE TRUNK?
UHHH...
YANKING YOUR MITTS OUT OF HANDCUFFS ISN'T GREAT FOR THE SKIN. TOUGH TO GRIP A WEAPON.
OF COURSE, NONE OF THIS WOULD'VE HAVE HAPPENED IF YOUR BOYS HAD KEPT THEIR MOUTHS SHUT COMING OUT OF MIAMI AND LET ME SLEEP.
LISTEN TO ME GO ON. IT'S WATER UNDER THE BRIDGE, RIGHT?
WHO'M I SUPPOSED TO KILL HERE ANYWAY?
KILL? OKAY, WAIT A MINUTE. I JUST WANTED TO GET A HANDLE ON THE WHOLE--
STOP RIGHT THERE, MEN'S WEARHOUSE.
I GET CALLED, SOMEONE GETS CAPPED. IT'S THE WAY OF THE WORLD.
TRUTH BE TOLD, I COULDN'T GIVE A FLYING FUCK ABOUT THE MONEY.
I'M A PISTOL, CHIEF, AND THE TRIGGER'S ALREADY BEEN PULLED.
YOU JUST POINT ME IN THE RIGHT DIRECTION.

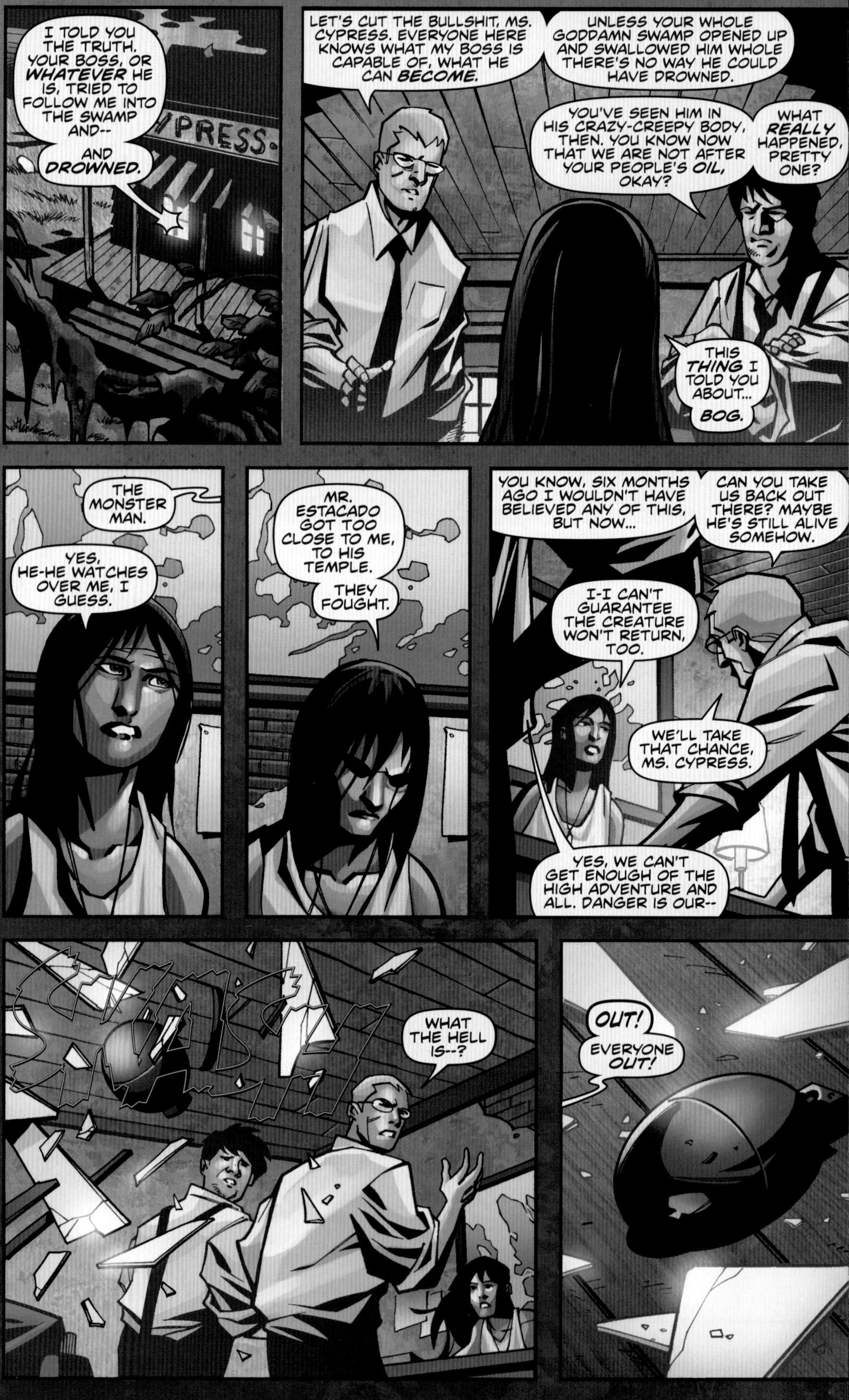

I TOLD YOU THE TRUTH. YOUR BOSS, OR WHATEVER HE IS, TRIED TO FOLLOW ME INTO THE SWAMP AND--
AND DROWNED.
PRESS
LET'S CUT THE BULLSHIT, MS. CYPRESS. EVERYONE HERE KNOWS WHAT MY BOSS IS CAPABLE OF, WHAT HE CAN BECOME.
UNLESS YOUR WHOLE GODDAMN SWAMP OPENED UP AND SWALLOWED HIM WHOLE THERE'S NO WAY HE COULD HAVE DROWNED.
YOU'VE SEEN HIM IN HIS CRAZY-CREEPY BODY, THEN. YOU KNOW NOW THAT WE ARE NOT AFTER YOUR PEOPLE'S OIL, OKAY?
WHAT REALLY HAPPENED, PRETTY ONE?
THIS THING I TOLD YOU ABOUT... BOG.
THE MONSTER MAN.
YES, HE-HE WATCHES OVER ME, I GUESS.
MR. ESTACADO GOT TOO CLOSE TO ME, TO HIS TEMPLE.
THEY FOUGHT.
YOU KNOW, SIX MONTHS AGO I WOULDN'T HAVE BELIEVED ANY OF THIS, BUT NOW...
CAN YOU TAKE US BACK OUT THERE? MAYBE HE'S STILL ALIVE SOMEHOW.
I-I CAN'T GUARANTEE THE CREATURE WON'T RETURN, TOO.
WE'LL TAKE THAT CHANCE, MS. CYPRESS.
YES, WE CAN'T GET ENOUGH OF THE HIGH ADVENTURE AND ALL. DANGER IS OUR--
WHAT THE HELL IS--?
OUT! EVERYONE OUT!

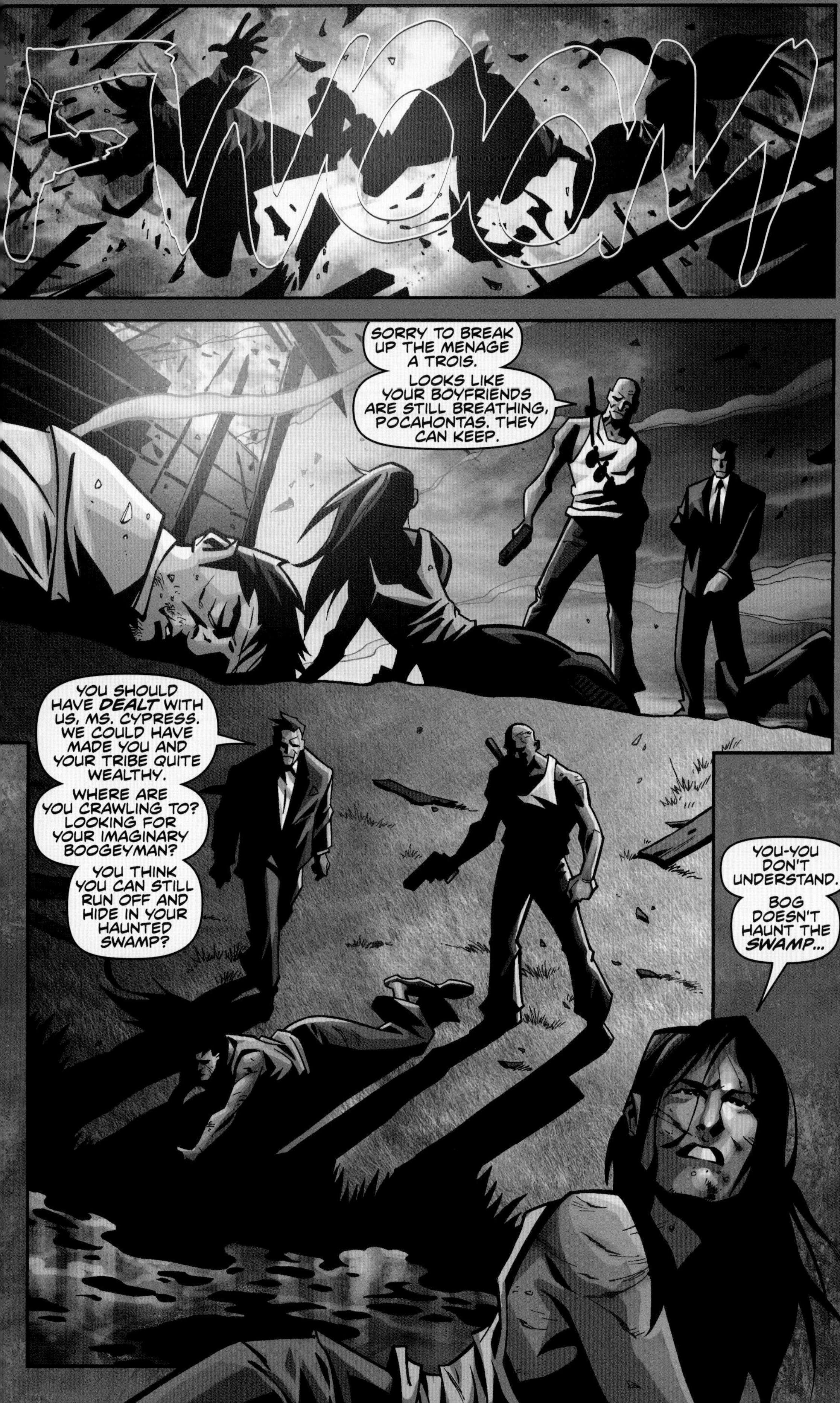
FWOOM
SORRY TO BREAK UP THE MENAGE A TROIS.
LOOKS LIKE YOUR BOYFRIENDS ARE STILL BREATHING, POCAHONTAS. THEY CAN KEEP.
YOU SHOULD HAVE DEALT WITH US, MS. CYPRESS. WE COULD HAVE MADE YOU AND YOUR TRIBE QUITE WEALTHY.
WHERE ARE YOU CRAWLING TO? LOOKING FOR YOUR IMAGINARY BOOGEYMAN?
YOU THINK YOU CAN STILL RUN OFF AND HIDE IN YOUR HAUNTED SWAMP?
YOU-YOU DON'T UNDERSTAND.
BOG DOESN'T HAUNT THE SWAMP...

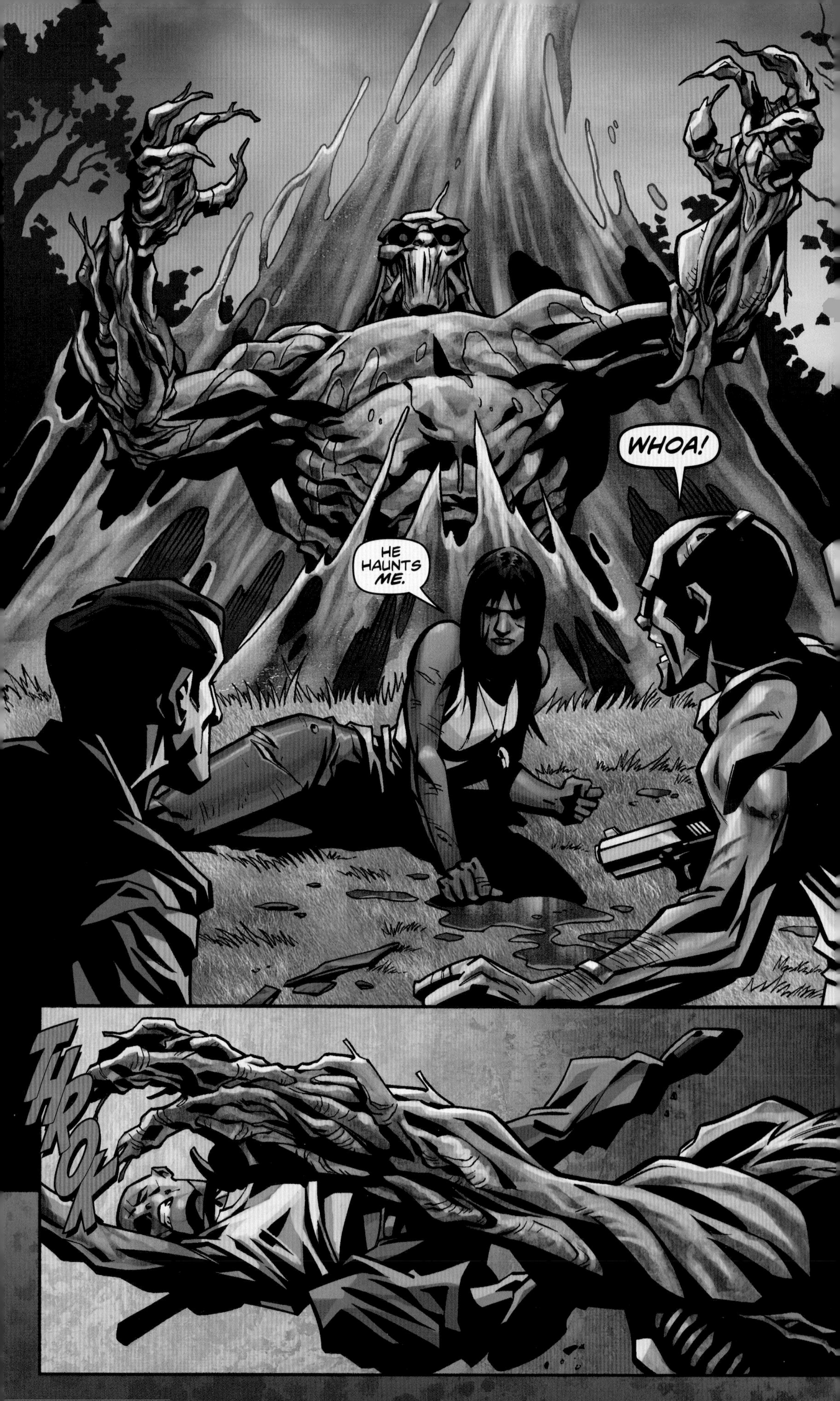
HE HAUNTS ME.
WHOA!
THROK

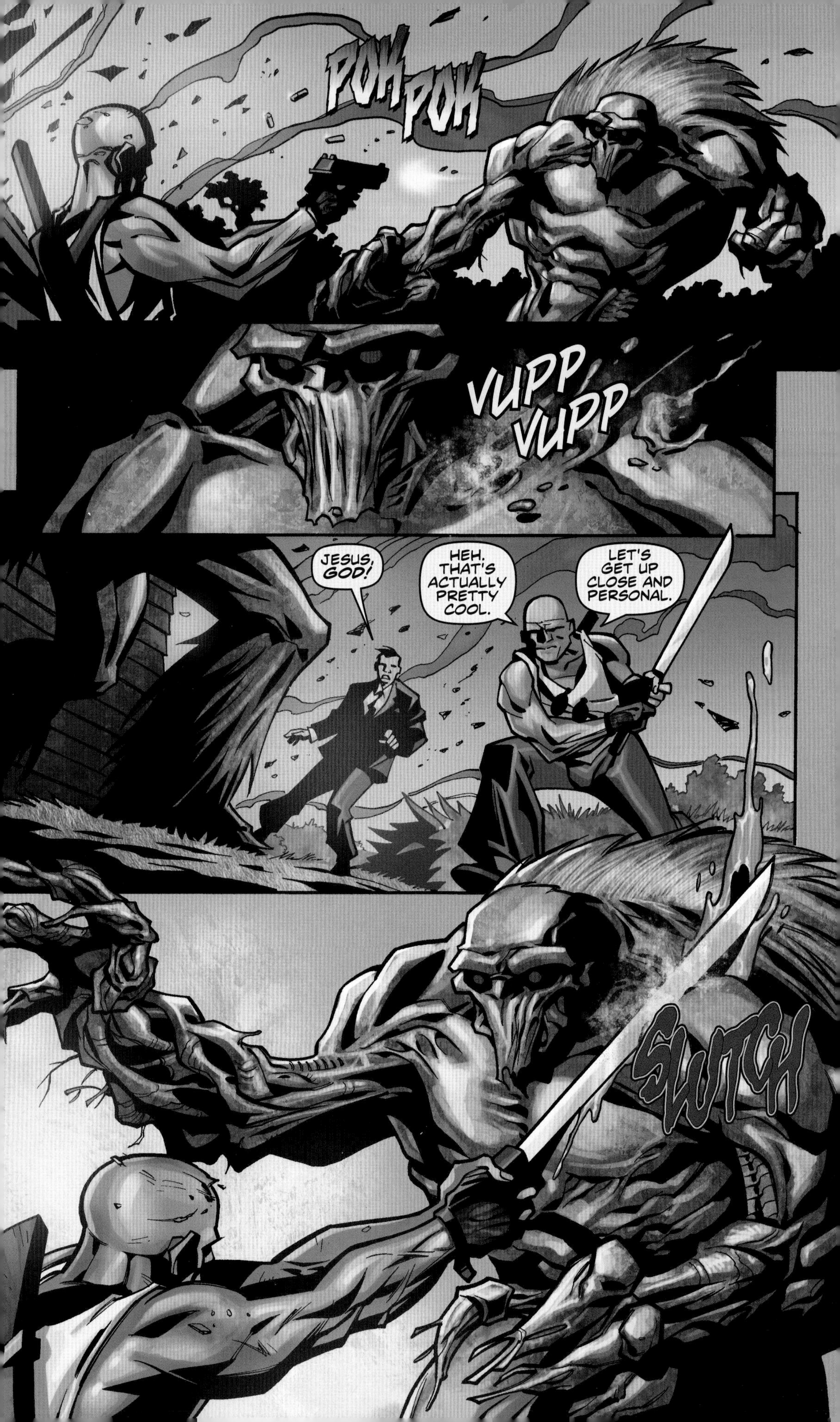
POK POK
VUPP VUPP
JESUS, GOD!
HEH. THAT'S ACTUALLY PRETTY COOL.
LET'S GET UP CLOSE AND PERSONAL.
SLUTCH

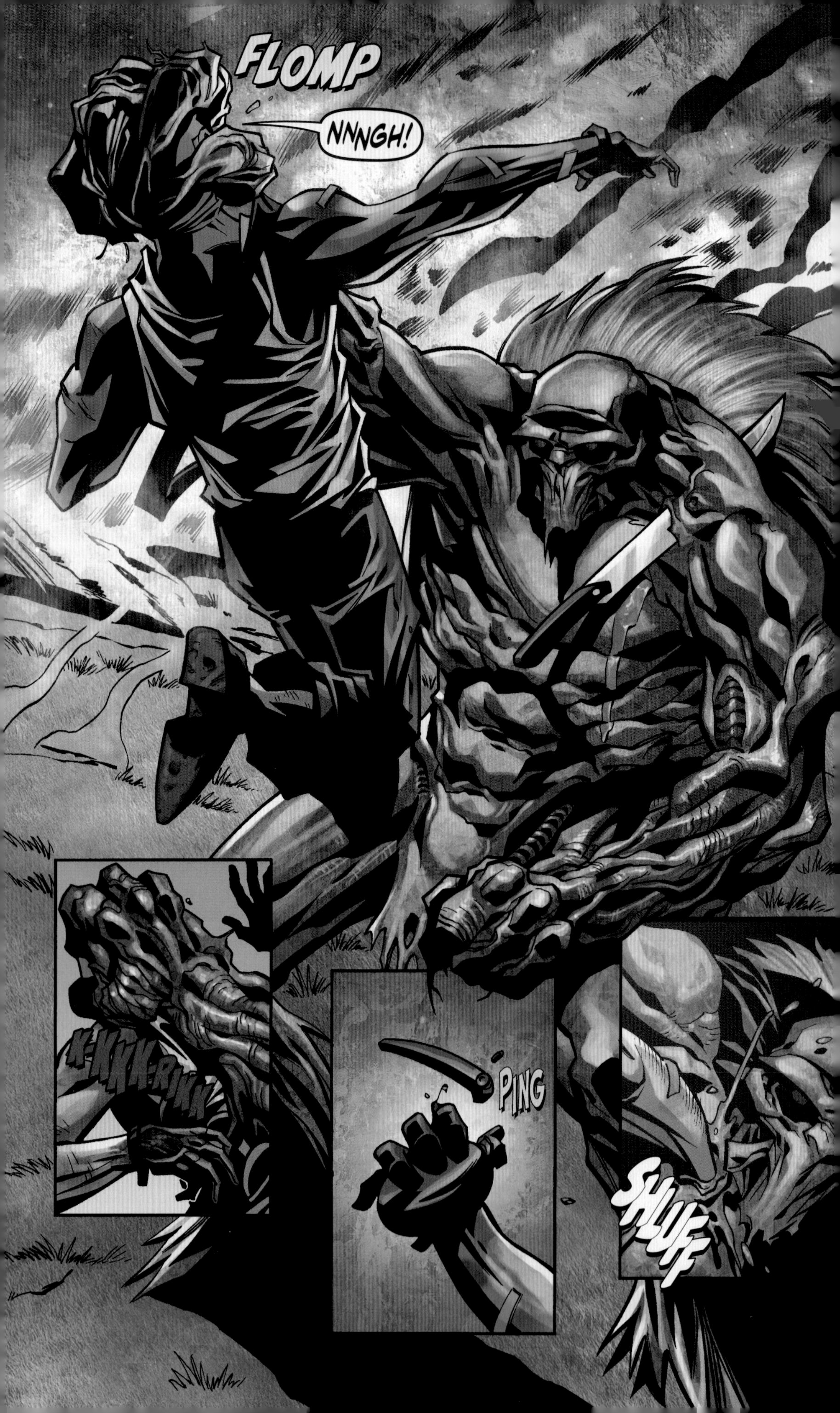
FLOMP
NNNGH!
K-KKK-RIKK
PING
SHUFF

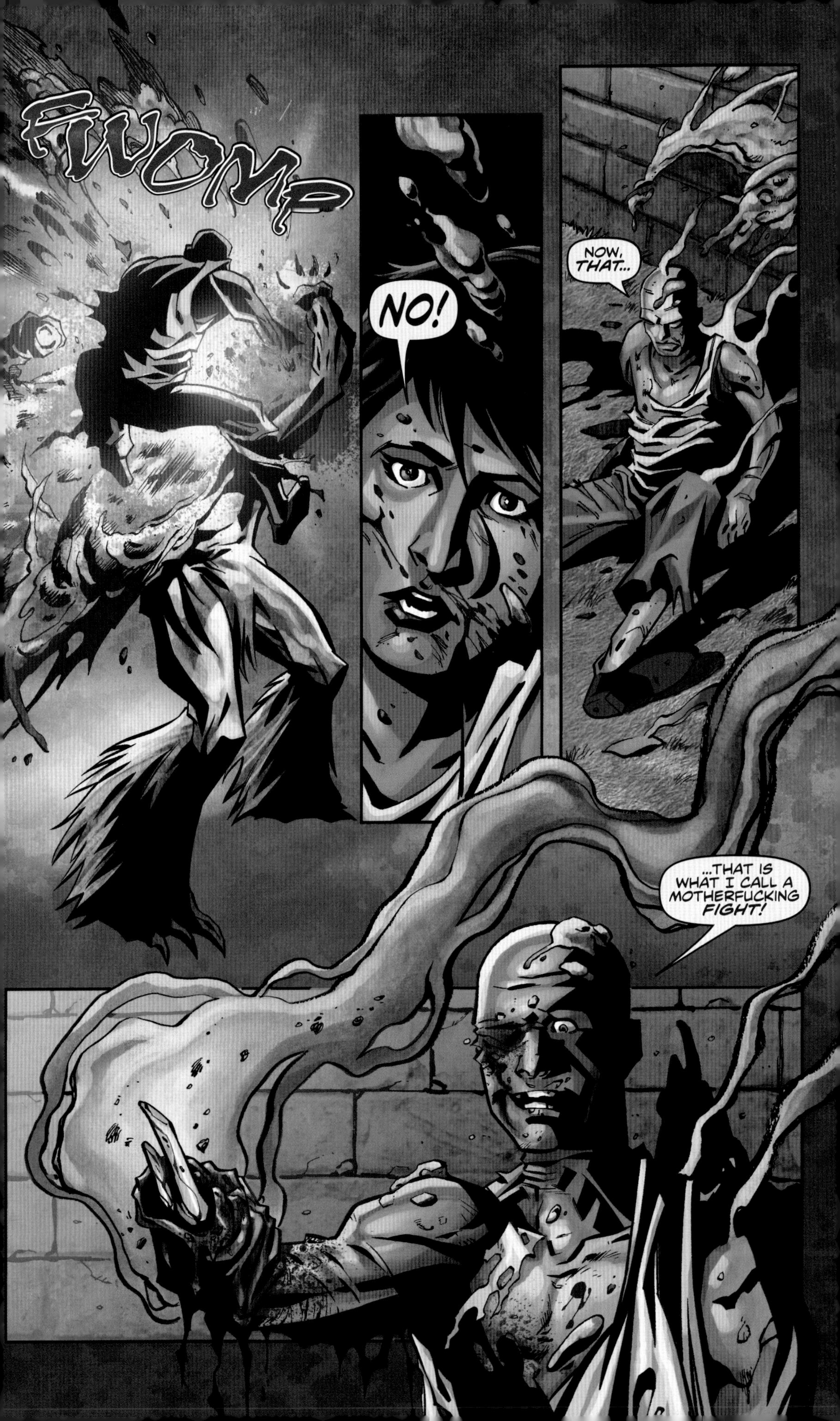
FWOMP
NO!
NOW, THAT...
...THAT IS WHAT I CALL A MOTHERFUCKING FIGHT!

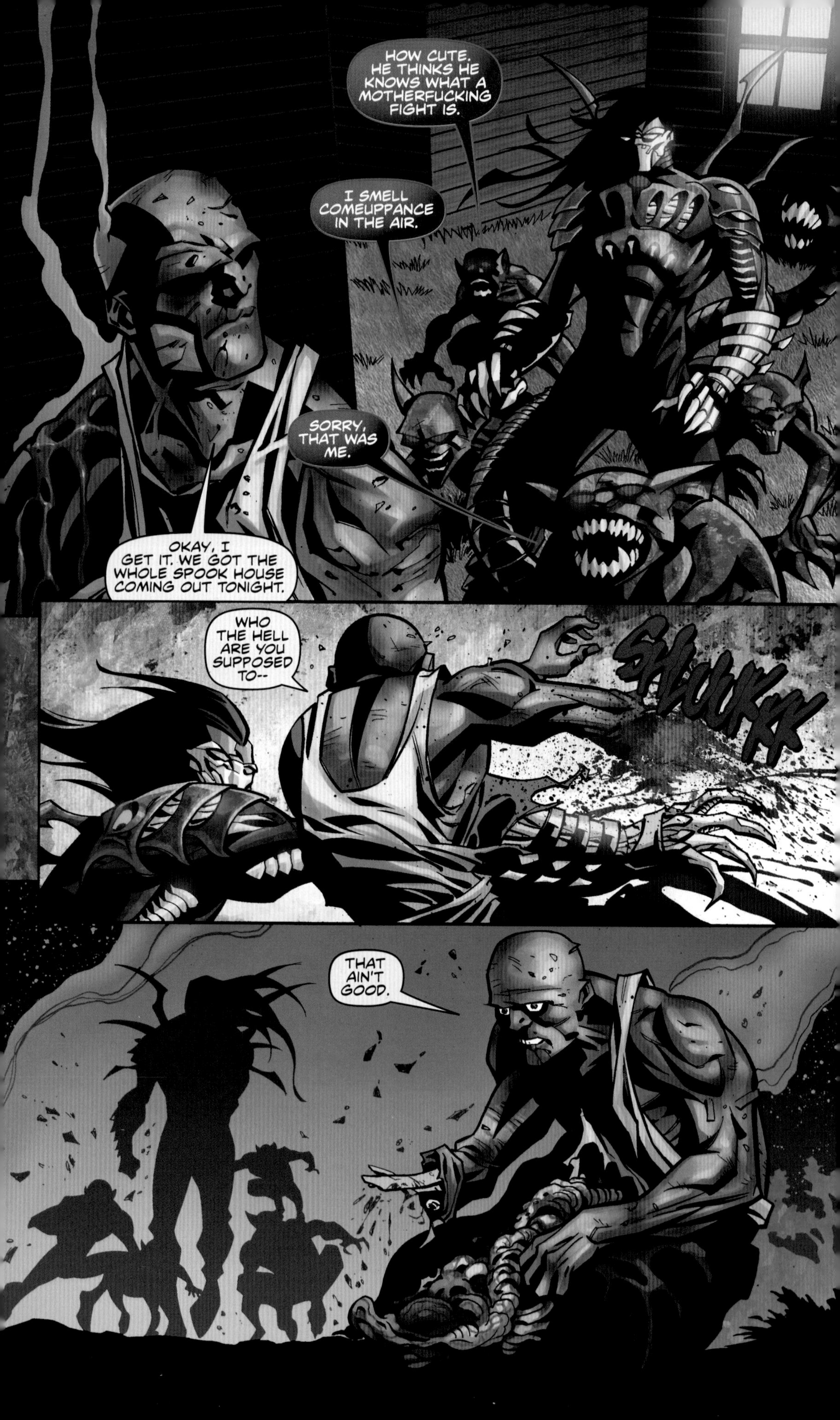
OKAY, I GET IT. WE GOT THE WHOLE SPOOK HOUSE COMING OUT TONIGHT.
HOW CUTE. HE THINKS HE KNOWS WHAT A MOTHERFUCKING FIGHT IS.
I SMELL COMEUPPANCE IN THE AIR.
SORRY, THAT WAS ME.
WHO THE HELL ARE YOU SUPPOSED TO--
SHLUKKK
THAT AIN'T GOOD.

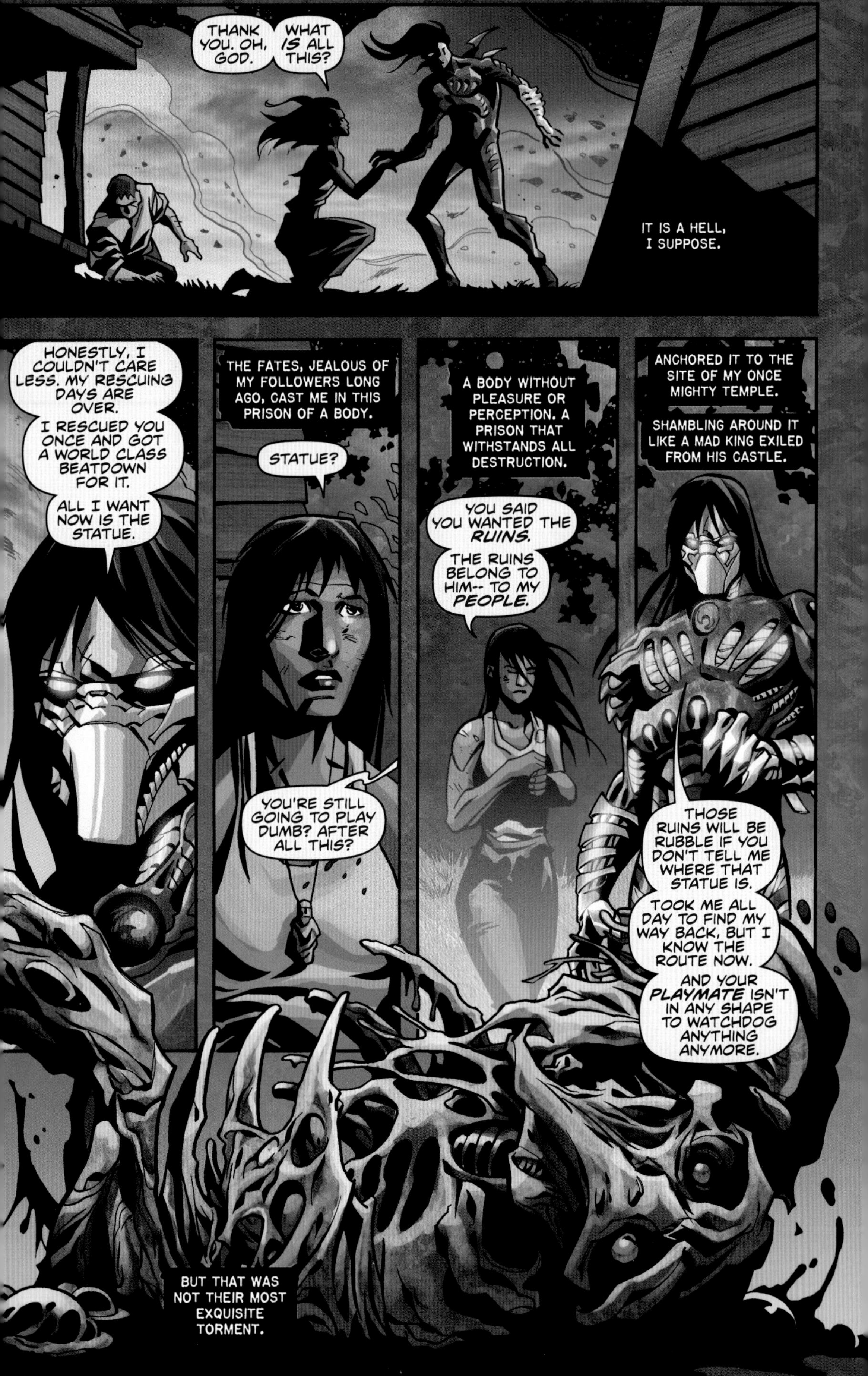
THANK YOU. OH, GOD.
WHAT IS ALL THIS?
IT IS A HELL, I SUPPOSE.
HONESTLY, I COULDN'T CARE LESS. MY RESCUING DAYS ARE OVER.
I RESCUED YOU ONCE AND GOT A WORLD CLASS BEATDOWN FOR IT.
ALL I WANT NOW IS THE STATUE.
THE FATES, JEALOUS OF MY FOLLOWERS LONG AGO, CAST ME IN THIS PRISON OF A BODY.
STATUE?
YOU'RE STILL GOING TO PLAY DUMB? AFTER ALL THIS?
A BODY WITHOUT PLEASURE OR PERCEPTION. A PRISON THAT WITHSTANDS ALL DESTRUCTION.
YOU SAID YOU WANTED THE RUINS.
THE RUINS BELONG TO HIM-- TO MY PEOPLE.
ANCHORED IT TO THE SITE OF MY ONCE MIGHTY TEMPLE.
SHAMBLING AROUND IT LIKE A MAD KING EXILED FROM HIS CASTLE.
THOSE RUINS WILL BE RUBBLE IF YOU DON'T TELL ME WHERE THAT STATUE IS.
TOOK ME ALL DAY TO FIND MY WAY BACK, BUT I KNOW THE ROUTE NOW.
AND YOUR PLAYMATE ISN'T IN ANY SHAPE TO WATCHDOG ANYTHING ANYMORE.
BUT THAT WAS NOT THEIR MOST EXQUISITE TORMENT.

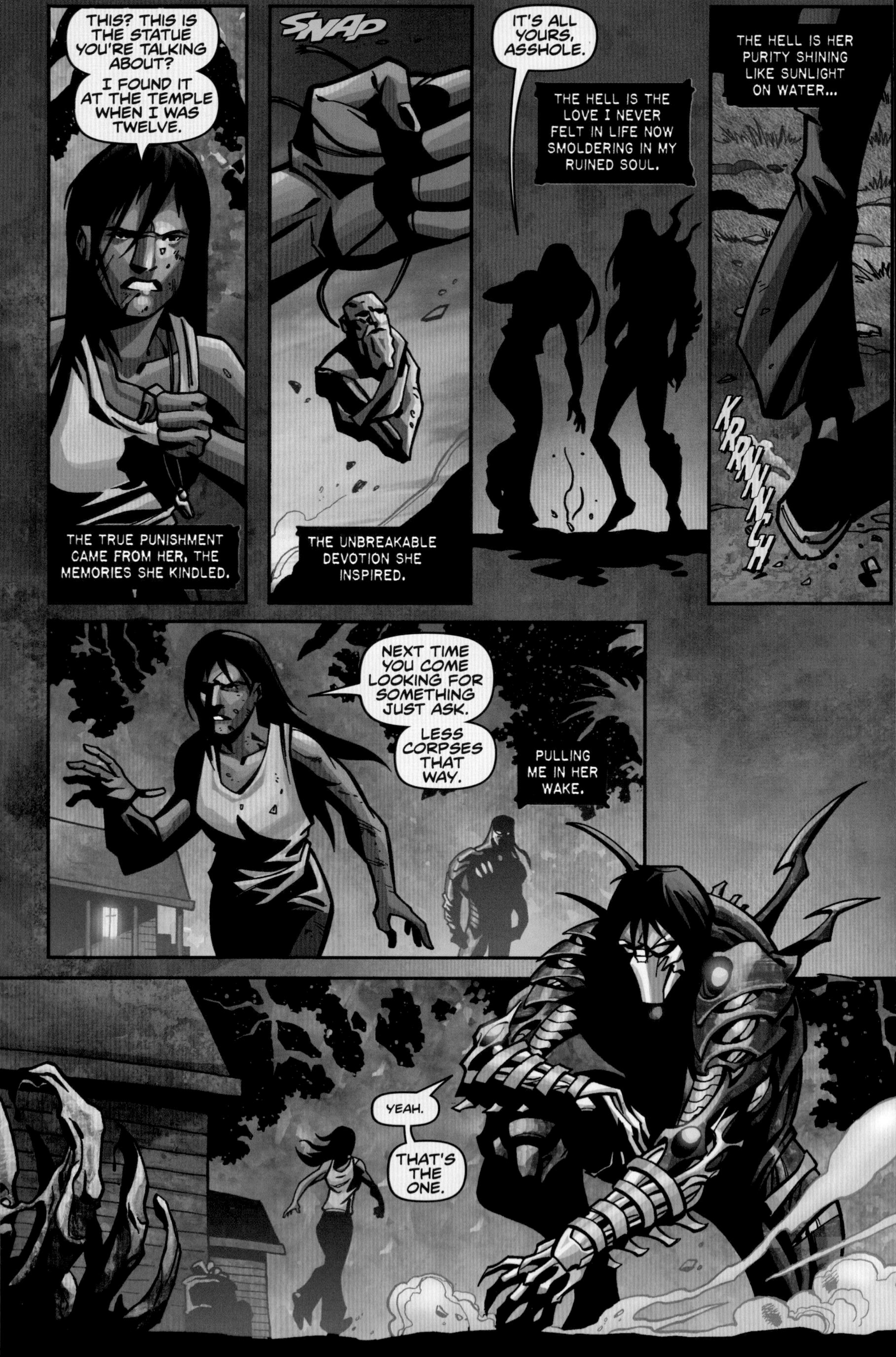

THIS? THIS IS THE STATUE YOU'RE TALKING ABOUT?
I FOUND IT AT THE TEMPLE WHEN I WAS TWELVE.
THE TRUE PUNISHMENT CAME FROM HER, THE MEMORIES SHE KINDLED.
SNAP
THE UNBREAKABLE DEVOTION SHE INSPIRED.
IT'S ALL YOURS, ASSHOLE.
THE HELL IS THE LOVE I NEVER FELT IN LIFE NOW SMOLDERING IN MY RUINED SOUL.
THE HELL IS HER PURITY SHINING LIKE SUNLIGHT ON WATER...
KRRNNNCH
NEXT TIME YOU COME LOOKING FOR SOMETHING JUST ASK.
LESS CORPSES THAT WAY.
PULLING ME IN HER WAKE.
YEAH.
THAT'S THE ONE.

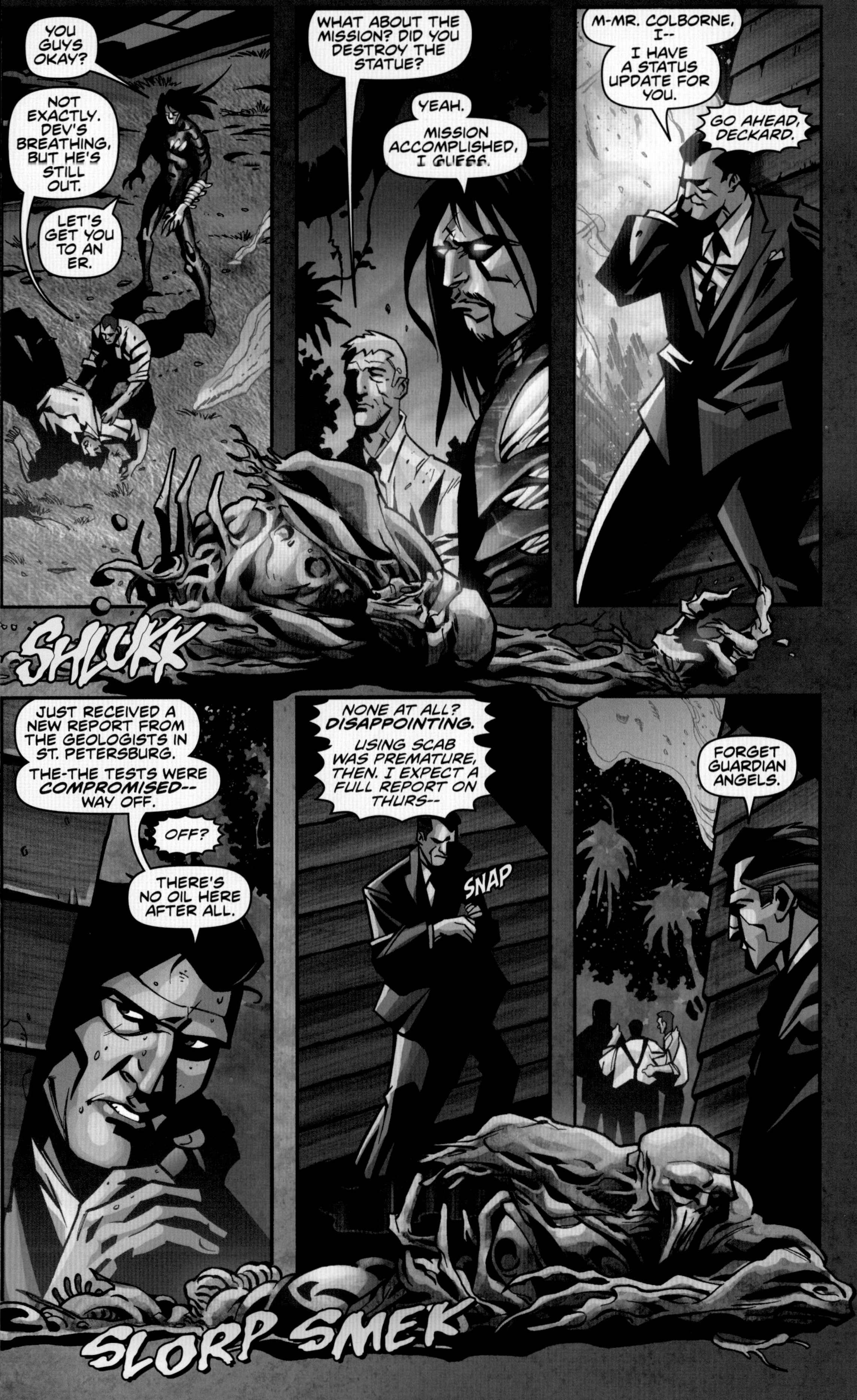
YOU GUYS OKAY?
NOT EXACTLY. DEV'S BREATHING, BUT HE'S STILL OUT.
LET'S GET YOU TO AN ER.
WHAT ABOUT THE MISSION? DID YOU DESTROY THE STATUE?
YEAH.
MISSION ACCOMPLISHED, I GUESS.
M-MR. COLBORNE, I--
I HAVE A STATUS UPDATE FOR YOU.
GO AHEAD, DECKARD.
SHLUKK
JUST RECEIVED A NEW REPORT FROM THE GEOLOGISTS IN ST. PETERSBURG.
THE-THE TESTS WERE COMPROMISED-- WAY OFF.
OFF?
THERE'S NO OIL HERE AFTER ALL.
NONE AT ALL? DISAPPOINTING.
USING SCAB WAS PREMATURE, THEN. I EXPECT A FULL REPORT ON THURS--
SNAP
FORGET GUARDIAN ANGELS.
SLORP SMEK

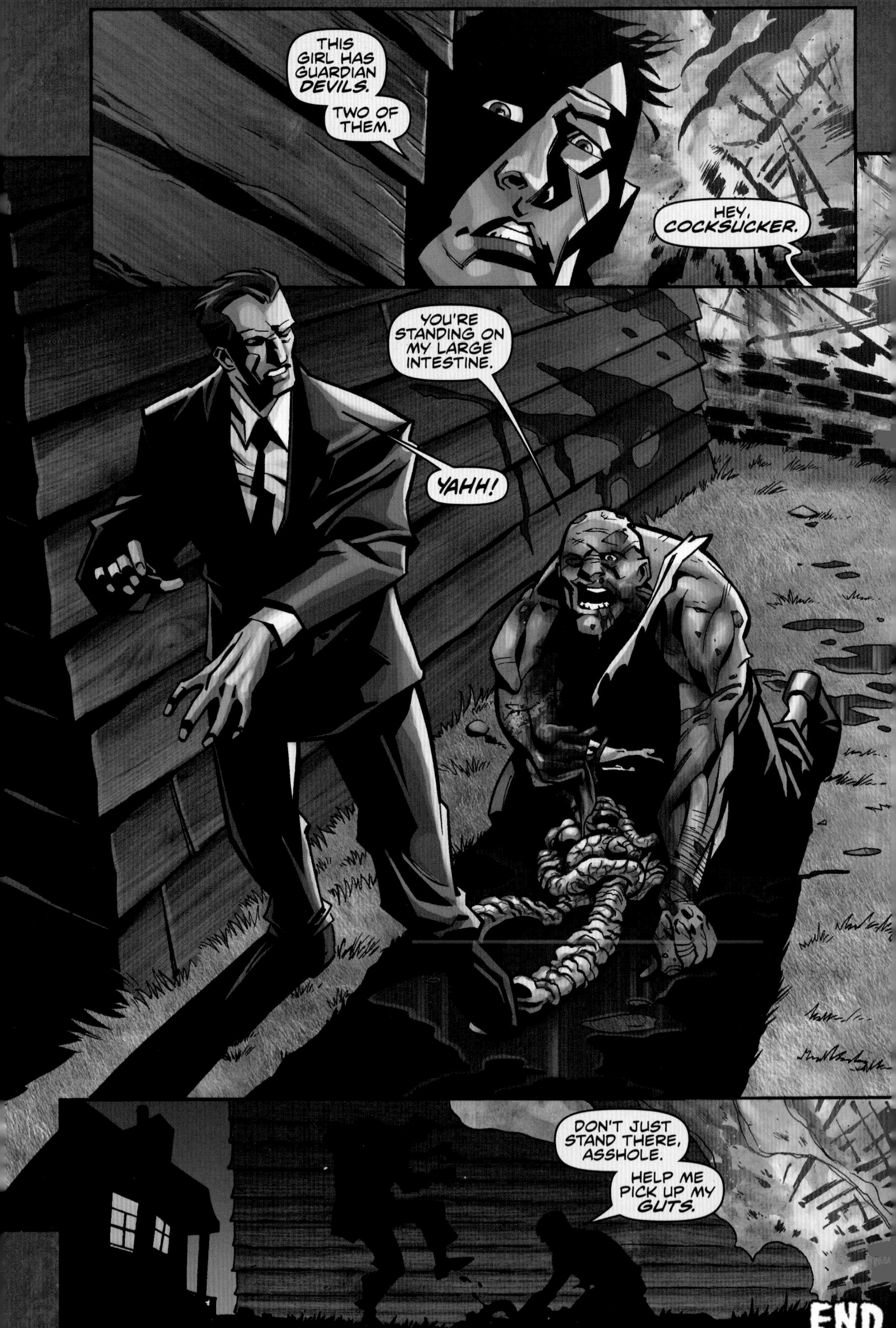
THIS GIRL HAS GUARDIAN DEVILS.
TWO OF THEM.
HEY, COCKSUCKER.
YOU'RE STANDING ON MY LARGE INTESTINE.
YAHH!
DON'T JUST STAND THERE, ASSHOLE.
HELP ME PICK UP MY GUTS.
END

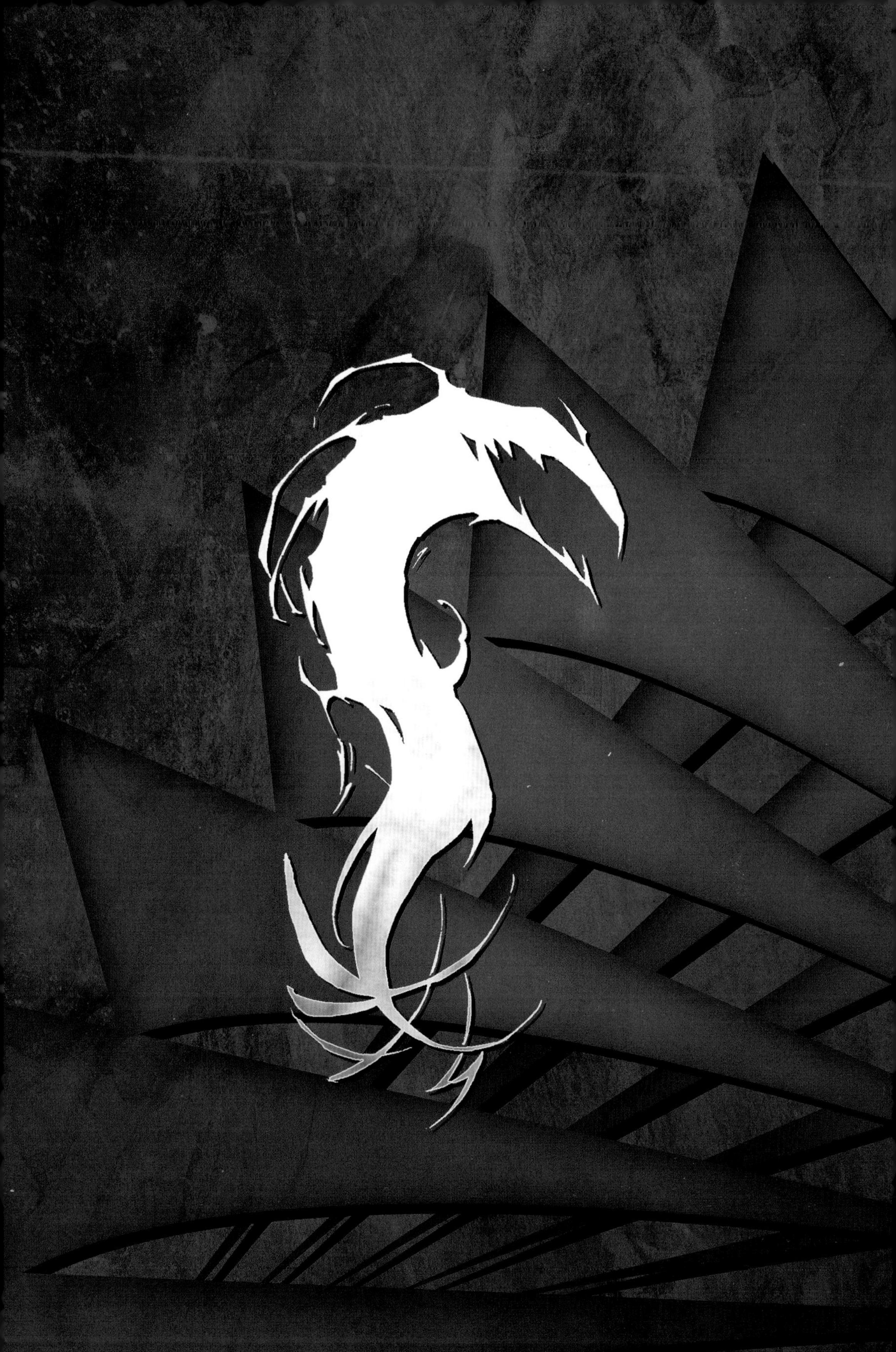

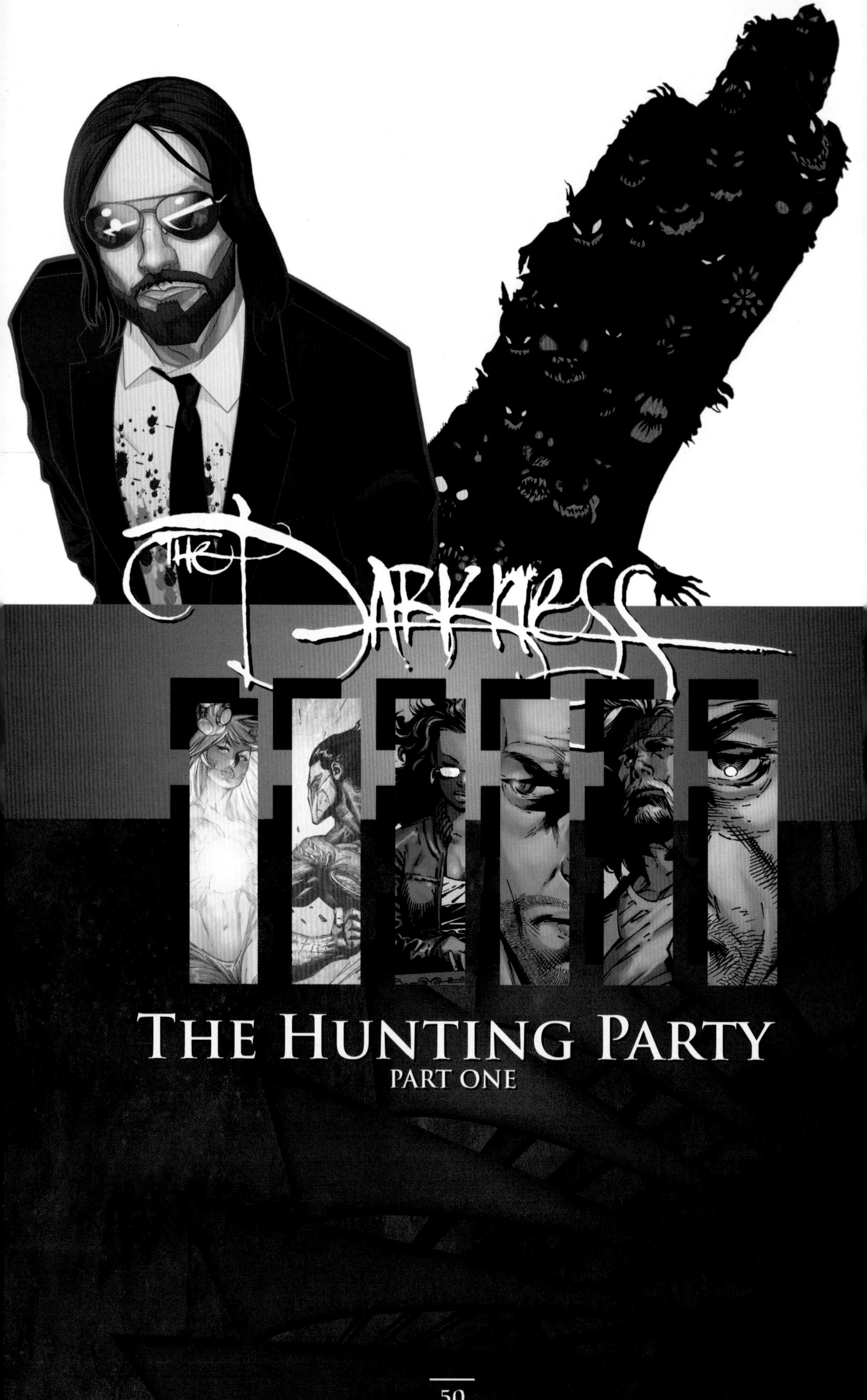
THE DARKNESS
THE HUNTING PARTY
PART ONE

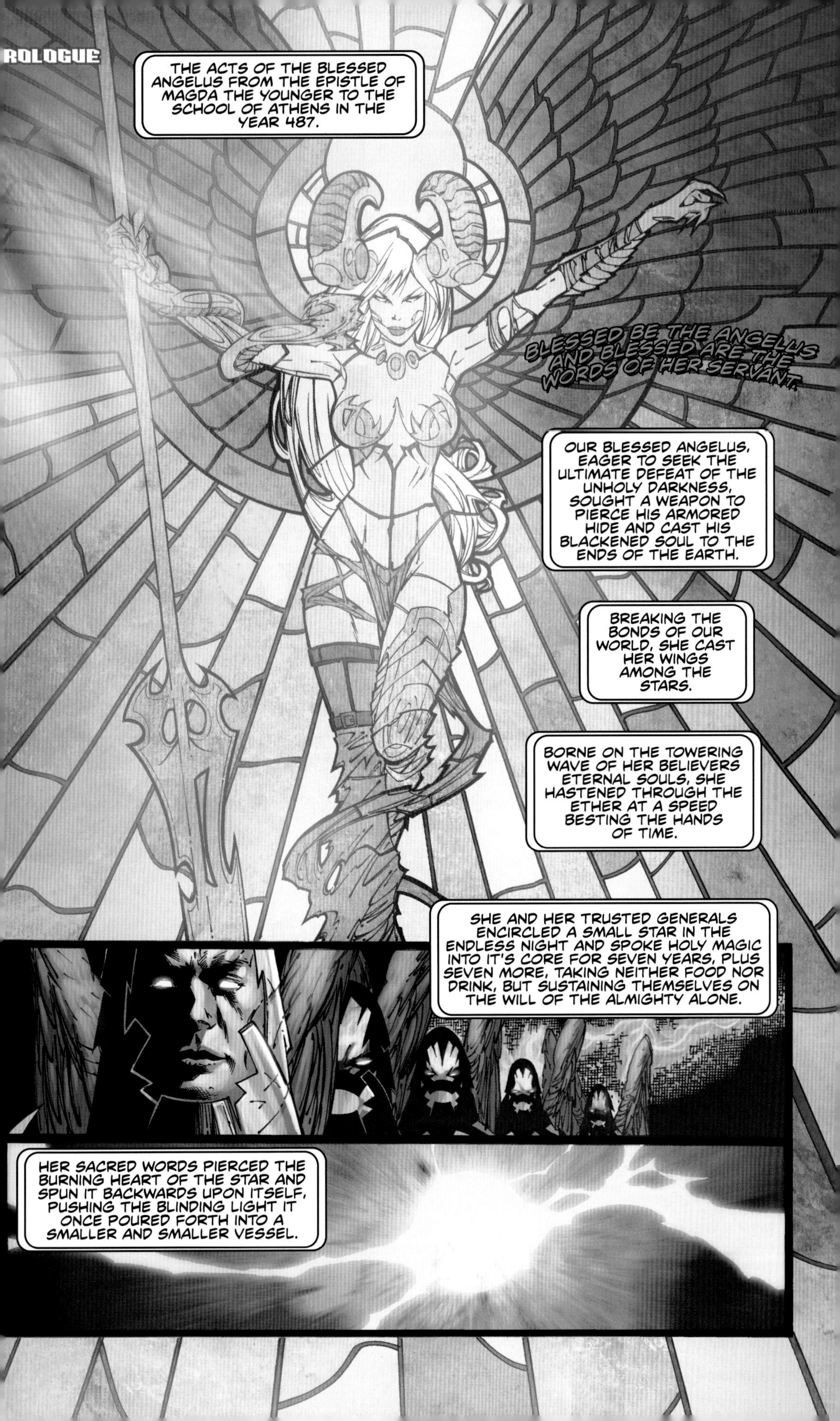
ROLOGUE
THE ACTS OF THE BLESSED ANGELUS FROM THE EPISTLE OF MAGDA THE YOUNGER TO THE SCHOOL OF ATHENS IN THE YEAR 487.
BLESSED BE THE ANGELUS AND BLESSED ARE THE WORDS OF HER SERVANT.
OUR BLESSED ANGELUS, EAGER TO SEEK THE ULTIMATE DEFEAT OF THE UNHOLY DARKNESS, SOUGHT A WEAPON TO PIERCE HIS ARMORED HIDE AND CAST HIS BLACKENED SOUL TO THE ENDS OF THE EARTH.
BREAKING THE BONDS OF OUR WORLD, SHE CAST HER WINGS AMONG THE STARS.
BORNE ON THE TOWERING WAVE OF HER BELIEVERS ETERNAL SOULS, SHE HASTENED THROUGH THE ETHER AT A SPEED BESTING THE HANDS OF TIME.
SHE AND HER TRUSTED GENERALS ENCIRCLED A SMALL STAR IN THE ENDLESS NIGHT AND SPOKE HOLY MAGIC INTO IT'S CORE FOR SEVEN YEARS, PLUS SEVEN MORE, TAKING NEITHER FOOD NOR DRINK, BUT SUSTAINING THEMSELVES ON THE WILL OF THE ALMIGHTY ALONE.
HER SACRED WORDS PIERCED THE BURNING HEART OF THE STAR AND SPUN IT BACKWARDS UPON ITSELF, PUSHING THE BLINDING LIGHT IT ONCE POURED FORTH INTO A SMALLER AND SMALLER VESSEL.

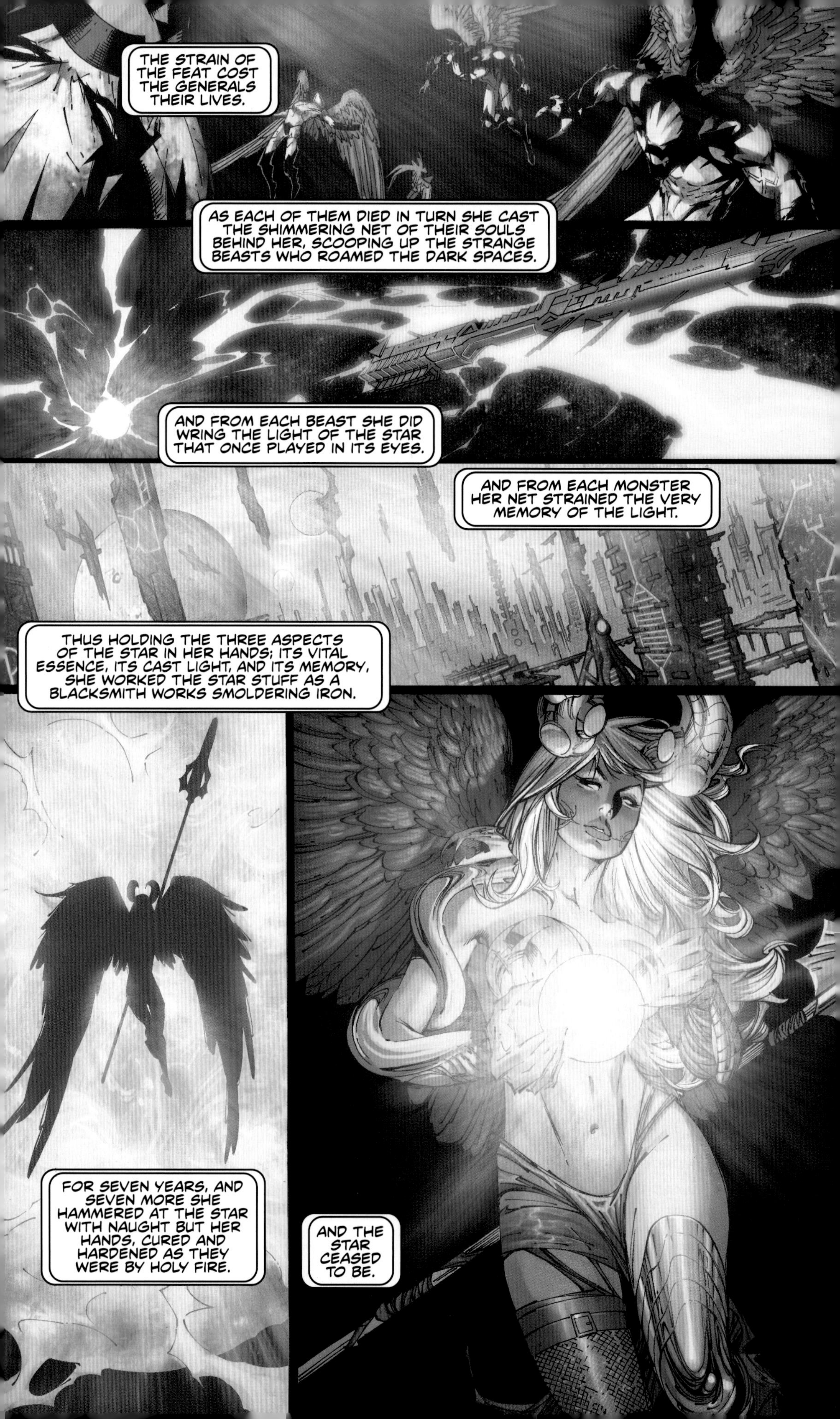
THE STRAIN OF THE FEAT COST THE GENERALS THEIR LIVES.
AS EACH OF THEM DIED IN TURN SHE CAST THE SHIMMERING NET OF THEIR SOULS BEHIND HER, SCOOPING UP THE STRANGE BEASTS WHO ROAMED THE DARK SPACES.
AND FROM EACH BEAST SHE DID WRING THE LIGHT OF THE STAR THAT ONCE PLAYED IN ITS EYES.
AND FROM EACH MONSTER HER NET STRAINED THE VERY MEMORY OF THE LIGHT.
THUS HOLDING THE THREE ASPECTS OF THE STAR IN HER HANDS; ITS VITAL ESSENCE, ITS CAST LIGHT, AND ITS MEMORY, SHE WORKED THE STAR STUFF AS A BLACKSMITH WORKS SMOLDERING IRON.
FOR SEVEN YEARS, AND SEVEN MORE SHE HAMMERED AT THE STAR WITH NAUGHT BUT HER HANDS, CURED AND HARDENED AS THEY WERE BY HOLY FIRE.
AND THE STAR CEASED TO BE.

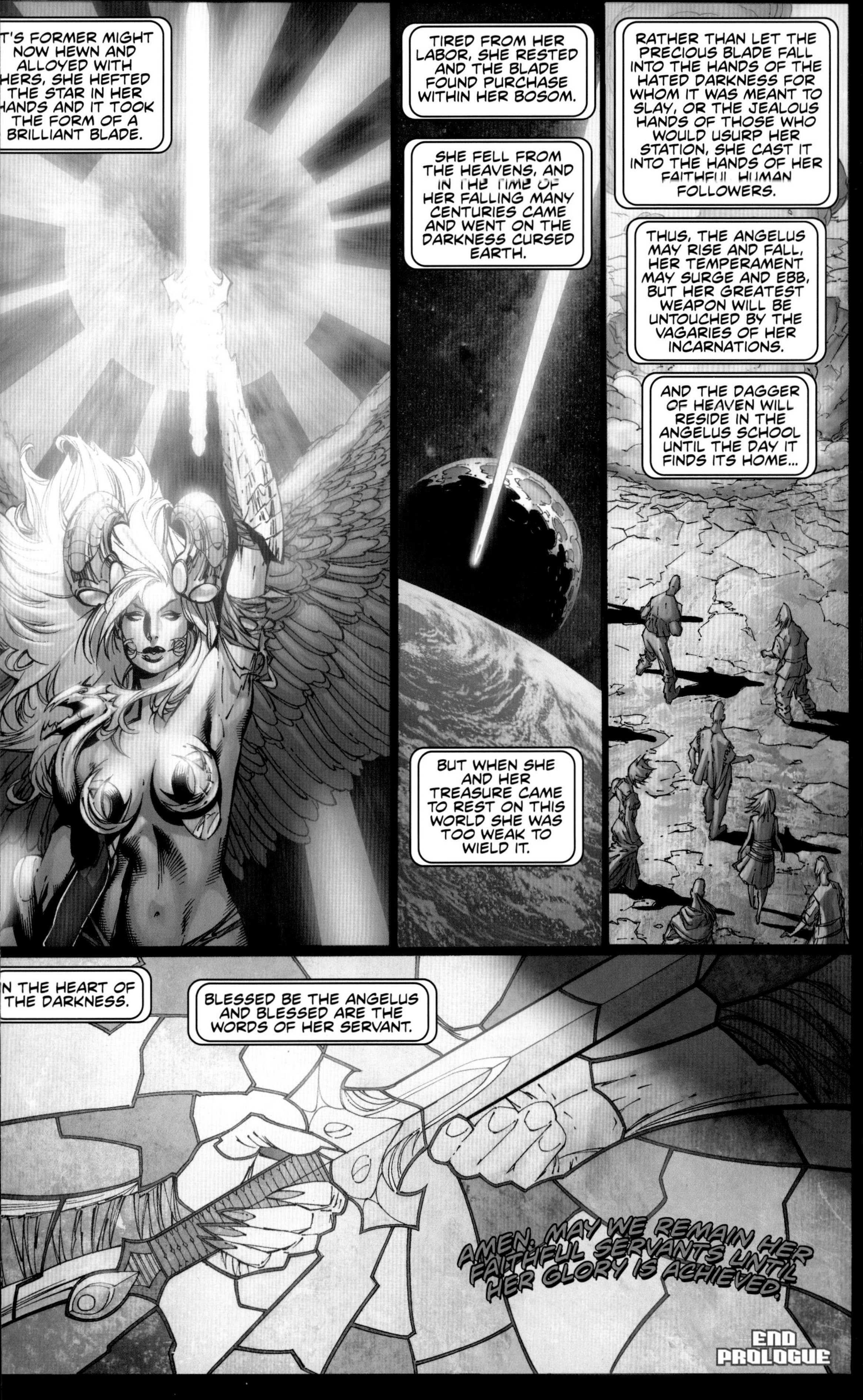
T'S FORMER MIGHT NOW HEWN AND ALLOYED WITH HERS, SHE HEFTED THE STAR IN HER HANDS AND IT TOOK THE FORM OF A BRILLIANT BLADE.
TIRED FROM HER LABOR, SHE RESTED AND THE BLADE FOUND PURCHASE WITHIN HER BOSOM.
SHE FELL FROM THE HEAVENS, AND IN THE TIME OF HER FALLING MANY CENTURIES CAME AND WENT ON THE DARKNESS CURSED EARTH.
BUT WHEN SHE AND HER TREASURE CAME TO REST ON THIS WORLD SHE WAS TOO WEAK TO WIELD IT.
RATHER THAN LET THE PRECIOUS BLADE FALL INTO THE HANDS OF THE HATED DARKNESS FOR WHOM IT WAS MEANT TO SLAY, OR THE JEALOUS HANDS OF THOSE WHO WOULD USURP HER STATION, SHE CAST IT INTO THE HANDS OF HER FAITHFUL HUMAN FOLLOWERS.
THUS, THE ANGELUS MAY RISE AND FALL, HER TEMPERAMENT MAY SURGE AND EBB, BUT HER GREATEST WEAPON WILL BE UNTOUCHED BY THE VAGARIES OF HER INCARNATIONS.
AND THE DAGGER OF HEAVEN WILL RESIDE IN THE ANGELUS SCHOOL UNTIL THE DAY IT FINDS ITS HOME...
N THE HEART OF THE DARKNESS.
BLESSED BE THE ANGELUS AND BLESSED ARE THE WORDS OF HER SERVANT.
AMEN. MAY WE REMAIN HER FAITHFUL SERVANTS UNTIL HER GLORY IS ACHIEVED.
END PROLOGUE

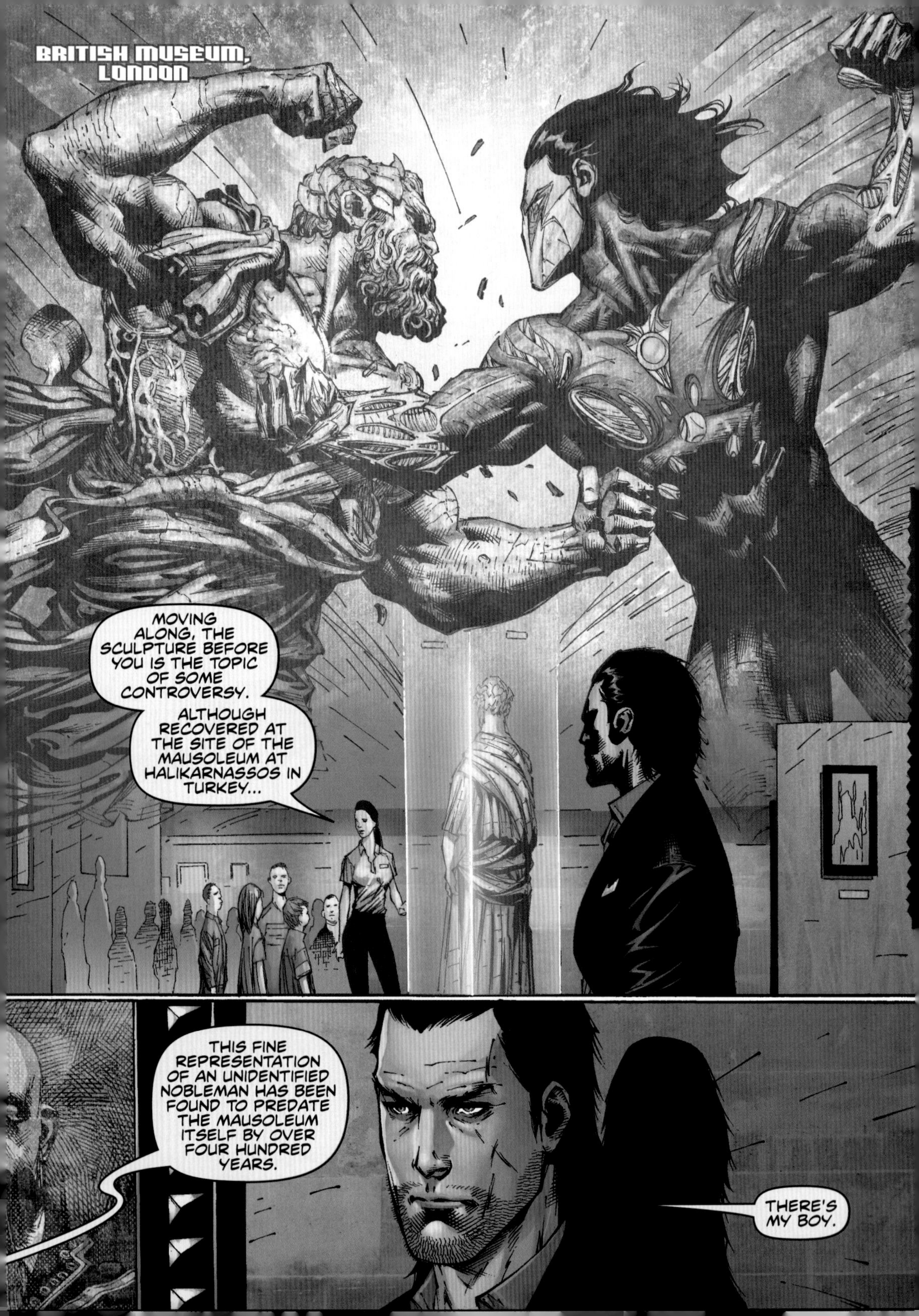
BRITISH MUSEUM, LONDON
MOVING ALONG, THE SCULPTURE BEFORE YOU IS THE TOPIC OF SOME CONTROVERSY.
ALTHOUGH RECOVERED AT THE SITE OF THE MAUSOLEUM AT HALIKARNASSOS IN TURKEY...
THIS FINE REPRESENTATION OF AN UNIDENTIFIED NOBLEMAN HAS BEEN FOUND TO PREDATE THE MAUSOLEUM ITSELF BY OVER FOUR HUNDRED YEARS.
THERE'S MY BOY.

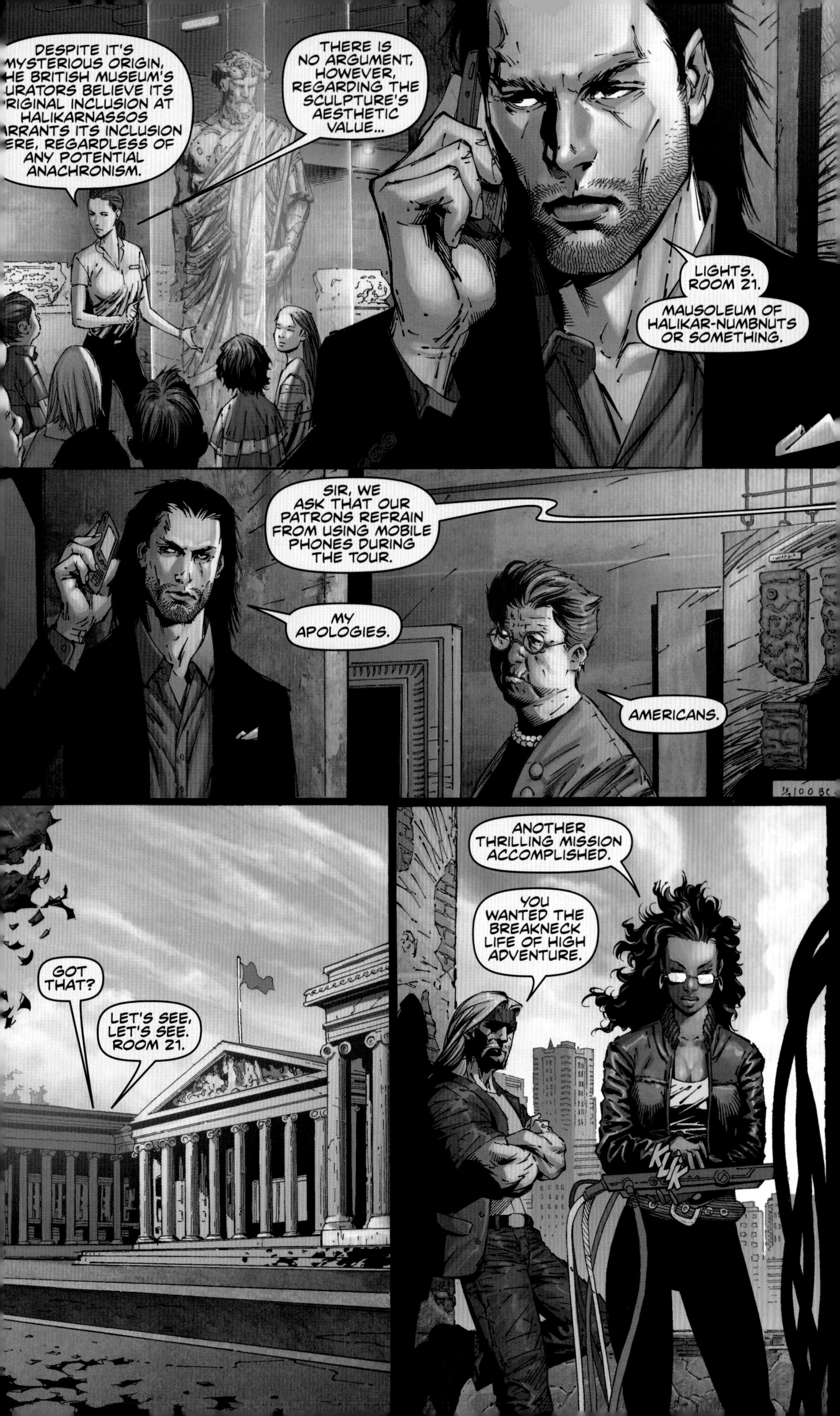
DESPITE IT'S MYSTERIOUS ORIGIN, HE BRITISH MUSEUM'S URATORS BELIEVE ITS RIGINAL INCLUSION AT HALIKARNASSOS ARRANTS ITS INCLUSION ERE, REGARDLESS OF ANY POTENTIAL ANACHRONISM.
THERE IS NO ARGUMENT, HOWEVER, REGARDING THE SCULPTURE'S AESTHETIC VALUE...
LIGHTS. ROOM 21.
MAUSOLEUM OF HALIKAR-NUMBNUTS OR SOMETHING.
SIR, WE ASK THAT OUR PATRONS REFRAIN FROM USING MOBILE PHONES DURING THE TOUR.
MY APOLOGIES.
AMERICANS.
GOT THAT?
LET'S SEE, LET'S SEE. ROOM 21.
ANOTHER THRILLING MISSION ACCOMPLISHED.
YOU WANTED THE BREAKNECK LIFE OF HIGH ADVENTURE.
KLIK

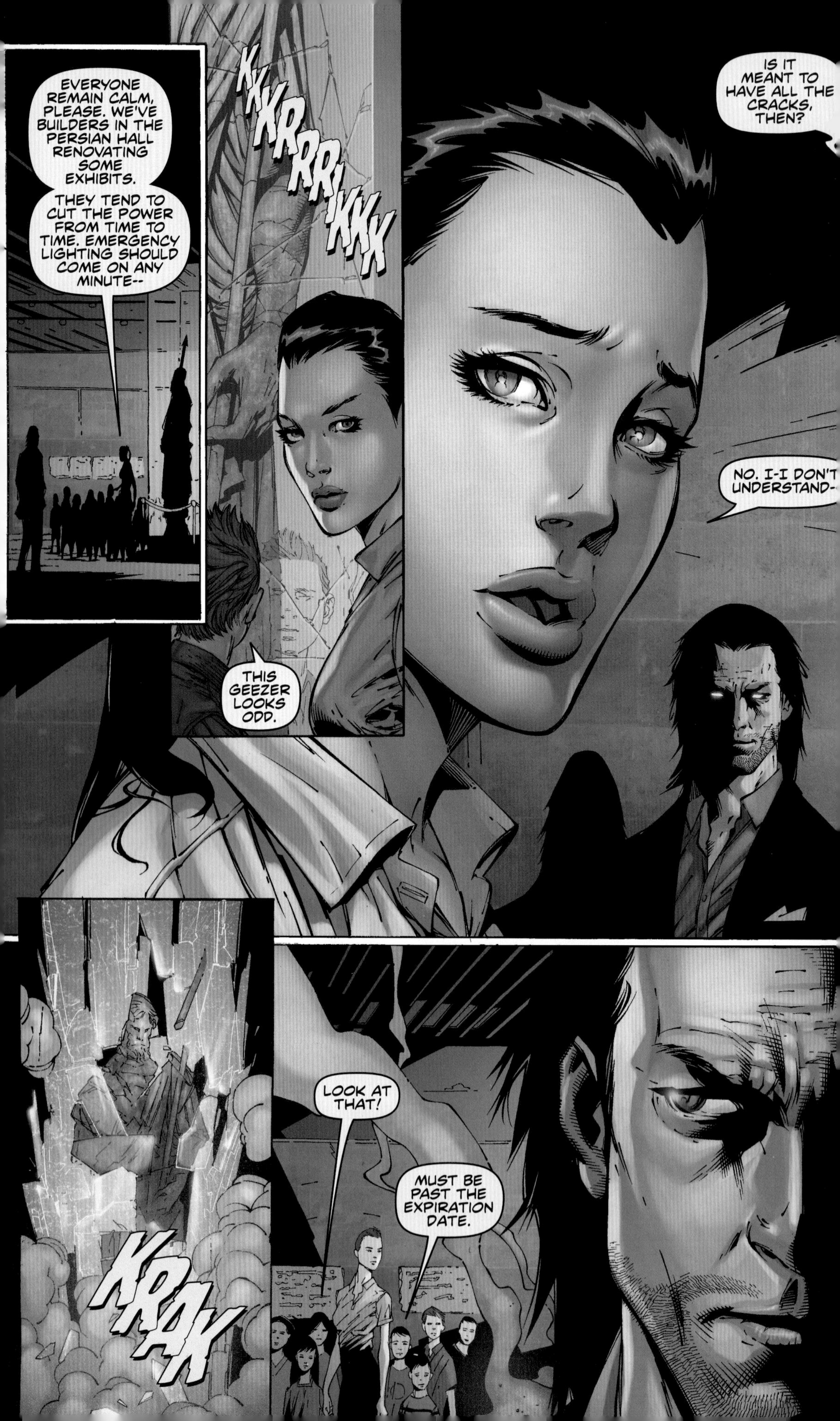
EVERYONE REMAIN CALM, PLEASE. WE'VE BUILDERS IN THE PERSIAN HALL RENOVATING SOME EXHIBITS.
THEY TEND TO CUT THE POWER FROM TIME TO TIME. EMERGENCY LIGHTING SHOULD COME ON ANY MINUTE--
KKKRRRRIKKKK
IS IT MEANT TO HAVE ALL THE CRACKS, THEN?
NO. I-I DON'T UNDERSTAND--
THIS GEEZER LOOKS ODD.
KRAK
LOOK AT THAT!
MUST BE PAST THE EXPIRATION DATE.

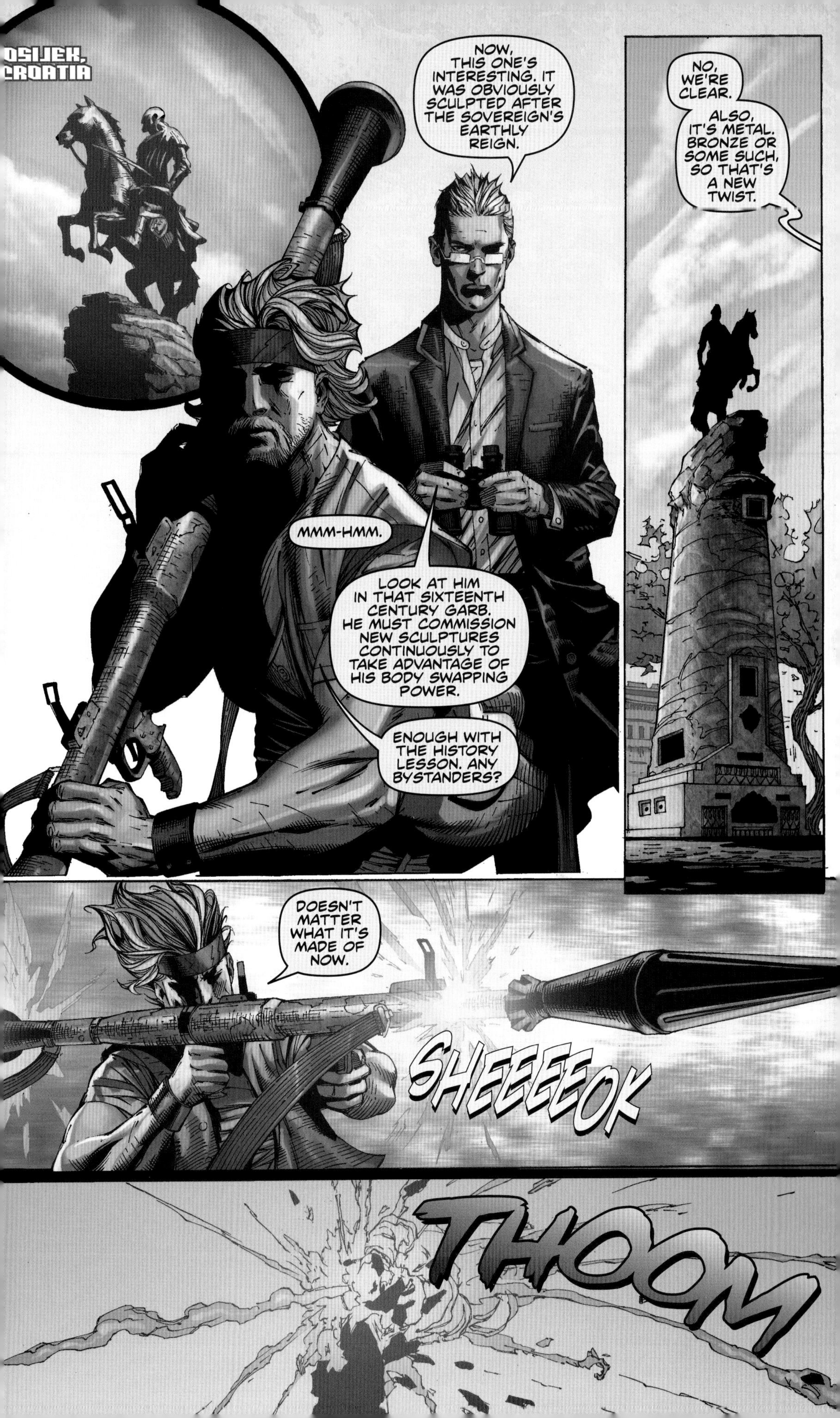
OSIJEK, CROATIA
NOW, THIS ONE'S INTERESTING. IT WAS OBVIOUSLY SCULPTED AFTER THE SOVEREIGN'S EARTHLY REIGN.
MMM-HMM.
LOOK AT HIM IN THAT SIXTEENTH CENTURY GARB. HE MUST COMMISSION NEW SCULPTURES CONTINUOUSLY TO TAKE ADVANTAGE OF HIS BODY SWAPPING POWER.
ENOUGH WITH THE HISTORY LESSON. ANY BYSTANDERS?
NO, WE'RE CLEAR.
ALSO, IT'S METAL. BRONZE OR SOME SUCH, SO THAT'S A NEW TWIST.
DOESN'T MATTER WHAT IT'S MADE OF NOW.
SHEEEEEOK
THOOM

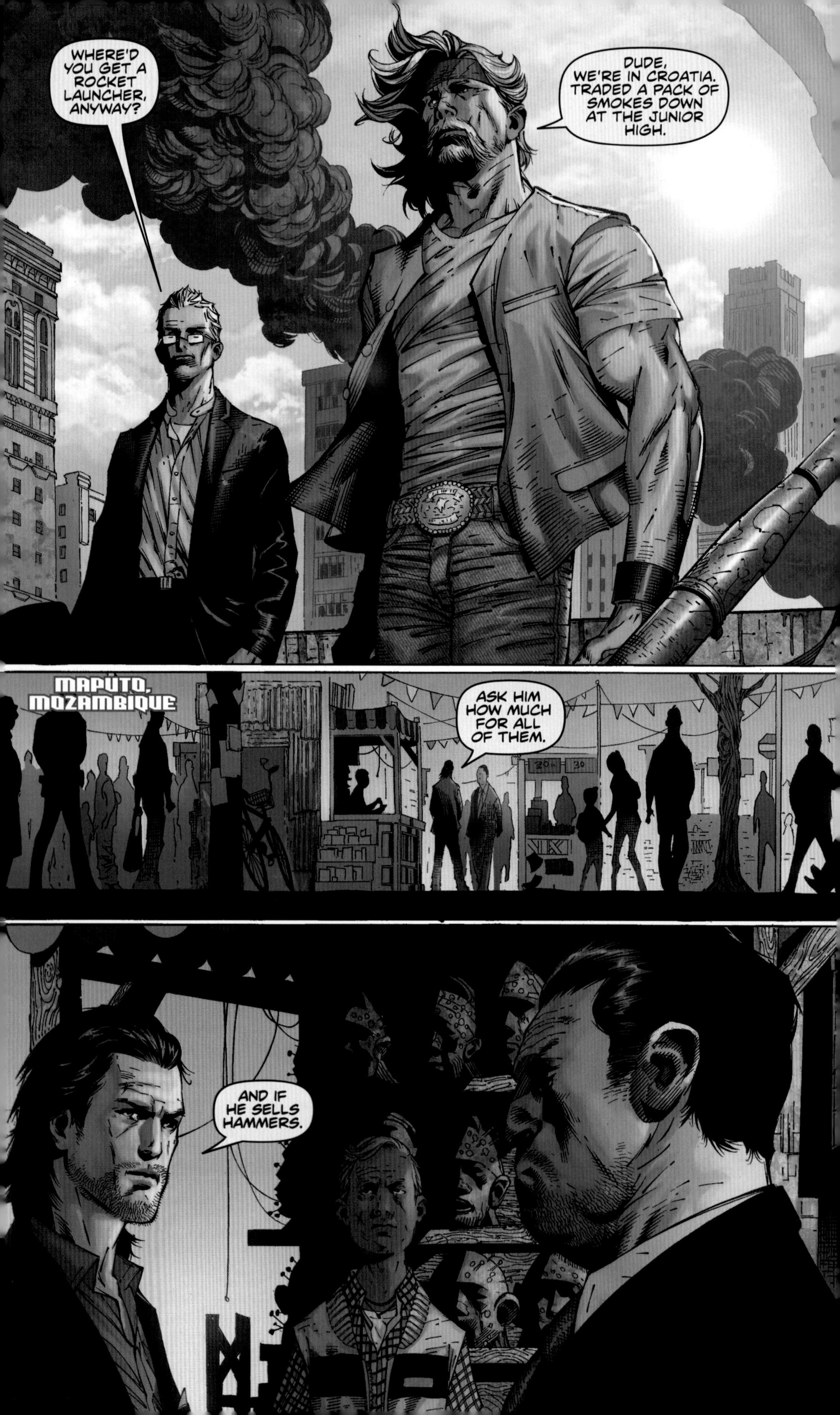
WHERE'D YOU GET A ROCKET LAUNCHER, ANYWAY?
DUDE, WE'RE IN CROATIA. TRADED A PACK OF SMOKES DOWN AT THE JUNIOR HIGH.
MAPUTO, MOZAMBIQUE
ASK HIM HOW MUCH FOR ALL OF THEM.
AND IF HE SELLS HAMMERS.

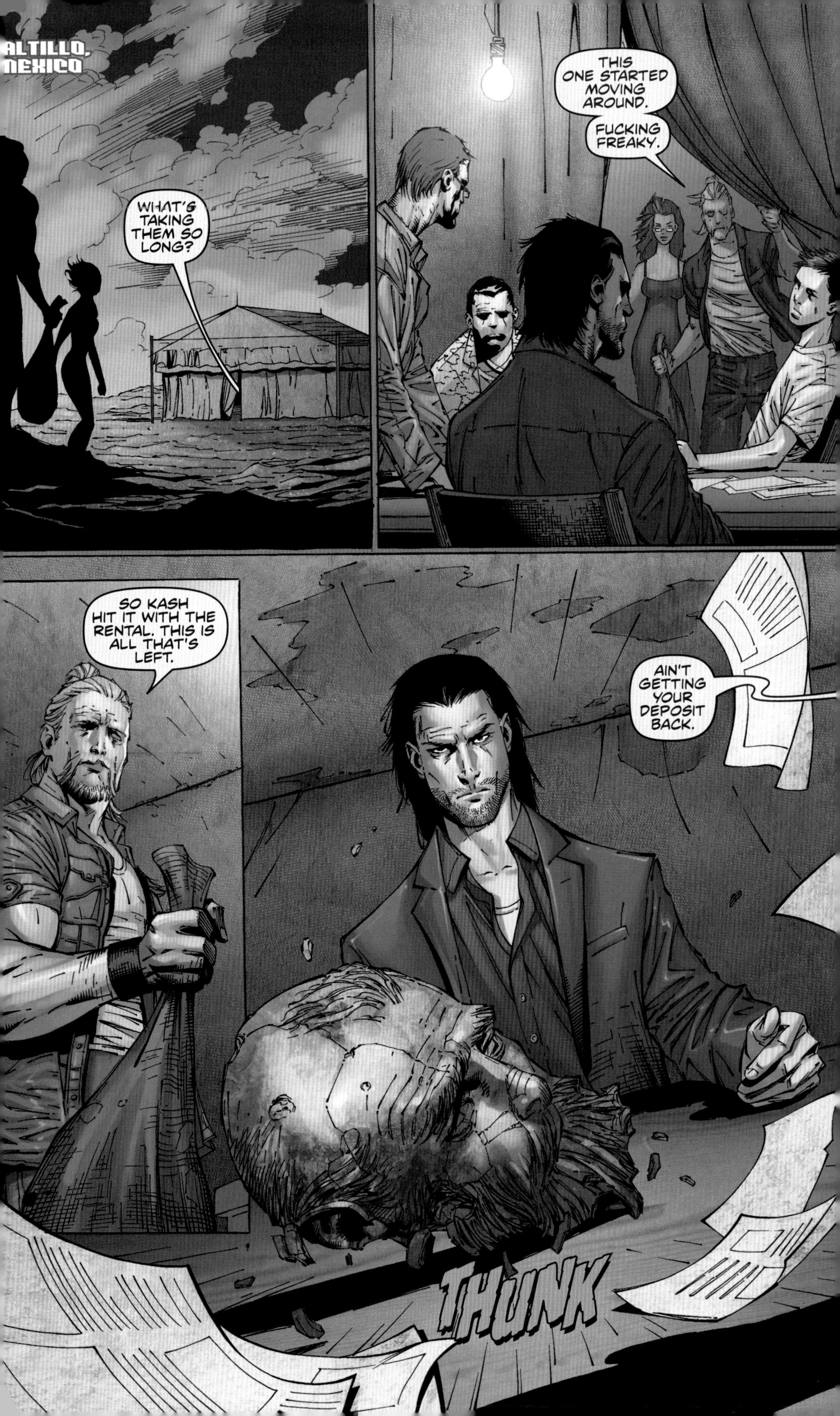
ALTILLO, MEXICO
WHAT'S TAKING THEM SO LONG?
THIS ONE STARTED MOVING AROUND.
FUCKING FREAKY.
SO KASH HIT IT WITH THE RENTAL. THIS IS ALL THAT'S LEFT.
AIN'T GETTING YOUR DEPOSIT BACK.
THUNK

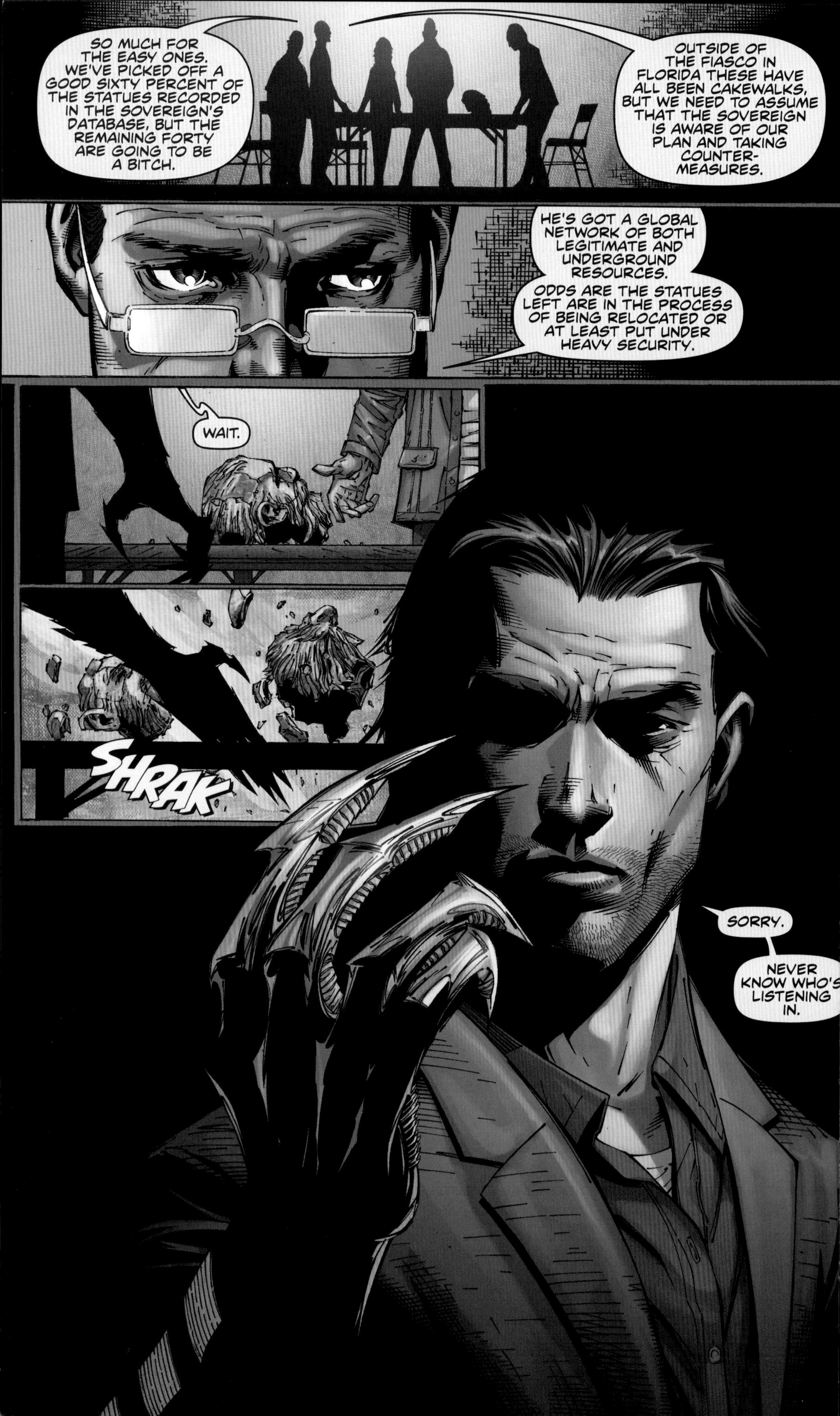
SO MUCH FOR THE EASY ONES. WE'VE PICKED OFF A GOOD SIXTY PERCENT OF THE STATUES RECORDED IN THE SOVEREIGN'S DATABASE, BUT THE REMAINING FORTY ARE GOING TO BE A BITCH.
OUTSIDE OF THE FIASCO IN FLORIDA THESE HAVE ALL BEEN CAKEWALKS, BUT WE NEED TO ASSUME THAT THE SOVEREIGN IS AWARE OF OUR PLAN AND TAKING COUNTER-MEASURES.
HE'S GOT A GLOBAL NETWORK OF BOTH LEGITIMATE AND UNDERGROUND RESOURCES.
ODDS ARE THE STATUES LEFT ARE IN THE PROCESS OF BEING RELOCATED OR AT LEAST PUT UNDER HEAVY SECURITY.
WAIT.
SHRAK
SORRY.
NEVER KNOW WHO'S LISTENING IN.

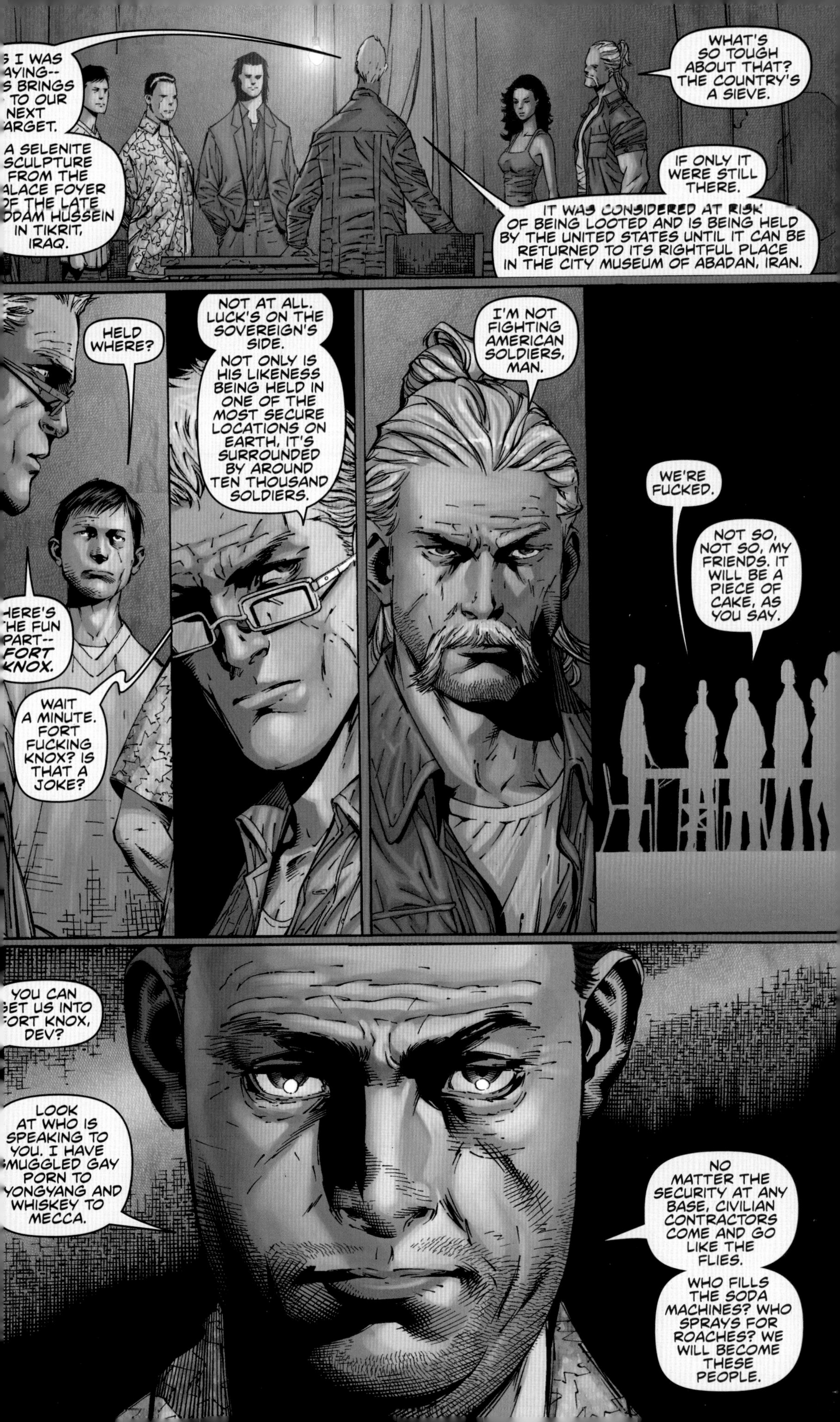

I WAS
AYING--
S BRINGS
TO OUR
NEXT
ARGET.
A SELENITE
SCULPTURE
FROM THE
ALACE FOYER
OF THE LATE
DDAM HUSSEIN
IN TIKRIT,
IRAQ.
WHAT'S SO TOUGH ABOUT THAT? THE COUNTRY'S A SIEVE.
IF ONLY IT WERE STILL THERE.
IT WAS CONSIDERED AT RISK OF BEING LOOTED AND IS BEING HELD BY THE UNITED STATES UNTIL IT CAN BE RETURNED TO ITS RIGHTFUL PLACE IN THE CITY MUSEUM OF ABADAN, IRAN.
HELD WHERE?
HERE'S
THE FUN
PART--
FORT
KNOX.
WAIT A MINUTE. FORT FUCKING KNOX? IS THAT A JOKE?
NOT AT ALL. LUCK'S ON THE SOVEREIGN'S SIDE.
NOT ONLY IS HIS LIKENESS BEING HELD IN ONE OF THE MOST SECURE LOCATIONS ON EARTH, IT'S SURROUNDED BY AROUND TEN THOUSAND SOLDIERS.
I'M NOT FIGHTING AMERICAN SOLDIERS, MAN.
WE'RE FUCKED.
NOT SO, NOT SO, MY FRIENDS. IT WILL BE A PIECE OF CAKE, AS YOU SAY.
YOU CAN
GET US INTO
FORT KNOX,
DEV?
LOOK
AT WHO IS
SPEAKING TO
YOU. I HAVE
SMUGGLED GAY
PORN TO
YONGYANG AND
WHISKEY TO
MECCA.
NO MATTER THE SECURITY AT ANY BASE, CIVILIAN CONTRACTORS COME AND GO LIKE THE FLIES.
WHO FILLS THE SODA MACHINES? WHO SPRAYS FOR ROACHES? WE WILL BECOME THESE PEOPLE.

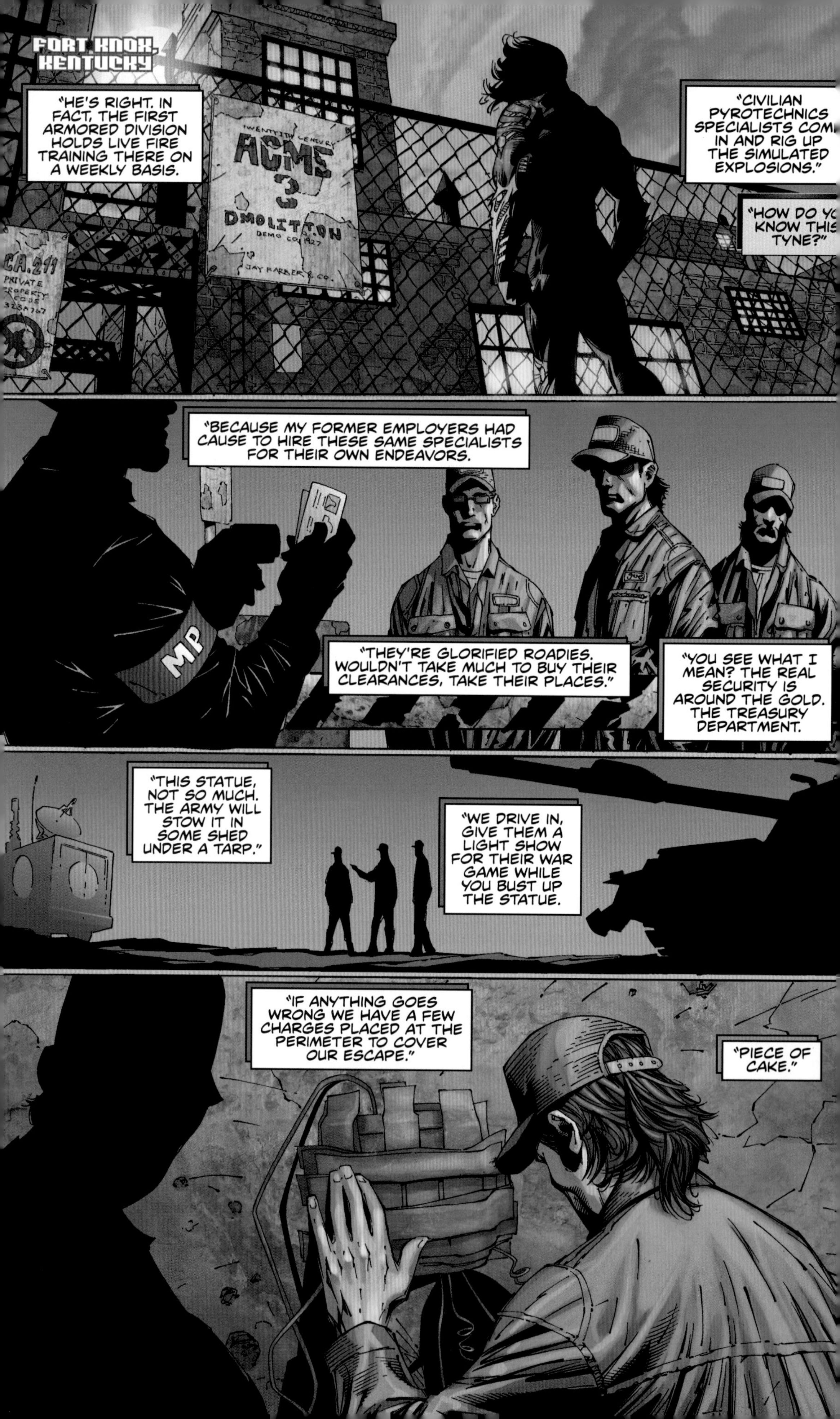
FORT KNOX, KENTUCKY
"HE'S RIGHT. IN FACT, THE FIRST ARMORED DIVISION HOLDS LIVE FIRE TRAINING THERE ON A WEEKLY BASIS.
ACME
3
DMOLITION
DEMO CO. 1927
JAY BARBER & CO.
PRIVATE
"CIVILIAN PYROTECHNICS SPECIALISTS COM IN AND RIG UP THE SIMULATED EXPLOSIONS."
"HOW DO YO KNOW THIS TYNE?"
"BECAUSE MY FORMER EMPLOYERS HAD CAUSE TO HIRE THESE SAME SPECIALISTS FOR THEIR OWN ENDEAVORS.
MP
"THEY'RE GLORIFIED ROADIES. WOULDN'T TAKE MUCH TO BUY THEIR CLEARANCES, TAKE THEIR PLACES."
"YOU SEE WHAT I MEAN? THE REAL SECURITY IS AROUND THE GOLD. THE TREASURY DEPARTMENT.
"THIS STATUE, NOT SO MUCH. THE ARMY WILL STOW IT IN SOME SHED UNDER A TARP."
"WE DRIVE IN, GIVE THEM A LIGHT SHOW FOR THEIR WAR GAME WHILE YOU BUST UP THE STATUE.
"IF ANYTHING GOES WRONG WE HAVE A FEW CHARGES PLACED AT THE PERIMETER TO COVER OUR ESCAPE."
"PIECE OF CAKE."

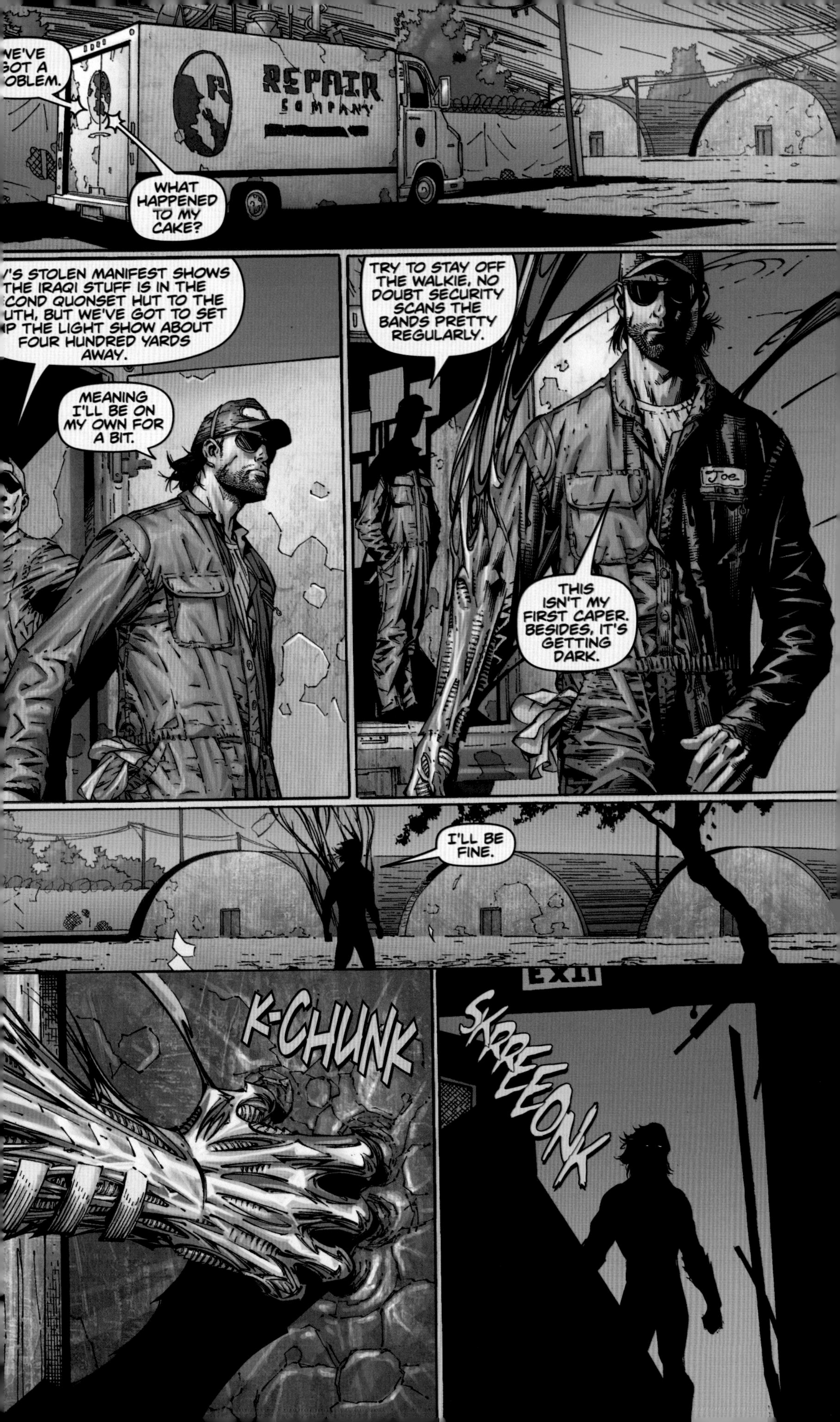

WE'VE GOT A PROBLEM.
REPAIR COMPANY
WHAT HAPPENED TO MY CAKE?
'S STOLEN MANIFEST SHOWS THE IRAQI STUFF IS IN THE SECOND QUONSET HUT TO THE SOUTH, BUT WE'VE GOT TO SET UP THE LIGHT SHOW ABOUT FOUR HUNDRED YARDS AWAY.
MEANING I'LL BE ON MY OWN FOR A BIT.
TRY TO STAY OFF THE WALKIE, NO DOUBT SECURITY SCANS THE BANDS PRETTY REGULARLY.
Joe
THIS ISN'T MY FIRST CAPER. BESIDES, IT'S GETTING DARK.
I'LL BE FINE.
K-CHUNK
EXIT
SKRREEONK

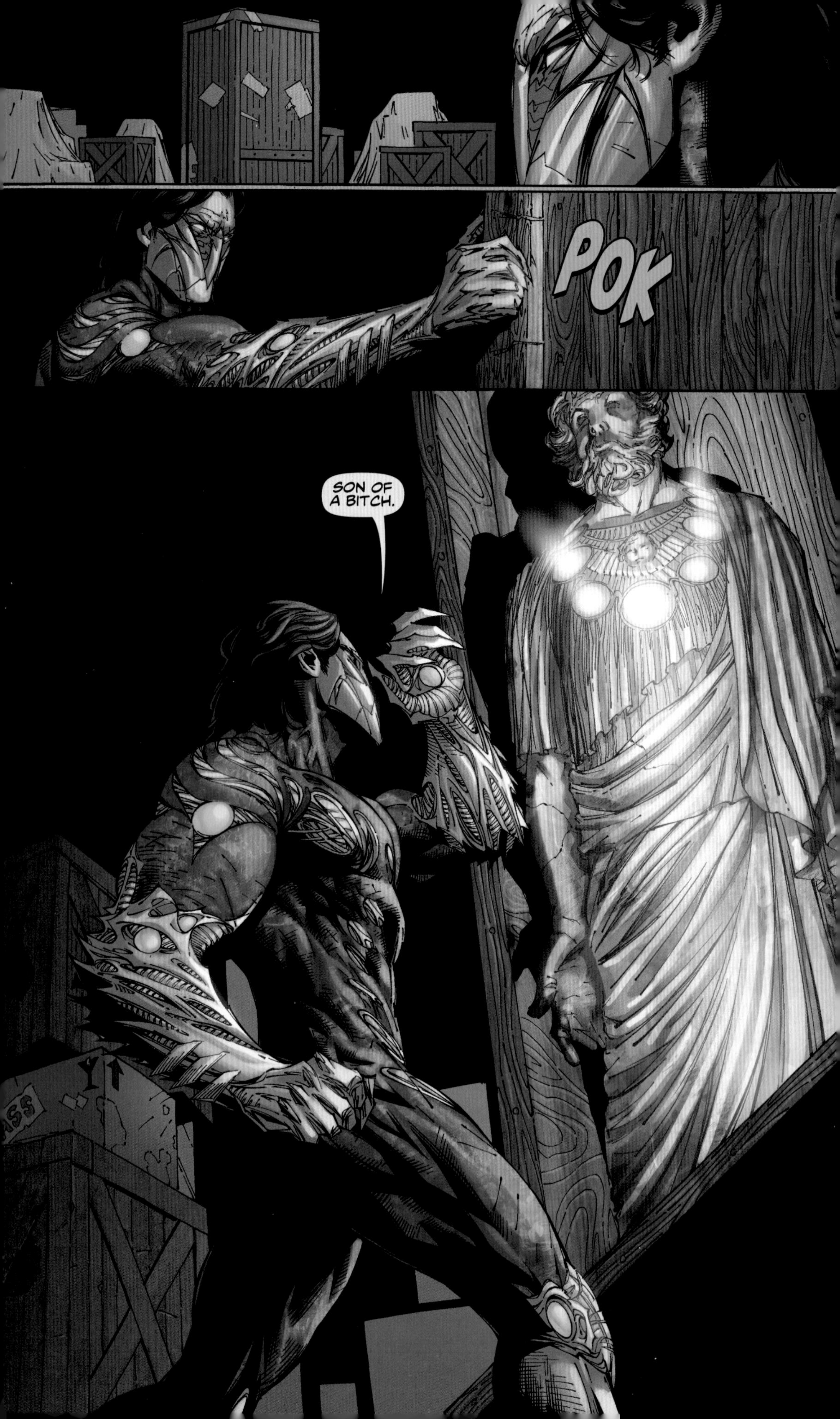
POK
SON OF A BITCH.

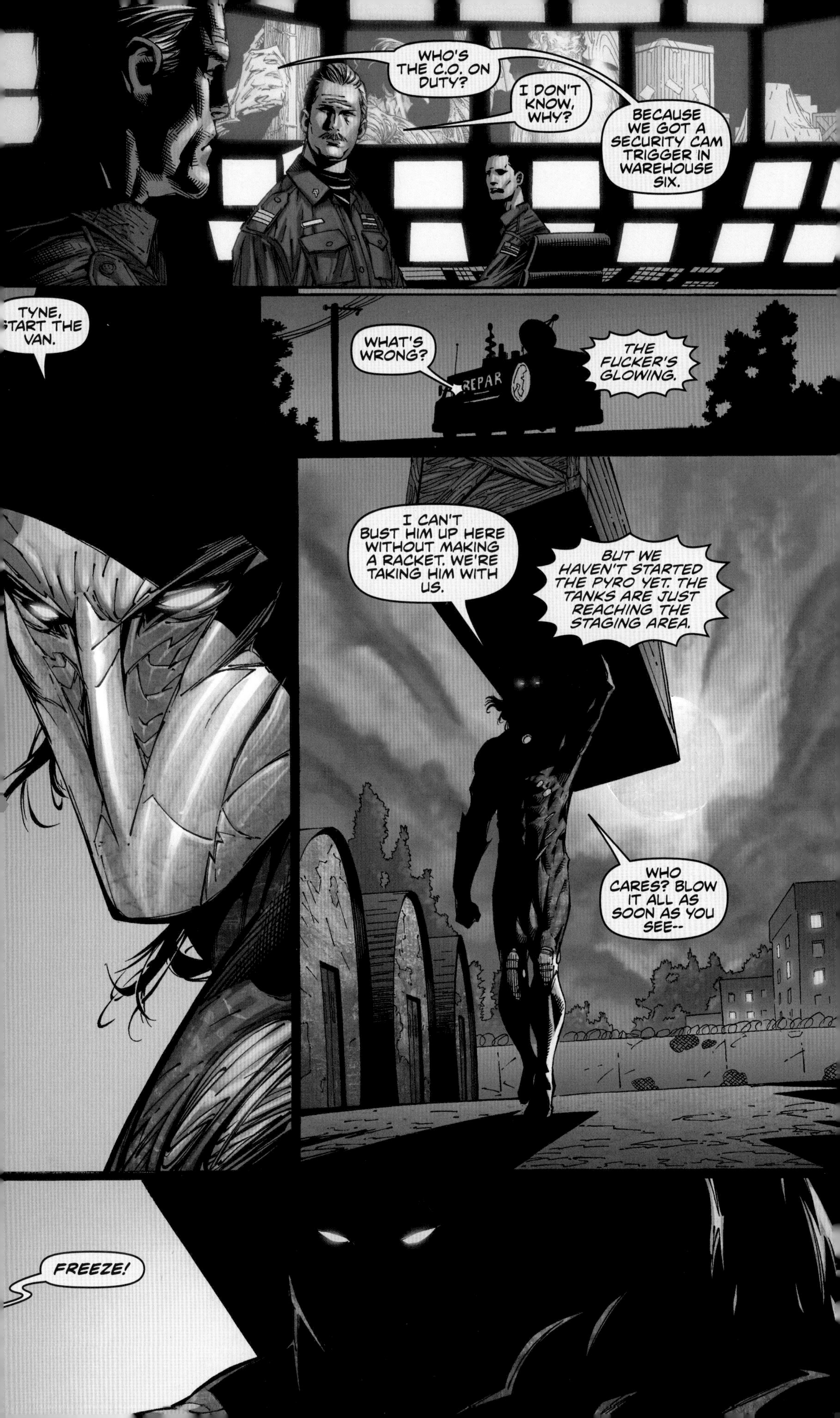
WHO'S THE C.O. ON DUTY?
I DON'T KNOW, WHY?
BECAUSE WE GOT A SECURITY CAM TRIGGER IN WAREHOUSE SIX.
TYNE, START THE VAN.
WHAT'S WRONG?
REPAR
THE FUCKER'S GLOWING.
I CAN'T BUST HIM UP HERE WITHOUT MAKING A RACKET. WE'RE TAKING HIM WITH US.
BUT WE HAVEN'T STARTED THE PYRO YET. THE TANKS ARE JUST REACHING THE STAGING AREA.
WHO CARES? BLOW IT ALL AS SOON AS YOU SEE--
FREEZE!

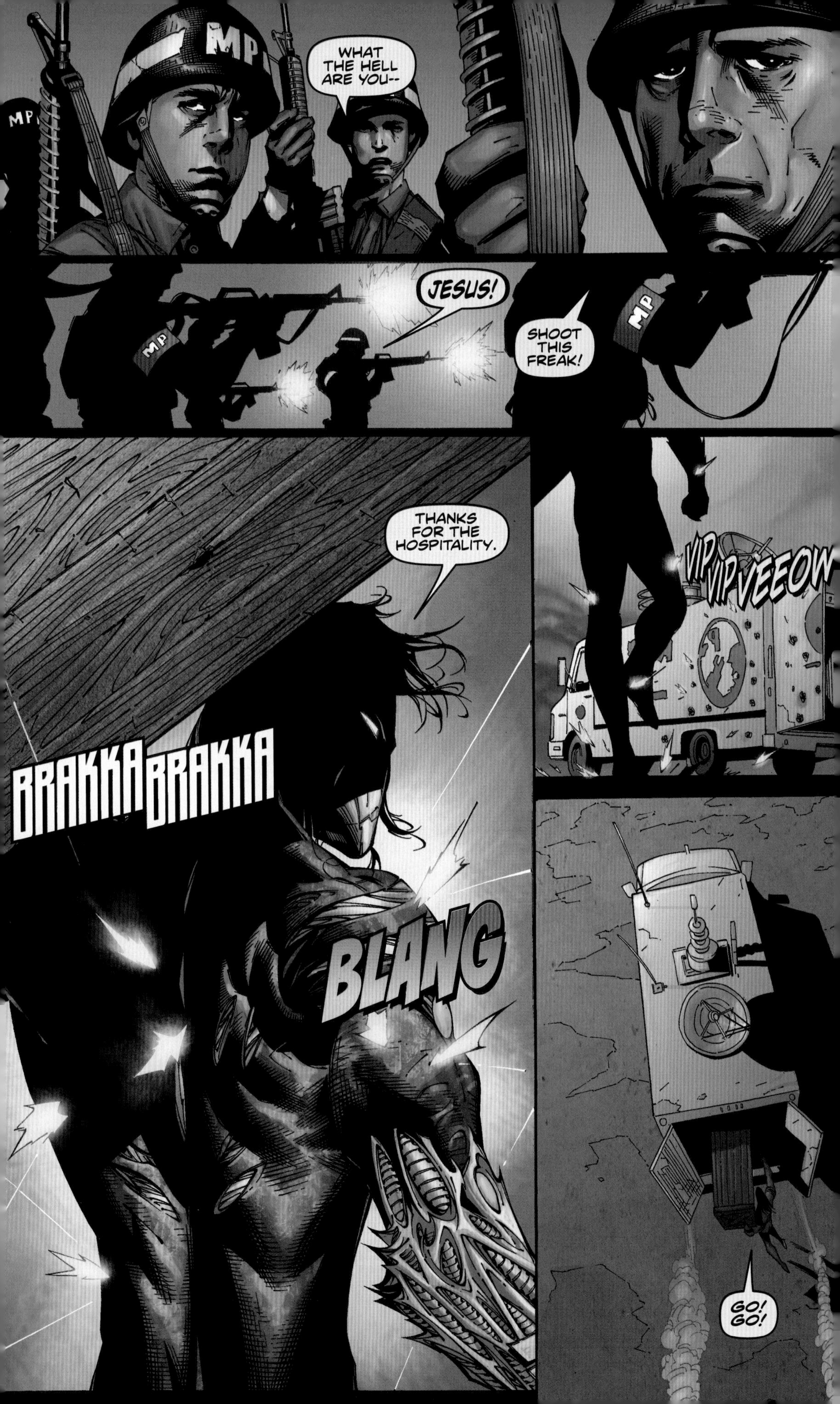
WHAT THE HELL ARE YOU--
JESUS!
SHOOT THIS FREAK!
THANKS FOR THE HOSPITALITY.
BRAKKA BRAKKA
BLANG
VIP VIP VEEOW
GO! GO!

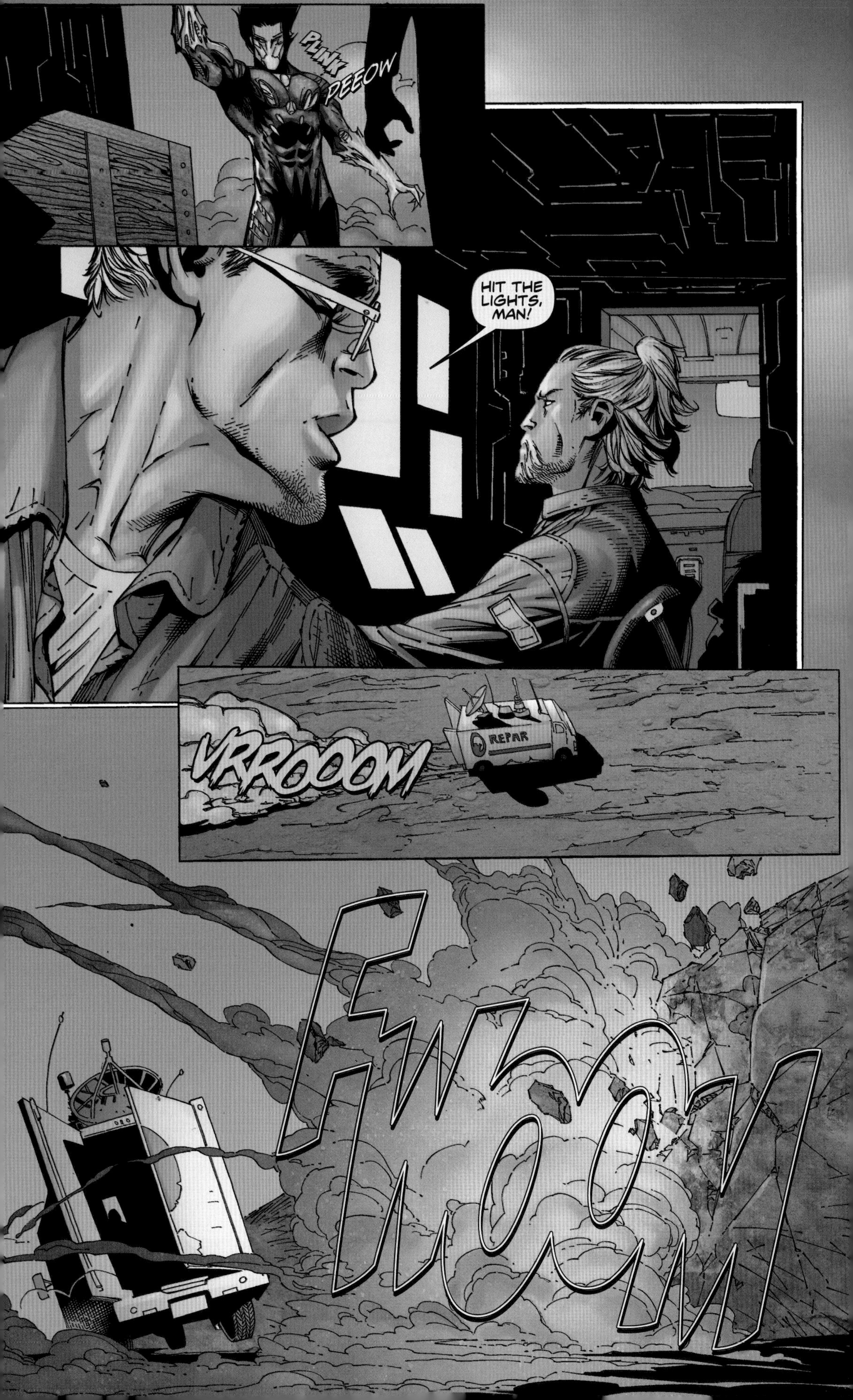
PLINK
PEEOW
HIT THE LIGHTS, MAN!
VRROOOM
REPAR
FWOOOM

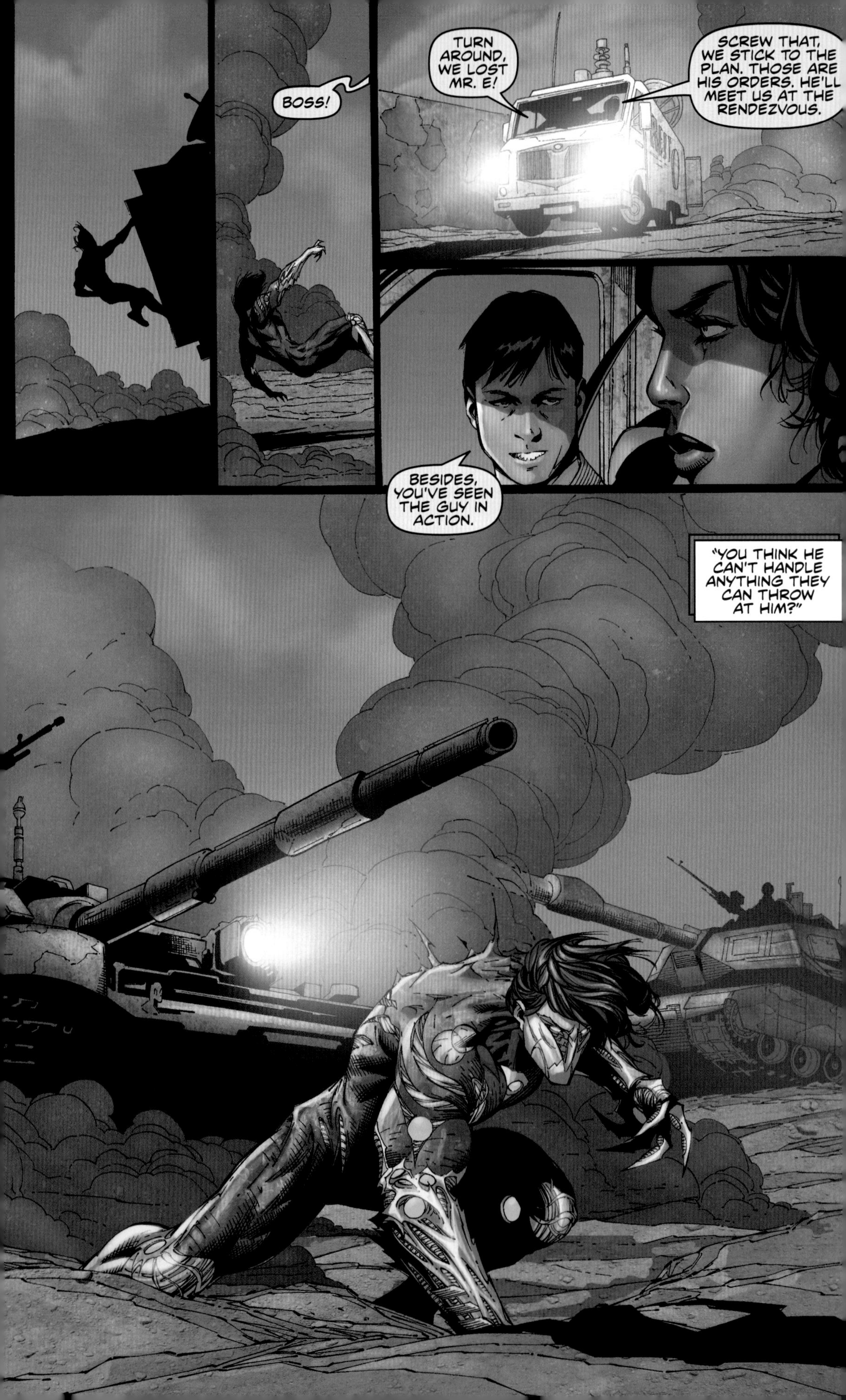
BOSS!
TURN AROUND, WE LOST MR. E!
SCREW THAT, WE STICK TO THE PLAN. THOSE ARE HIS ORDERS. HE'LL MEET US AT THE RENDEZVOUS.
BESIDES, YOU'VE SEEN THE GUY IN ACTION.
"YOU THINK HE CAN'T HANDLE ANYTHING THEY CAN THROW AT HIM?"

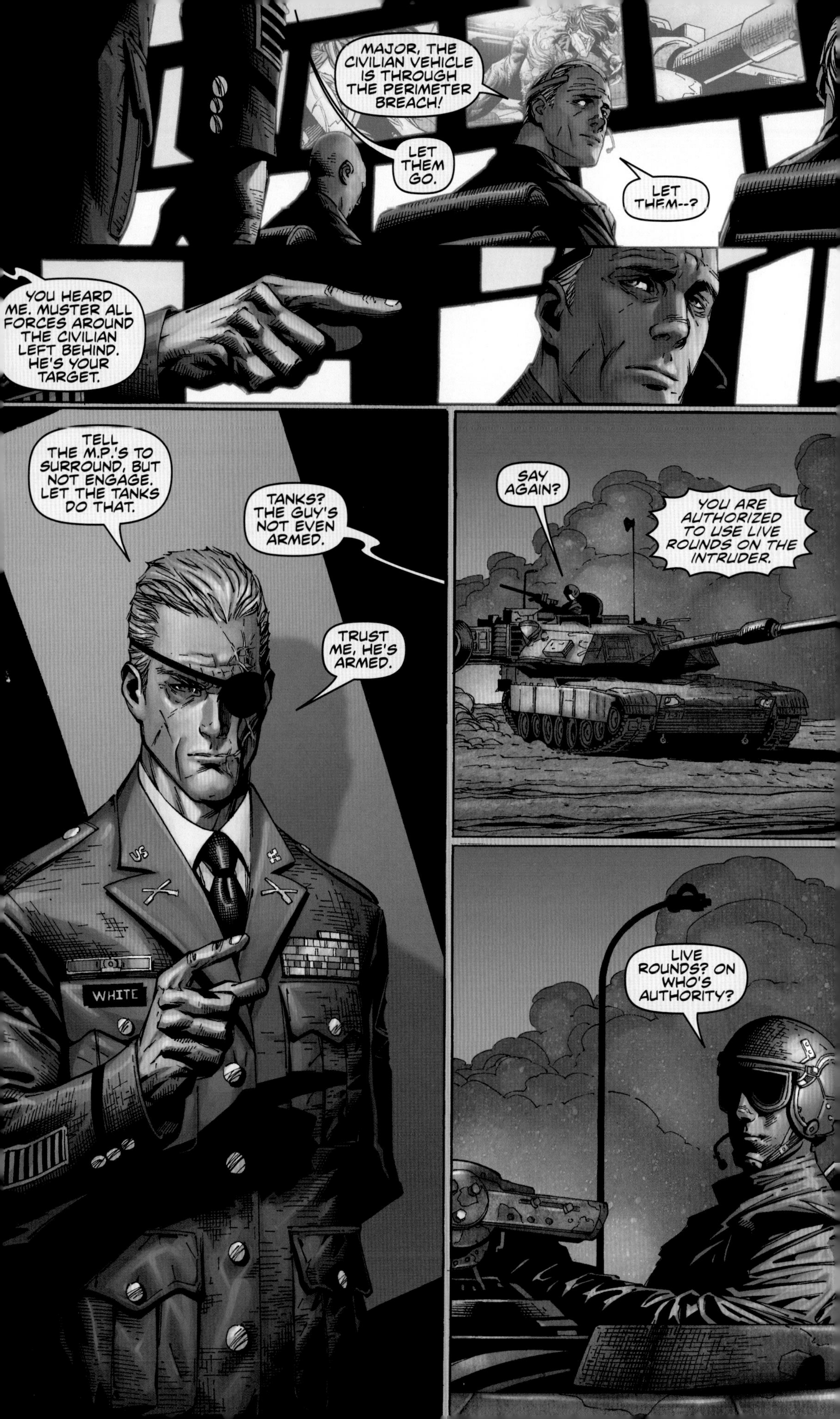
MAJOR, THE CIVILIAN VEHICLE IS THROUGH THE PERIMETER BREACH!
LET THEM GO.
LET THEM--?
YOU HEARD ME. MUSTER ALL FORCES AROUND THE CIVILIAN LEFT BEHIND. HE'S YOUR TARGET.
TELL THE M.P.'S TO SURROUND, BUT NOT ENGAGE. LET THE TANKS DO THAT.
TANKS? THE GUY'S NOT EVEN ARMED.
TRUST ME, HE'S ARMED.
WHITE
SAY AGAIN?
YOU ARE AUTHORIZED TO USE LIVE ROUNDS ON THE INTRUDER.
LIVE ROUNDS? ON WHO'S AUTHORITY?

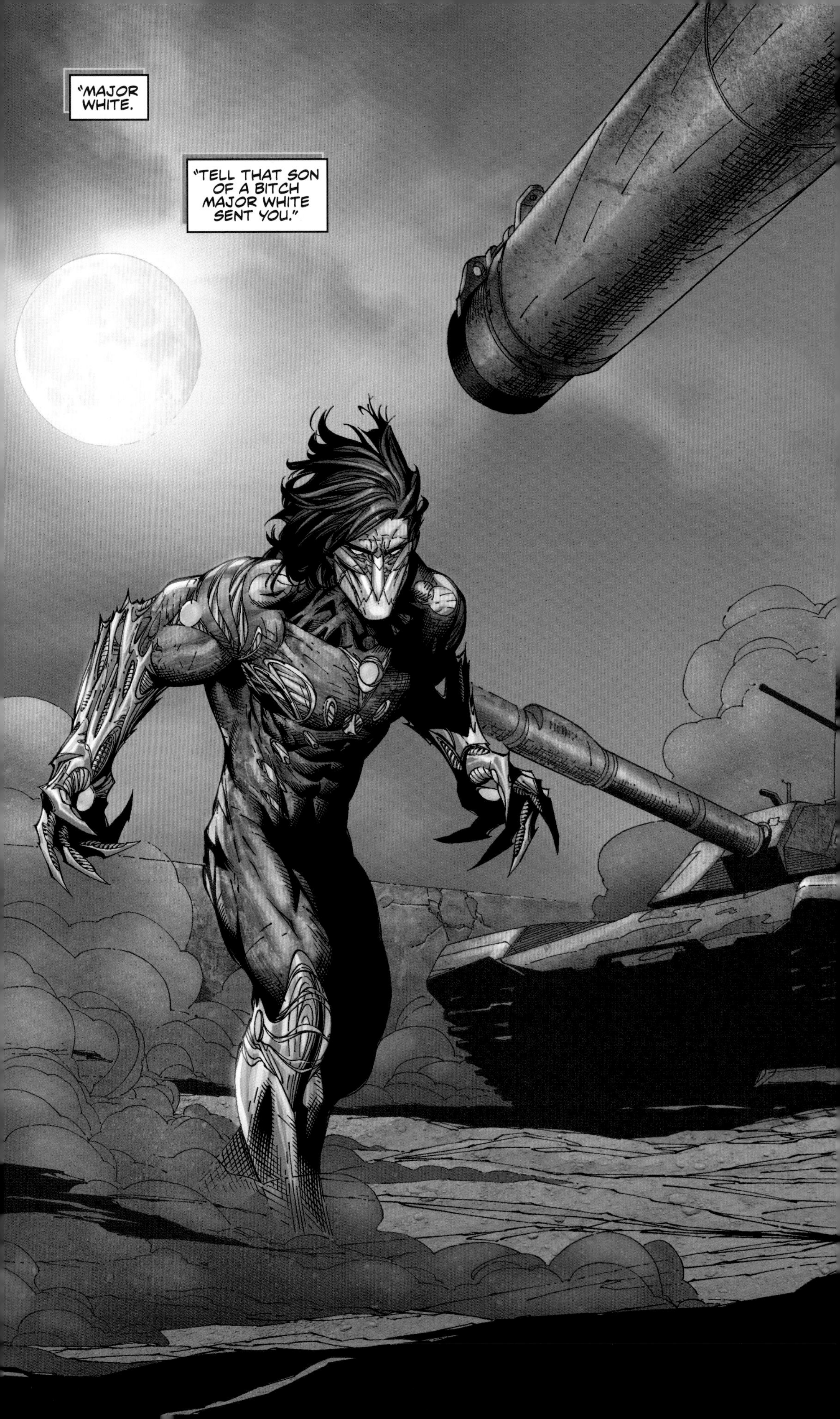
"MAJOR WHITE.
"TELL THAT SON OF A BITCH MAJOR WHITE SENT YOU."

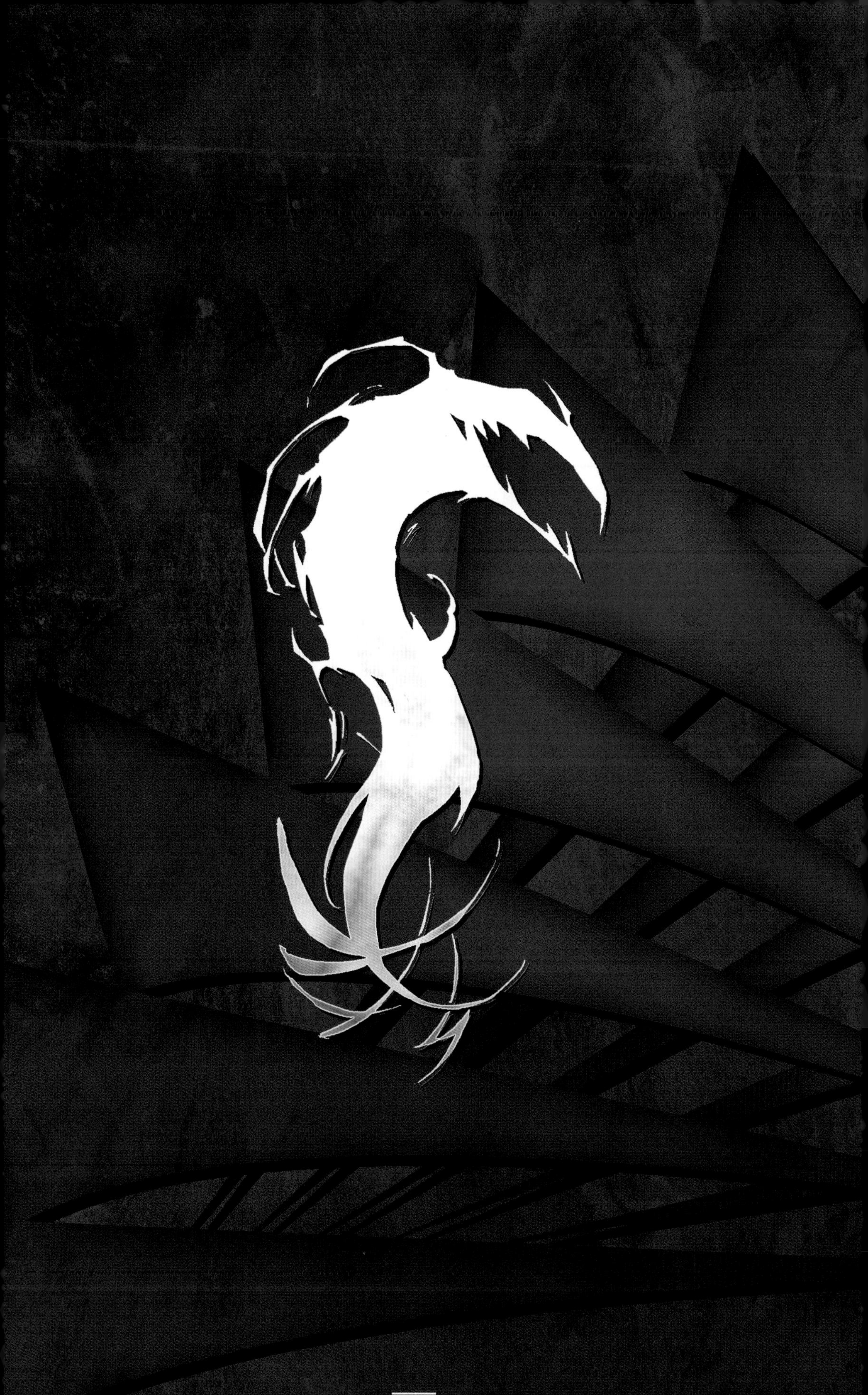

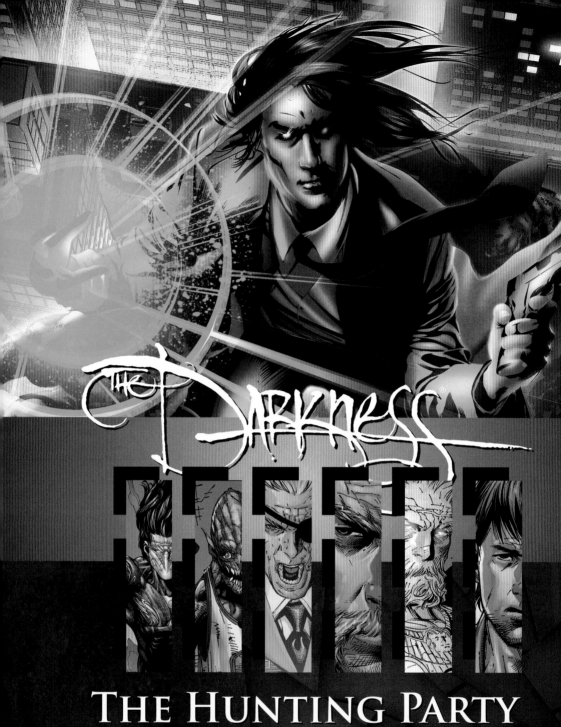

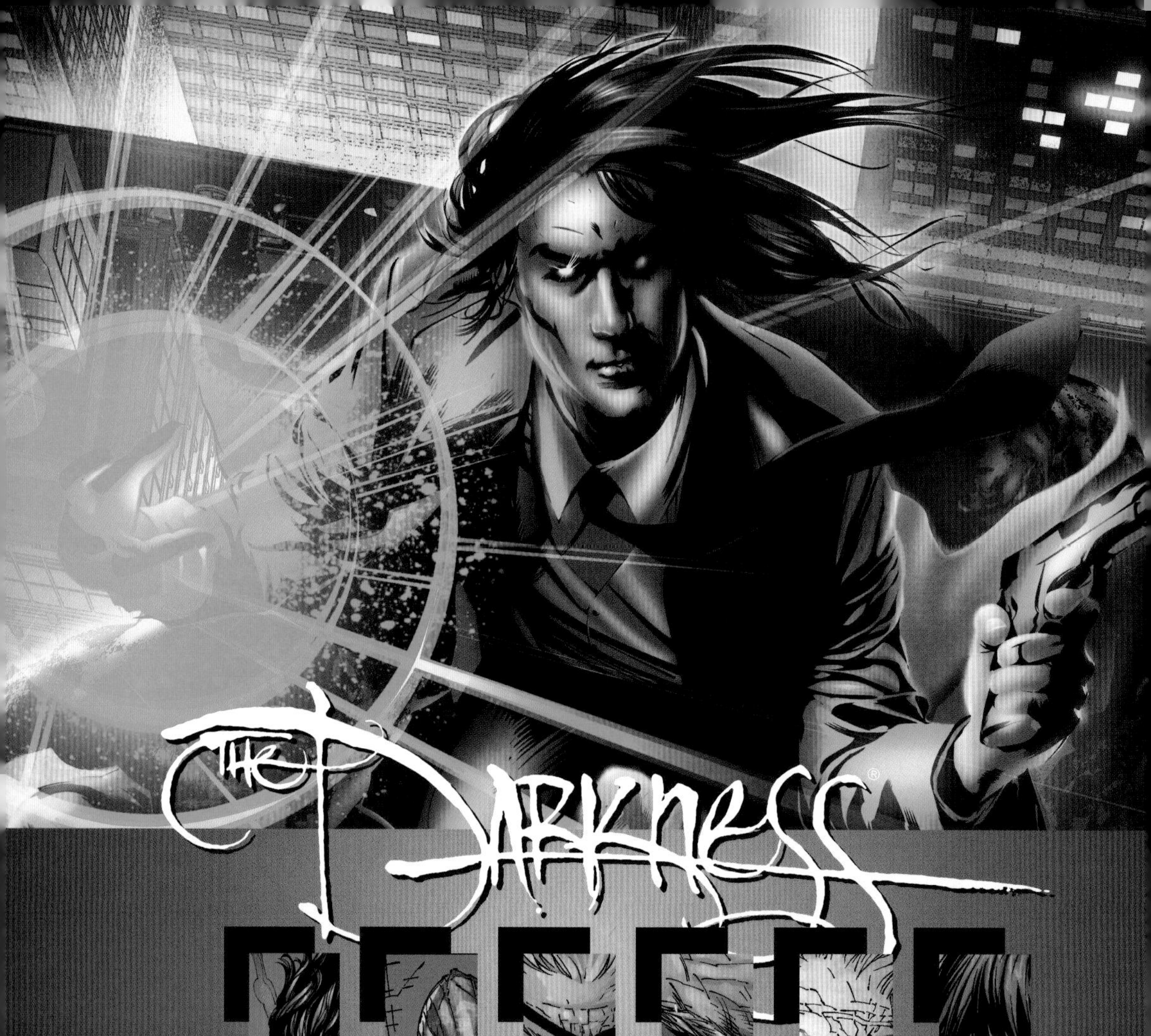
The Darkness

THE HUNTING PARTY
PART TWO

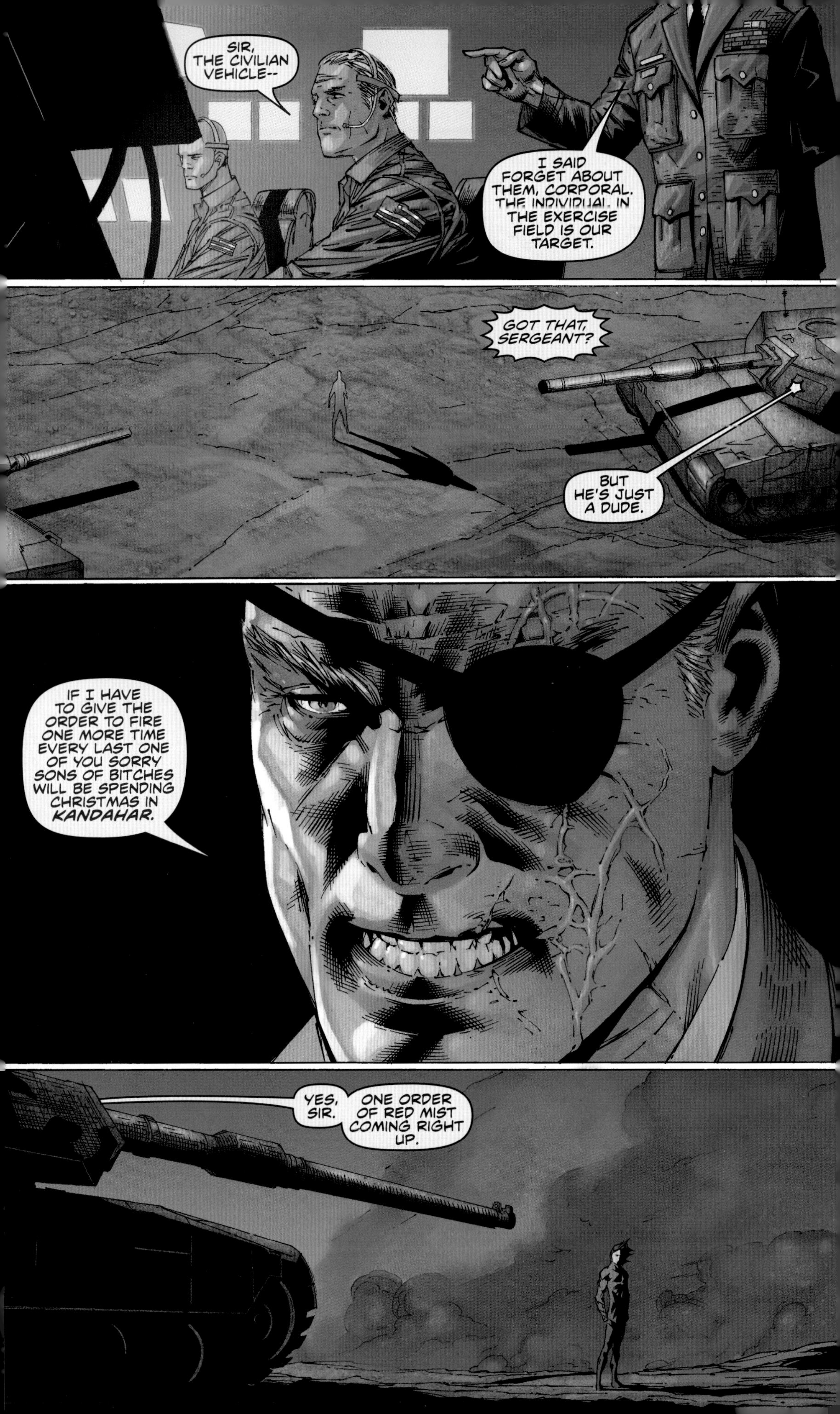
SIR, THE CIVILIAN VEHICLE--
I SAID FORGET ABOUT THEM, CORPORAL. THE INDIVIDUAL IN THE EXERCISE FIELD IS OUR TARGET.
GOT THAT, SERGEANT?
BUT HE'S JUST A DUDE.
IF I HAVE TO GIVE THE ORDER TO FIRE ONE MORE TIME EVERY LAST ONE OF YOU SORRY SONS OF BITCHES WILL BE SPENDING CHRISTMAS IN KANDAHAR.
YES, SIR.
ONE ORDER OF RED MIST COMING RIGHT UP.

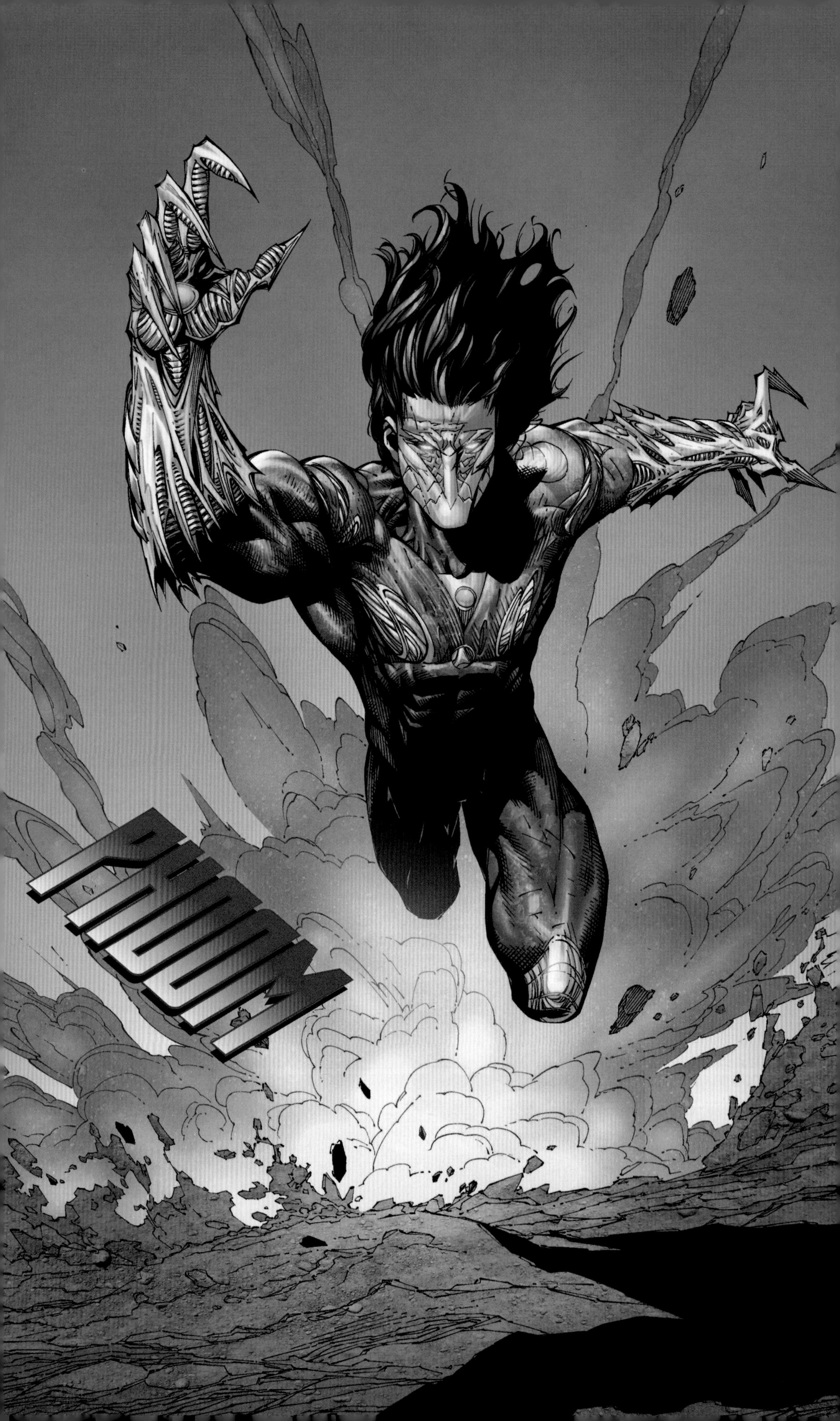
PHOOM

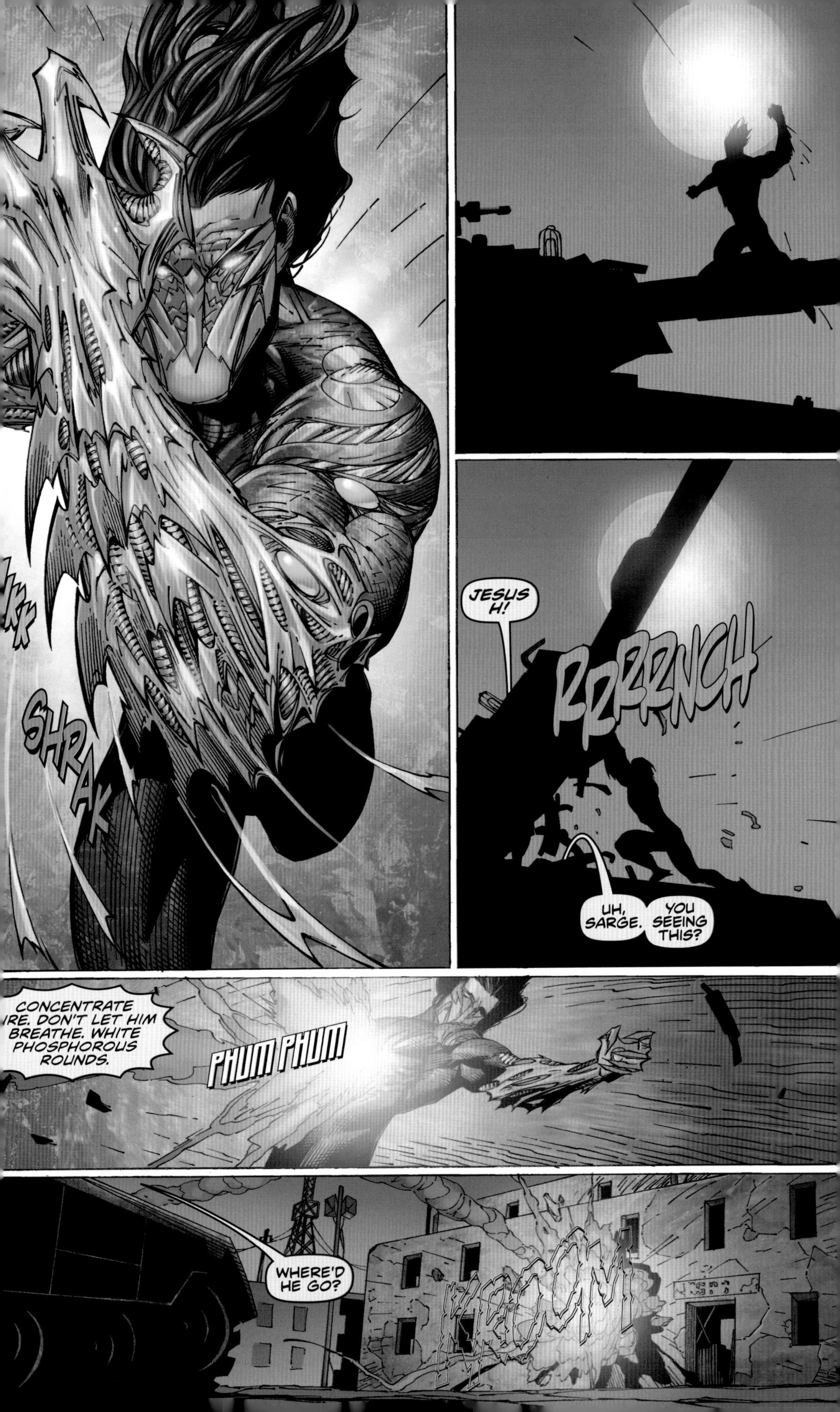
SHRAK
JESUS H!
RRRRNCH
UH, SARGE.
YOU SEEING THIS?
CONCENTRATE IRE. DON'T LET HIM BREATHE. WHITE PHOSPHOROUS ROUNDS.
PHUM PHUM
WHERE'D HE GO?

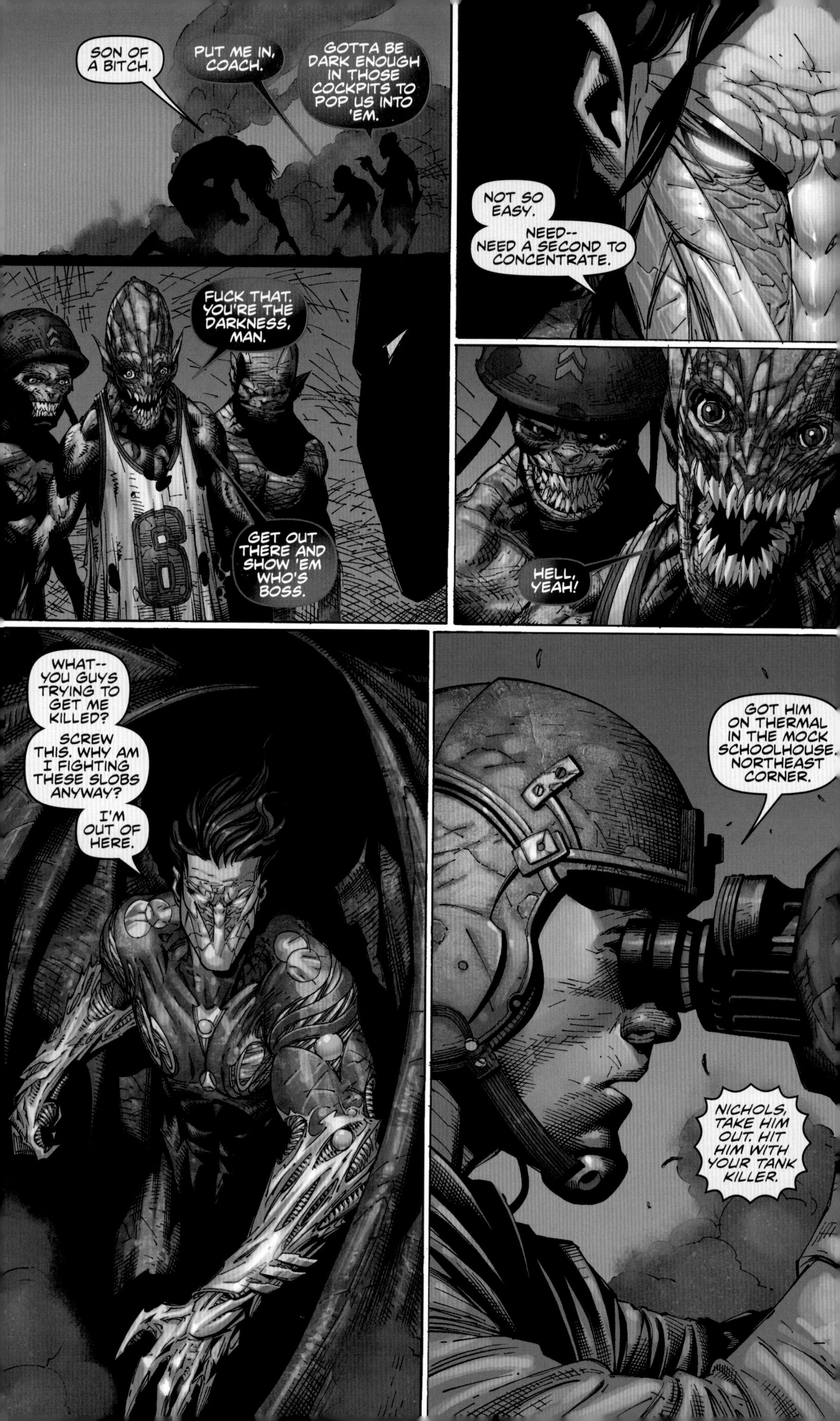
SON OF A BITCH.
PUT ME IN, COACH.
GOTTA BE DARK ENOUGH IN THOSE COCKPITS TO POP US INTO 'EM.
NOT SO EASY.
NEED-- NEED A SECOND TO CONCENTRATE.
FUCK THAT. YOU'RE THE DARKNESS, MAN.
GET OUT THERE AND SHOW 'EM WHO'S BOSS.
HELL, YEAH!
WHAT-- YOU GUYS TRYING TO GET ME KILLED?
SCREW THIS. WHY AM I FIGHTING THESE SLOBS ANYWAY?
I'M OUT OF HERE.
GOT HIM ON THERMAL IN THE MOCK SCHOOLHOUSE. NORTHEAST CORNER.
NICHOLS, TAKE HIM OUT. HIT HIM WITH YOUR TANK KILLER.

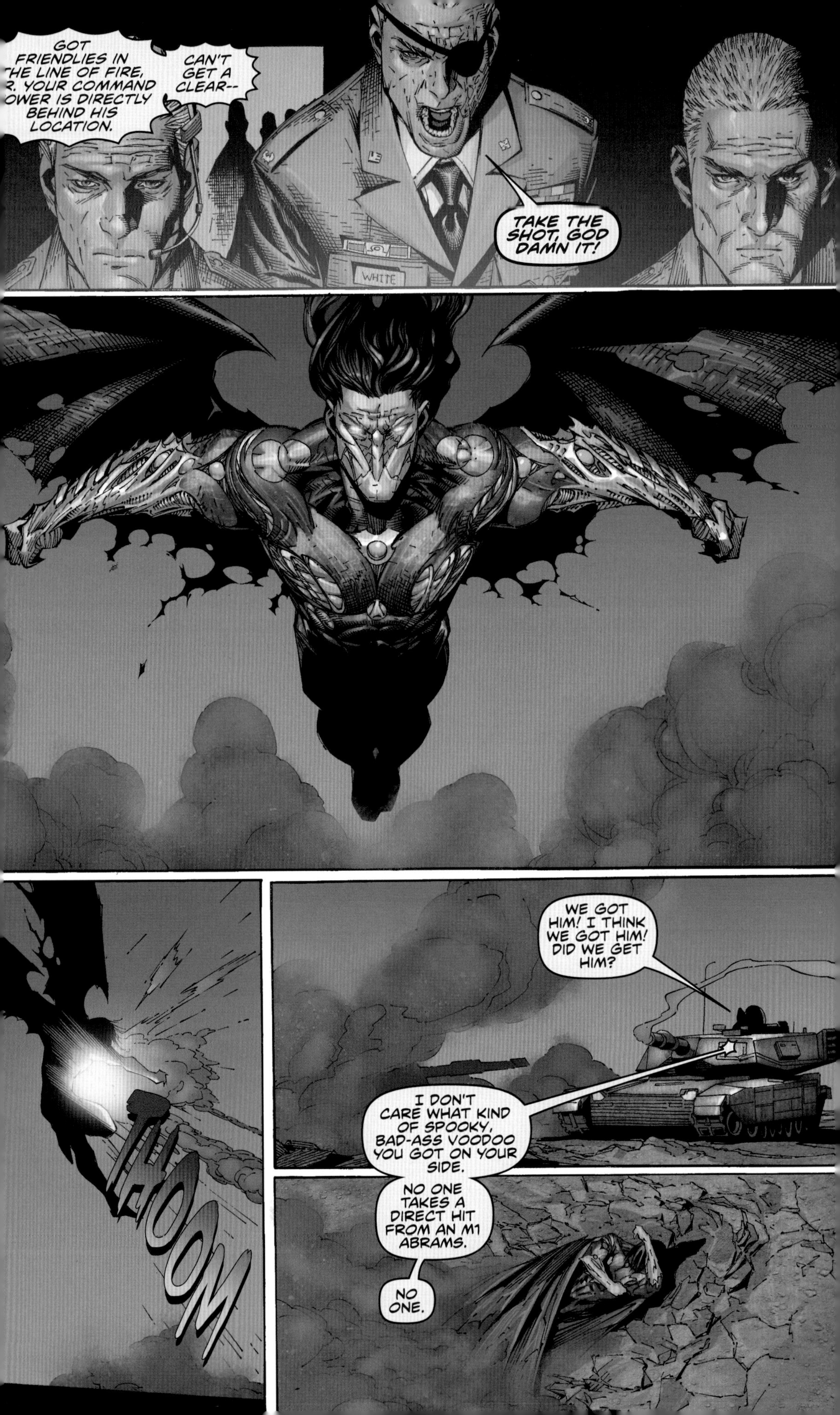
GOT FRIENDLIES IN THE LINE OF FIRE, R. YOUR COMMAND OWER IS DIRECTLY BEHIND HIS LOCATION.
CAN'T GET A CLEAR--
TAKE THE SHOT, GOD DAMN IT!
WHITE
THOOM
WE GOT HIM! I THINK WE GOT HIM! DID WE GET HIM?
I DON'T CARE WHAT KIND OF SPOOKY, BAD-ASS VOODOO YOU GOT ON YOUR SIDE.
NO ONE TAKES A DIRECT HIT FROM AN M1 ABRAMS.
NO ONE.

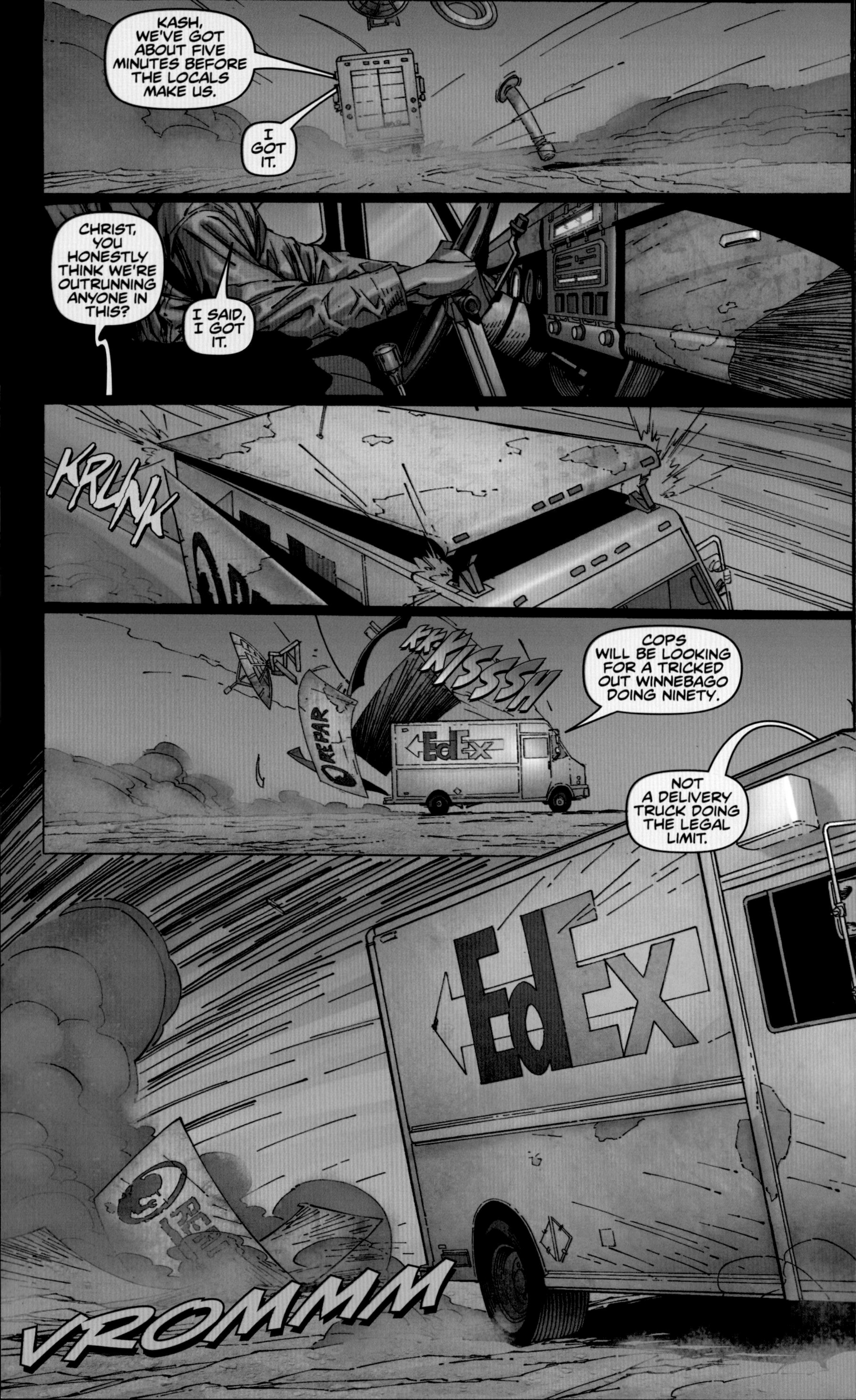
KASH, WE'VE GOT ABOUT FIVE MINUTES BEFORE THE LOCALS MAKE US.
I GOT IT.
CHRIST, YOU HONESTLY THINK WE'RE OUTRUNNING ANYONE IN THIS?
I SAID, I GOT IT.
KRUNK
KKKKISSSH
REPAIR
FedEx
COPS WILL BE LOOKING FOR A TRICKED OUT WINNEBAGO DOING NINETY.
NOT A DELIVERY TRUCK DOING THE LEGAL LIMIT.
FedEx
VROMMMM

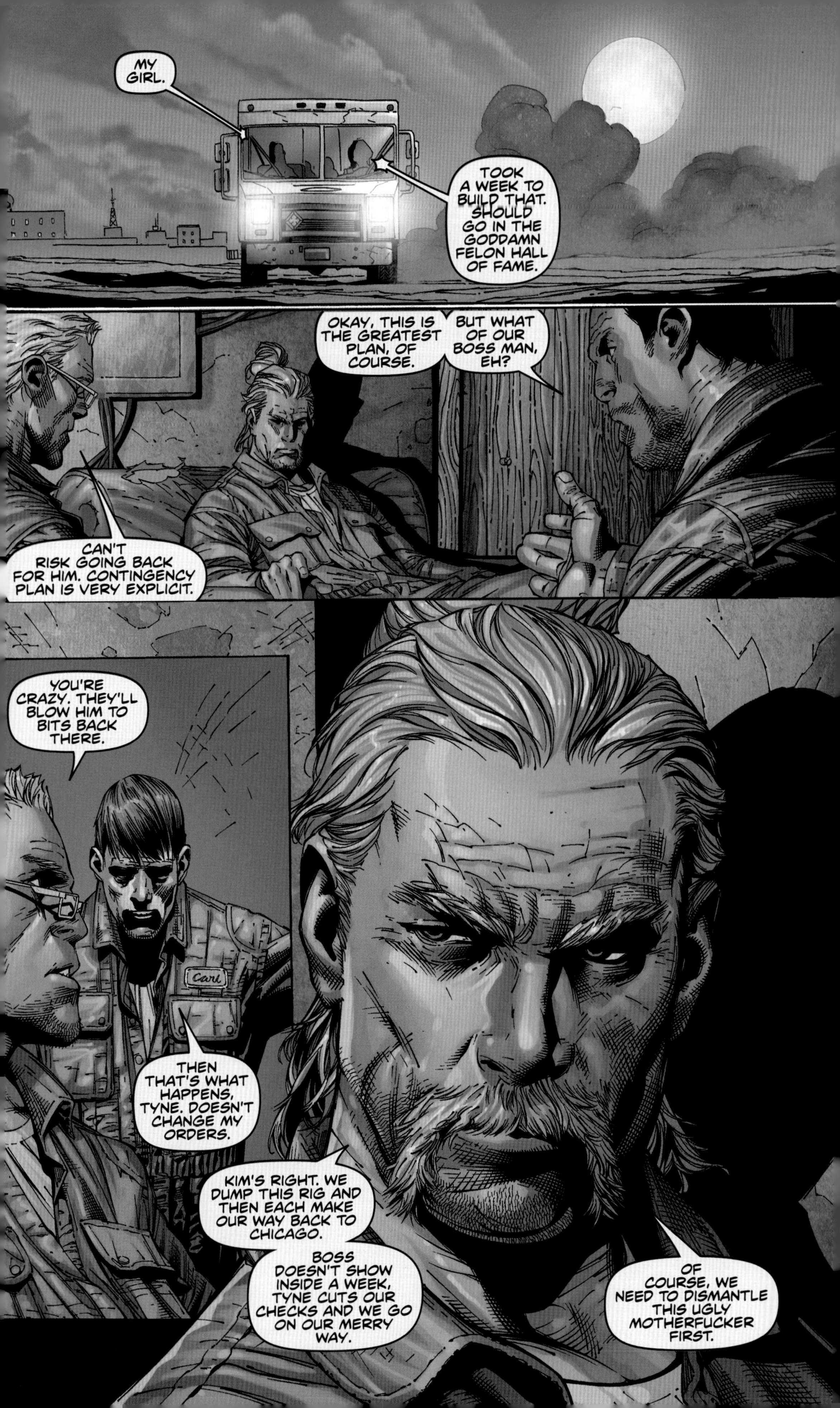
MY GIRL.
TOOK A WEEK TO BUILD THAT. SHOULD GO IN THE GODDAMN FELON HALL OF FAME.
OKAY, THIS IS THE GREATEST PLAN, OF COURSE.
BUT WHAT OF OUR BOSS MAN, EH?
CAN'T RISK GOING BACK FOR HIM. CONTINGENCY PLAN IS VERY EXPLICIT.
YOU'RE CRAZY. THEY'LL BLOW HIM TO BITS BACK THERE.
Carl
THEN THAT'S WHAT HAPPENS, TYNE. DOESN'T CHANGE MY ORDERS.
KIM'S RIGHT. WE DUMP THIS RIG AND THEN EACH MAKE OUR WAY BACK TO CHICAGO.
BOSS DOESN'T SHOW INSIDE A WEEK, TYNE CUTS OUR CHECKS AND WE GO ON OUR MERRY WAY.
OF COURSE, WE NEED TO DISMANTLE THIS UGLY MOTHERFUCKER FIRST.

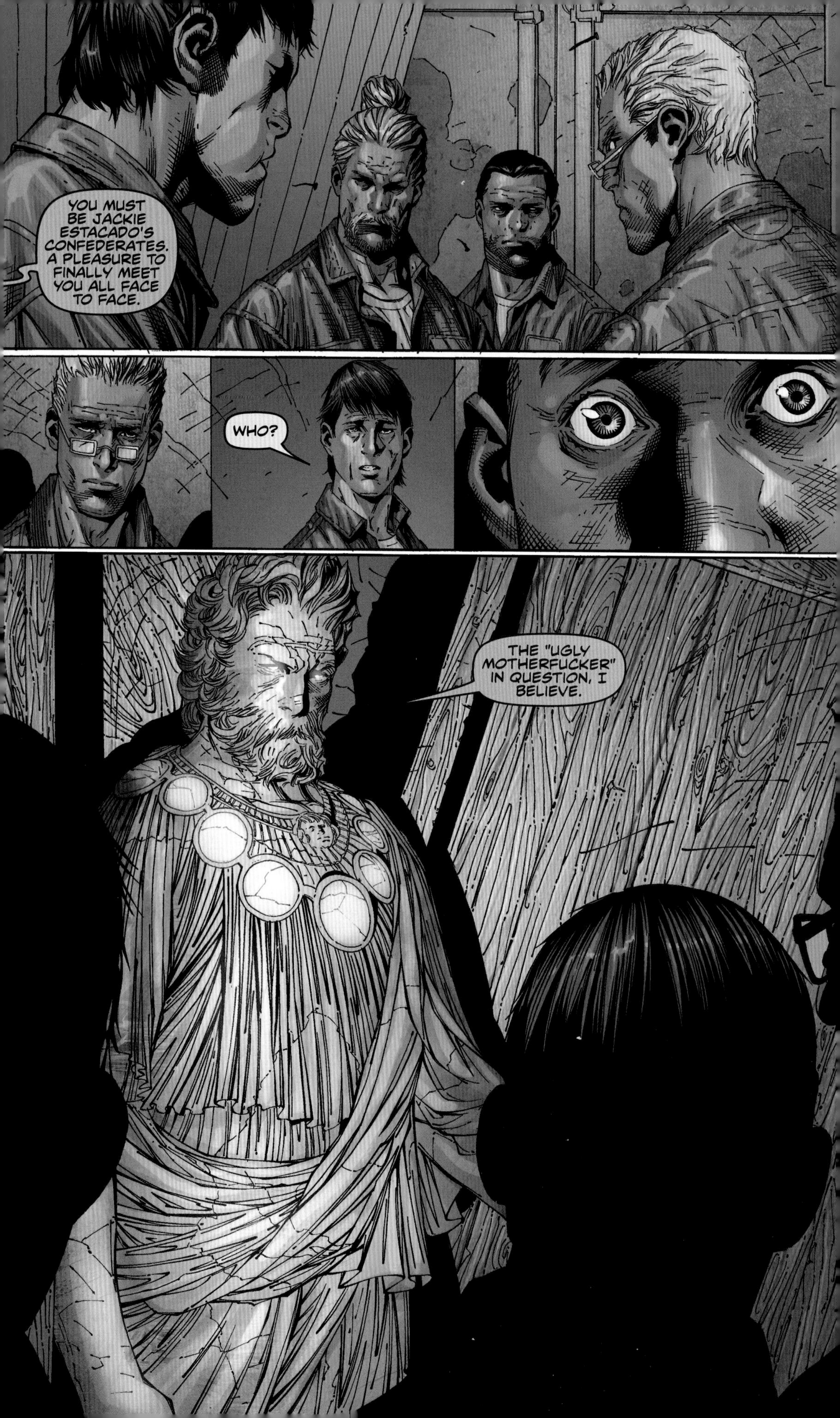
YOU MUST BE JACKIE ESTACADO'S CONFEDERATES. A PLEASURE TO FINALLY MEET YOU ALL FACE TO FACE.
WHO?
THE "UGLY MOTHERFUCKER" IN QUESTION, I BELIEVE.

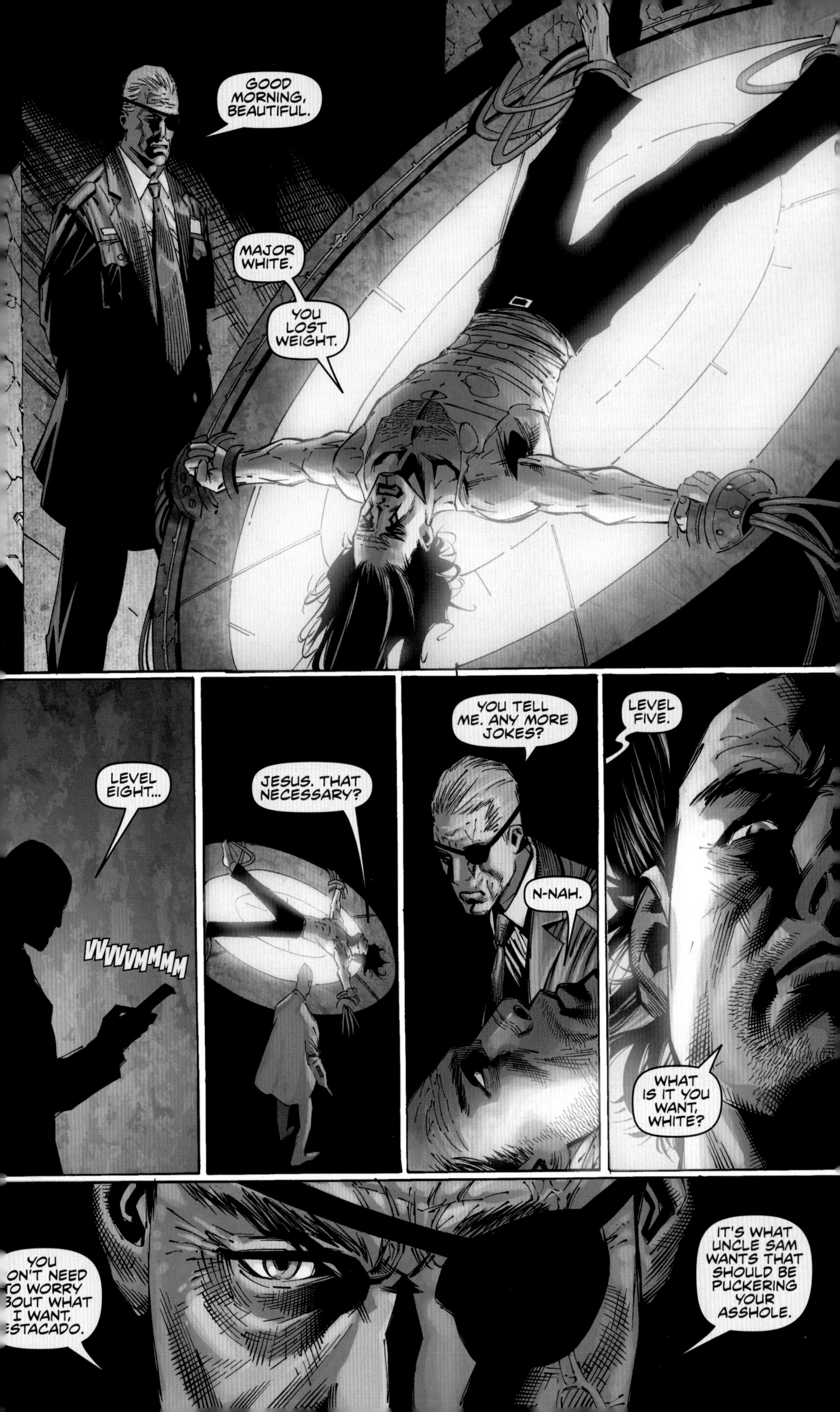
GOOD MORNING, BEAUTIFUL.
MAJOR WHITE.
YOU LOST WEIGHT.
LEVEL EIGHT...
VVVVVMMMM
JESUS. THAT NECESSARY?
YOU TELL ME. ANY MORE JOKES?
N-NAH.
LEVEL FIVE.
WHAT IS IT YOU WANT, WHITE?
YOU ON'T NEED TO WORRY BOUT WHAT I WANT, STACADO.
IT'S WHAT UNCLE SAM WANTS THAT SHOULD BE PUCKERING YOUR ASSHOLE.

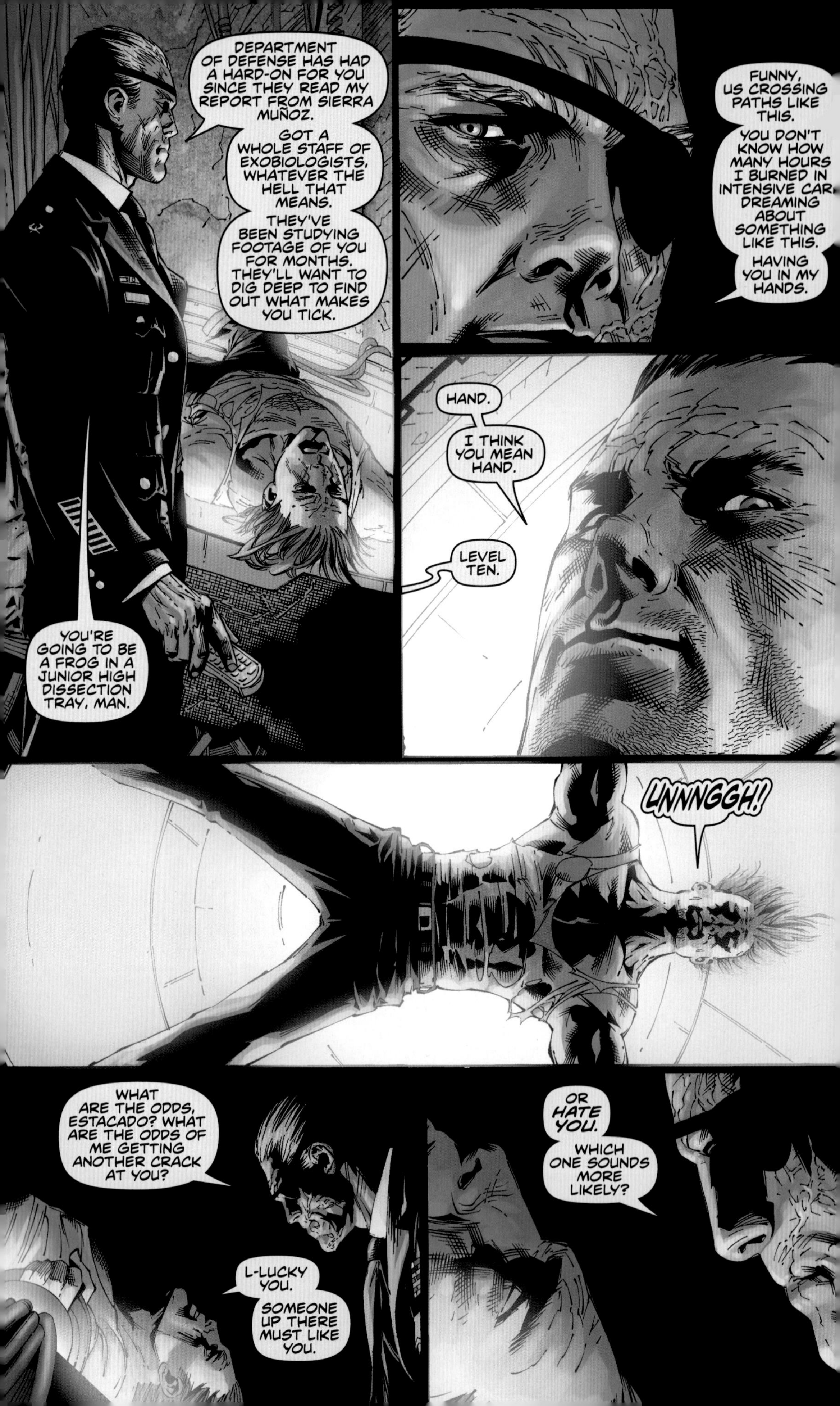
DEPARTMENT OF DEFENSE HAS HAD A HARD-ON FOR YOU SINCE THEY READ MY REPORT FROM SIERRA MUÑOZ.
GOT A WHOLE STAFF OF EXOBIOLOGISTS, WHATEVER THE HELL THAT MEANS.
THEY'VE BEEN STUDYING FOOTAGE OF YOU FOR MONTHS. THEY'LL WANT TO DIG DEEP TO FIND OUT WHAT MAKES YOU TICK.
YOU'RE GOING TO BE A FROG IN A JUNIOR HIGH DISSECTION TRAY, MAN.
FUNNY, US CROSSING PATHS LIKE THIS.
YOU DON'T KNOW HOW MANY HOURS I BURNED IN INTENSIVE CAR DREAMING ABOUT SOMETHING LIKE THIS.
HAVING YOU IN MY HANDS.
HAND.
I THINK YOU MEAN HAND.
LEVEL TEN.
UNNNGGH!
WHAT ARE THE ODDS, ESTACADO? WHAT ARE THE ODDS OF ME GETTING ANOTHER CRACK AT YOU?
L-LUCKY YOU.
SOMEONE UP THERE MUST LIKE YOU.
OR HATE YOU.
WHICH ONE SOUNDS MORE LIKELY?

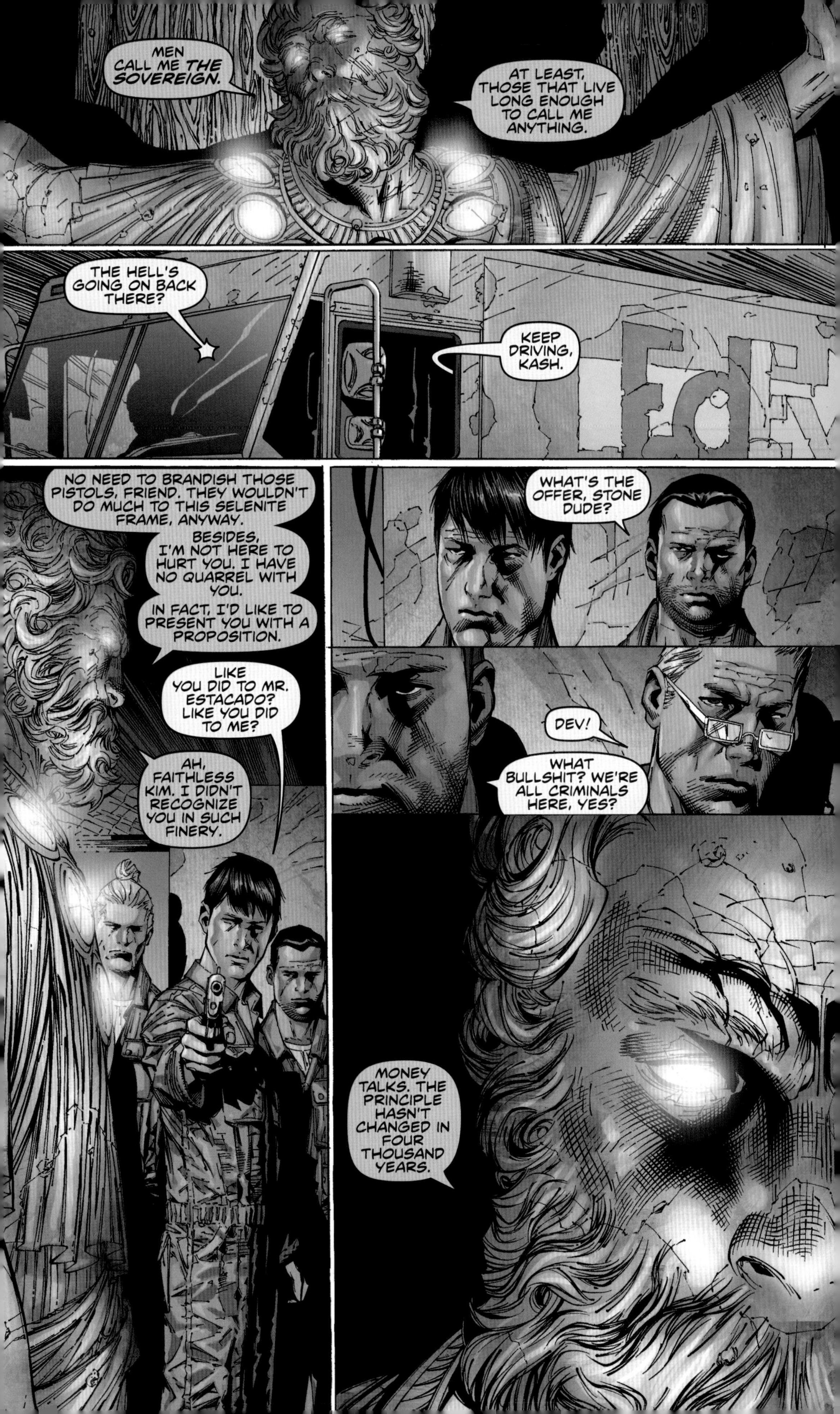
MEN CALL ME *THE SOVEREIGN.*
AT LEAST, THOSE THAT LIVE LONG ENOUGH TO CALL ME ANYTHING.
THE HELL'S GOING ON BACK THERE?
KEEP DRIVING, KASH.
NO NEED TO BRANDISH THOSE PISTOLS, FRIEND. THEY WOULDN'T DO MUCH TO THIS SELENITE FRAME, ANYWAY.
BESIDES, I'M NOT HERE TO HURT YOU. I HAVE NO QUARREL WITH YOU.
IN FACT, I'D LIKE TO PRESENT YOU WITH A PROPOSITION.
LIKE YOU DID TO MR. ESTACADO? LIKE YOU DID TO ME?
AH, FAITHLESS KIM. I DIDN'T RECOGNIZE YOU IN SUCH FINERY.
WHAT'S THE OFFER, STONE DUDE?
DEV!
WHAT BULLSHIT? WE'RE ALL CRIMINALS HERE, YES?
MONEY TALKS. THE PRINCIPLE HASN'T CHANGED IN FOUR THOUSAND YEARS.

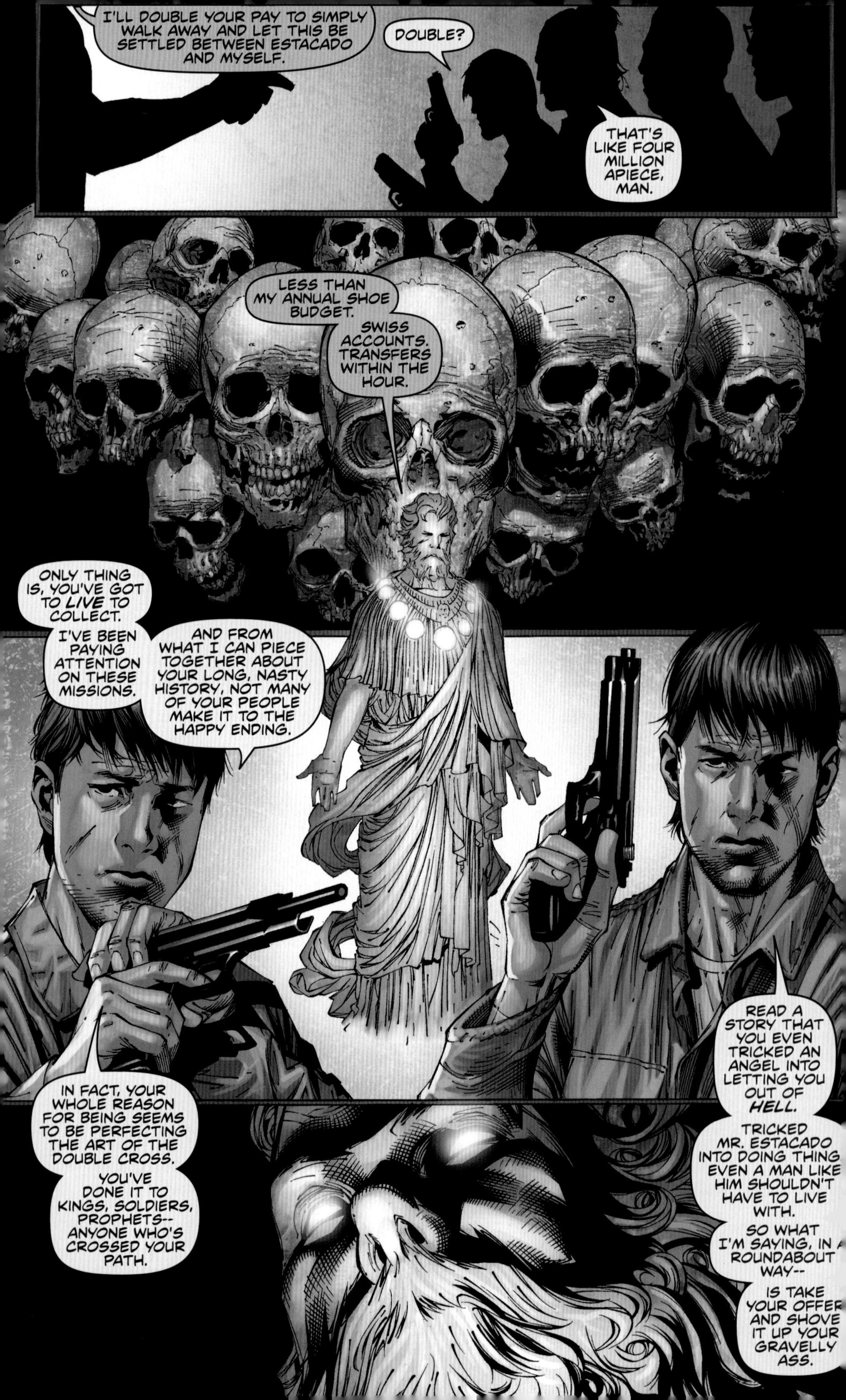
I'LL DOUBLE YOUR PAY TO SIMPLY WALK AWAY AND LET THIS BE SETTLED BETWEEN ESTACADO AND MYSELF.
DOUBLE?
THAT'S LIKE FOUR MILLION APIECE, MAN.
LESS THAN MY ANNUAL SHOE BUDGET.
SWISS ACCOUNTS. TRANSFERS WITHIN THE HOUR.
ONLY THING IS, YOU'VE GOT TO LIVE TO COLLECT.
I'VE BEEN PAYING ATTENTION ON THESE MISSIONS.
AND FROM WHAT I CAN PIECE TOGETHER ABOUT YOUR LONG, NASTY HISTORY, NOT MANY OF YOUR PEOPLE MAKE IT TO THE HAPPY ENDING.
IN FACT, YOUR WHOLE REASON FOR BEING SEEMS TO BE PERFECTING THE ART OF THE DOUBLE CROSS.
YOU'VE DONE IT TO KINGS, SOLDIERS, PROPHETS-- ANYONE WHO'S CROSSED YOUR PATH.
READ A STORY THAT YOU EVEN TRICKED AN ANGEL INTO LETTING YOU OUT OF HELL.
TRICKED MR. ESTACADO INTO DOING THING EVEN A MAN LIKE HIM SHOULDN'T HAVE TO LIVE WITH.
SO WHAT I'M SAYING, IN A ROUNDABOUT WAY--
IS TAKE YOUR OFFER AND SHOVE IT UP YOUR GRAVELLY ASS.

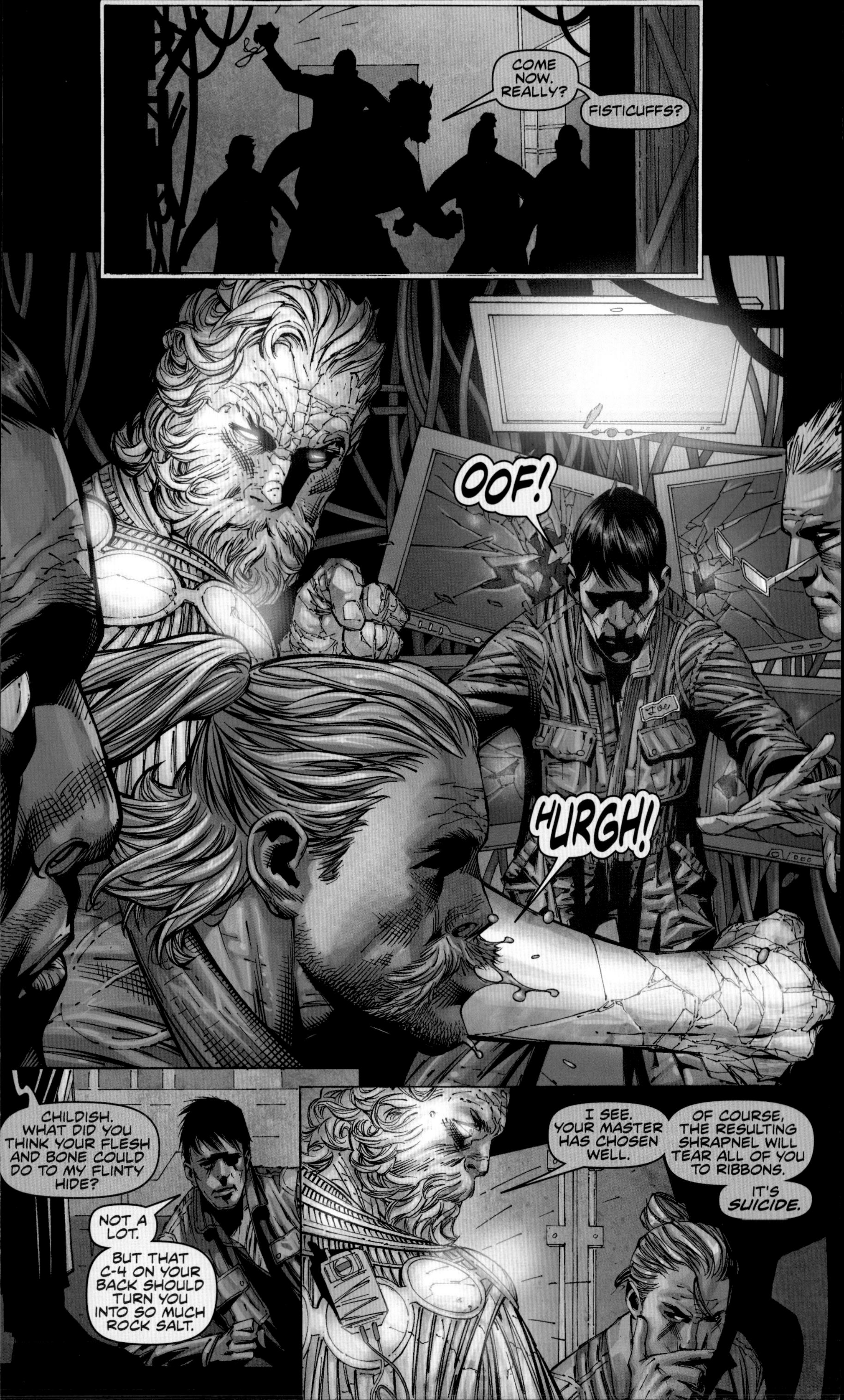
COME NOW. REALLY?
FISTICUFFS?
OOF!
HURGH!
CHILDISH. WHAT DID YOU THINK YOUR FLESH AND BONE COULD DO TO MY FLINTY HIDE?
NOT A LOT.
BUT THAT C-4 ON YOUR BACK SHOULD TURN YOU INTO SO MUCH ROCK SALT.
I SEE. YOUR MASTER HAS CHOSEN WELL.
OF COURSE, THE RESULTING SHRAPNEL WILL TEAR ALL OF YOU TO RIBBONS.
IT'S SUICIDE.

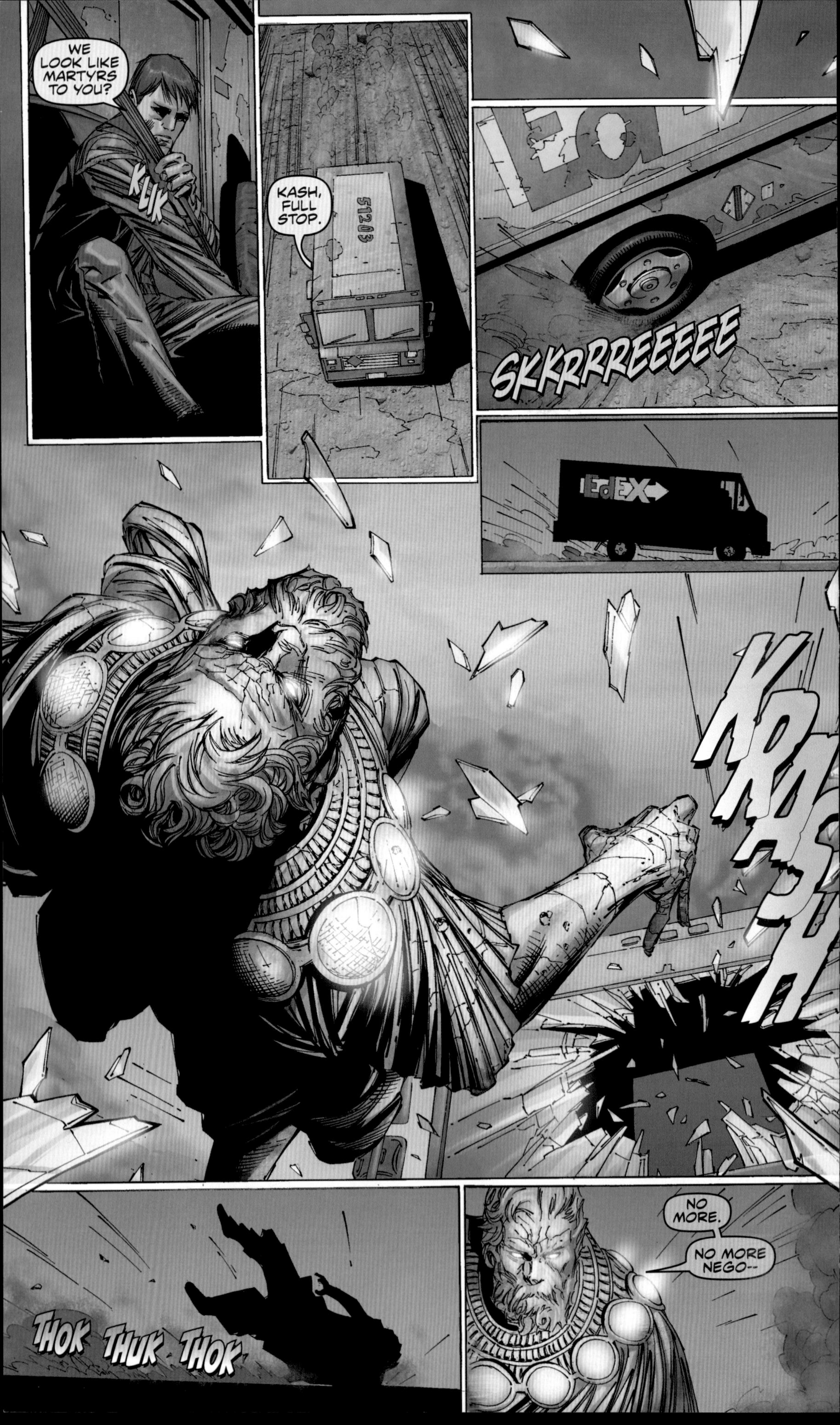
WE LOOK LIKE MARTYRS TO YOU?
KLIK
KASH, FULL STOP.
51203
SKKRRREEEEEE
FEDEX
KRASH
THOK THUK THOK
NO MORE.
NO MORE NEGO--

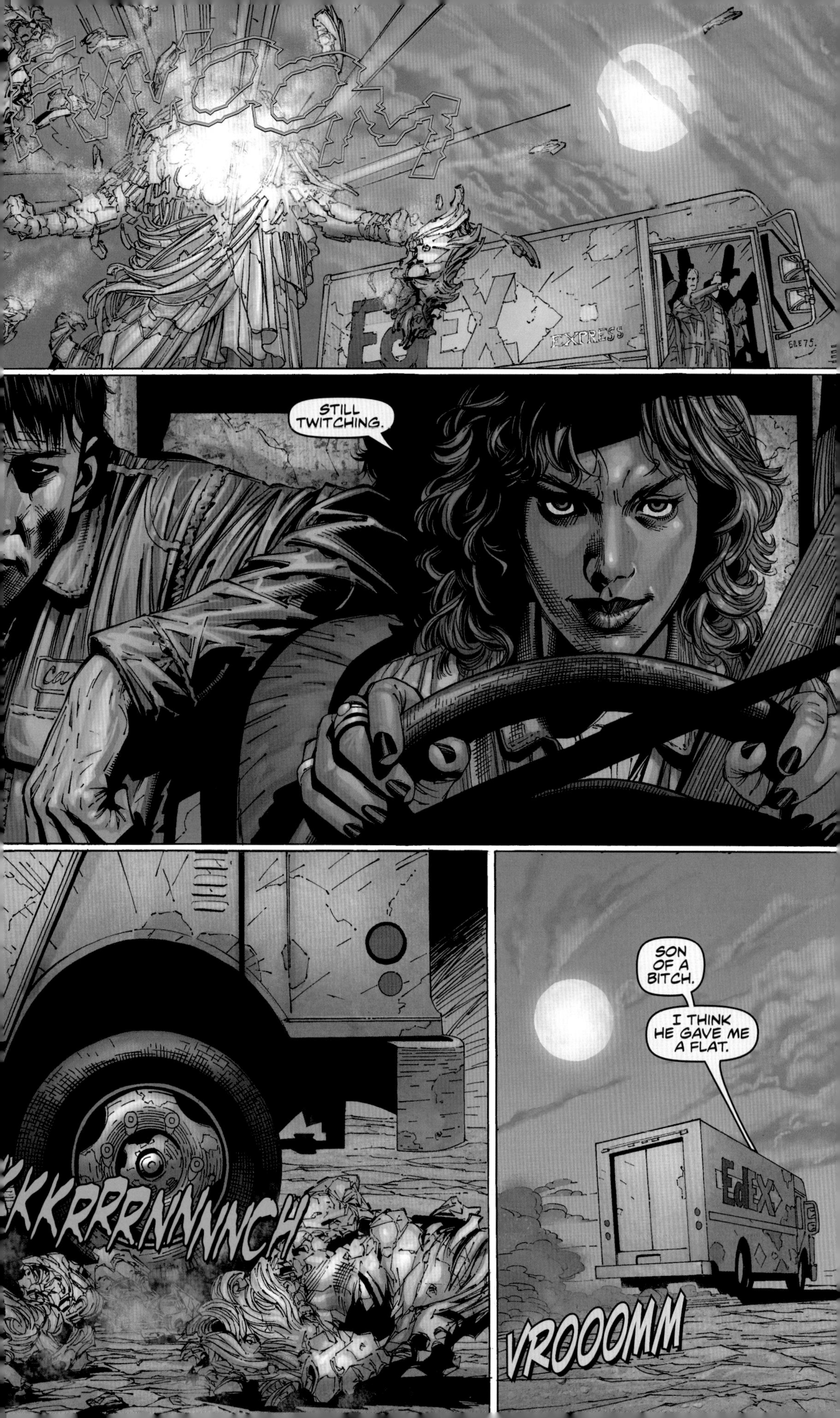
STILL TWITCHING.
KKRRRNNNNNCH
SON OF A BITCH.
I THINK HE GAVE ME A FLAT.
VROOOMM

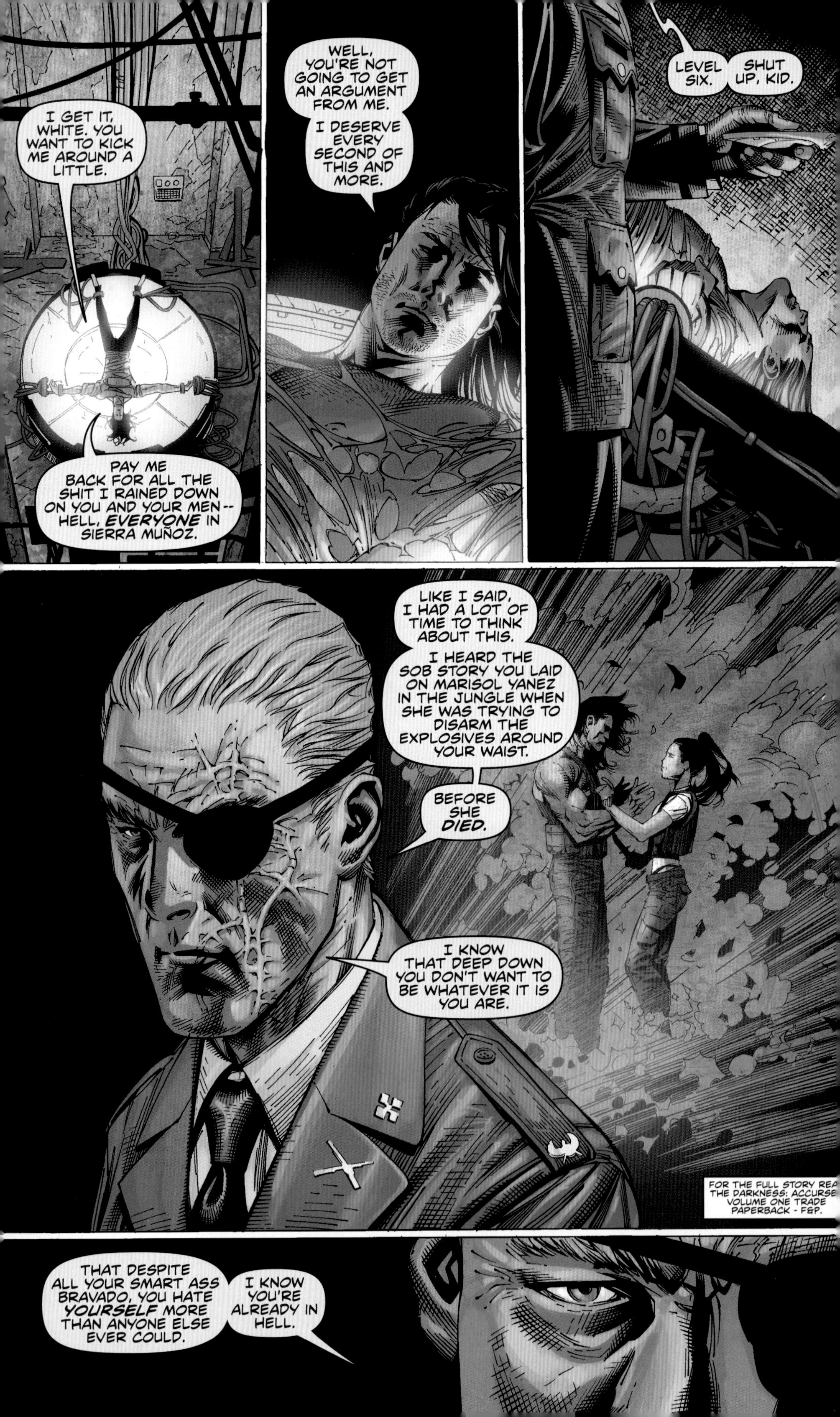
I GET IT, WHITE. YOU WANT TO KICK ME AROUND A LITTLE.
PAY ME BACK FOR ALL THE SHIT I RAINED DOWN ON YOU AND YOUR MEN-- HELL, EVERYONE IN SIERRA MUÑOZ.
WELL, YOU'RE NOT GOING TO GET AN ARGUMENT FROM ME.
I DESERVE EVERY SECOND OF THIS AND MORE.
LEVEL SIX.
SHUT UP, KID.
LIKE I SAID, I HAD A LOT OF TIME TO THINK ABOUT THIS.
I HEARD THE SOB STORY YOU LAID ON MARISOL YANEZ IN THE JUNGLE WHEN SHE WAS TRYING TO DISARM THE EXPLOSIVES AROUND YOUR WAIST.
BEFORE SHE DIED.
I KNOW THAT DEEP DOWN YOU DON'T WANT TO BE WHATEVER IT IS YOU ARE.
FOR THE FULL STORY REA THE DARKNESS: ACCURSE VOLUME ONE TRADE PAPERBACK - F&P.
THAT DESPITE ALL YOUR SMART ASS BRAVADO, YOU HATE YOURSELF MORE THAN ANYONE ELSE EVER COULD.
I KNOW YOU'RE ALREADY IN HELL.

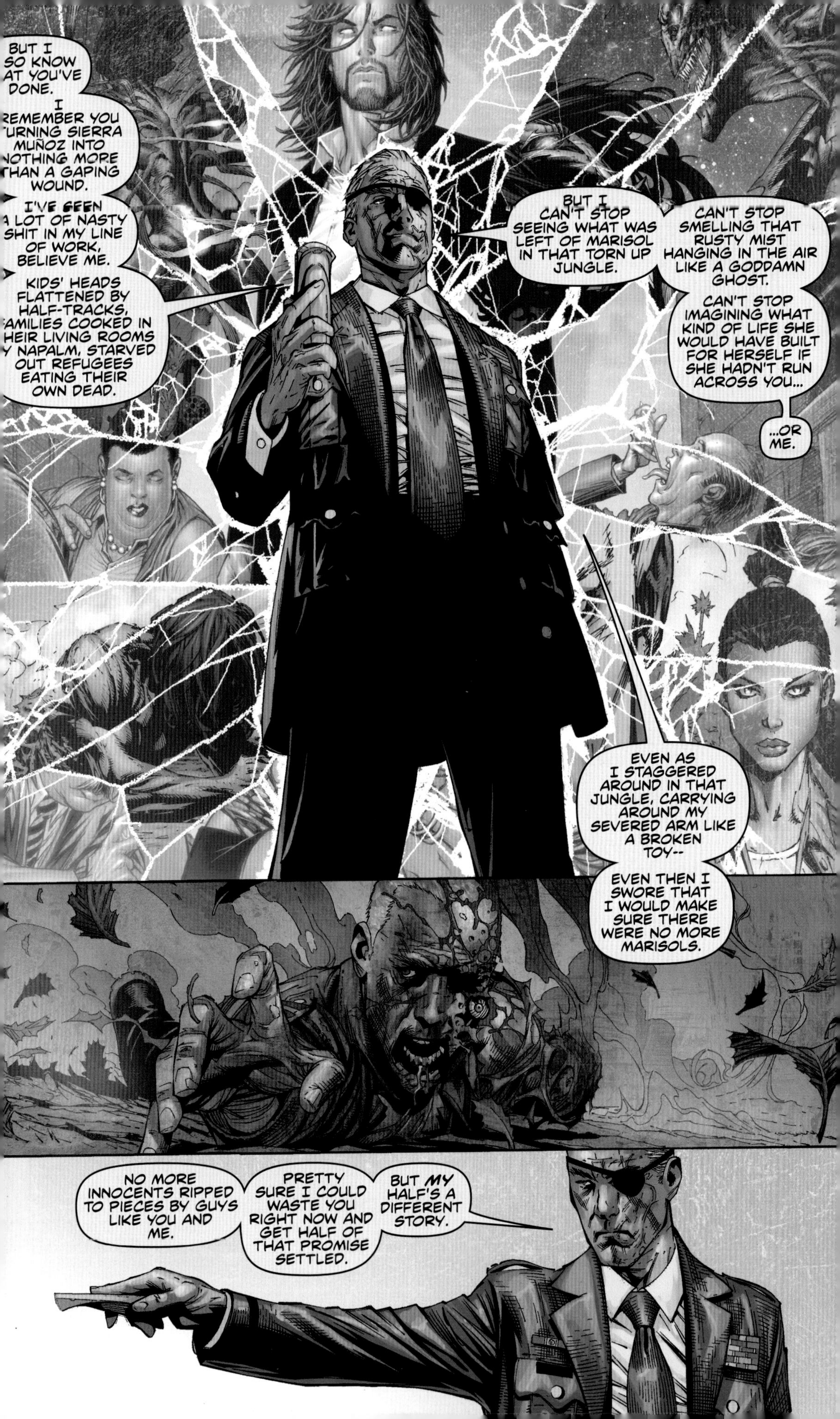

BUT I SO KNOW AT YOU'VE DONE.
I REMEMBER YOU TURNING SIERRA MUÑOZ INTO NOTHING MORE THAN A GAPING WOUND.
I'VE SEEN A LOT OF NASTY SHIT IN MY LINE OF WORK, BELIEVE ME.
KIDS' HEADS FLATTENED BY HALF-TRACKS, FAMILIES COOKED IN THEIR LIVING ROOMS Y NAPALM, STARVED OUT REFUGEES EATING THEIR OWN DEAD.
BUT I CAN'T STOP SEEING WHAT WAS LEFT OF MARISOL IN THAT TORN UP JUNGLE.
CAN'T STOP SMELLING THAT RUSTY MIST HANGING IN THE AIR LIKE A GODDAMN GHOST.
CAN'T STOP IMAGINING WHAT KIND OF LIFE SHE WOULD HAVE BUILT FOR HERSELF IF SHE HADN'T RUN ACROSS YOU...
...OR ME.
EVEN AS I STAGGERED AROUND IN THAT JUNGLE, CARRYING AROUND MY SEVERED ARM LIKE A BROKEN TOY--
EVEN THEN I SWORE THAT I WOULD MAKE SURE THERE WERE NO MORE MARISOLS.
NO MORE INNOCENTS RIPPED TO PIECES BY GUYS LIKE YOU AND ME.
PRETTY SURE I COULD WASTE YOU RIGHT NOW AND GET HALF OF THAT PROMISE SETTLED.
BUT MY HALF'S A DIFFERENT STORY.

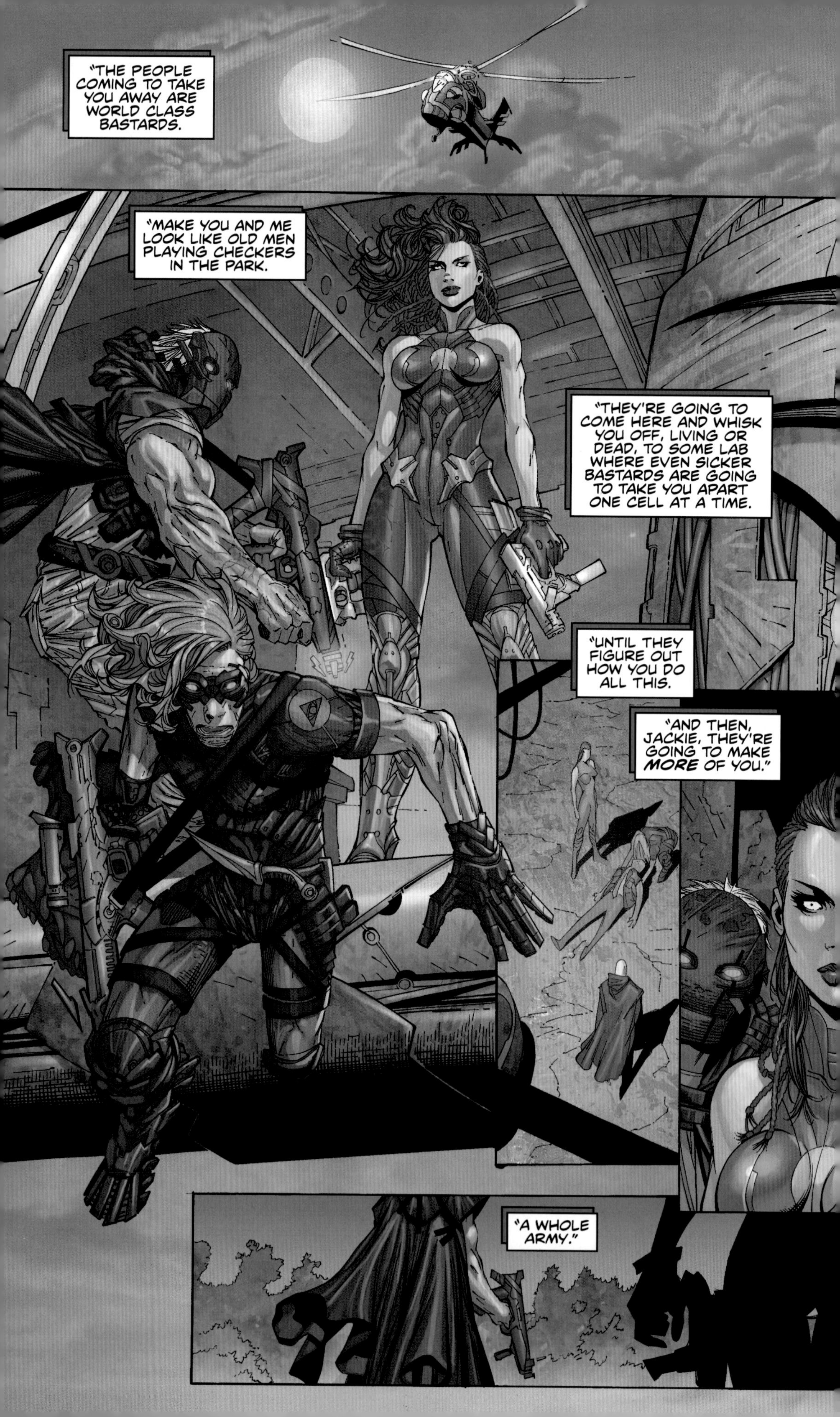
"THE PEOPLE COMING TO TAKE YOU AWAY ARE WORLD CLASS BASTARDS.
"MAKE YOU AND ME LOOK LIKE OLD MEN PLAYING CHECKERS IN THE PARK.
"THEY'RE GOING TO COME HERE AND WHISK YOU OFF, LIVING OR DEAD, TO SOME LAB WHERE EVEN SICKER BASTARDS ARE GOING TO TAKE YOU APART ONE CELL AT A TIME.
"UNTIL THEY FIGURE OUT HOW YOU DO ALL THIS.
"AND THEN, JACKIE, THEY'RE GOING TO MAKE *MORE* OF YOU."
"A WHOLE ARMY."

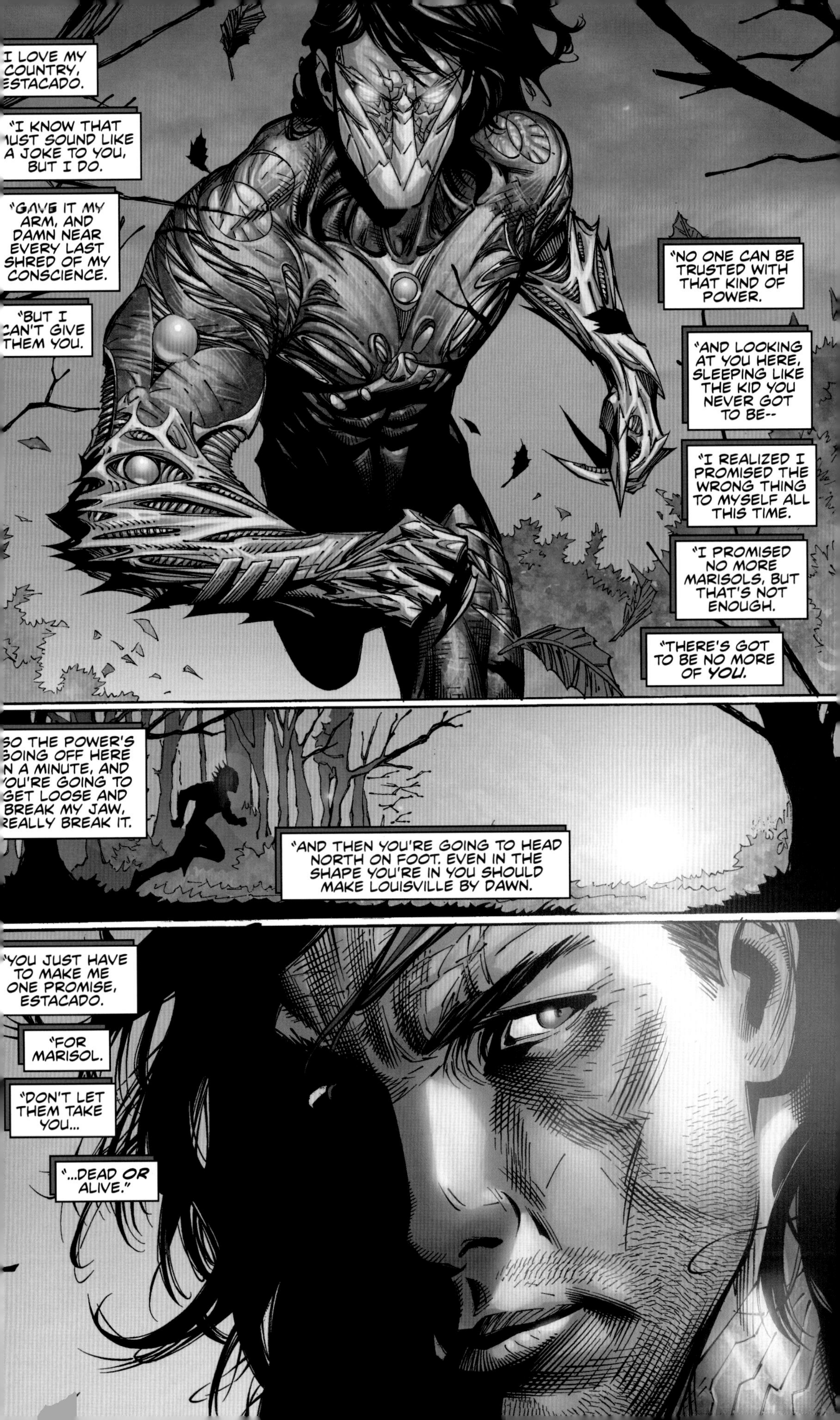
I LOVE MY COUNTRY, ESTACADO.
"I KNOW THAT MUST SOUND LIKE A JOKE TO YOU, BUT I DO.
"GAVE IT MY ARM, AND DAMN NEAR EVERY LAST SHRED OF MY CONSCIENCE.
"BUT I CAN'T GIVE THEM YOU.
"NO ONE CAN BE TRUSTED WITH THAT KIND OF POWER.
"AND LOOKING AT YOU HERE, SLEEPING LIKE THE KID YOU NEVER GOT TO BE--
"I REALIZED I PROMISED THE WRONG THING TO MYSELF ALL THIS TIME.
"I PROMISED NO MORE MARISOLS, BUT THAT'S NOT ENOUGH.
"THERE'S GOT TO BE NO MORE OF YOU.
SO THE POWER'S GOING OFF HERE IN A MINUTE, AND YOU'RE GOING TO GET LOOSE AND BREAK MY JAW, REALLY BREAK IT.
"AND THEN YOU'RE GOING TO HEAD NORTH ON FOOT. EVEN IN THE SHAPE YOU'RE IN YOU SHOULD MAKE LOUISVILLE BY DAWN.
"YOU JUST HAVE TO MAKE ME ONE PROMISE, ESTACADO.
"FOR MARISOL.
"DON'T LET THEM TAKE YOU...
"...DEAD OR ALIVE."

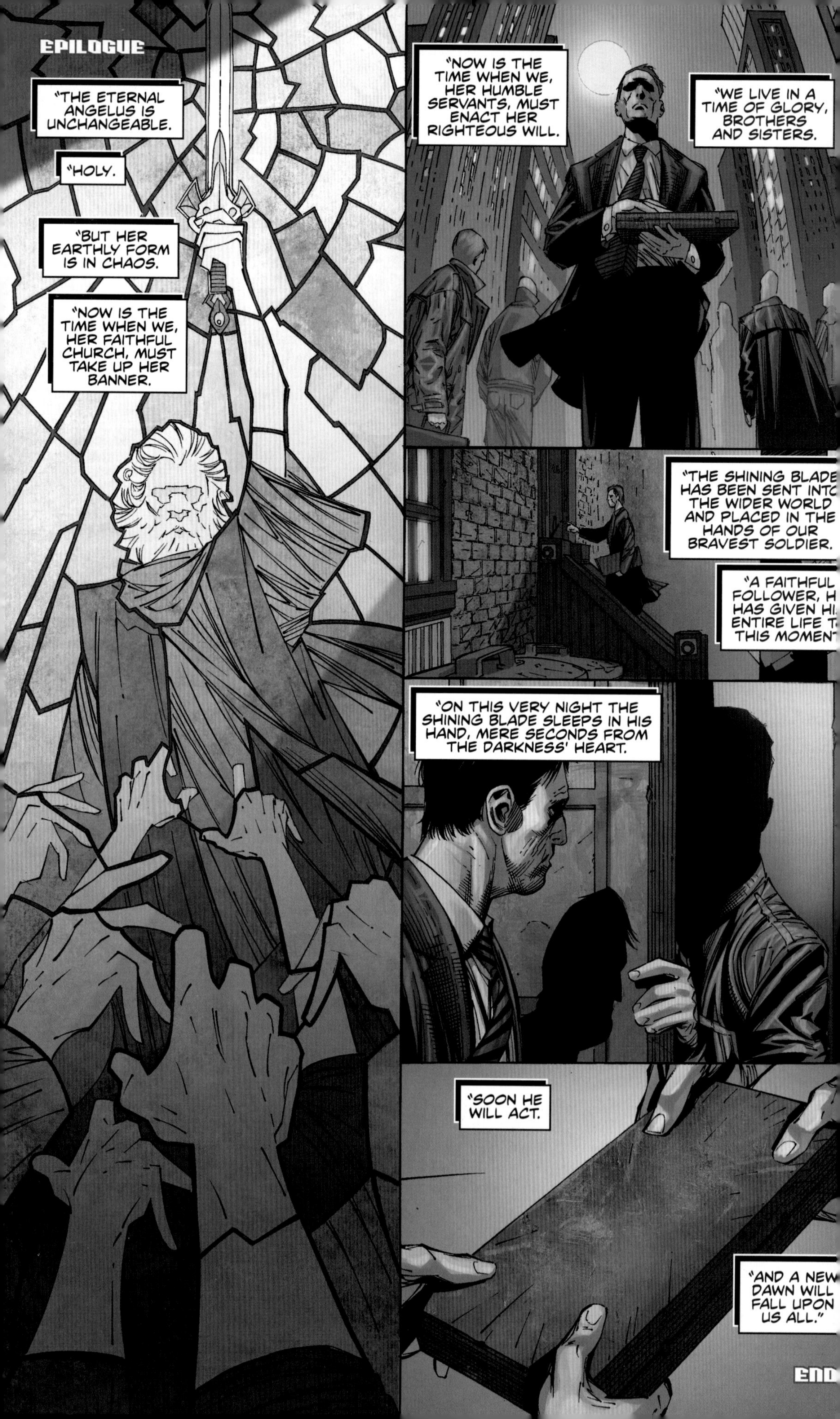
EPILOGUE
"THE ETERNAL ANGELUS IS UNCHANGEABLE.
"HOLY.
"BUT HER EARTHLY FORM IS IN CHAOS.
"NOW IS THE TIME WHEN WE, HER FAITHFUL CHURCH, MUST TAKE UP HER BANNER.
"NOW IS THE TIME WHEN WE, HER HUMBLE SERVANTS, MUST ENACT HER RIGHTEOUS WILL.
"WE LIVE IN A TIME OF GLORY, BROTHERS AND SISTERS.
"THE SHINING BLADE HAS BEEN SENT INTO THE WIDER WORLD AND PLACED IN THE HANDS OF OUR BRAVEST SOLDIER.
"A FAITHFUL FOLLOWER, H HAS GIVEN HI ENTIRE LIFE T THIS MOMENT
"ON THIS VERY NIGHT THE SHINING BLADE SLEEPS IN HIS HAND, MERE SECONDS FROM THE DARKNESS' HEART.
"SOON HE WILL ACT.
"AND A NEW DAWN WILL FALL UPON US ALL."
END

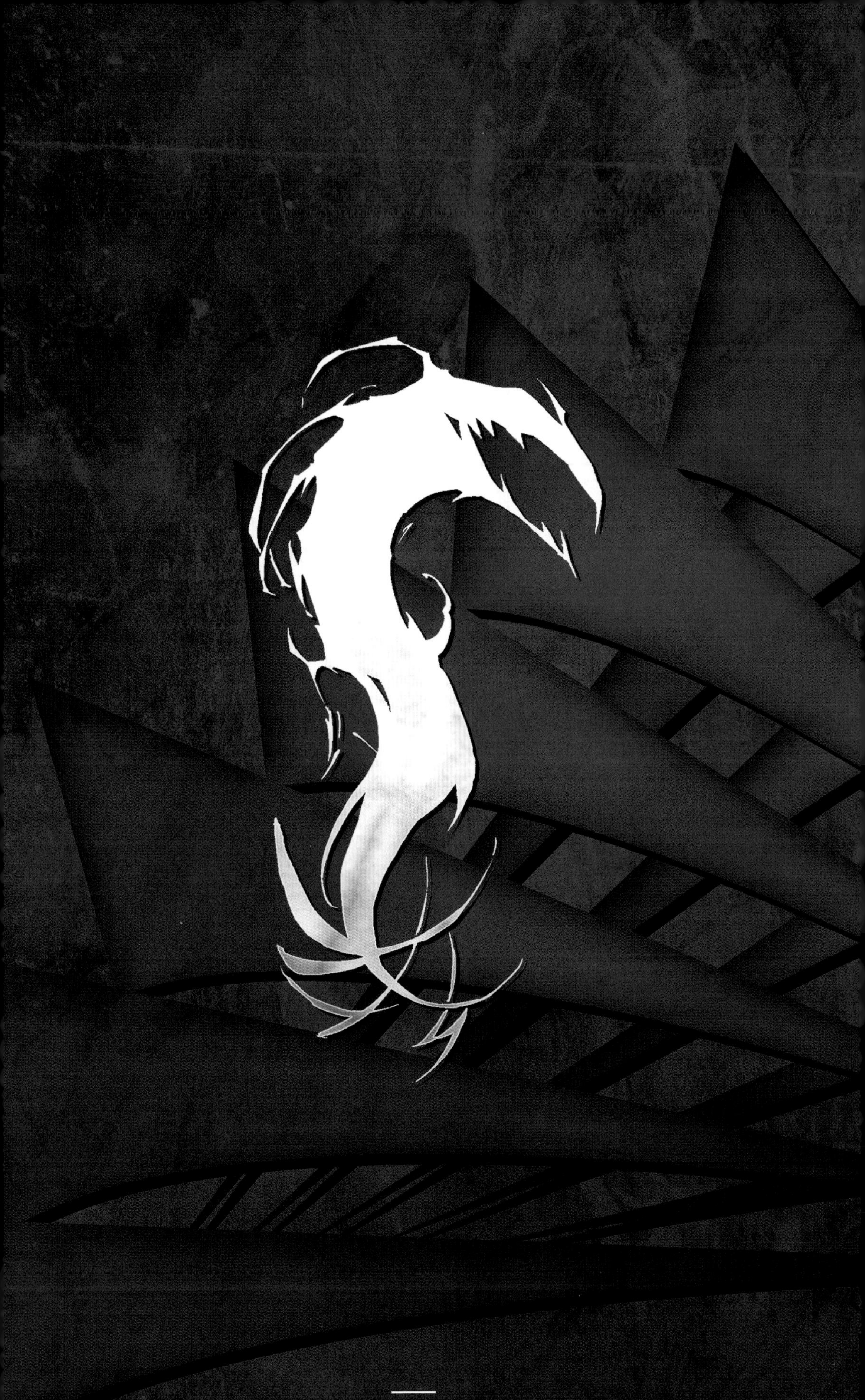

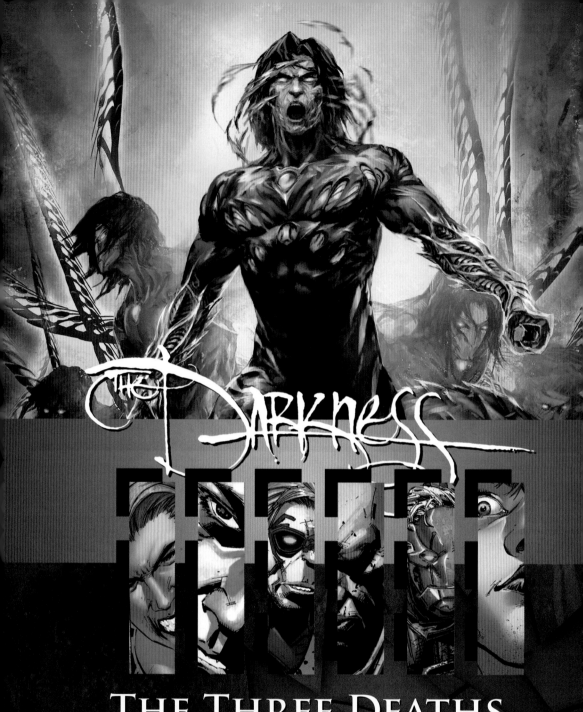

THE THREE DEATHS
OF JACKIE ESTACADO

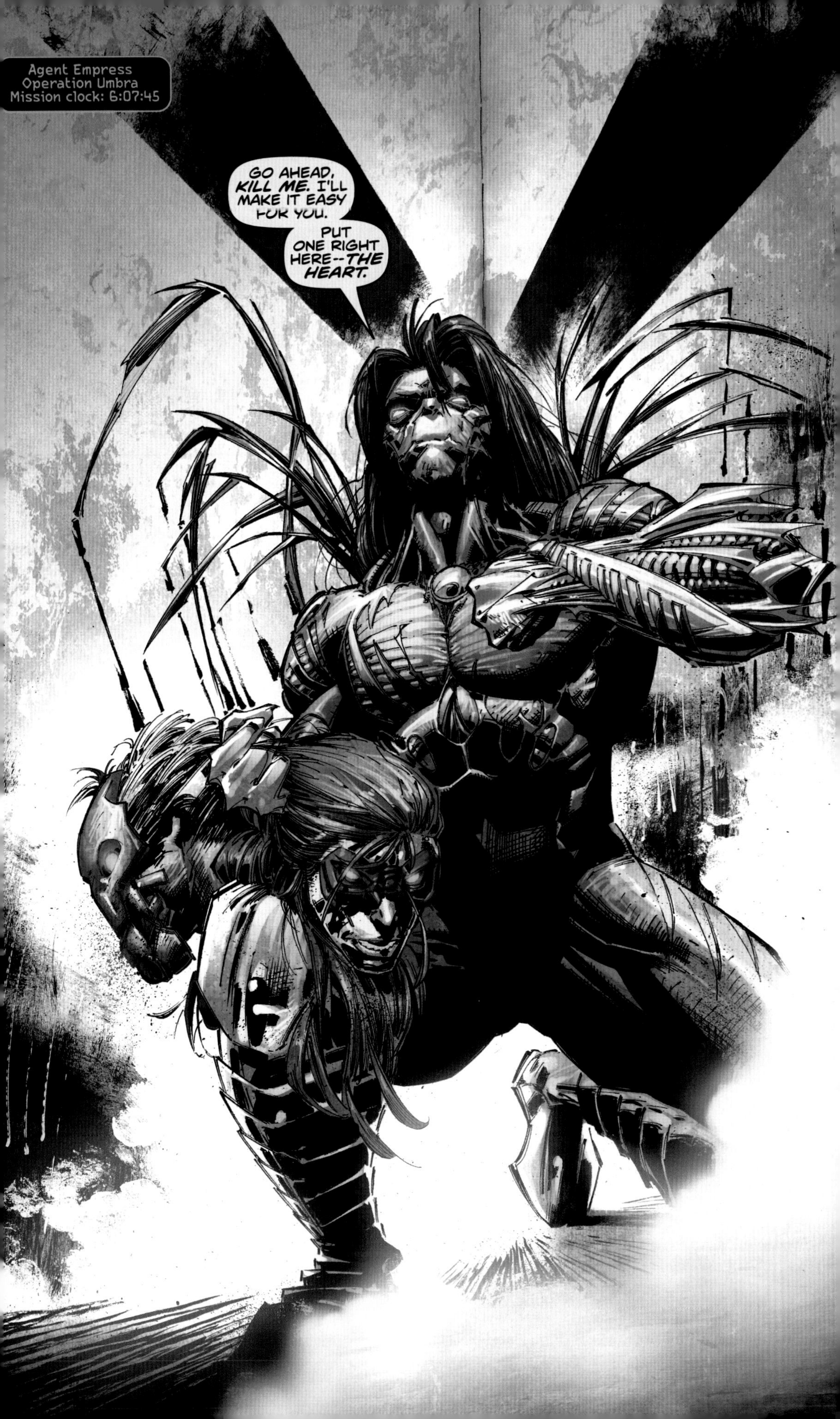
Agent Empress
Operation Umbra
Mission clock: 6:07:45
GO AHEAD, KILL ME. I'LL MAKE IT EASY FOR YOU.
PUT ONE RIGHT HERE--THE HEART.

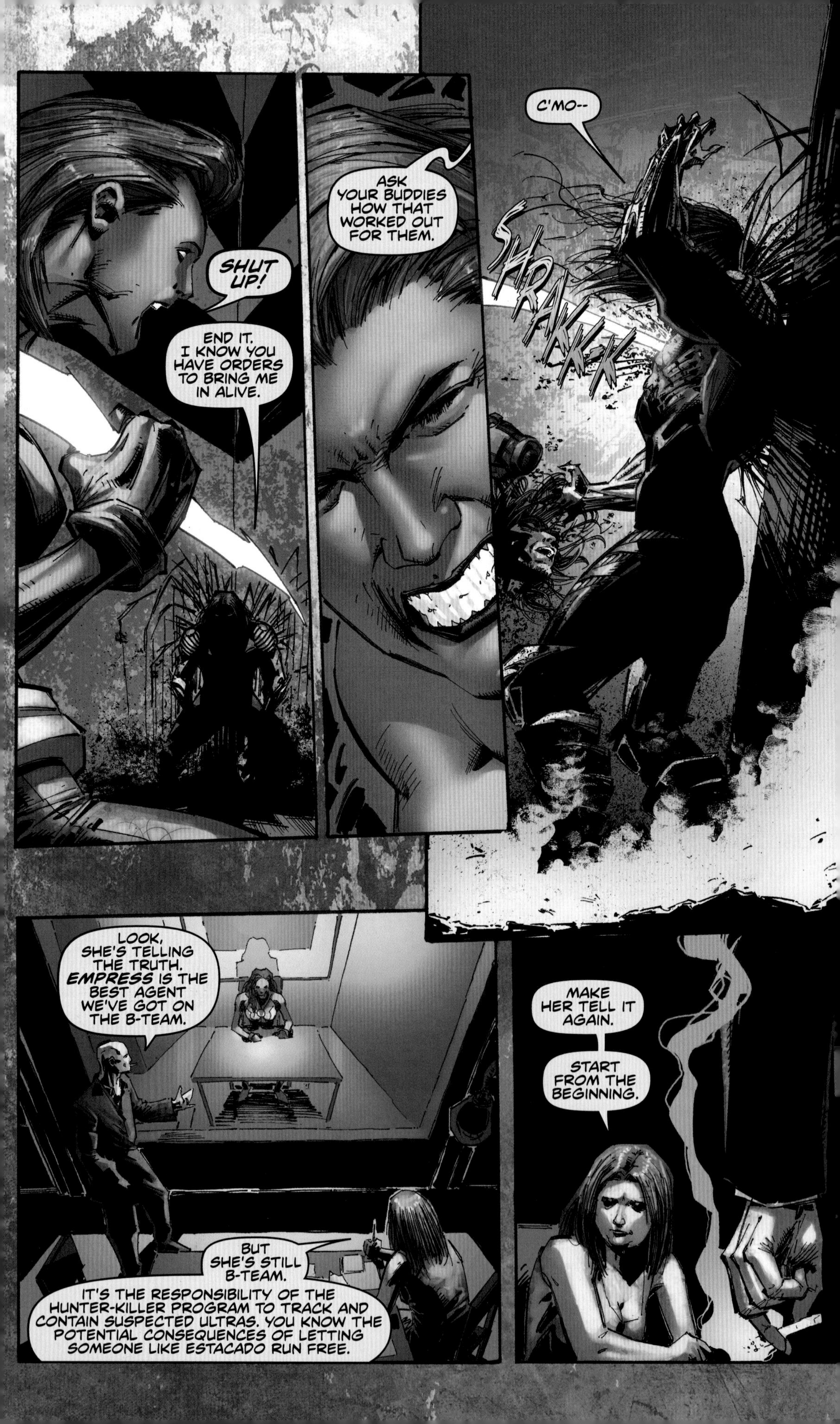
SHUT UP!
END IT. I KNOW YOU HAVE ORDERS TO BRING ME IN ALIVE.
ASK YOUR BUDDIES HOW THAT WORKED OUT FOR THEM.
C'MO--
SHRAKKKK
LOOK, SHE'S TELLING THE TRUTH. EMPRESS IS THE BEST AGENT WE'VE GOT ON THE B-TEAM.
BUT SHE'S STILL B-TEAM.
IT'S THE RESPONSIBILITY OF THE HUNTER-KILLER PROGRAM TO TRACK AND CONTAIN SUSPECTED ULTRAS. YOU KNOW THE POTENTIAL CONSEQUENCES OF LETTING SOMEONE LIKE ESTACADO RUN FREE.
MAKE HER TELL IT AGAIN.
START FROM THE BEGINNING.

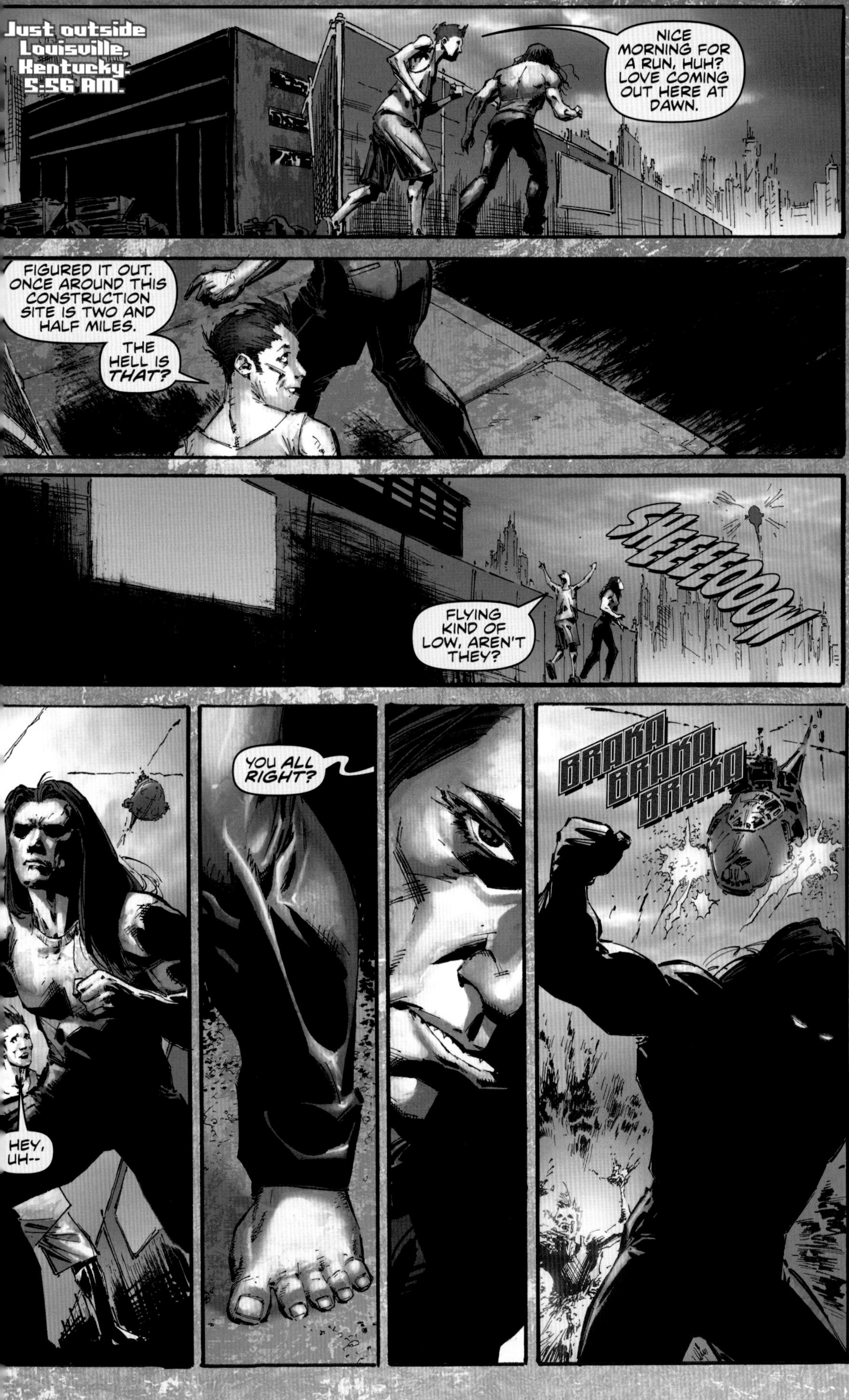
Just outside Louisville, Kentucky. 5:56 AM.
NICE MORNING FOR A RUN, HUH? LOVE COMING OUT HERE AT DAWN.
FIGURED IT OUT. ONCE AROUND THIS CONSTRUCTION SITE IS TWO AND HALF MILES.
THE HELL IS *THAT?*
SHEEEOOOM
FLYING KIND OF LOW, AREN'T THEY?
HEY, UH--
YOU *ALL* *RIGHT?*
BRAKA BRAKA BRAKA

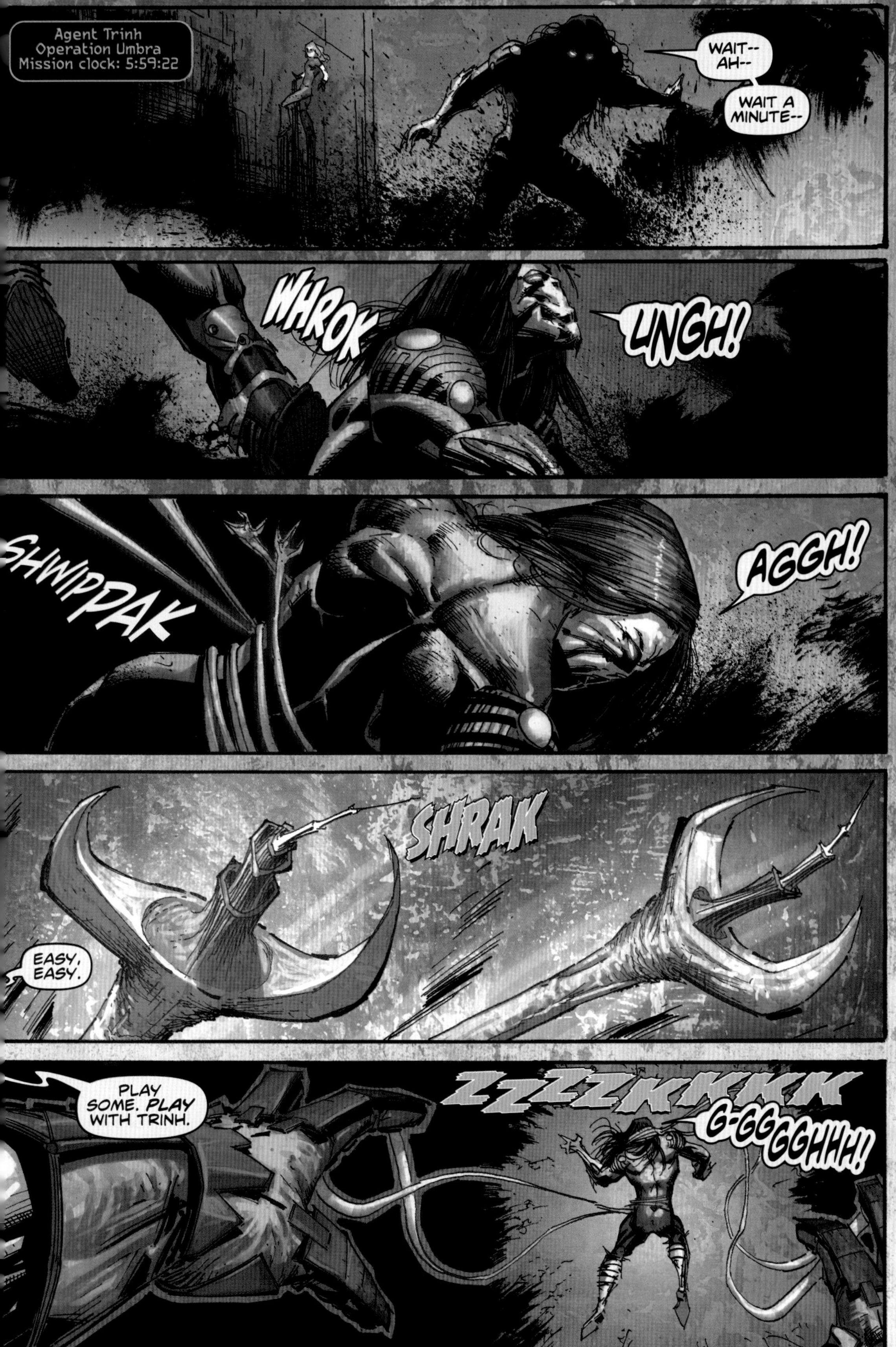
Agent Trinh
Operation Umbra
Mission clock: 5:59:22
WAIT-- AH--
WAIT A MINUTE--
WHROK
UNGH!
SHWIPPAK
AGGH!
SHRAK
EASY, EASY.
PLAY SOME. PLAY WITH TRINH.
ZZZZKKKKK
G-GGGGHHH!

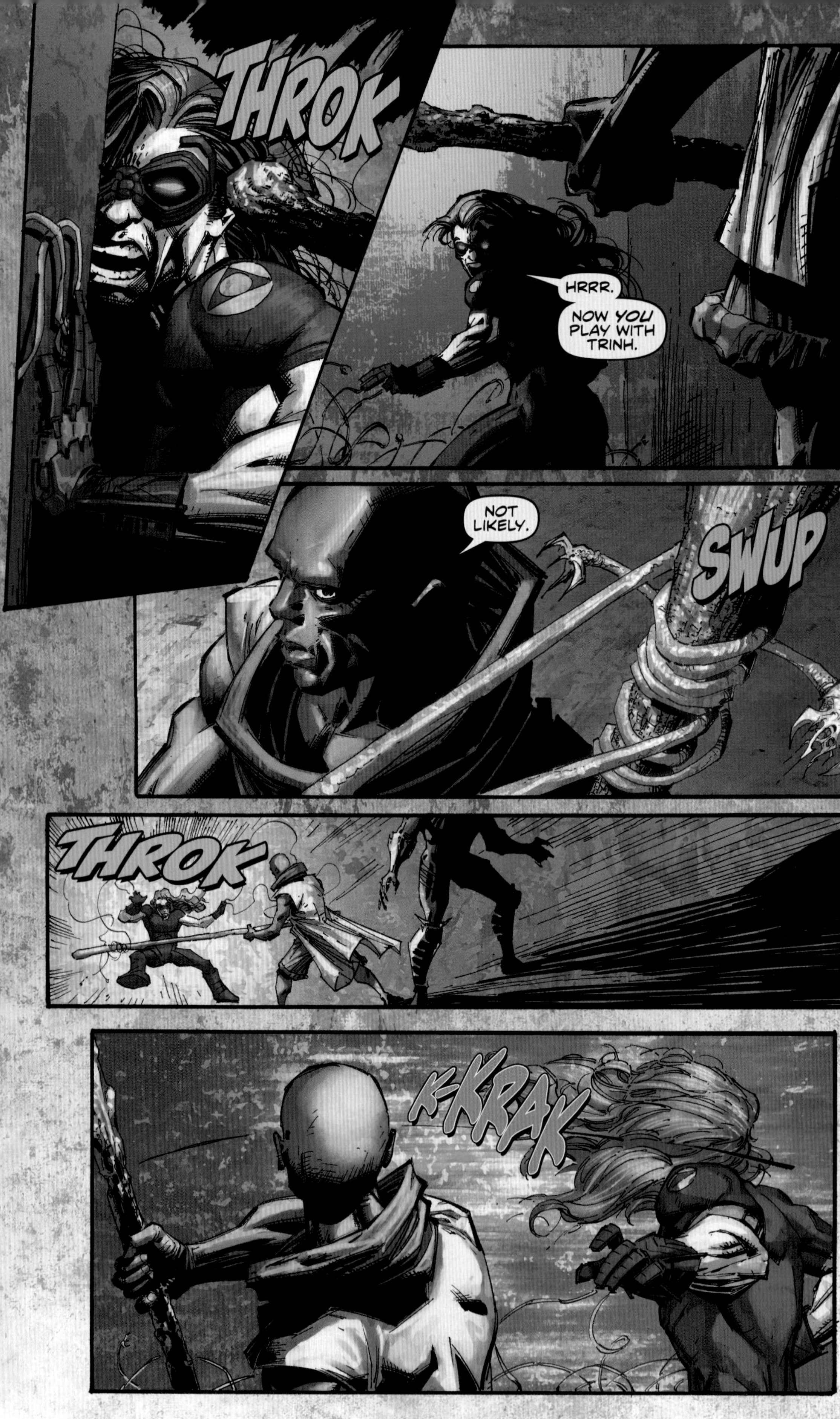
THROK
HRRR.
NOW YOU PLAY WITH TRINH.
NOT LIKELY.
SWUP
THROK
K-KRAK

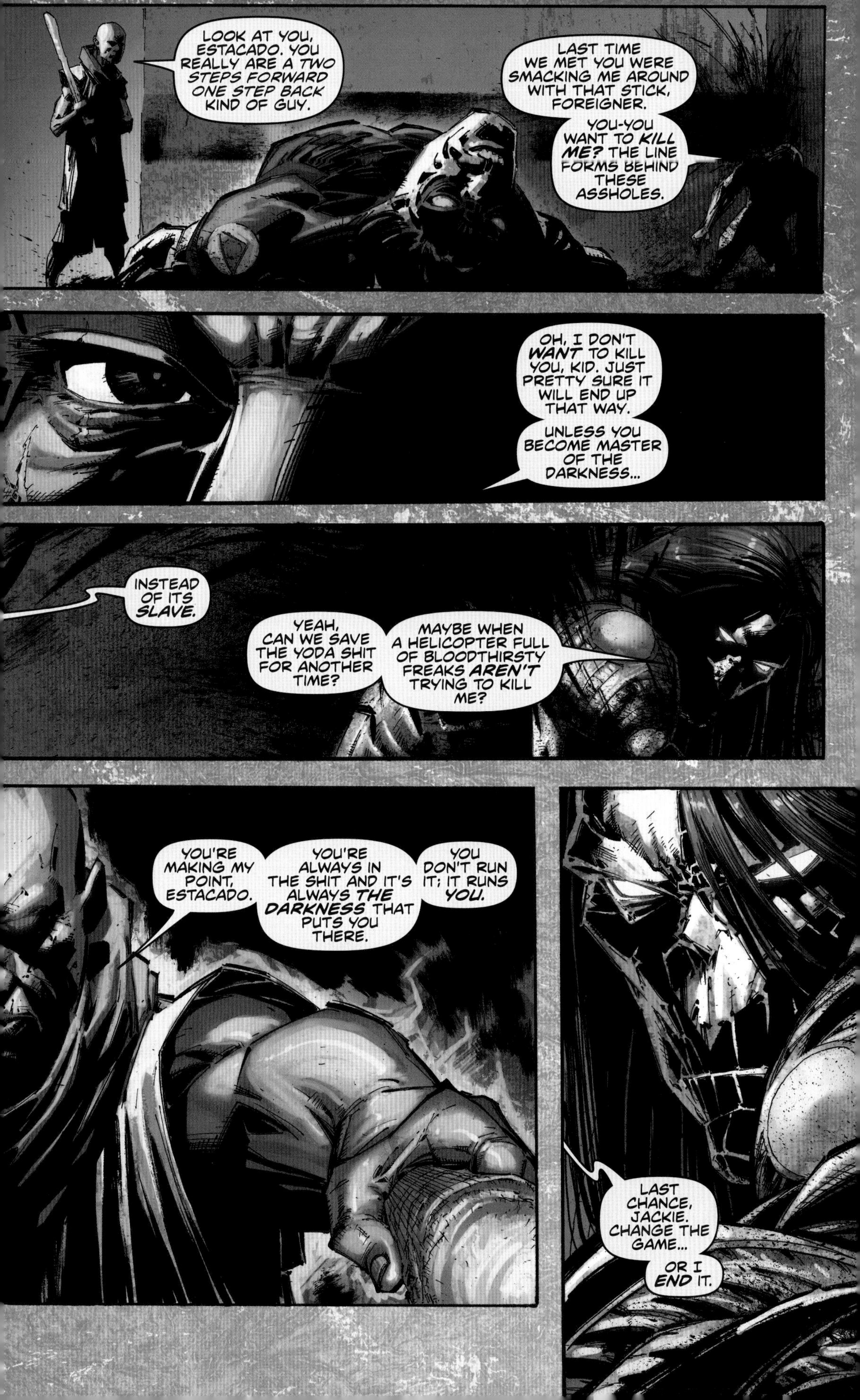
LOOK AT YOU, ESTACADO. YOU REALLY ARE A *TWO STEPS FORWARD ONE STEP BACK* KIND OF GUY.
LAST TIME WE MET YOU WERE SMACKING ME AROUND WITH THAT STICK, FOREIGNER.
YOU-YOU WANT TO ***KILL ME?*** THE LINE FORMS BEHIND THESE ASSHOLES.
OH, I DON'T ***WANT*** TO KILL YOU, KID. JUST PRETTY SURE IT WILL END UP THAT WAY.
UNLESS YOU BECOME MASTER OF THE DARKNESS...
INSTEAD OF ITS ***SLAVE.***
YEAH, CAN WE SAVE THE YODA SHIT FOR ANOTHER TIME?
MAYBE WHEN A HELICOPTER FULL OF BLOODTHIRSTY FREAKS ***AREN'T*** TRYING TO KILL ME?
YOU'RE MAKING MY POINT, ESTACADO.
YOU'RE ALWAYS IN THE SHIT AND IT'S ALWAYS ***THE DARKNESS*** THAT PUTS YOU THERE.
YOU DON'T RUN IT; IT RUNS ***YOU.***
LAST CHANCE, JACKIE. CHANGE THE GAME...
OR I ***END*** IT.

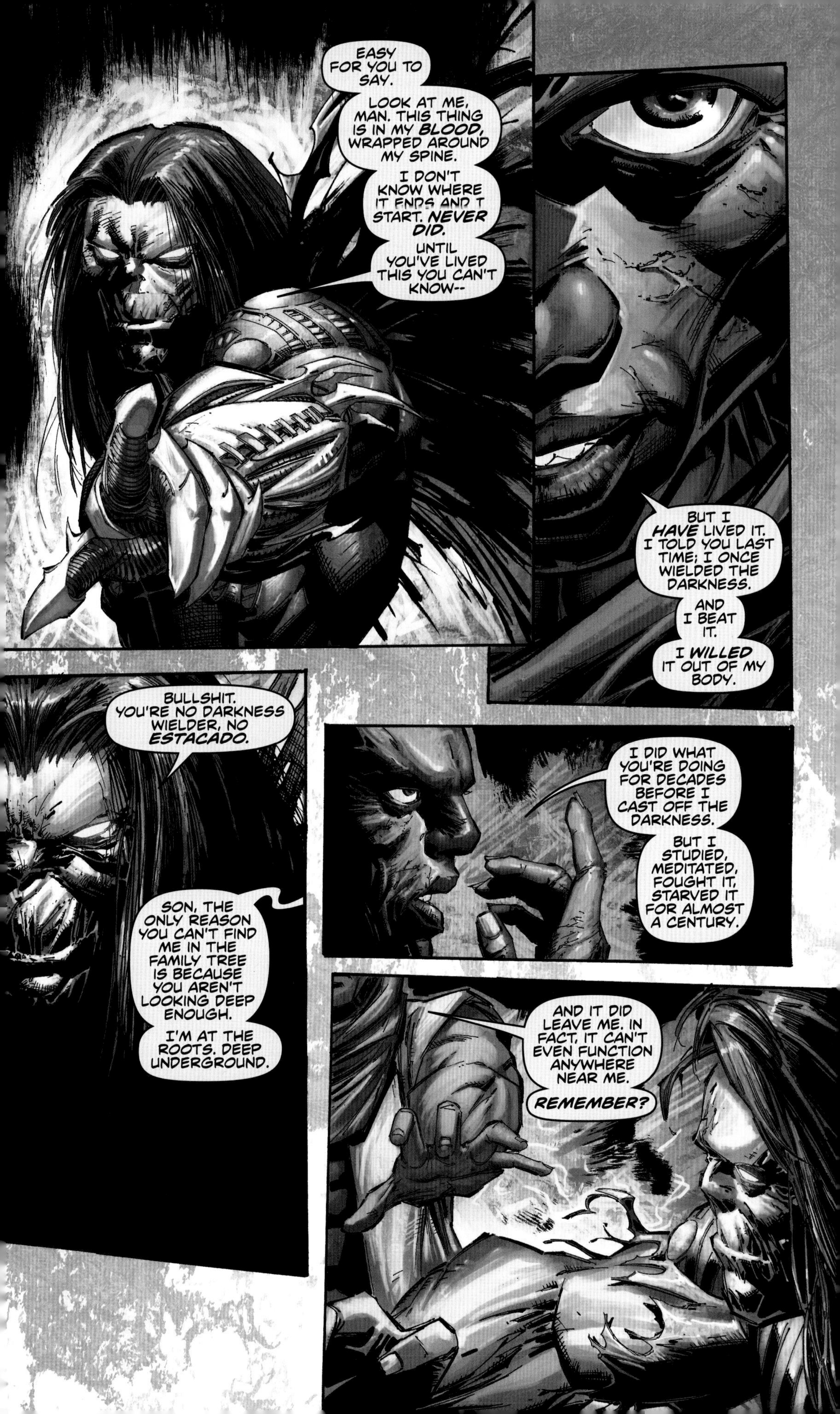
EASY FOR YOU TO SAY.
LOOK AT ME, MAN. THIS THING IS IN MY *BLOOD,* WRAPPED AROUND MY SPINE.
I DON'T KNOW WHERE IT ENDS AND I START. ***NEVER DID.***
UNTIL YOU'VE LIVED THIS YOU CAN'T KNOW--
BUT I ***HAVE*** LIVED IT. I TOLD YOU LAST TIME; I ONCE WIELDED THE DARKNESS.
AND I BEAT IT.
I ***WILLED*** IT OUT OF MY BODY.
BULLSHIT. YOU'RE NO DARKNESS WIELDER, NO ***ESTACADO.***
I DID WHAT YOU'RE DOING FOR DECADES BEFORE I CAST OFF THE DARKNESS.
BUT I STUDIED, MEDITATED, FOUGHT IT, STARVED IT FOR ALMOST A CENTURY.
SON, THE ONLY REASON YOU CAN'T FIND ME IN THE FAMILY TREE IS BECAUSE YOU AREN'T LOOKING DEEP ENOUGH.
I'M AT THE ROOTS. DEEP UNDERGROUND.
AND IT DID LEAVE ME. IN FACT, IT CAN'T EVEN FUNCTION ANYWHERE NEAR ME.
REMEMBER?

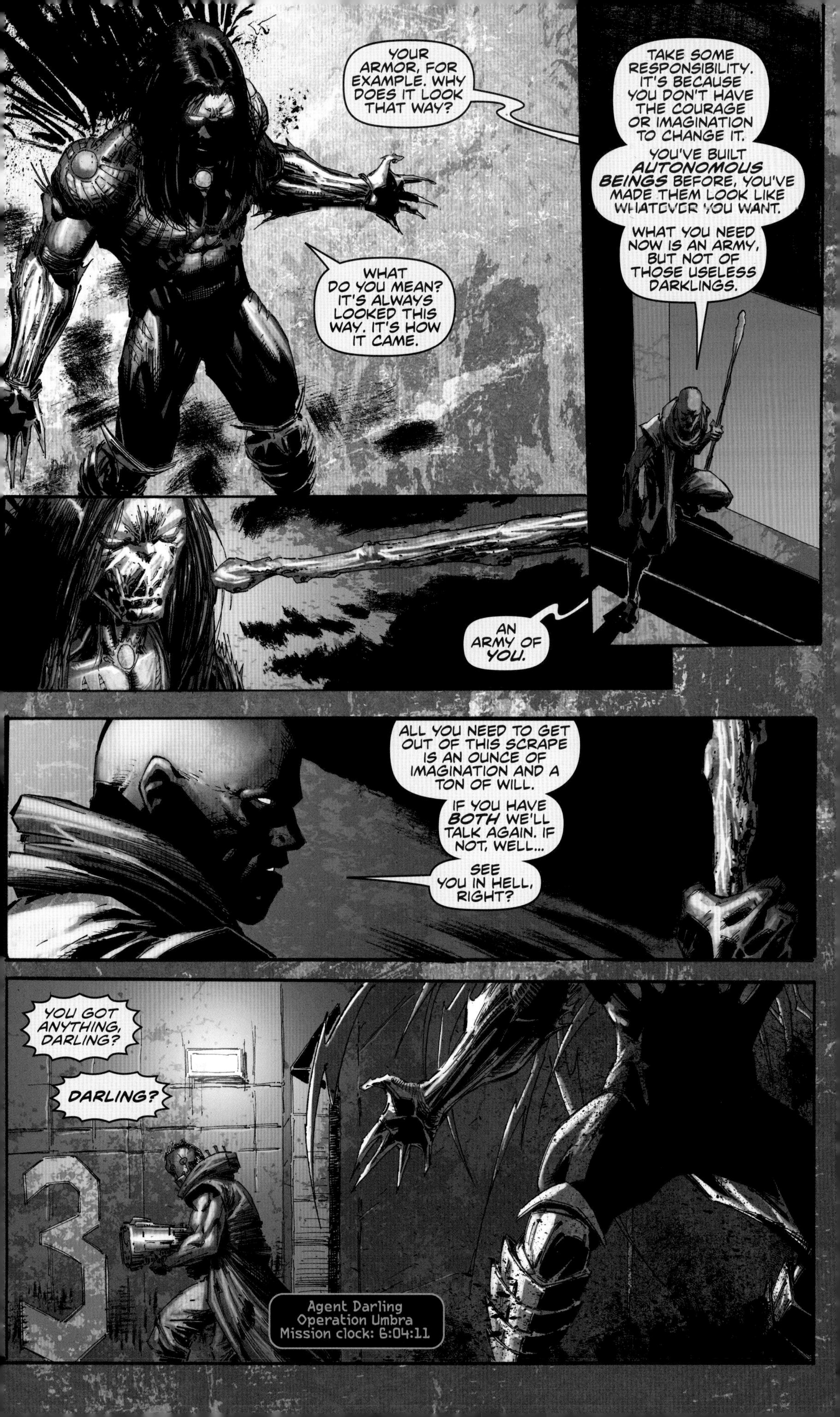
YOUR ARMOR, FOR EXAMPLE. WHY DOES IT LOOK THAT WAY?
TAKE SOME RESPONSIBILITY. IT'S BECAUSE YOU DON'T HAVE THE COURAGE OR IMAGINATION TO CHANGE IT.
YOU'VE BUILT AUTONOMOUS BEINGS BEFORE, YOU'VE MADE THEM LOOK LIKE WHATEVER YOU WANT.
WHAT YOU NEED NOW IS AN ARMY, BUT NOT OF THOSE USELESS DARKLINGS.
WHAT DO YOU MEAN? IT'S ALWAYS LOOKED THIS WAY. IT'S HOW IT CAME.
AN ARMY OF YOU.
ALL YOU NEED TO GET OUT OF THIS SCRAPE IS AN OUNCE OF IMAGINATION AND A TON OF WILL.
IF YOU HAVE BOTH WE'LL TALK AGAIN. IF NOT, WELL...
SEE YOU IN HELL, RIGHT?
YOU GOT ANYTHING, DARLING?
DARLING?
Agent Darling
Operation Umbra
Mission clock: 6:04:11

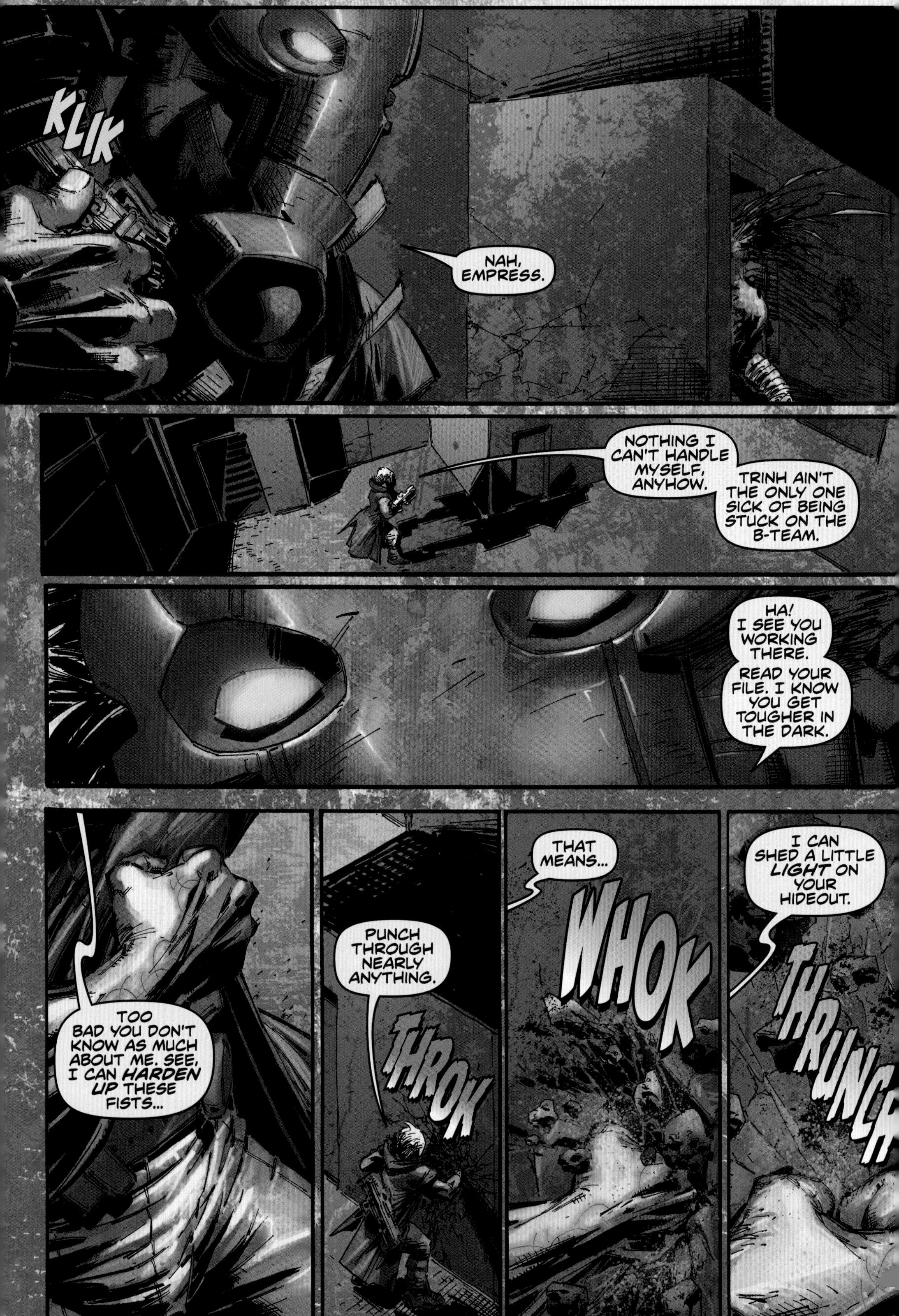
KLIK
NAH, EMPRESS.
NOTHING I CAN'T HANDLE MYSELF, ANYHOW.
TRINH AIN'T THE ONLY ONE SICK OF BEING STUCK ON THE B-TEAM.
HA! I SEE YOU WORKING THERE.
READ YOUR FILE. I KNOW YOU GET TOUGHER IN THE DARK.
TOO BAD YOU DON'T KNOW AS MUCH ABOUT ME. SEE, I CAN *HARDEN UP* THESE FISTS...
PUNCH THROUGH NEARLY ANYTHING.
THROK
THAT MEANS...
WHOK
I CAN SHED A LITTLE *LIGHT* ON YOUR HIDEOUT.
THRUNCH

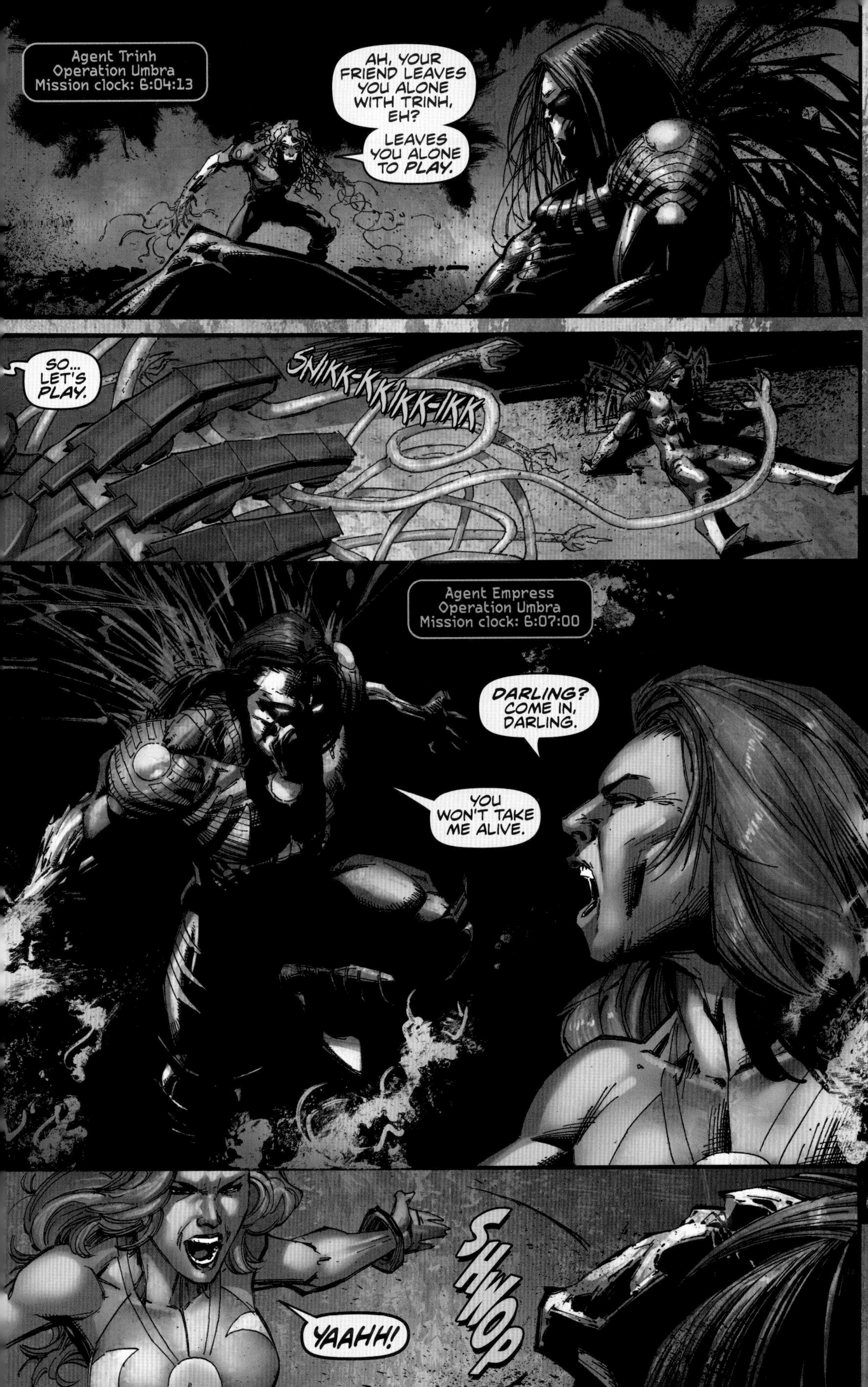
Agent Trinh
Operation Umbra
Mission clock: 6:04:13
AH, YOUR FRIEND LEAVES YOU ALONE WITH TRINH, EH?
LEAVES YOU ALONE TO PLAY.
SO... LET'S PLAY.
SNIKK-KKIKK-IKK
Agent Empress
Operation Umbra
Mission clock: 6:07:00
DARLING? COME IN, DARLING.
YOU WON'T TAKE ME ALIVE.
SHWOP
YAAHH!

NICE MOVES, BUT IT WON'T HELP YOU.

WHAT-- WHAT ARE YOU HOLDING?

I TOLD YOU. I'M NOT LETTING YOU PEOPLE TAKE ME IN.

I'D RATHER DIE. RATHER WE ALL DIE.

D-DARLING?

TRINH?

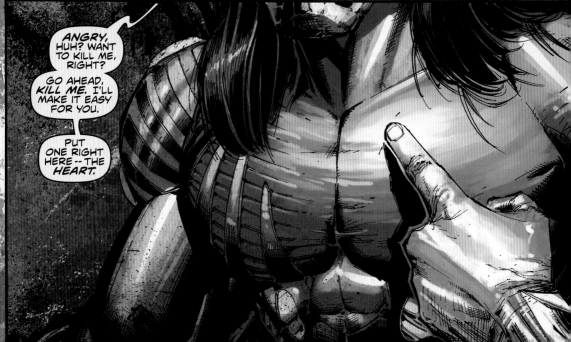

ANGRY, HUH? WANT TO KILL ME, RIGHT?

GO AHEAD, KILL ME. I'LL MAKE IT EASY FOR YOU.

PUT ONE RIGHT HERE -- THE HEART.

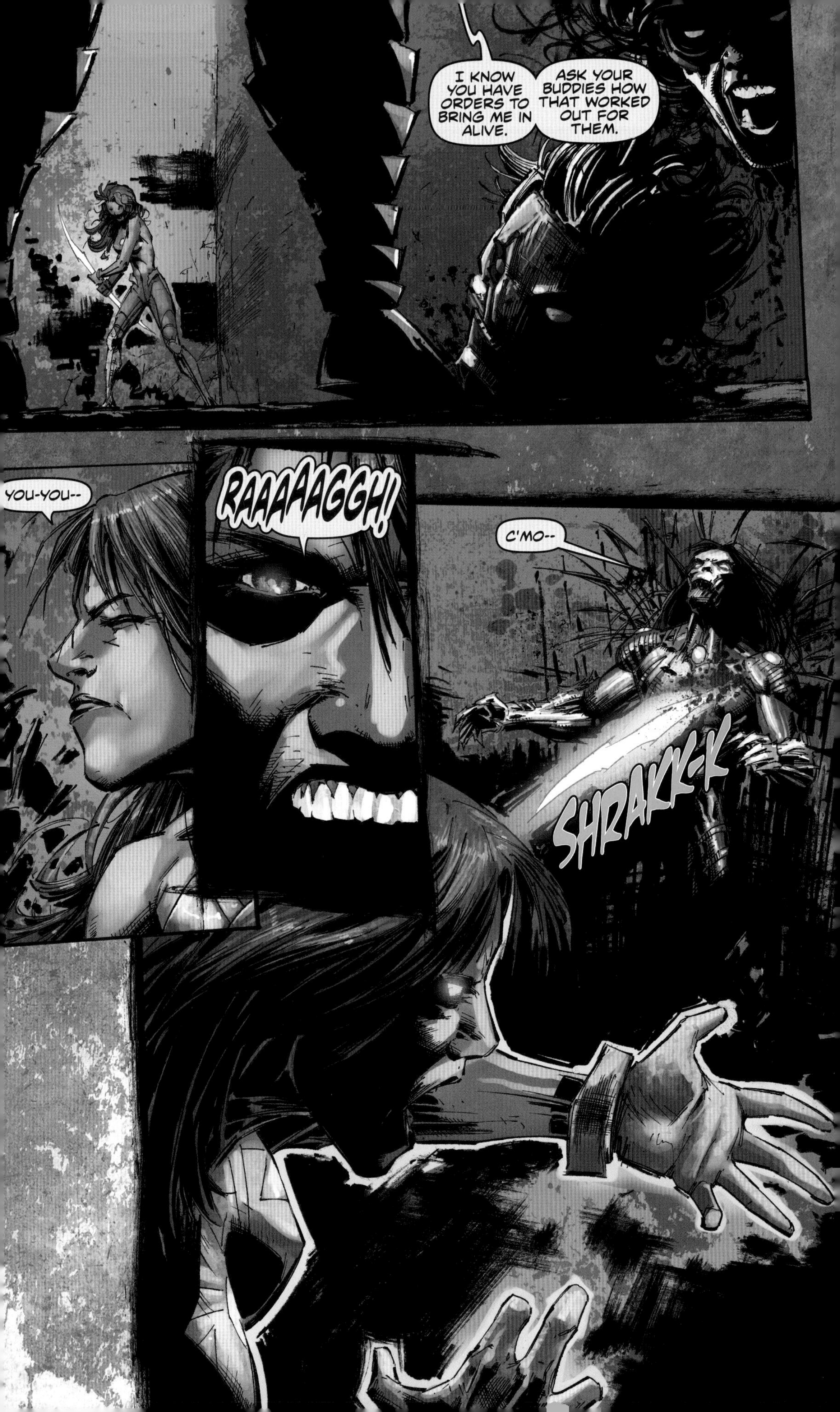
I KNOW YOU HAVE ORDERS TO BRING ME IN ALIVE.
ASK YOUR BUDDIES HOW THAT WORKED OUT FOR THEM.
YOU-YOU--
RAAAAAGGH!
C'MO--
SHRAKK-K

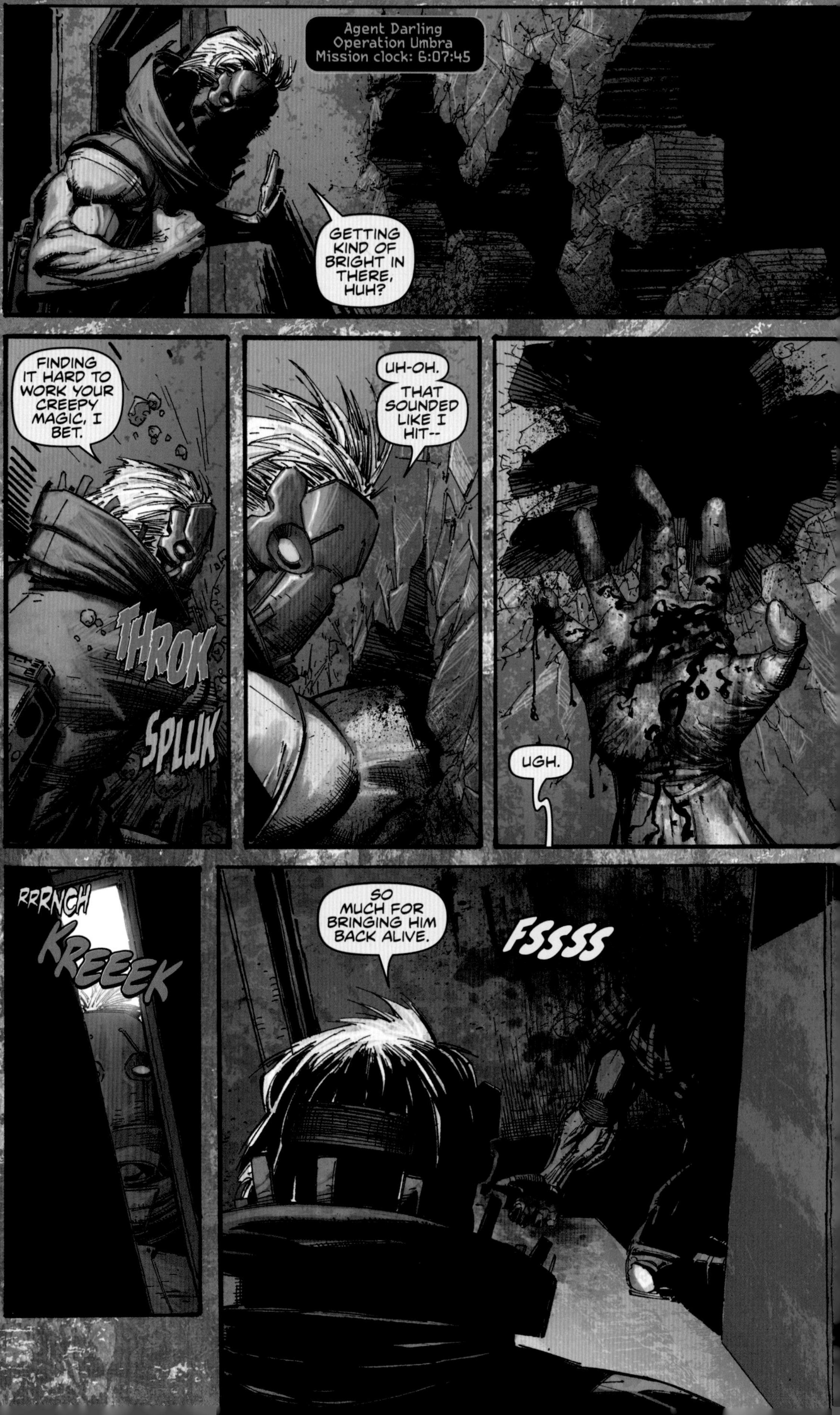
Agent Darling
Operation Umbra
Mission clock: 6:07:45
GETTING KIND OF BRIGHT IN THERE, HUH?
FINDING IT HARD TO WORK YOUR CREEPY MAGIC, I BET.
THROK
SPLUK
UH-OH. THAT SOUNDED LIKE I HIT--
UGH.
RRRNCH
KREEEK
SO MUCH FOR BRINGING HIM BACK ALIVE.
FSSSS

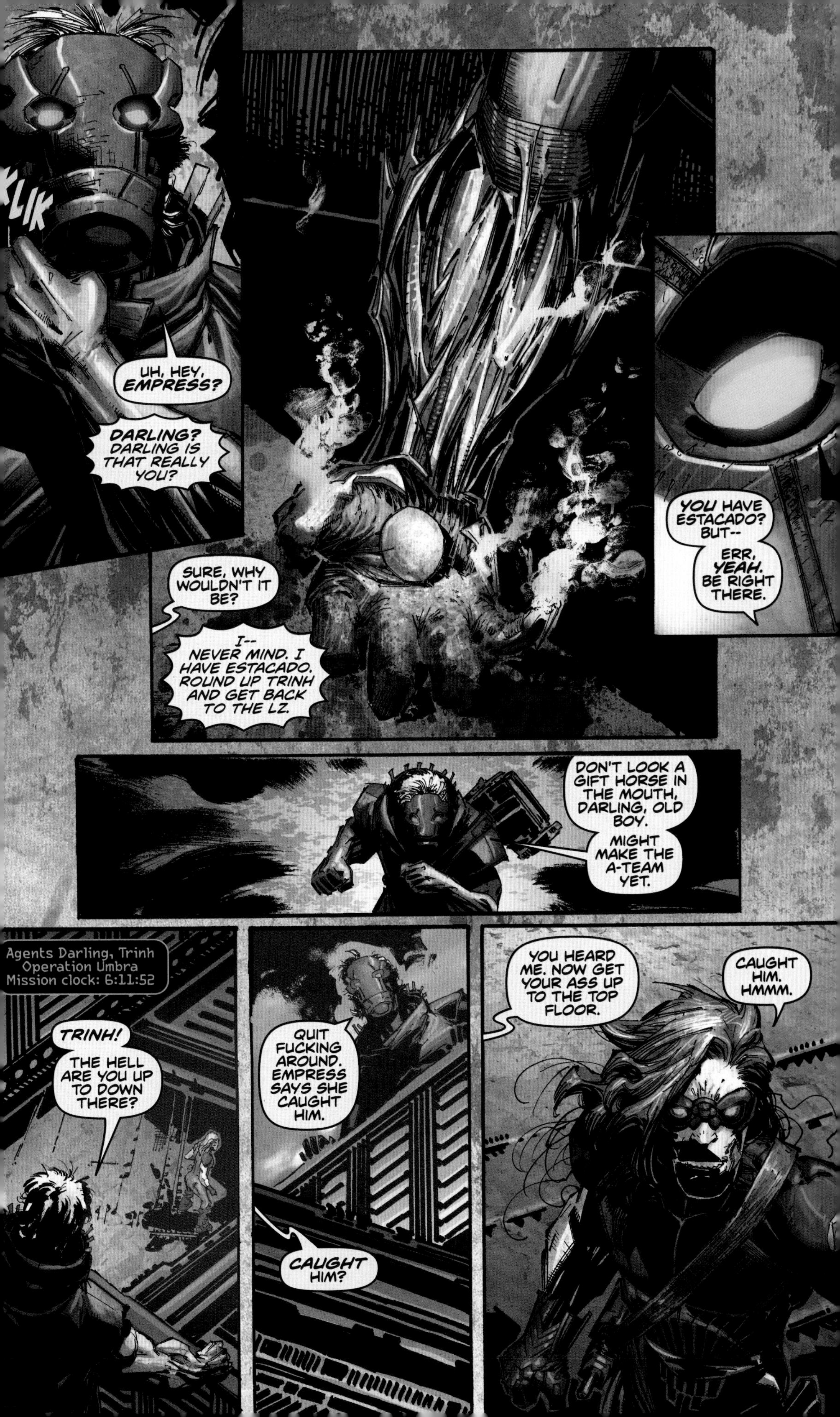
KLIK
UH, HEY, EMPRESS?
DARLING? DARLING IS THAT REALLY YOU?
SURE, WHY WOULDN'T IT BE?
I-- NEVER MIND. I HAVE ESTACADO. ROUND UP TRINH AND GET BACK TO THE LZ.
YOU HAVE ESTACADO? BUT--
ERR, YEAH. BE RIGHT THERE.
DON'T LOOK A GIFT HORSE IN THE MOUTH, DARLING, OLD BOY.
MIGHT MAKE THE A-TEAM YET.
Agents Darling, Trinh
Operation Umbra
Mission clock: 6:11:52
TRINH!
THE HELL ARE YOU UP TO DOWN THERE?
QUIT FUCKING AROUND. EMPRESS SAYS SHE CAUGHT HIM.
CAUGHT HIM?
YOU HEARD ME. NOW GET YOUR ASS UP TO THE TOP FLOOR.
CAUGHT HIM. HMMM.

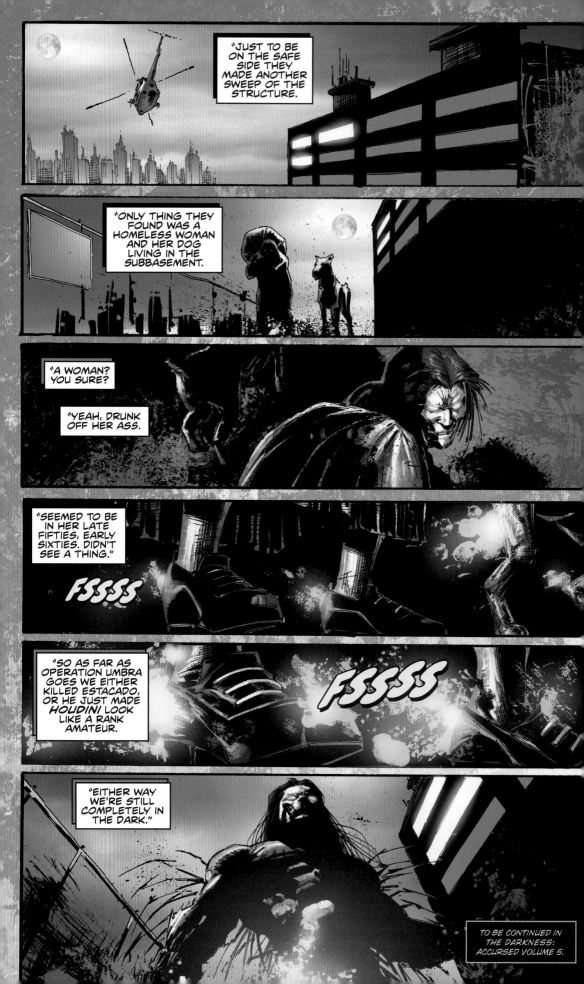

"JUST TO BE ON THE SAFE SIDE THEY MADE ANOTHER SWEEP OF THE STRUCTURE.

"ONLY THING THEY FOUND WAS A HOMELESS WOMAN AND HER DOG LIVING IN THE SUBBASEMENT.

"A WOMAN? YOU SURE?"

"YEAH, DRUNK OFF HER ASS.

"SEEMED TO BE IN HER LATE FIFTIES, EARLY SIXTIES. DIDN'T SEE A THING."

FSSSS

"SO AS FAR AS OPERATION UMBRA GOES WE EITHER KILLED ESTACADO, OR HE JUST MADE HOUDINI LOOK LIKE A RANK AMATEUR.

FSSSS

"EITHER WAY WE'RE STILL COMPLETELY IN THE DARK."

TO BE CONTINUED IN THE DARKNESS: ACCURSED VOLUME 5.

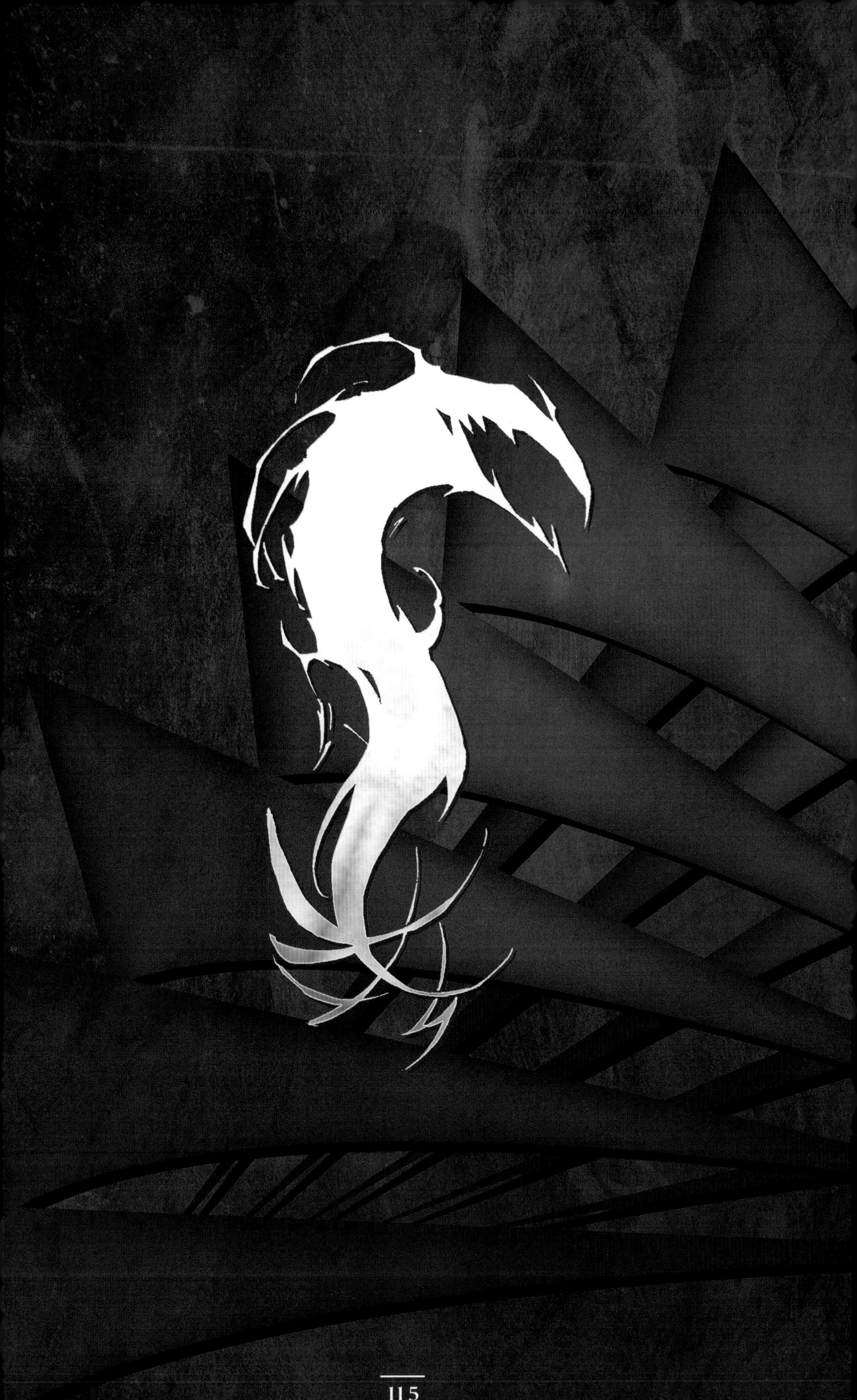

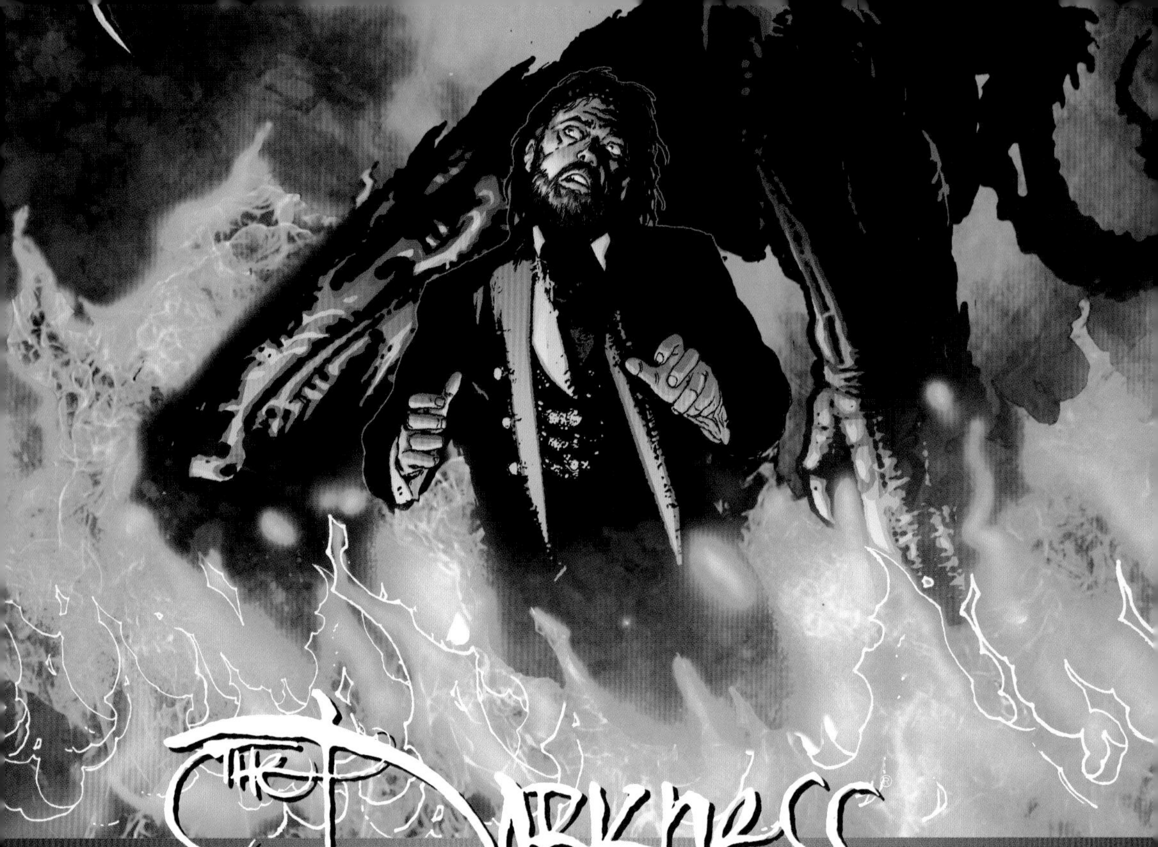

The Darkness

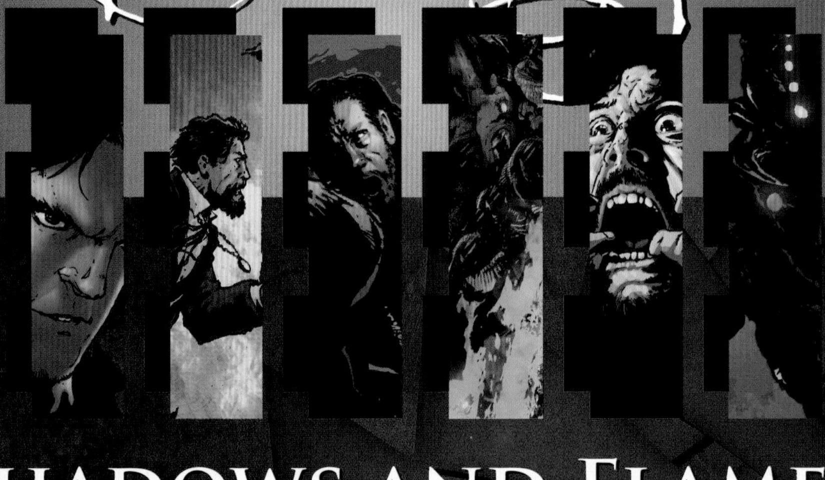

Shadows and Flame

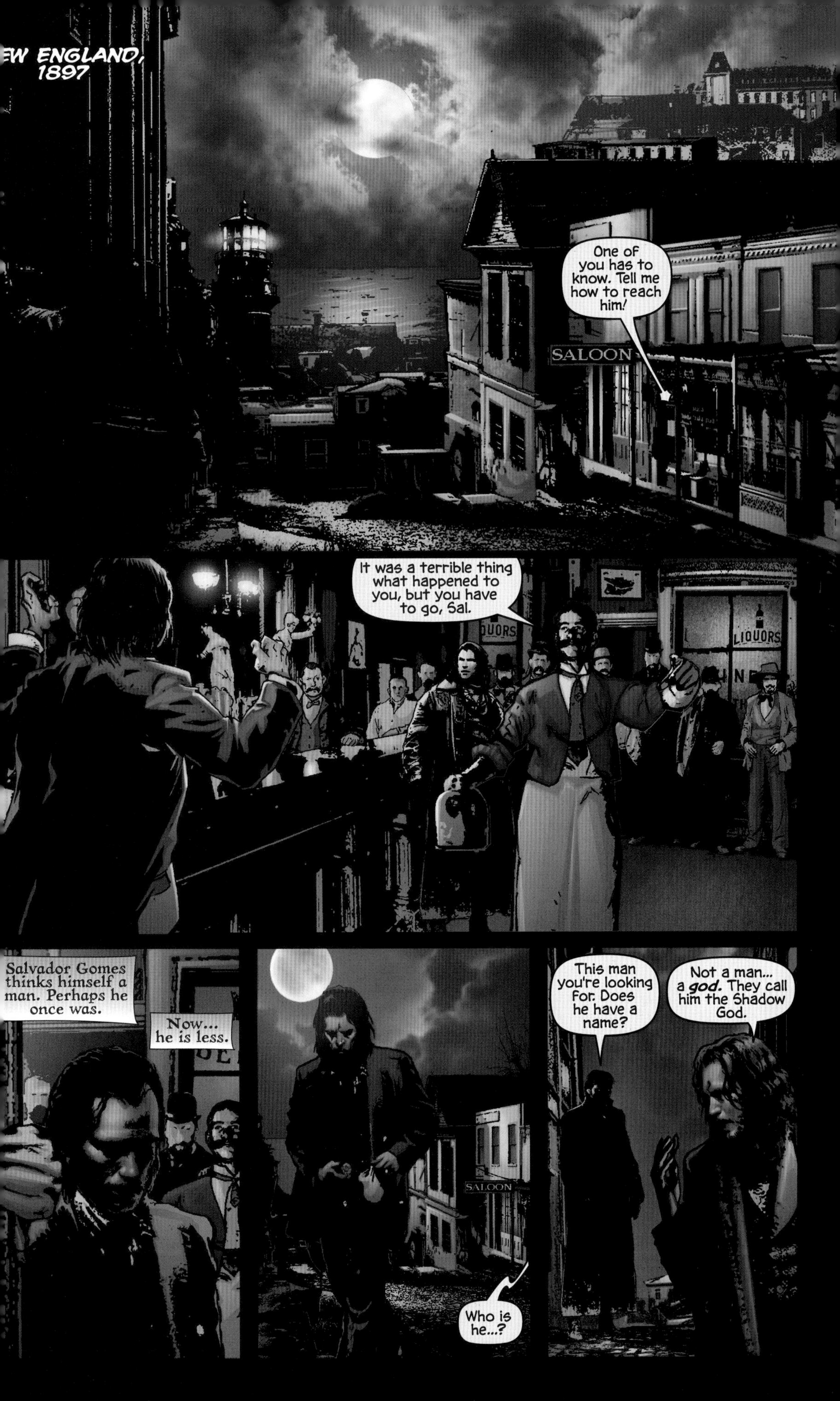
EW ENGLAND, 1897
One of you has to know. Tell me how to reach him!
SALOON
It was a terrible thing what happened to you, but you have to go, Sal.
LIQUORS
Salvador Gomes thinks himself a man. Perhaps he once was.
Now... he is less.
SALOON
Who is he...?
This man you're looking for. Does he have a name?
Not a man... a ***god.*** They call him the Shadow God.

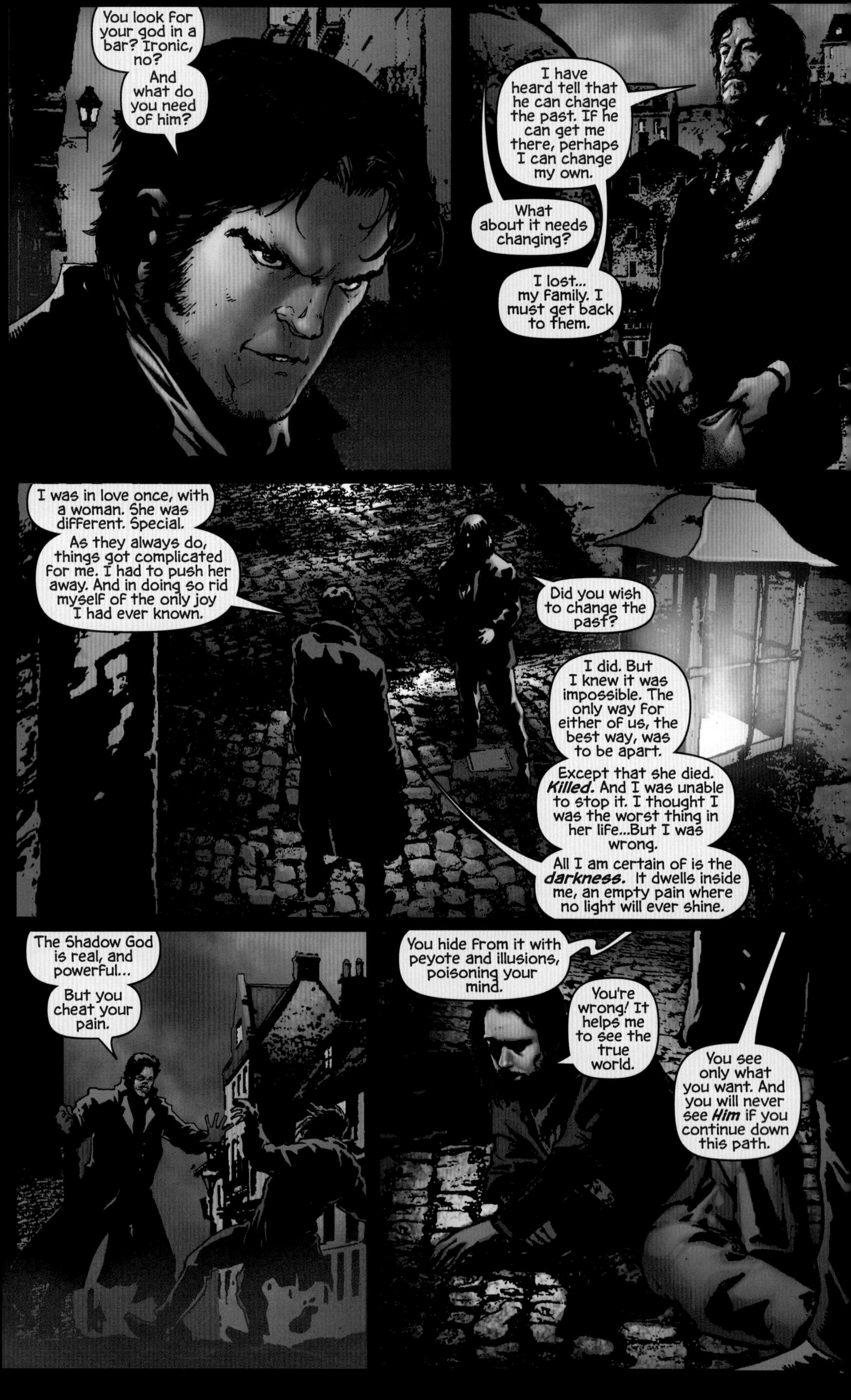
You look for your god in a bar? Ironic, no?
And what do you need of him?
I have heard tell that he can change the past. If he can get me there, perhaps I can change my own.
What about it needs changing?
I lost... my family. I must get back to them.
I was in love once, with a woman. She was different. Special.
As they always do, things got complicated for me. I had to push her away. And in doing so rid myself of the only joy I had ever known.
Did you wish to change the past?
I did. But I knew it was impossible. The only way for either of us, the best way, was to be apart.
Except that she died. ***Killed.*** And I was unable to stop it. I thought I was the worst thing in her life...But I was wrong.
All I am certain of is the ***darkness.*** It dwells inside me, an empty pain where no light will ever shine.
The Shadow God is real, and powerful...
But you cheat your pain.
You hide from it with peyote and illusions, poisoning your mind.
You're wrong! It helps me to see the true world.
You see only what you want. And you will never see ***Him*** if you continue down this path.

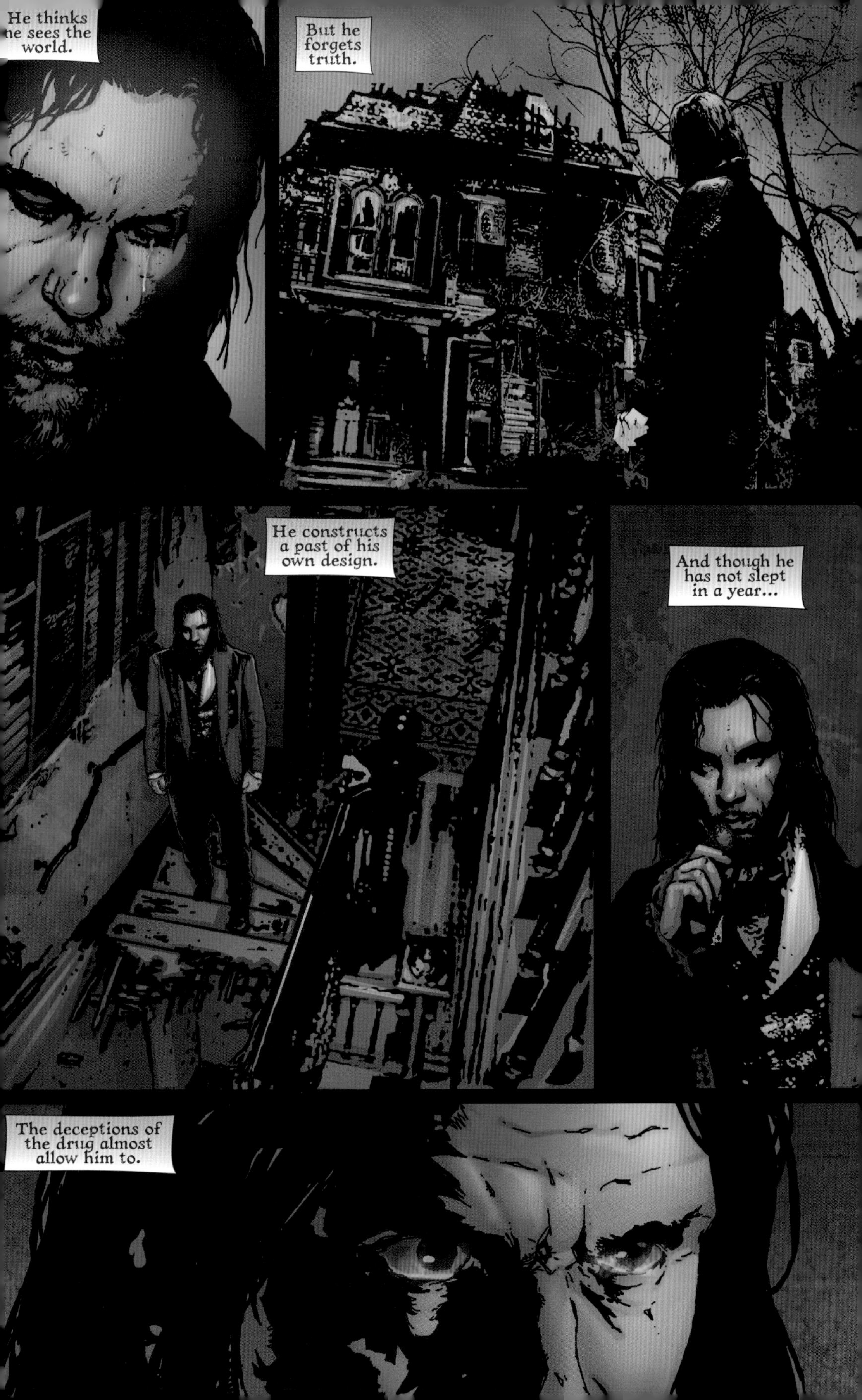
He thinks he sees the world.
But he forgets truth.
He constructs a past of his own design.
And though he has not slept in a year...
The deceptions of the drug almost allow him to.

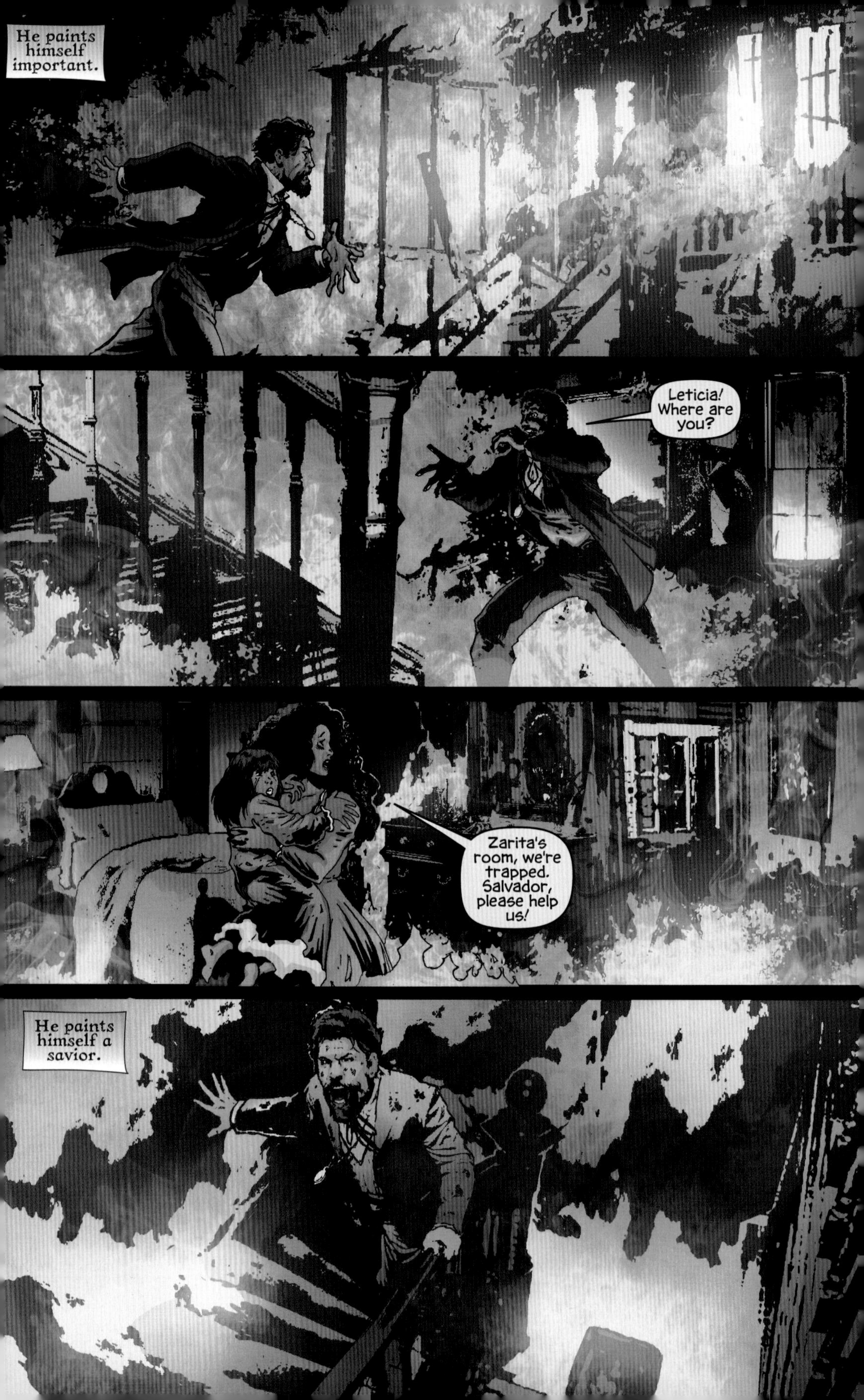
He paints himself important.
Leticia! Where are you?
Zarita's room, we're trapped. Salvador, please help us!
He paints himself a savior.

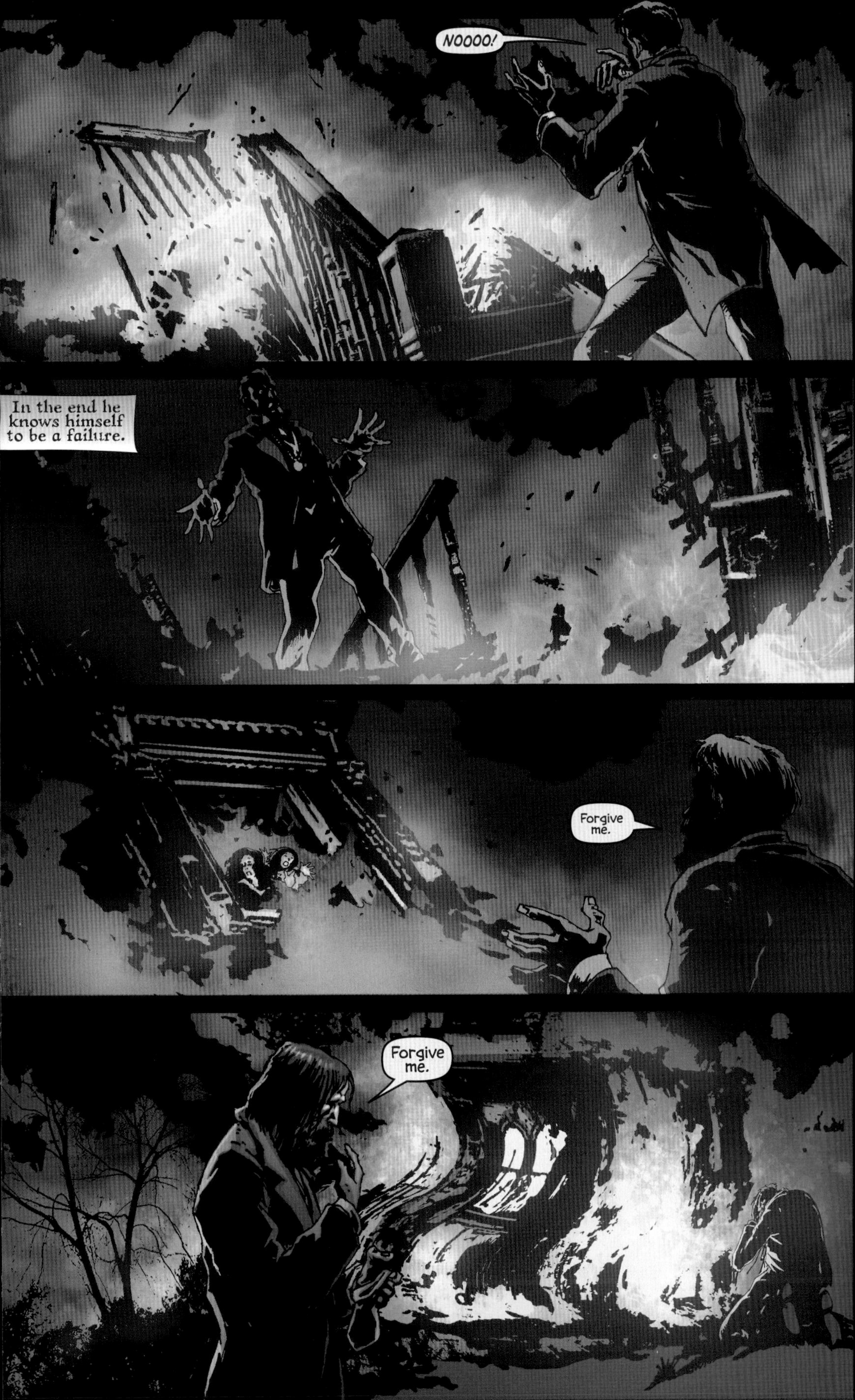
NOOOO!
In the end he knows himself to be a failure.
Forgive me.
Forgive me.

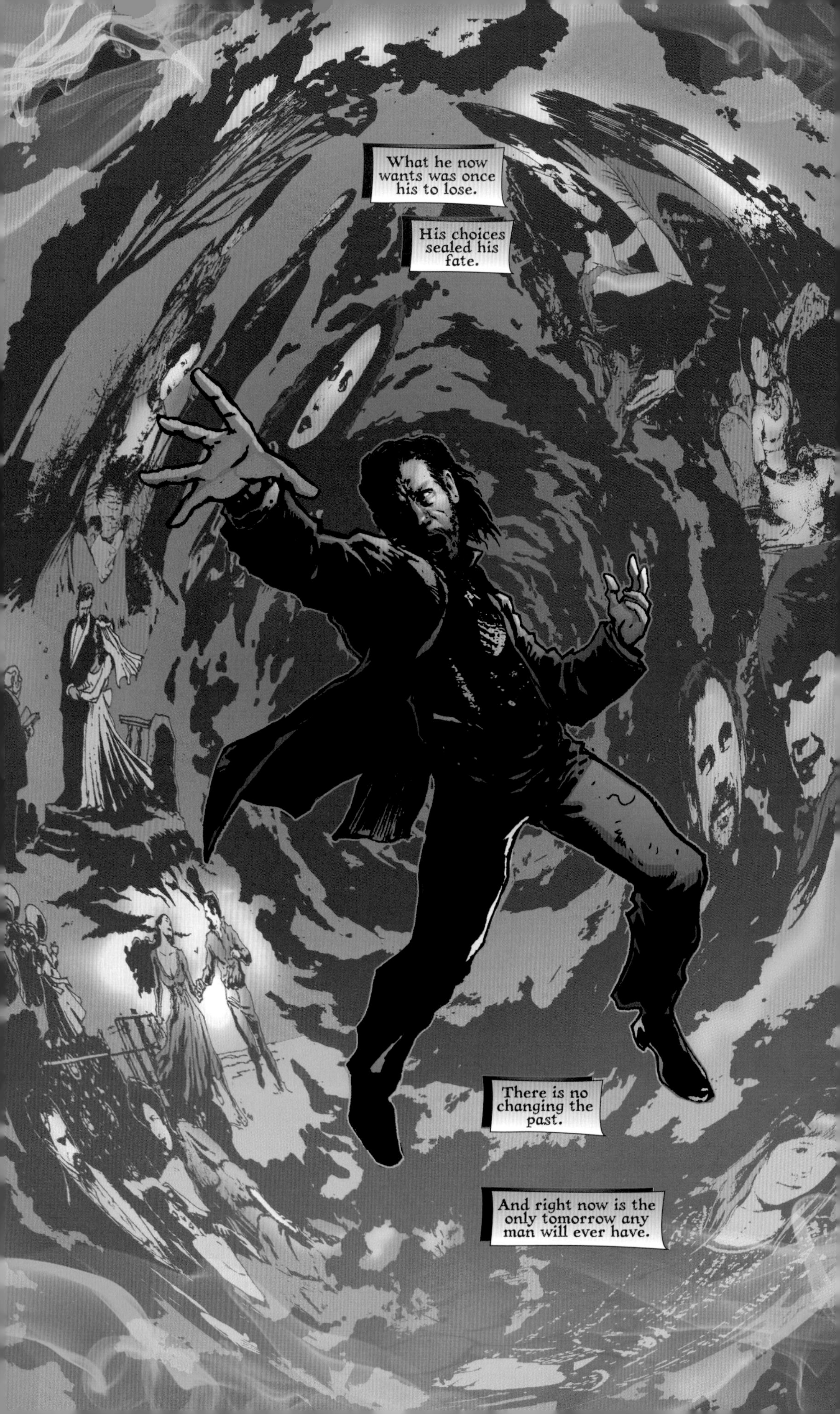
What he now wants was once his to lose.
His choices sealed his fate.
There is no changing the past.
And right now is the only tomorrow any man will ever have.

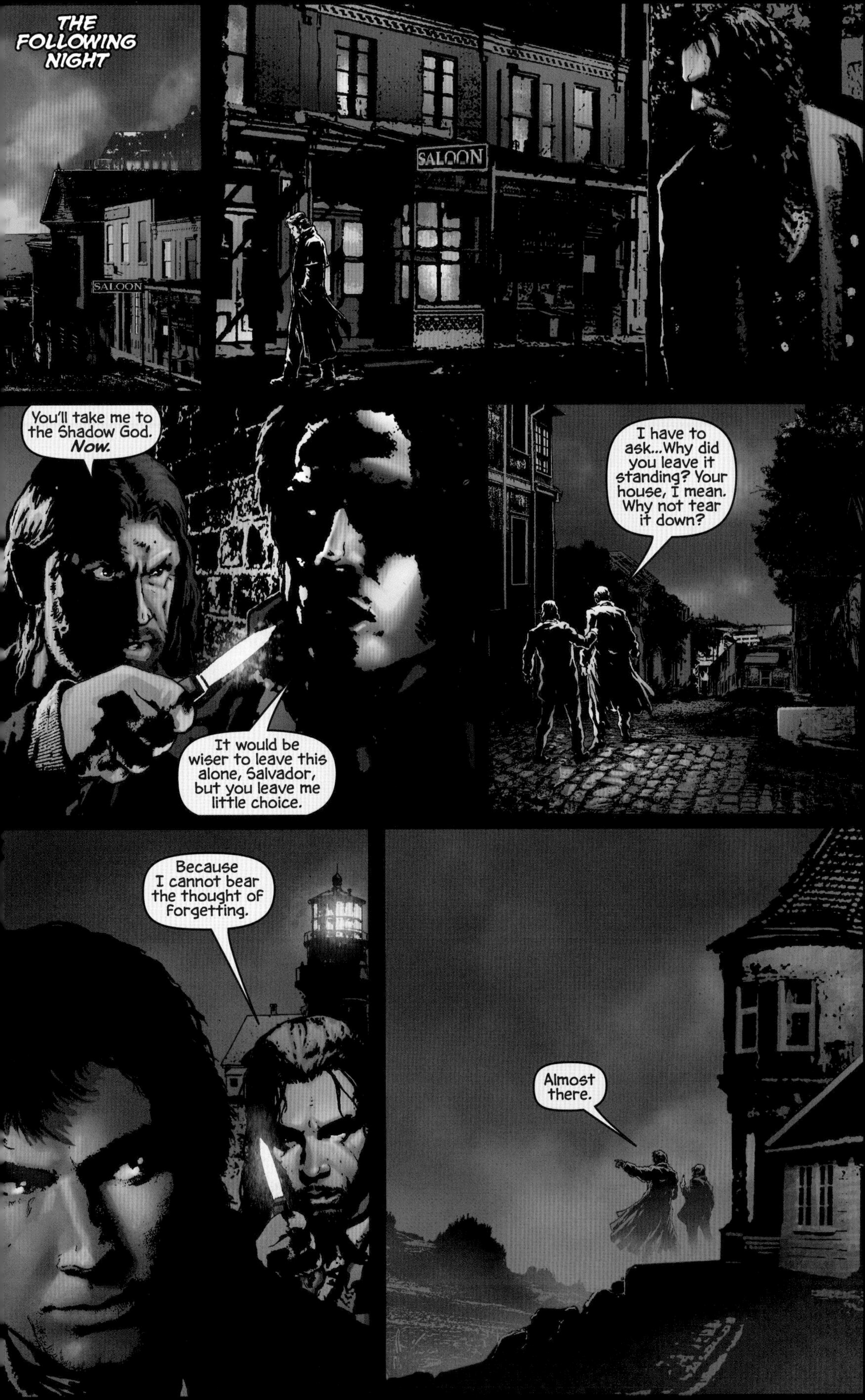
THE FOLLOWING NIGHT
SALOON
SALOON
You'll take me to the Shadow God. *Now.*
It would be wiser to leave this alone, Salvador, but you leave me little choice.
I have to ask...Why did you leave it standing? Your house, I mean. Why not tear it down?
Because I cannot bear the thought of forgetting.
Almost there.

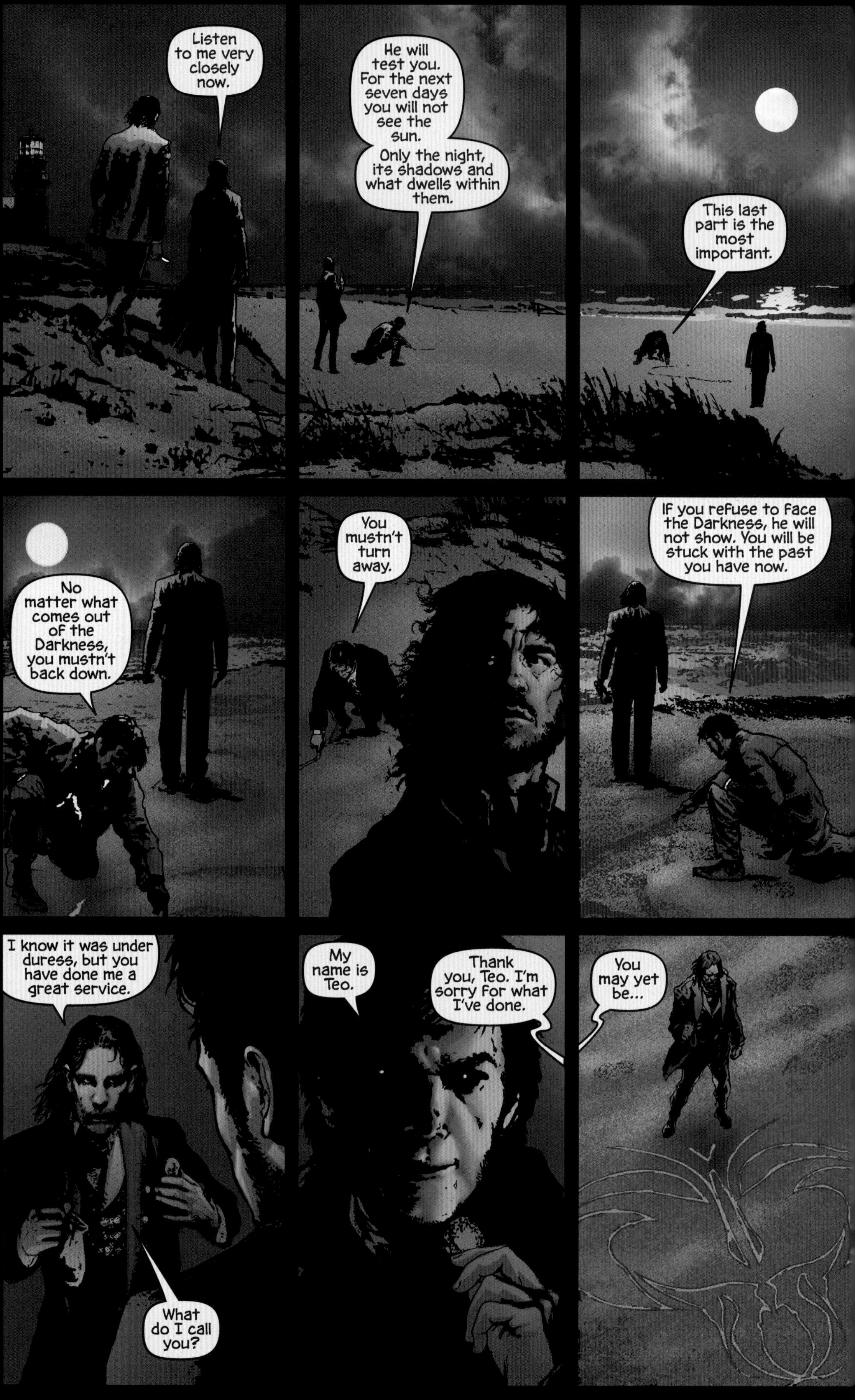
Listen to me very closely now.
He will test you. For the next seven days you will not see the sun.
Only the night, its shadows and what dwells within them.
This last part is the most important.
No matter what comes out of the Darkness, you mustn't back down.
You mustn't turn away.
If you refuse to face the Darkness, he will not show. You will be stuck with the past you have now.
I know it was under duress, but you have done me a great service.
What do I call you?
My name is Teo.
Thank you, Teo. I'm sorry for what I've done.
You may yet be...

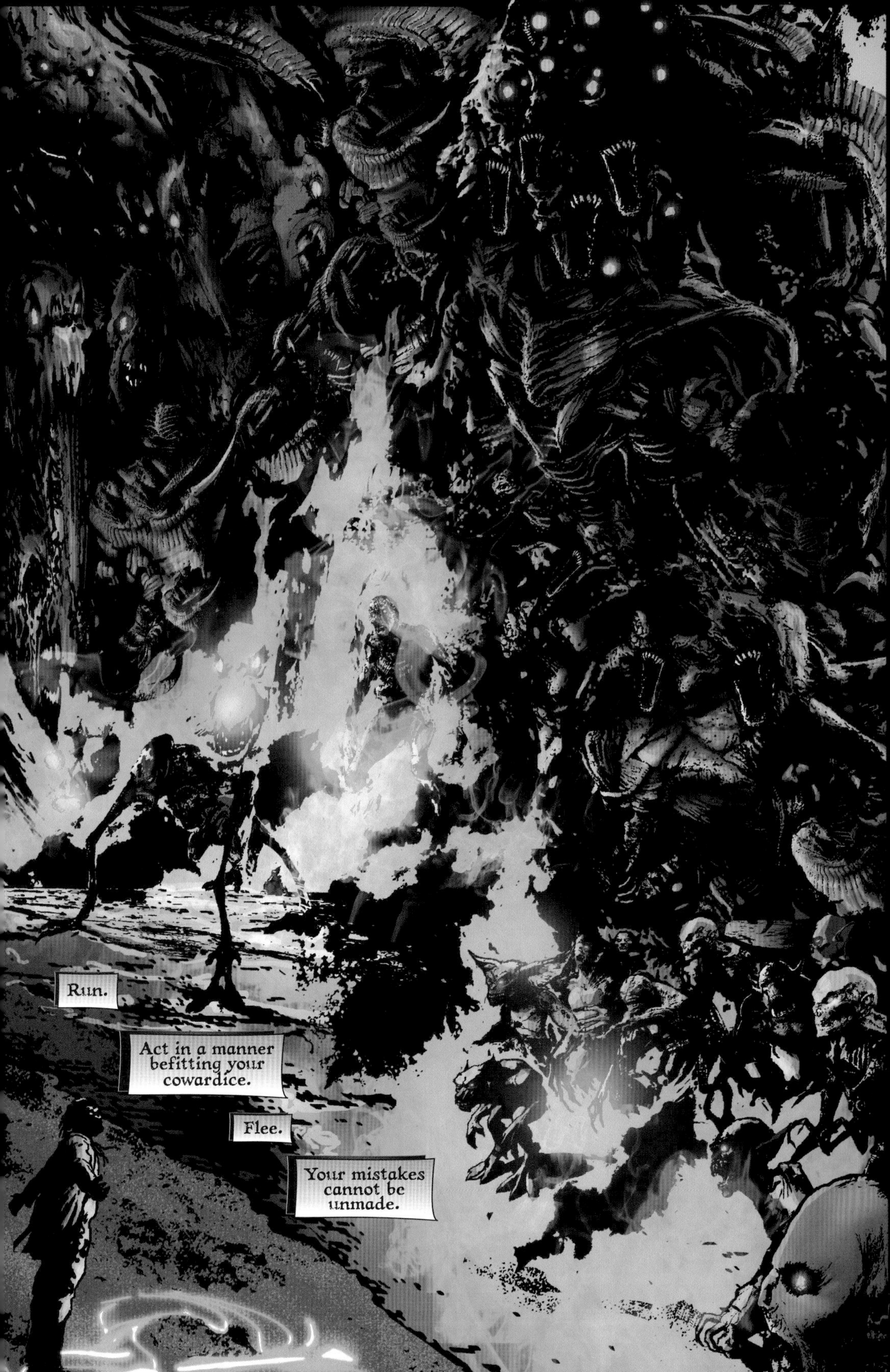
Run.
Act in a manner befitting your cowardice.
Flee.
Your mistakes cannot be unmade.

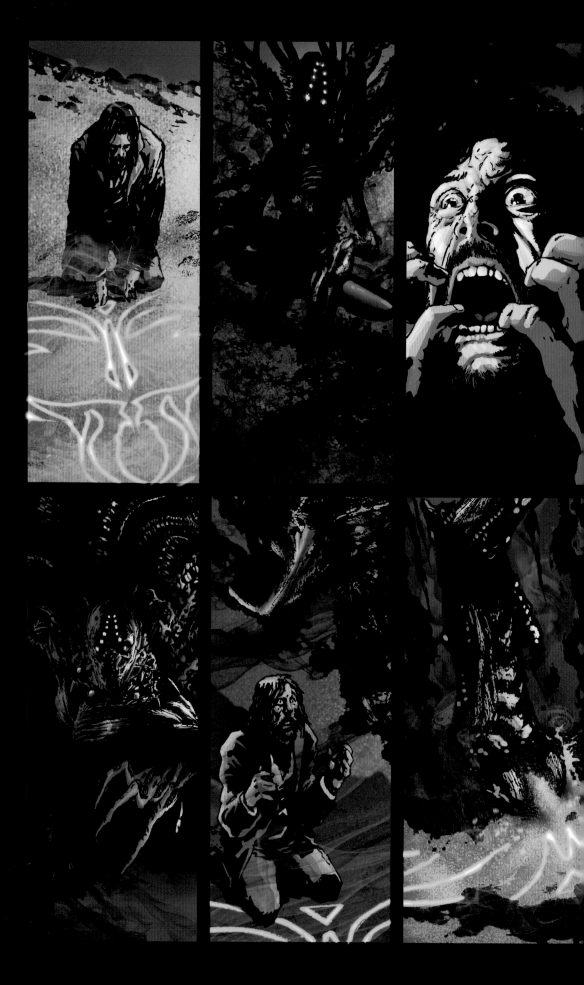

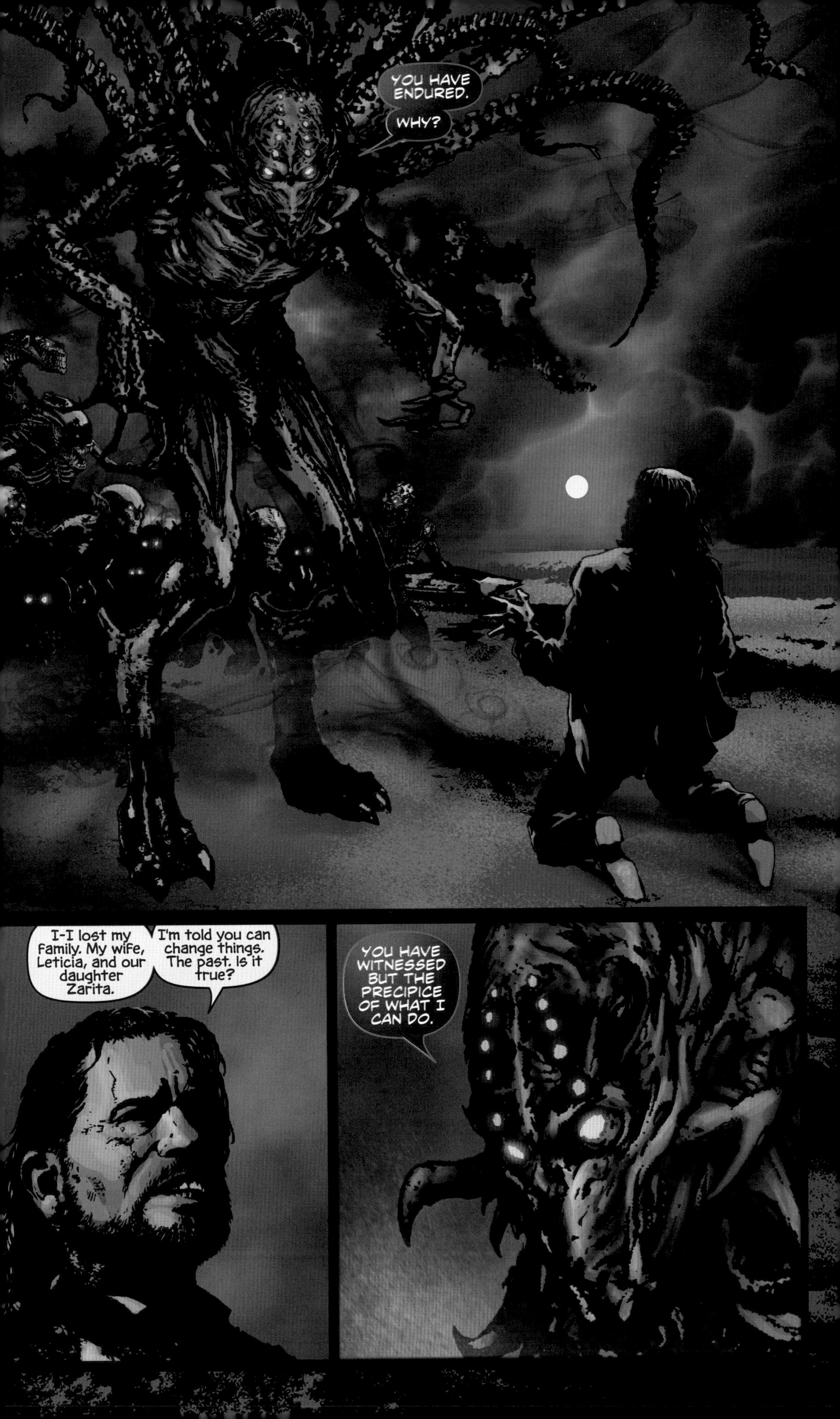
YOU HAVE ENDURED.
WHY?
I-I lost my family. My wife, Leticia, and our daughter Zarita.
I'm told you can change things. The past. Is it true?
YOU HAVE WITNESSED BUT THE PRECIPICE OF WHAT I CAN DO.

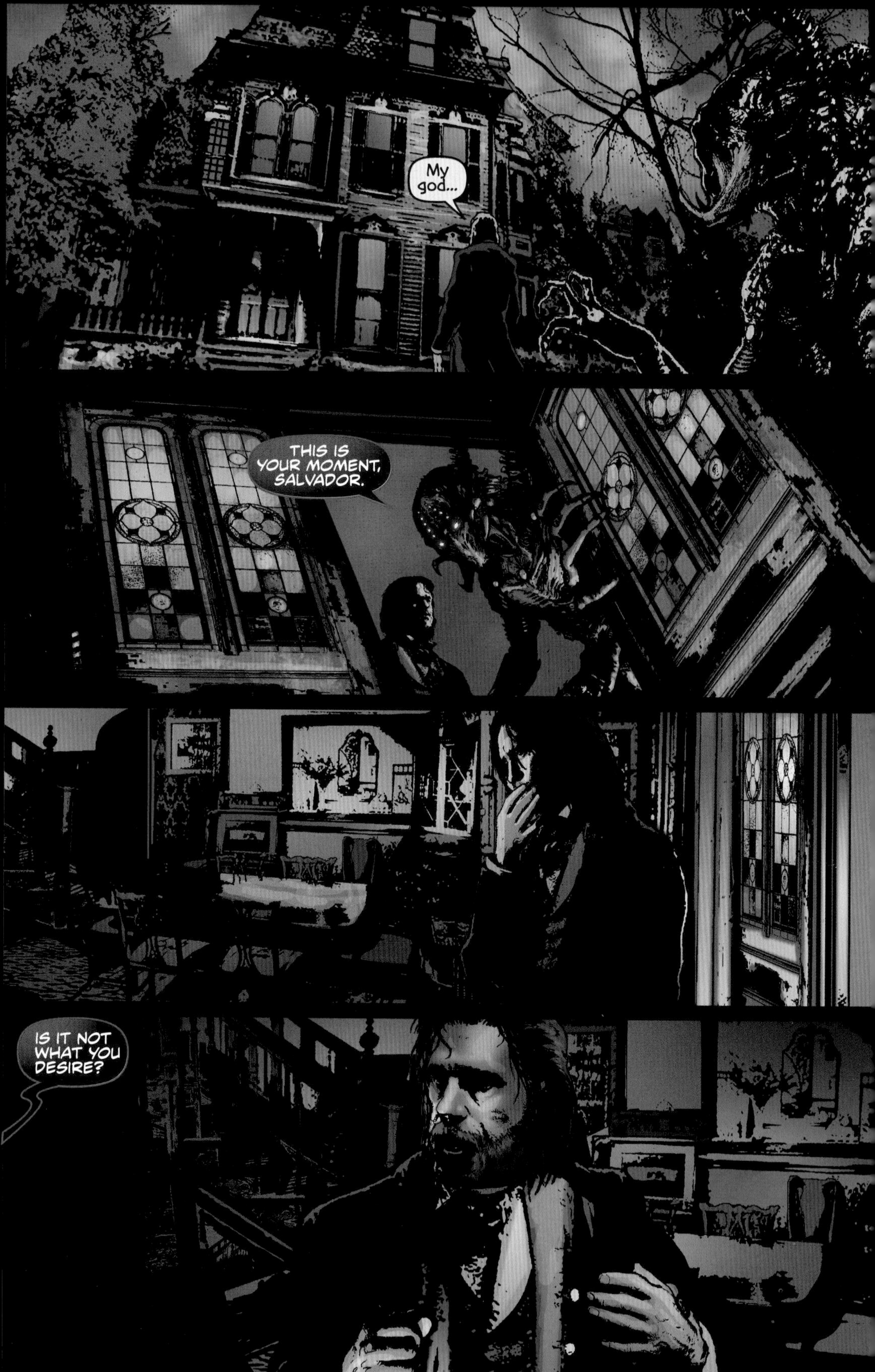
My god...
THIS IS YOUR MOMENT, SALVADOR.
IS IT NOT WHAT YOU DESIRE?

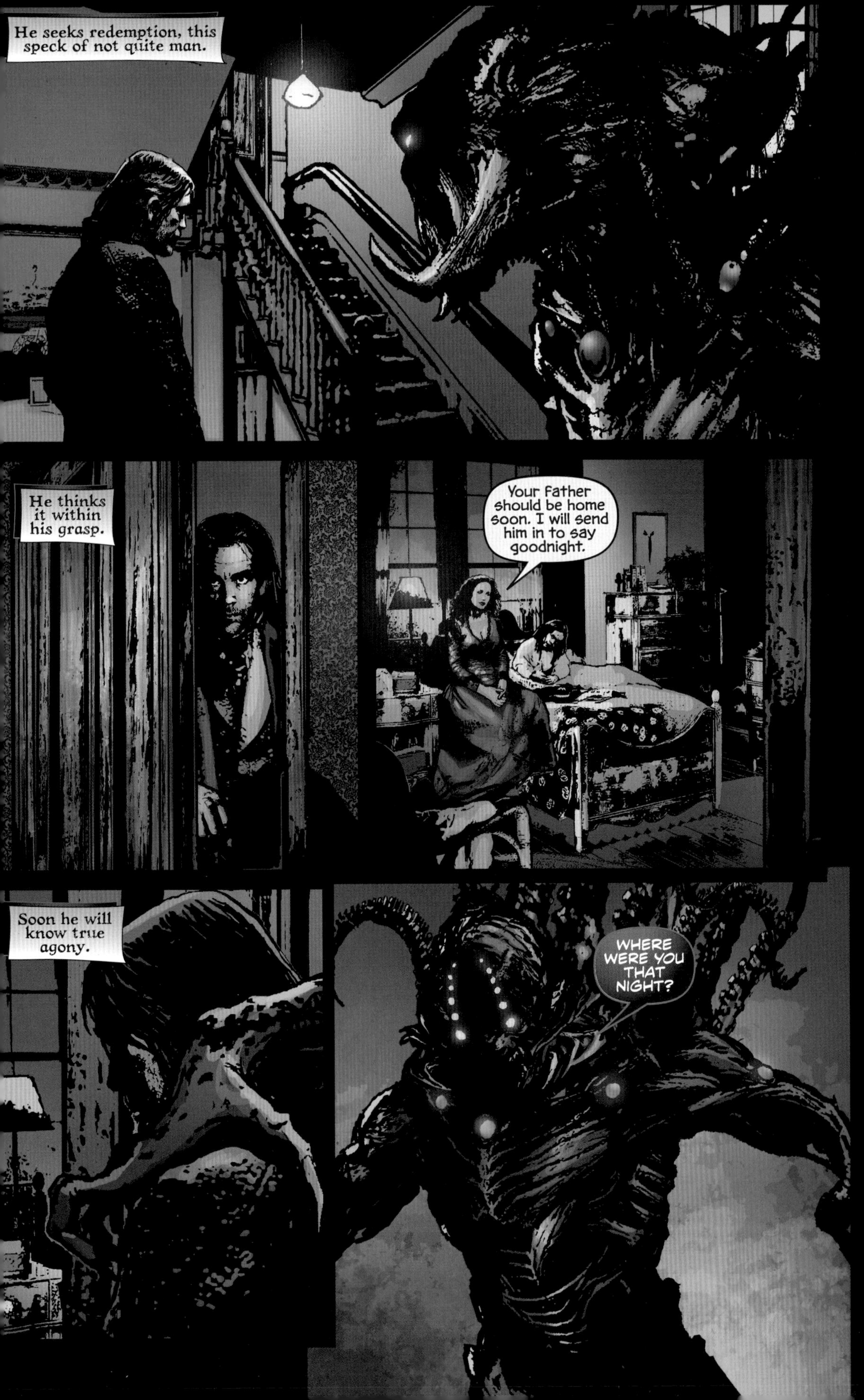
He seeks redemption, this speck of not quite man.
He thinks it within his grasp.
Your father should be home soon. I will send him in to say goodnight.
Soon he will know true agony.
WHERE WERE YOU THAT NIGHT?

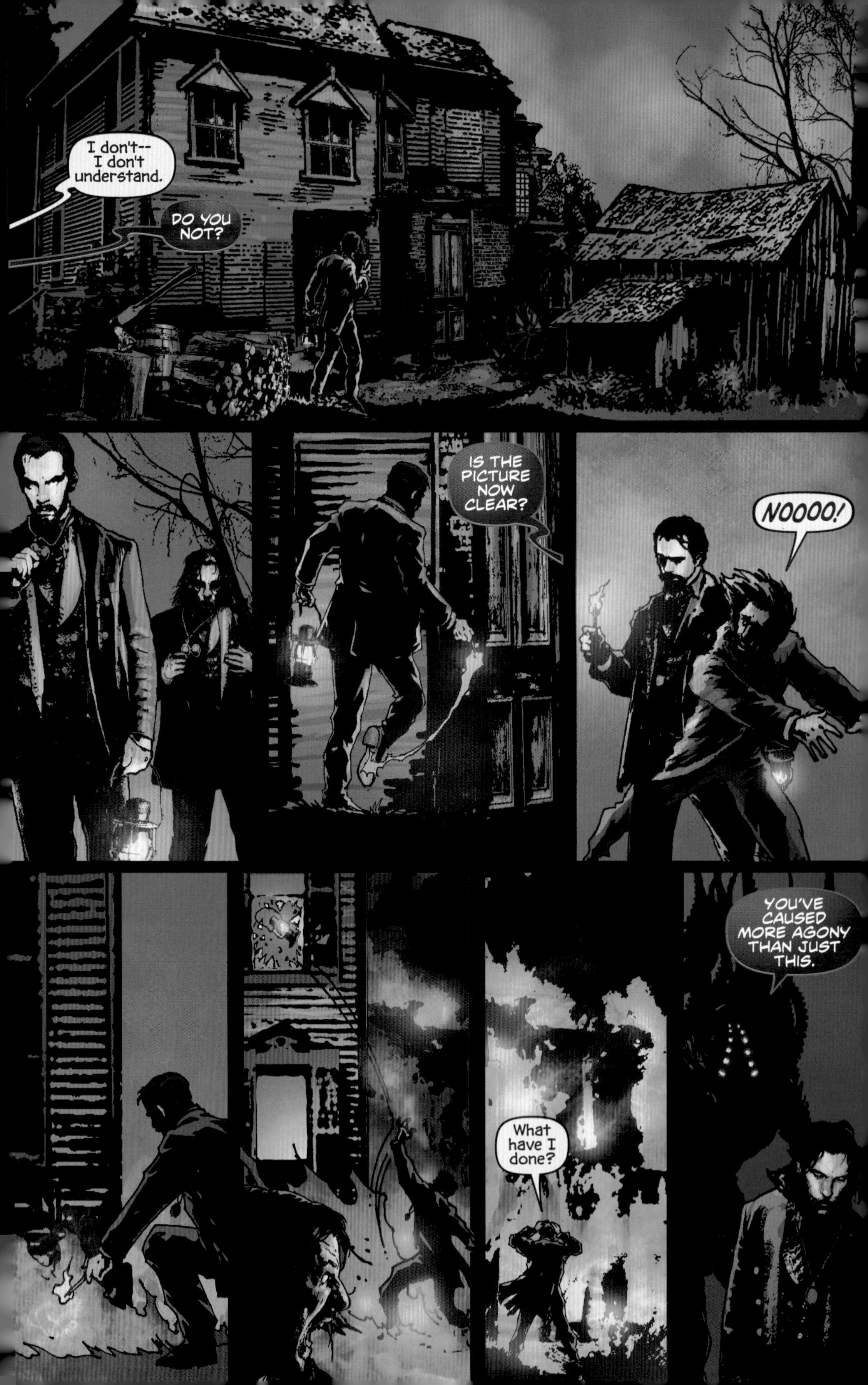
I don't-- I don't understand.
DO YOU NOT?
IS THE PICTURE NOW CLEAR?
NOOOO!
What have I done?
YOU'VE CAUSED MORE AGONY THAN JUST THIS.

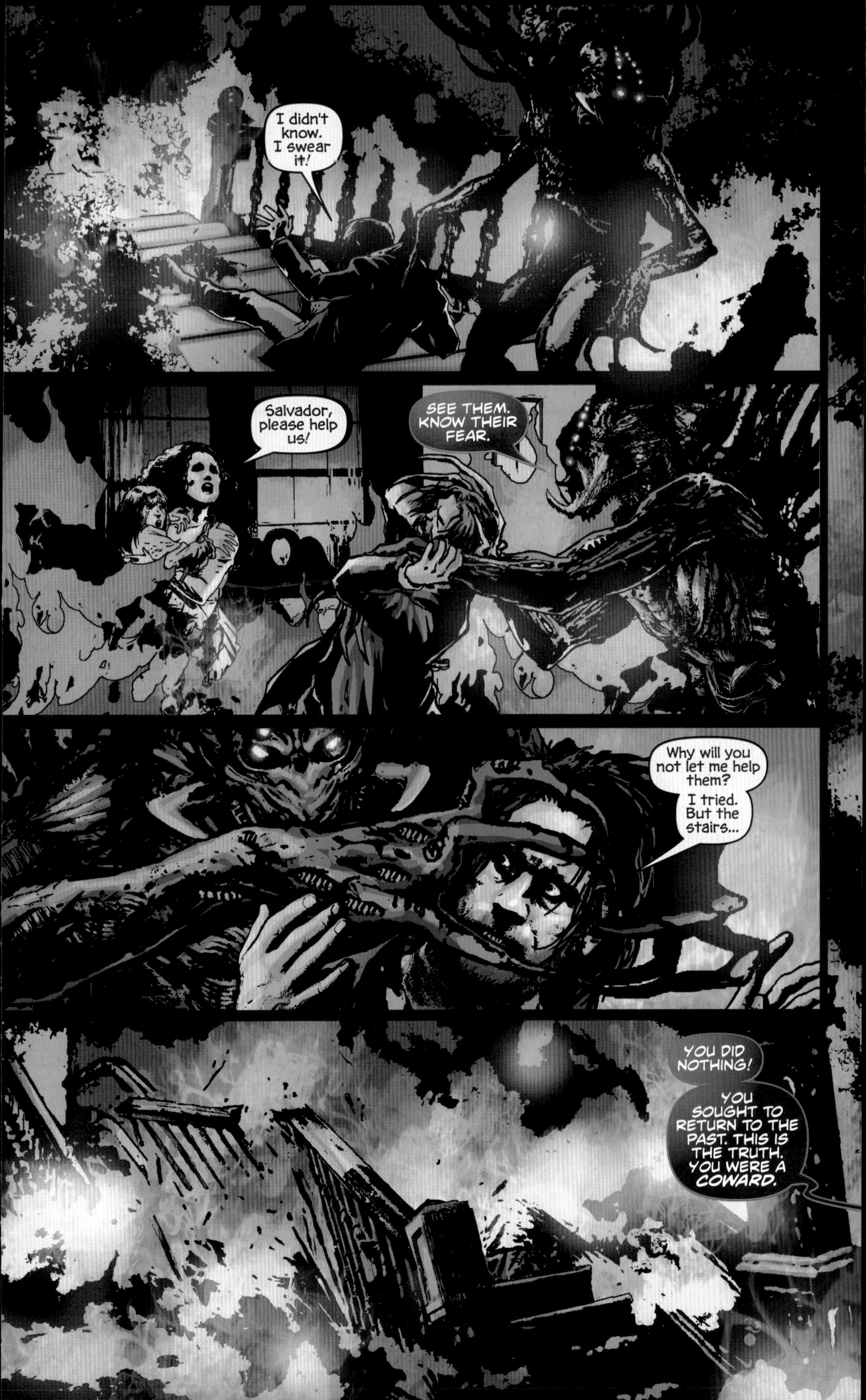
I didn't know. I swear it!
Salvador, please help us!
SEE THEM. KNOW THEIR FEAR.
Why will you not let me help them?
I tried. But the stairs...
YOU DID NOTHING!
YOU SOUGHT TO RETURN TO THE PAST. THIS IS THE TRUTH. YOU WERE A COWARD.

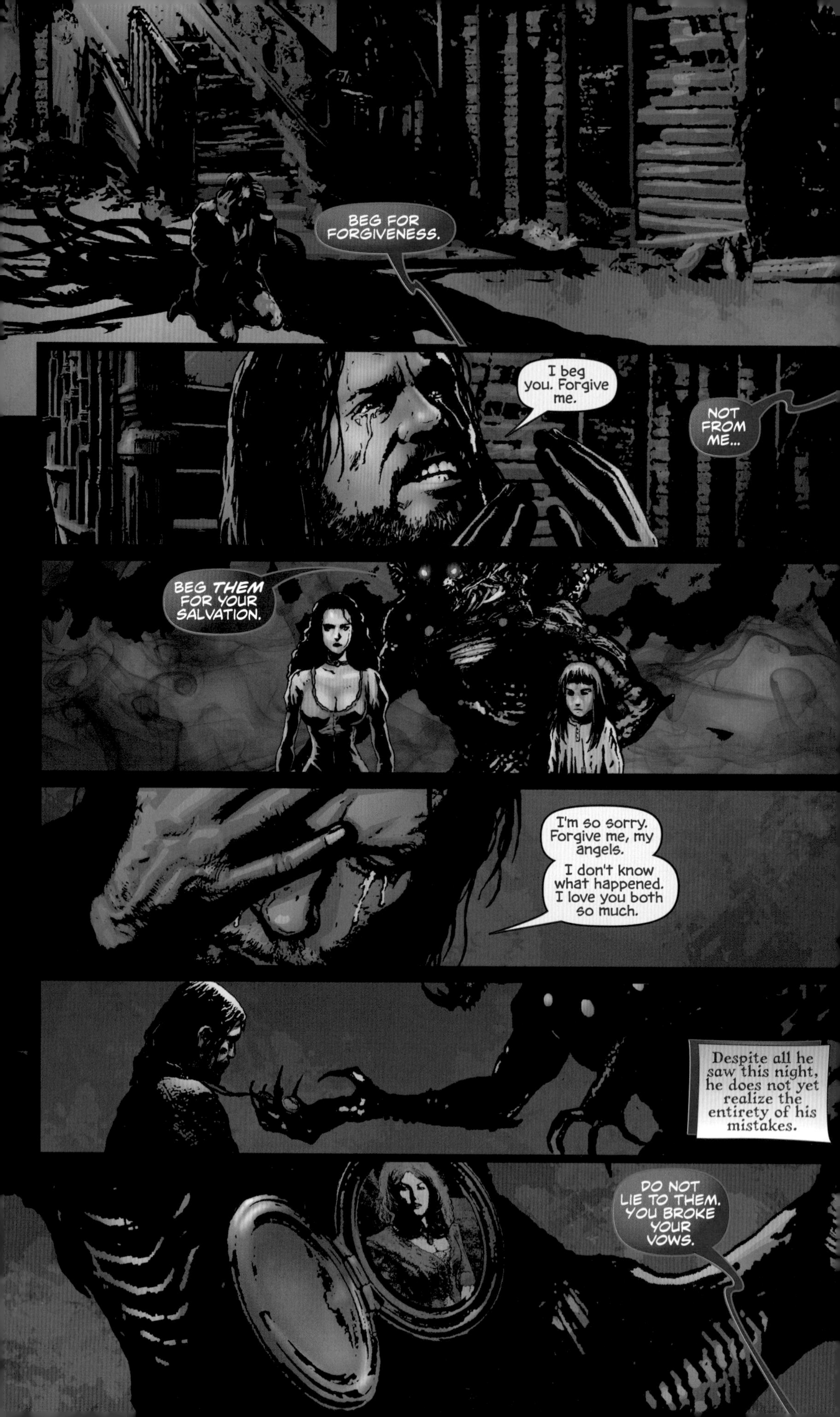
BEG FOR FORGIVENESS.
I beg you. Forgive me.
NOT FROM ME...
BEG THEM FOR YOUR SALVATION.
I'm so sorry. Forgive me, my angels.
I don't know what happened. I love you both so much.
Despite all he saw this night, he does not yet realize the entirety of his mistakes.
DO NOT LIE TO THEM. YOU BROKE YOUR VOWS.

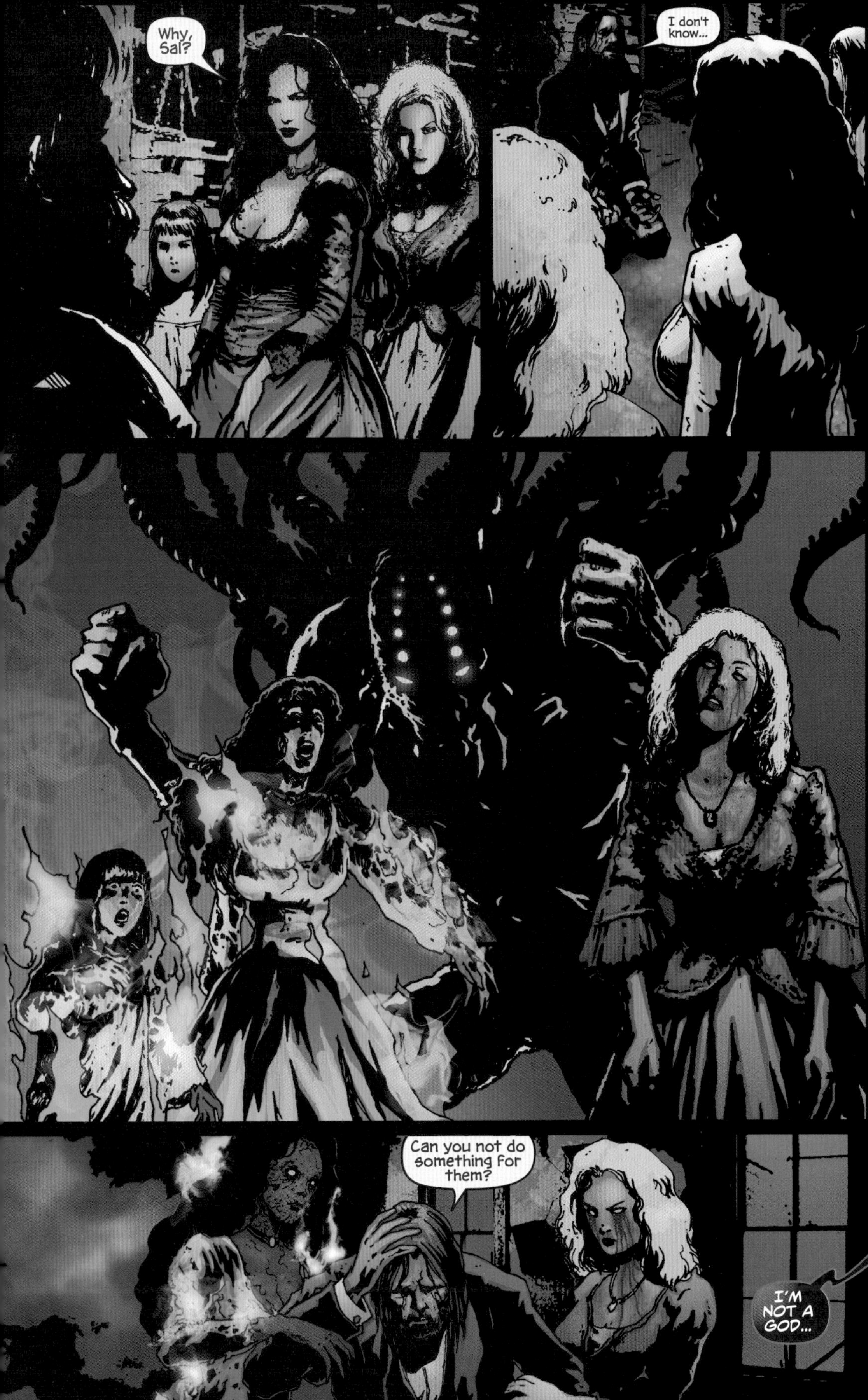
Why, Sal?
I don't know...
Can you not do something for them?
I'M NOT A GOD...

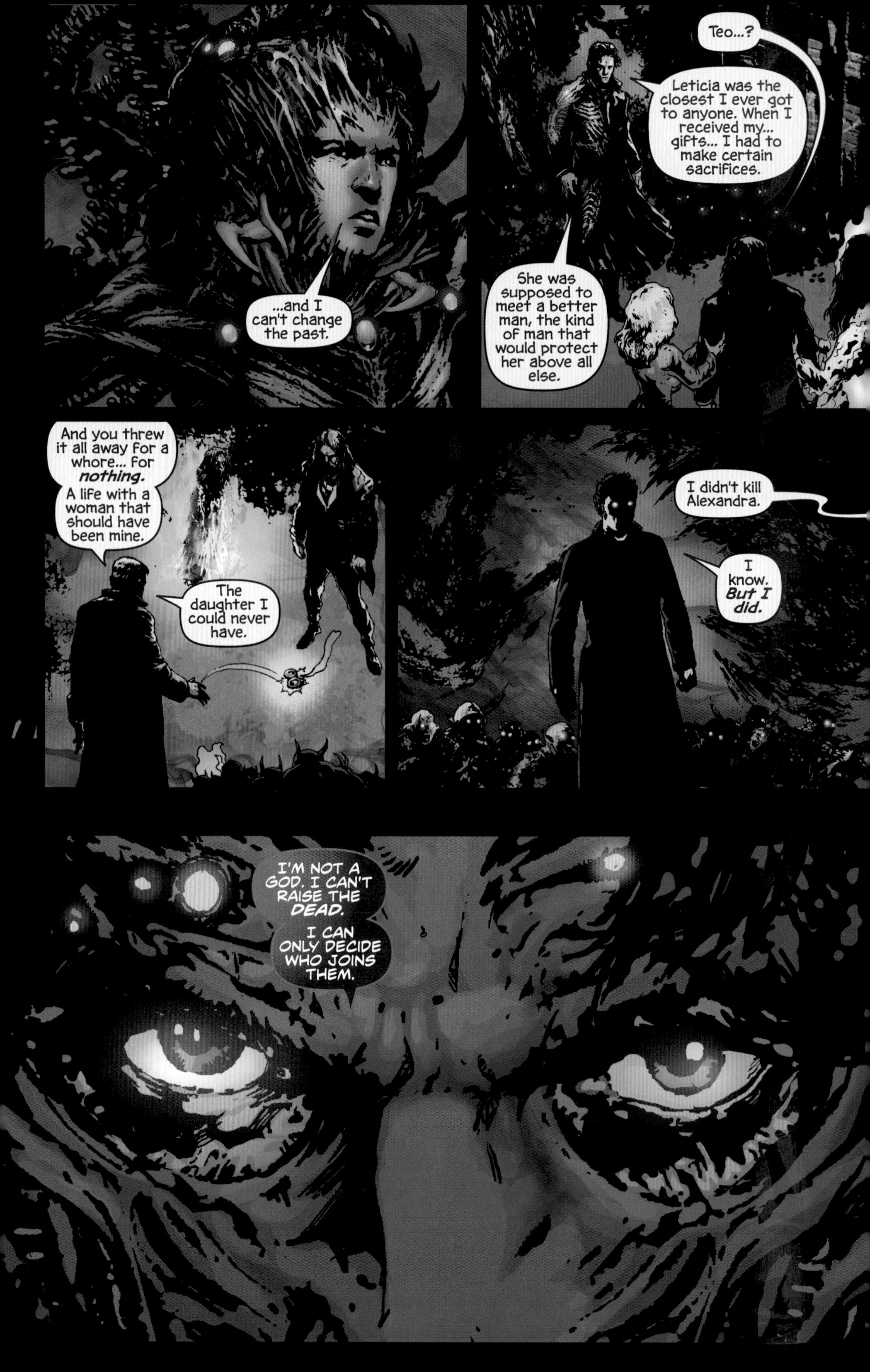

...and I can't change the past.
Teo...?
Leticia was the closest I ever got to anyone. When I received my... gifts... I had to make certain sacrifices.
She was supposed to meet a better man, the kind of man that would protect her above all else.
And you threw it all away for a whore... for *nothing.*
A life with a woman that should have been mine.
The daughter I could never have.
I didn't kill Alexandra.
I know. *But I did.*
I'M NOT A GOD. I CAN'T RAISE THE *DEAD.*
I CAN ONLY DECIDE WHO JOINS THEM.

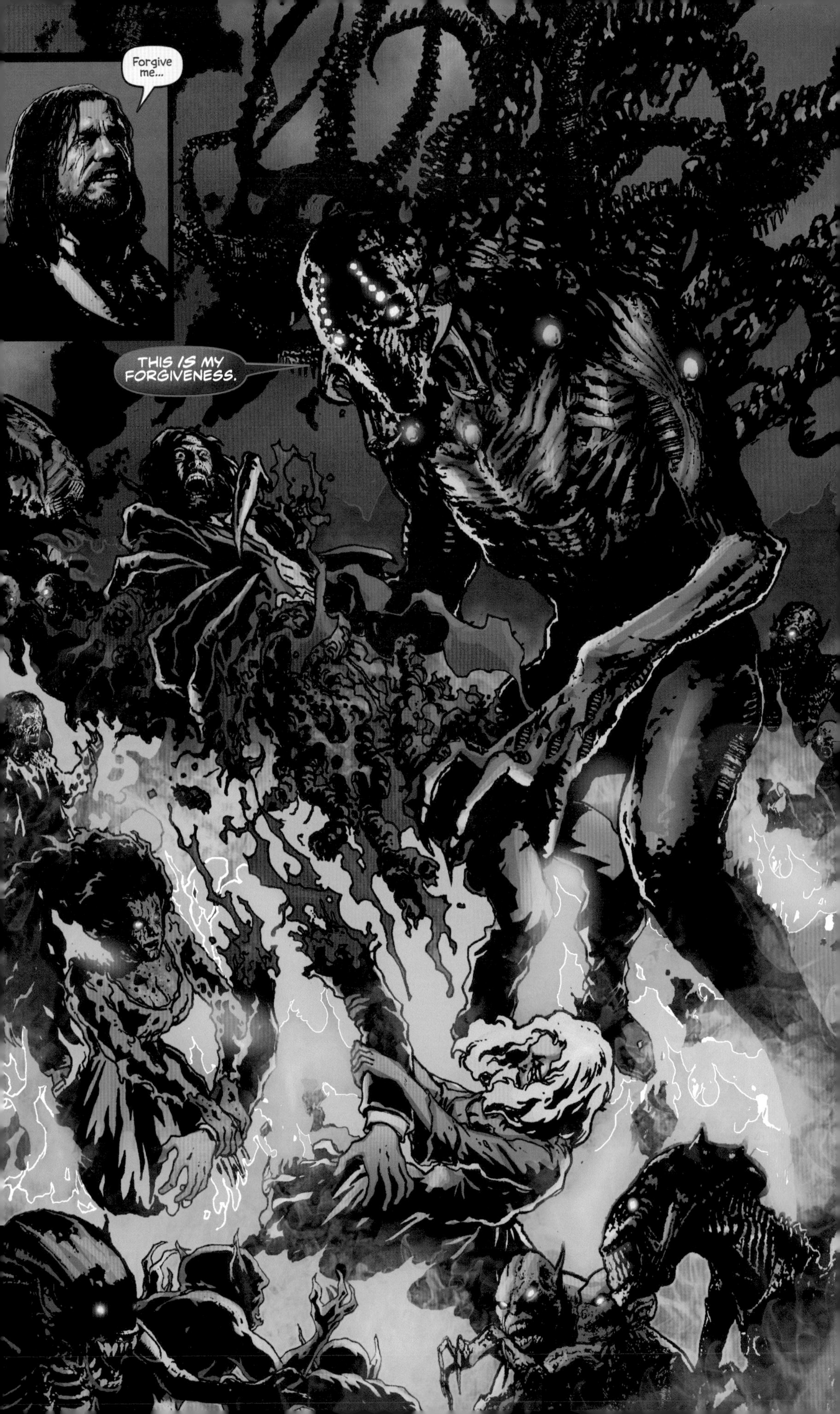
Forgive me...
THIS IS MY FORGIVENESS.

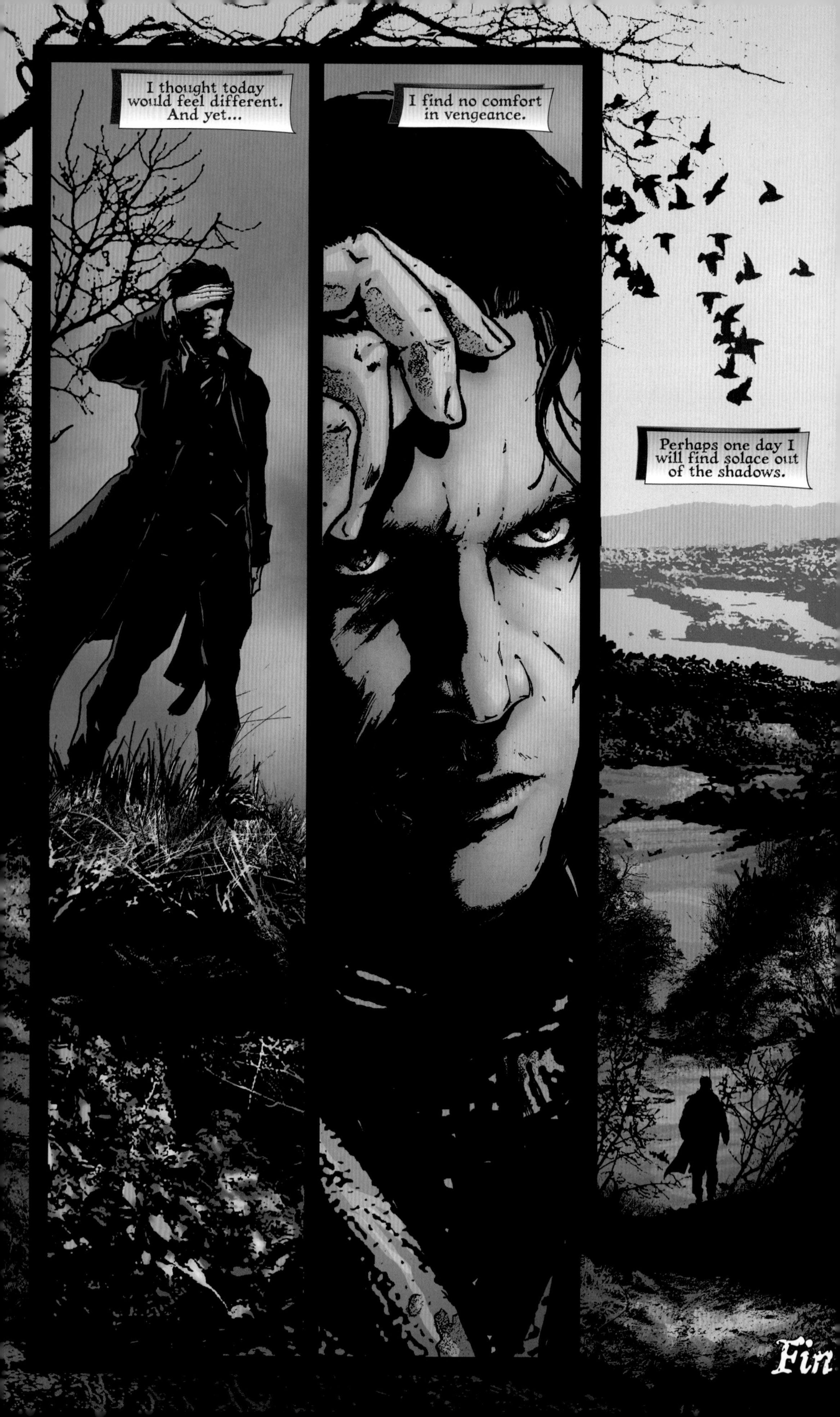
I thought today would feel different. And yet...
I find no comfort in vengeance.
Perhaps one day I will find solace out of the shadows.
Fin

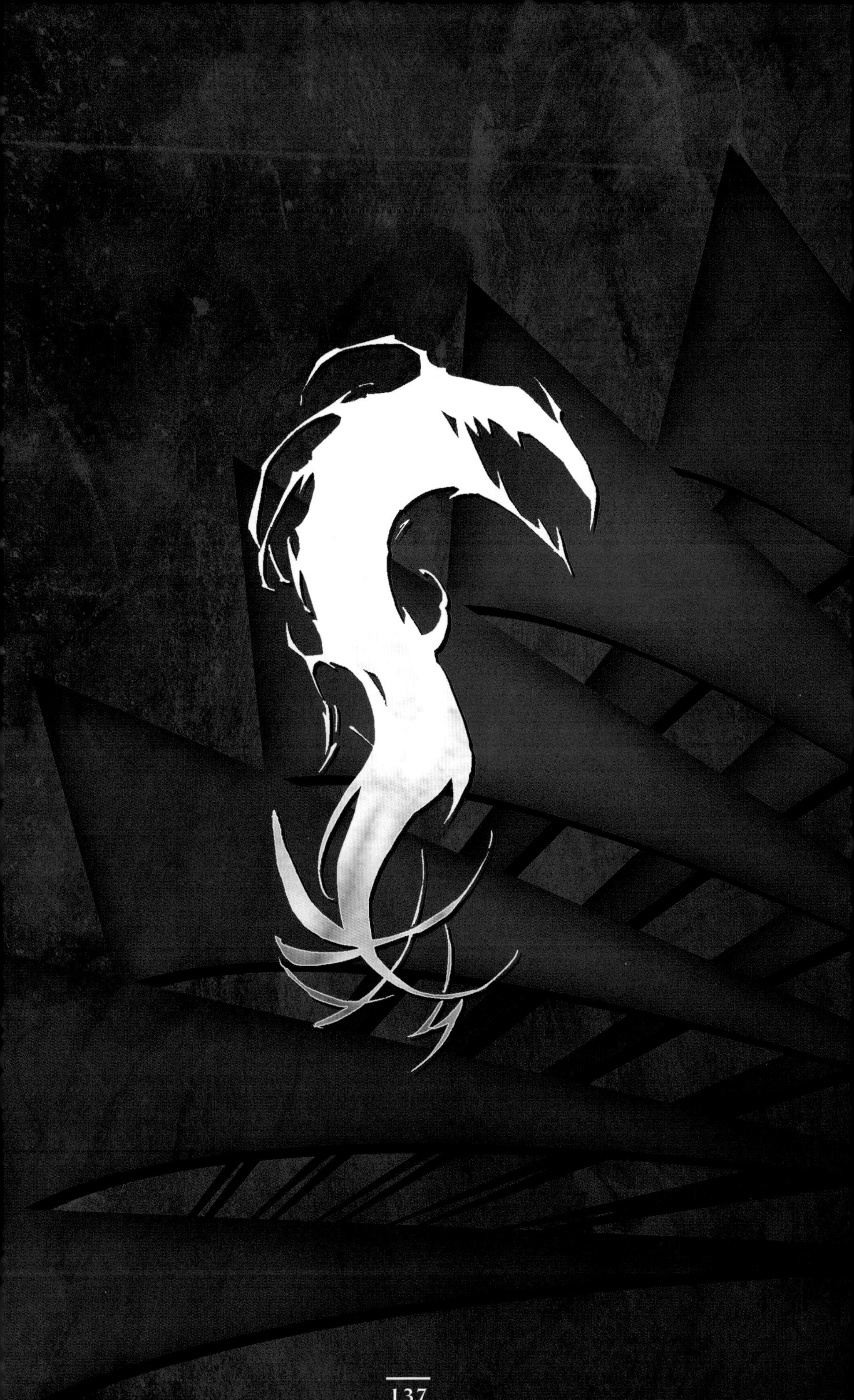

The Darkness®
Accursed Volume 4
COVER GALLERY

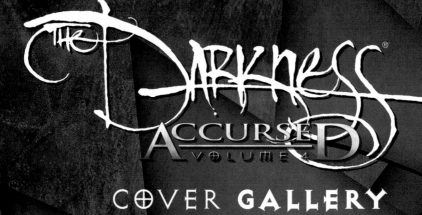

The Darkness, issue #80 cover A
Art by: Phil Hester & Admira Wijaya

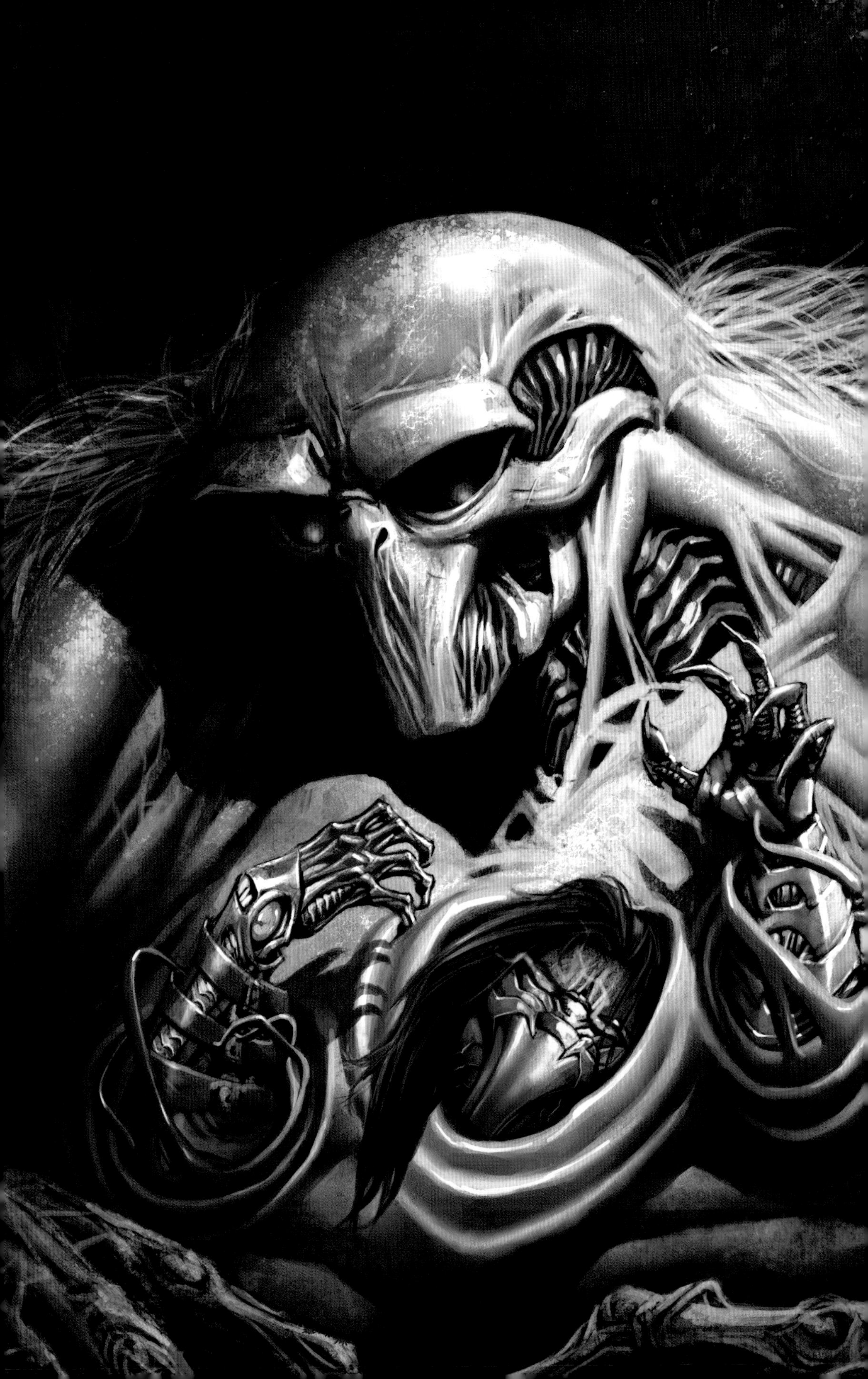

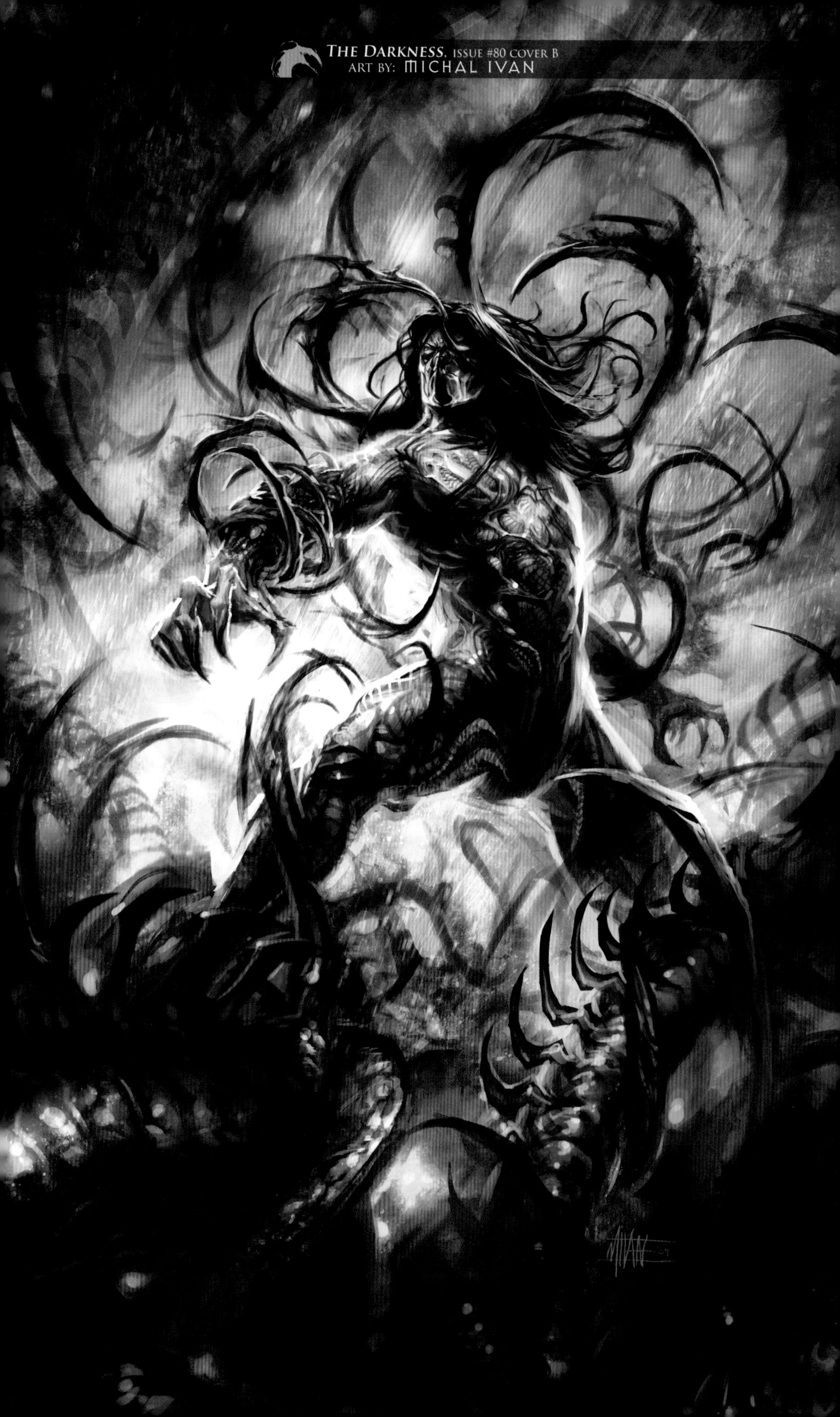

THE DARKNESS, ISSUE #80 COVER B
ART BY: MICHAL IVAN

The Darkness, issue #80 cover C
art by: PHIL HESTER & ANDE PARKS design by: PHIL SMITH

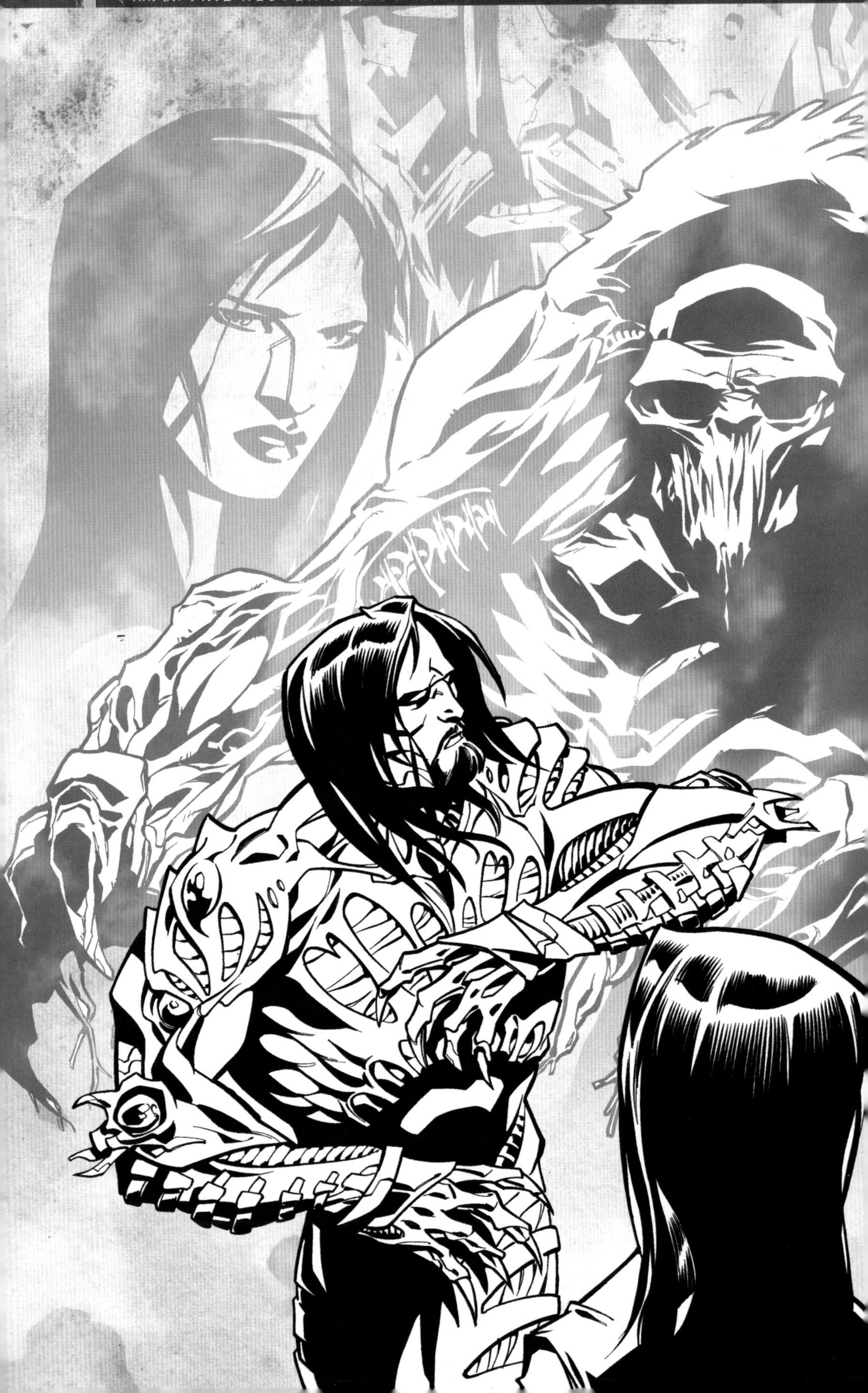

THE DARKNESS, ISSUE #81 COVER
ART BY: MICHAEL BROUSSARD & ERIC BASALDUA

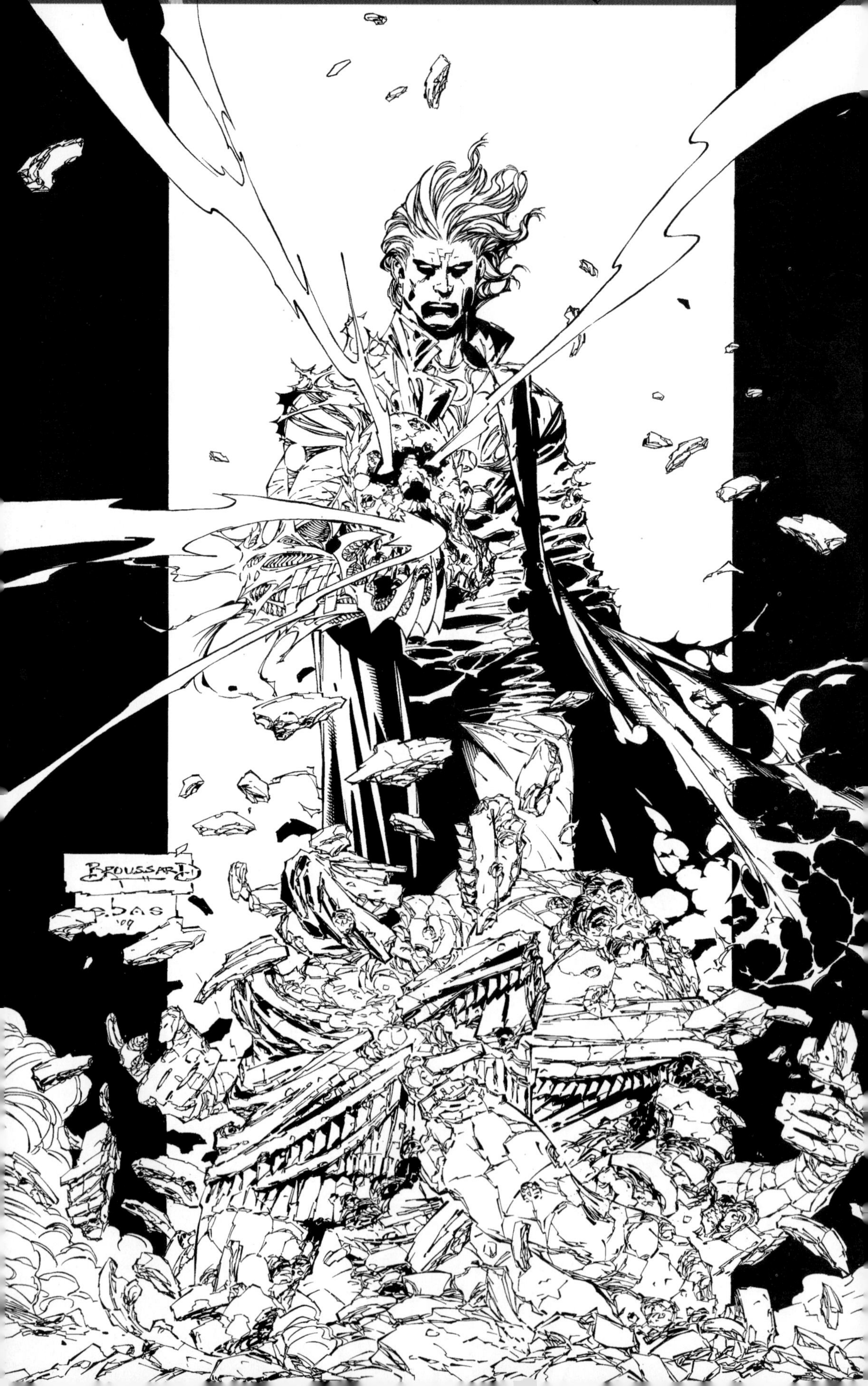
BROUSSARD
B.BAS '09

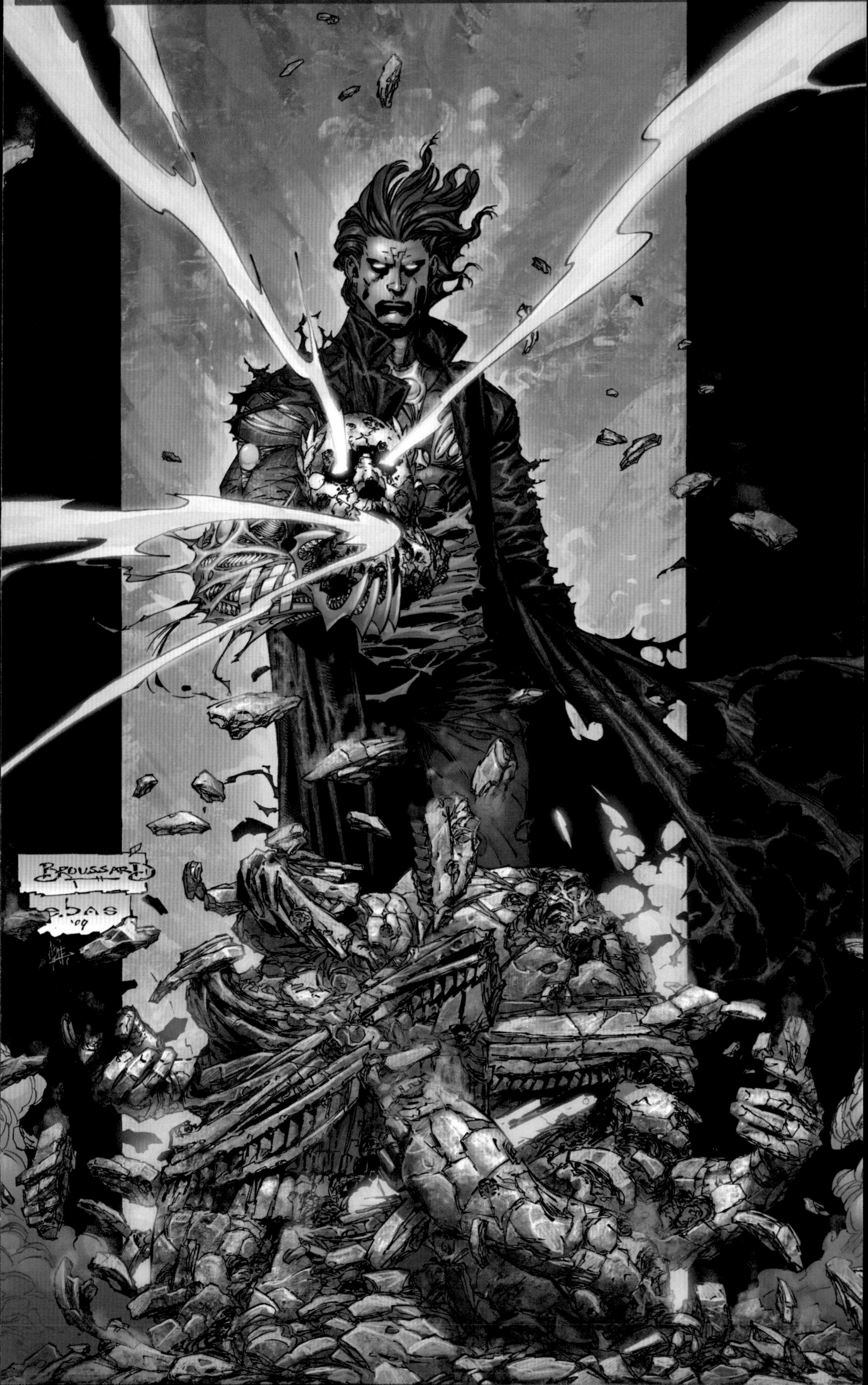
BROUSSARD
E.BAS '09

The Darkness, issue #81 cover
Art by: Michael Broussard, Eric Basaldua & Arif Prianto of IFS

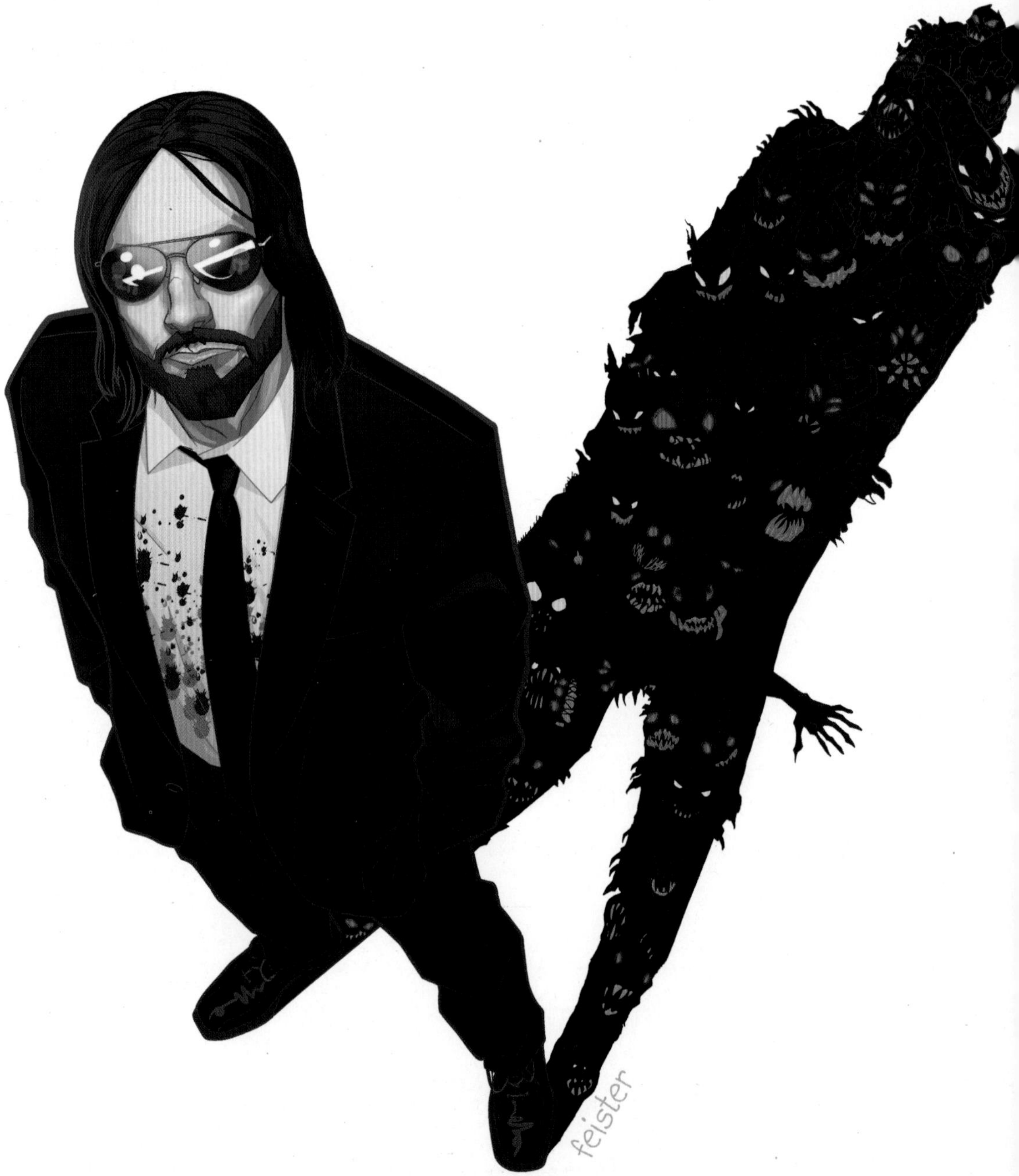
feister

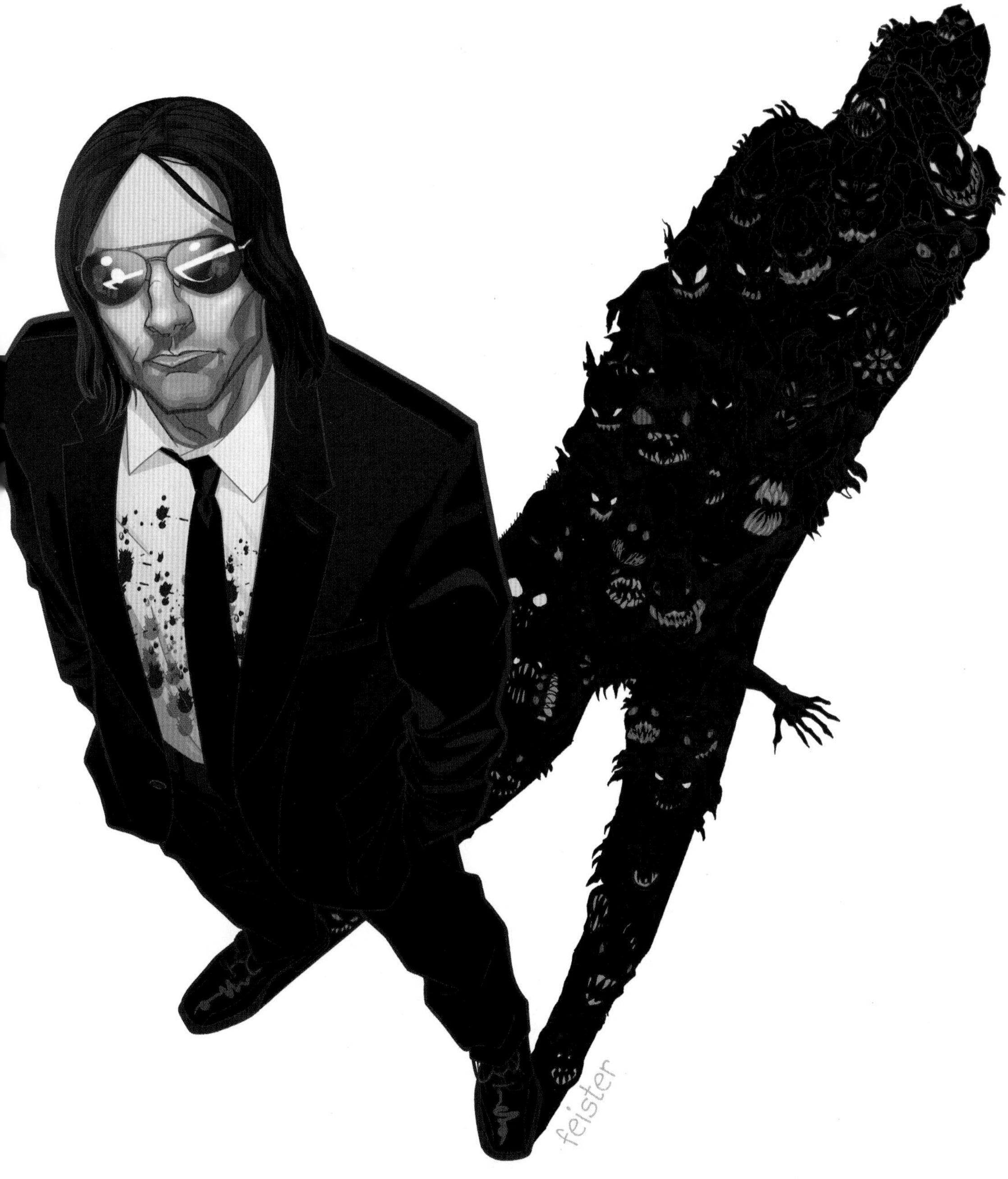
feister

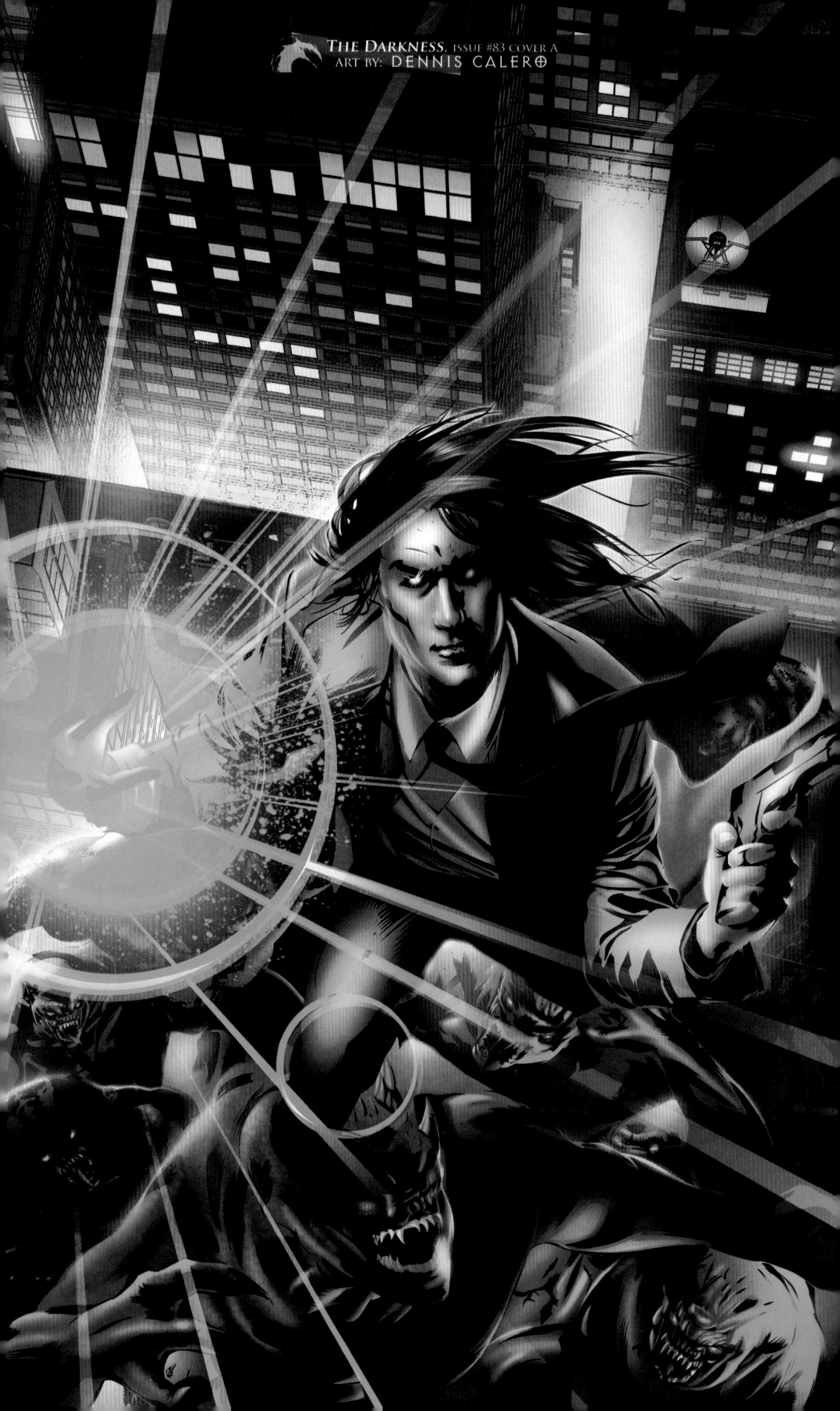

THE DARKNESS, ISSUE #83 COVER A
ART BY: DENNIS CALERO

The Darkness, issue #83 cover B, Emerald City Comic-Con variant
Art by: Whilce Portacio & Arif Prianto of IFS

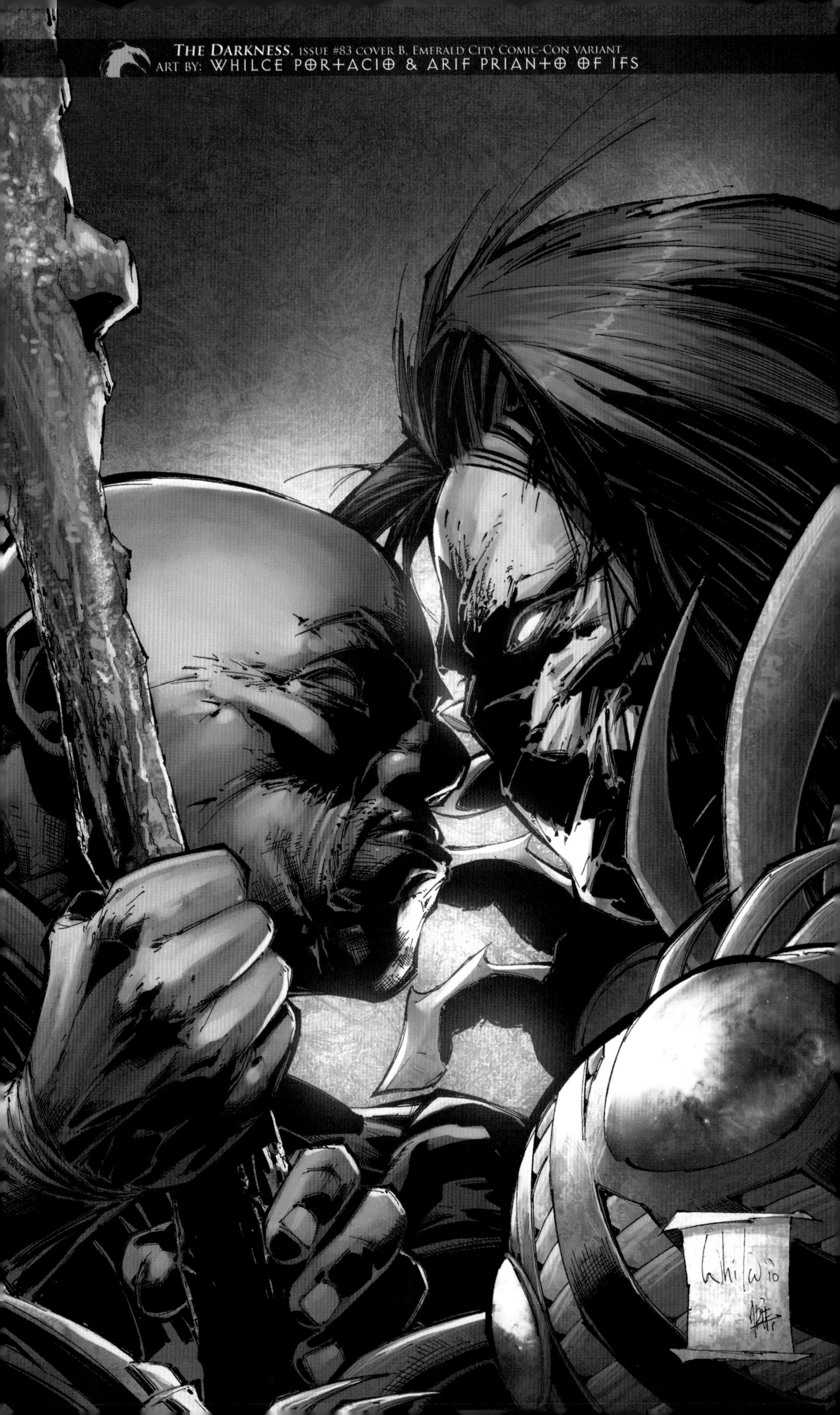

THE DARKNESS, ISSUE #84 COVER A
ART BY: BAGUS HUTOMO OF IFS

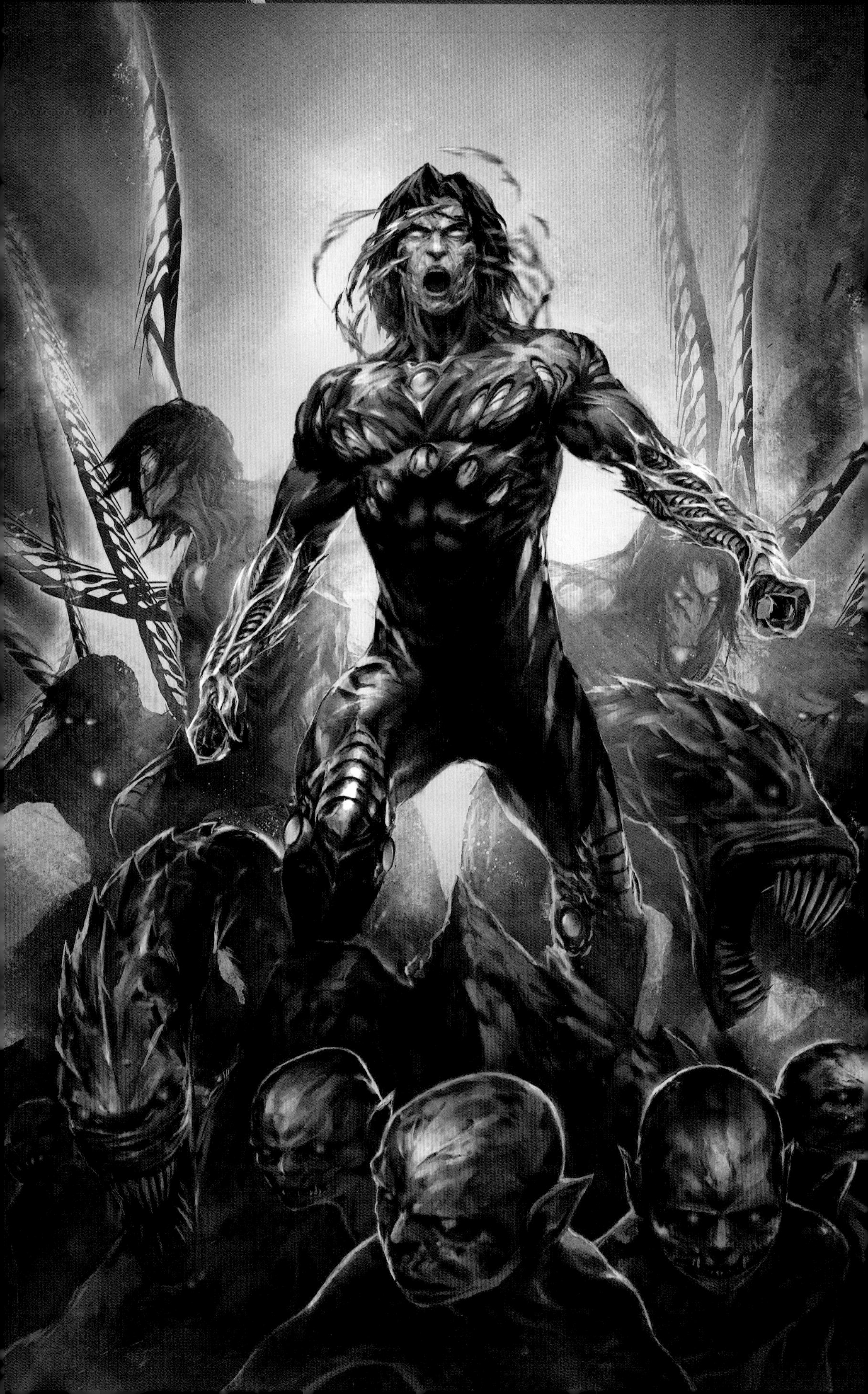

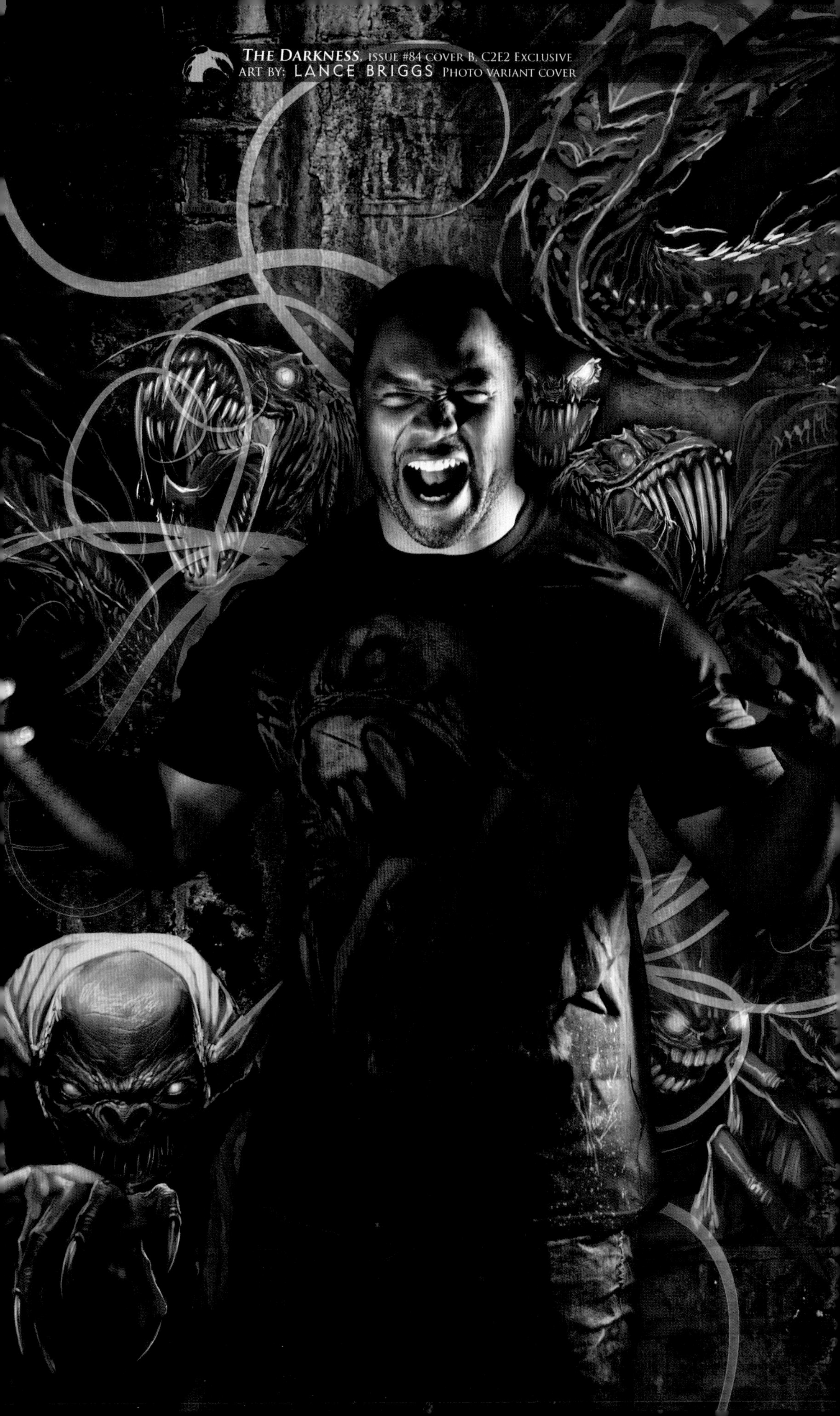

THE DARKNESS, ISSUE #84 COVER B, C2E2 EXCLUSIVE
ART BY: LANCE BRIGGS PHOTO VARIANT COVER

The Darkness: Shadows and Flame, issue #1 cover
Art by: Jorge Lucas & Felix Serrano

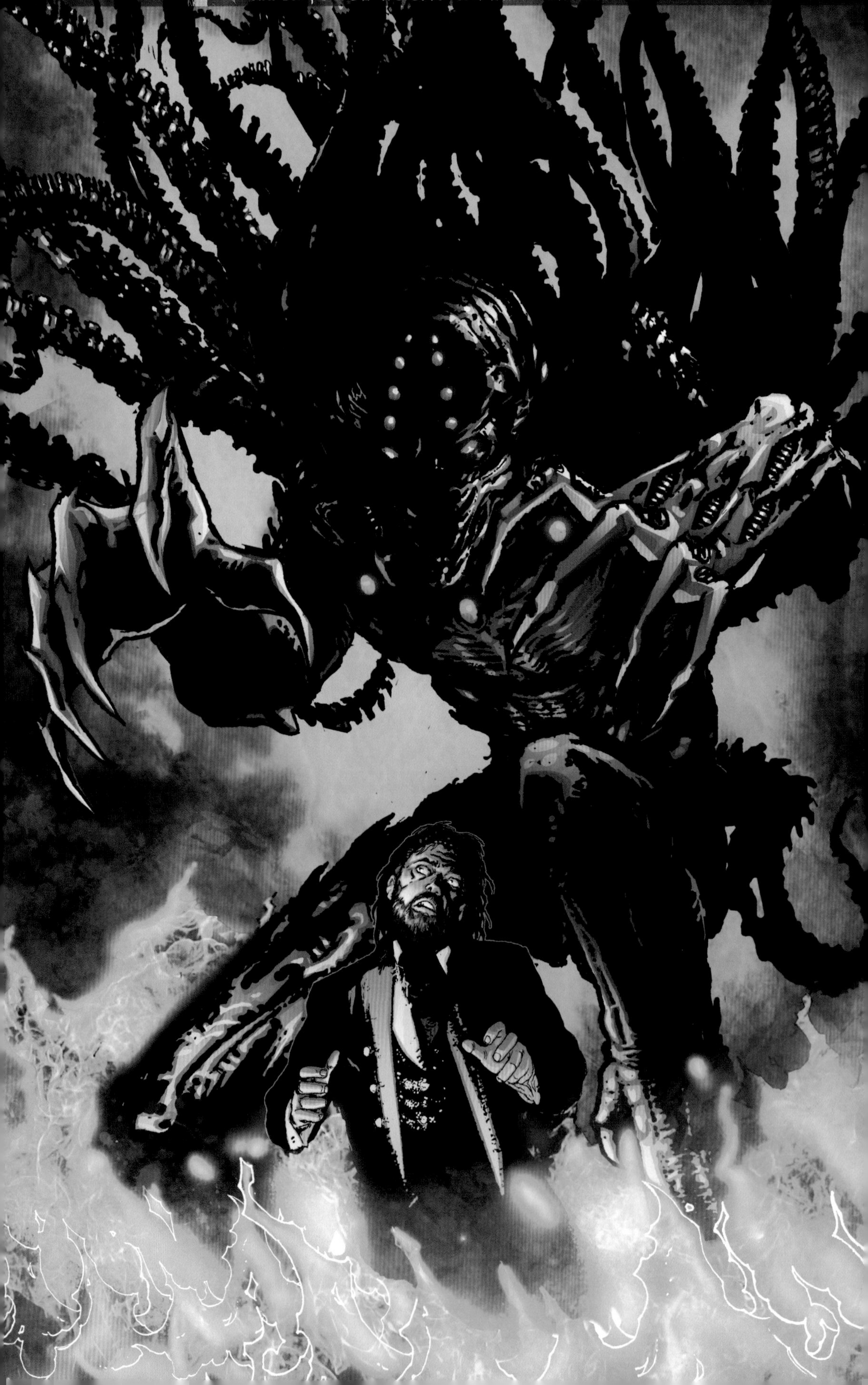

THE DARKNESS: ACCURSED, TRADE PAPERBACK VOLUME #4 COVER
ART BY: MICHAEL BROUSSARD, EKO PUTEH & SUNNY GHO OF IFS

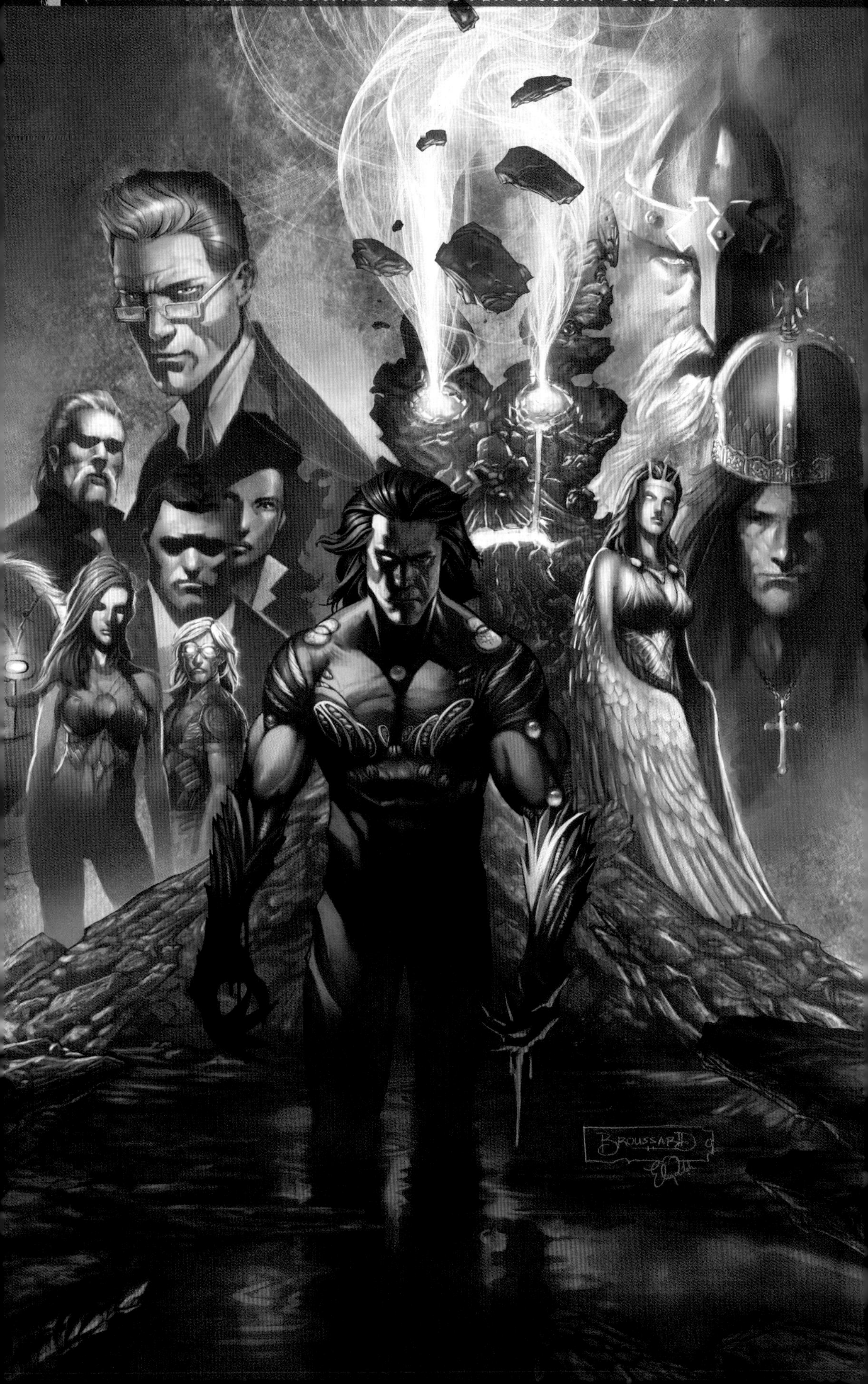

SCRIPT TO PAGE

On the following pages take a look at the script for *The Darkness* issue #84 written by Phil Hester along with inks and page layouts from the production process.

The Darkness issue #84 script:

CHARACTERS TO BE DESIGNED THIS ISSUE: NONE, BUT IT FEATURES THE H/K B-TEAM OF EMPRESS, DARLING AND TRINH WHICH MICHAEL MAY HAVE DESIGNED ALREADY FOR #83. IF NOT, MAYBE WHILCE CAN DESIGN AND FEED TO MICHAEL AS THEY ONLY APPEAR ON THE LAST FEW PAGES OF #83. DESCRIBED BELOW:

HUNTER-KILLER B TEAM
DARLING- White guy. He's 45 (one of the first Ultras) and vaguely out of shape. Huge arms and torso. Tattoo on forearms forms rock hard matrix around his fists for punching through buildings, cars, other Ultras, etc. Amiable and world weary. It's just a gig to Darling. Carries many high tech guns specially fitted for his ham-like hands. Not afraid to work drunk.

EMPRESS- Incredibly tall (6'6") African-American lady in her late twenties. The brains of the outfit. Lisa Leslie physically. She wears an icy white body suit. Her tattoo covers her arms and legs and even the sides of her neck and ribcage. She has raspy skin that she can harden at will to a razor's edge along her hands and arms, legs, etc. Any exposed flesh. She also carries a javelin that she throws with deadly accuracy. All business.

TRINH- Race indeterminable. 5'4". Always crouched over. Pure white, long, lank hair hangs in front of his face. Silent. Frog like body with splayed hands and toes. Tattoo is gnarly, bulging blue beneath his translucent white skin. Hands and feet bare. He can manipulate friction so that he can stick to walls and skitter up and down them, or cancel friction altogether and slide across surfaces like ice. Fast and agile. Equipped with powerful taser-like whips that uncoil from his forearms into multiple tendrils, like a cat o' nine tails.

NOTE: I'm presenting this DC/full script style. If Whilce wants thumbnails & placements I can provide, but he might want to get a jump on everything with this.

2.1 Splash. This entire issue takes place in or around a five story parking garage that is under construction. So, it's basically an empty, darkened parking garage with no cars, empty elevator shafts, etc. It is just after dawn, so it's pretty dark inside the garage, but there is sunlight outside and cutting across some levels of the garage in long arcs of light and dark. In this splash we see Jackie in his Darkness armor. He is holding the severed heads of Darling and Trinh with one hand and with the other is gesturing toward his heart. His armor is receding away from his heart, leaving his chest exposed. He's offering himself up. He's backed against a concrete wall.

1- CAP: Agent Empress
Operation Umbra
Mission clock: 6:07:45

2- TITLE: The Three Deaths of Jackie Estacado
Credits, etc.

3- JACKIE: Go ahead, kill me. I'll make it easy for you.

4- JACKIE: Put one right here- the heart.

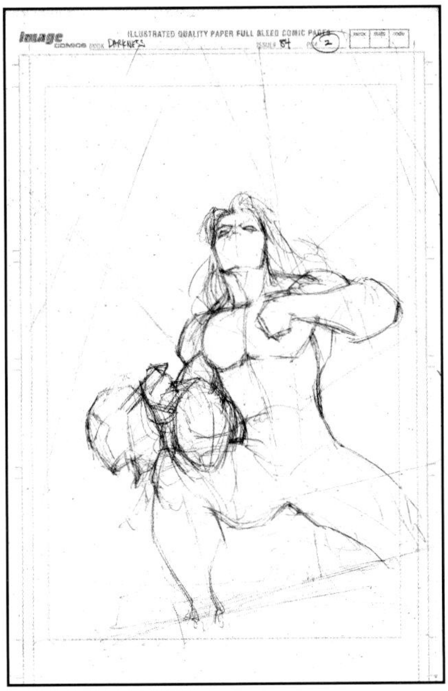
ILLUSTRATED QUALITY PAPER FULL BLEED COMIC PAGES

thumbnail

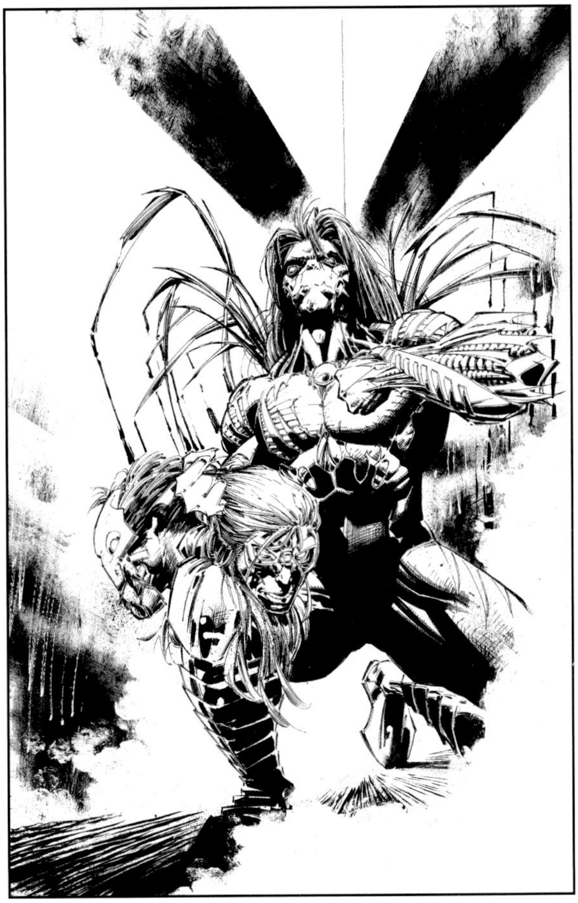

line art

3.1 Wide shot. Pull back to show Empress in the FG with her javelin cocked back to throw at the cornered Jackie in the BG.

1- JACKIE: End it. I know you have orders to bring me in alive.

3.2 Close up on the horrified, angry, sad Empress as she holds her javelin, trembling.

2- JACKIE OP: Ask your buddies how that worked out for them.

3.3 MCU Jackie as the javelin pierces his chest dead center, obviously killing him.

4- Jackie: C'mo-

5- SFX: Shrakk-k!

3.4 Wide, high angle. We're in a conference room at Hunter-Killer headquarters. We're above and behind Bureaucrat #2, a male who stands and seems more animated, and Bureaucrat #1, an older female in a business suit who remains seated. They both look through a wide one-way mirror to a holding cell/room. Inside the room we see Empress, looking tired, sitting at a table with two MiB looking goons standing over her.

6 BUREAUCRAT #2: Look, she's telling the truth. Empress is the best agent we've got on the B-team.

7 BUREAUCRAT #1: But she's still B-team.

8 BUREAUCRAT #1: We're responsible for tracking and containing suspected Ultras. You know the potential consequences of letting someone like Estacado run free.

3.5 Low angle MCU at the emotionless bureaucrats as they scrutinize Empress past the glass.

9 BUREAUCRAT #1: Make her tell it again.

10 BUREAUCRAT #1: Start from the beginning.

thumbnail   line art

1 Wide angle. Mere seconds after dawn. The scene is an industrial park area. There is a mall under construction and we're closest to its nearly finished parking amp. We're just outside a security fence that surrounds the whole thing. In the MG we see Jackie as he was last issue. Torn up and bleeding, wearing only a torn air of pants and the shredded remains of a white shirt. He is barefoot. He is running for his life from something we can't see. Just behind him a yuppie jogger the latest gear (ipod, running shoes, etc.) is catching up to him. Yuppie jogger thinks Jackie is just another jogger.

CAP: Just outside Louisville, Kentucky. 5:56 AM.

JOGGER: Nice morning for a run, huh? Love coming out here at dawn.

.2 Above and behind the two runners as jogger looks back at an unknown sound from above.

JOGGER: Figured it out. Once around this construction site is two and half miles.

JOGGER: The hell is that?

.3 repeat of 4.1, but pulled back so the figures are tiny. The high tech Hunter/Killer helicopter from last issue screams over their heads, almost swooping right own on them.

SFX: Sheeeeooow!

JOGGER: Flying kind of low, aren't they?

.4 Low angle from behind the two runners. The jogger finally seems to notice something is amiss about Jackie. In the BG we see the chopper bank to come ack around.

JOGGER: Hey, uh-

.5 Shot down at Jackie's bare and bloody feet in the mud of the construction site.

JOGGER OP: You all right?

.6 CU Jackie. He's smiling in a grim, defeated kind of way, as if to say, "No one's all right in this world, especially not me."

.7 Wide panel. A small missile arcs from the helicopter in the BG and blows up at Jackie's feet. No one is blown to bits or anything, but the blast throws Jackie nd the jogger into the air. The fence near them is ripped out of the ground.

SFX: Braka-braka-braka!

thumbnail

line art

5.1 Camera just behind the nose of the chopper. On the ground below we can see the dust cloud from the explosion. The jogger is sprawled on the ground, but alive. The dust cloud extends to the base of the parking ramp.

1 CAP: Agents Empress, Darling, Trinh; Pilot Claymoore
Operation Umbra
Mission clock: 5:57:01

2 EMPRESS OP: Watch it, Darling. This is a capture mission, not a termination.

5.2 Wide semi-splash. Looking into the open side door of the chopper. Inside are Empress, standing behind Darling and Trinh. Darling holds a smoking Cable Judge Dredd-like gun and is grinning. Trinh crouches at the very edge of the helicopter door, eager to spring into action. Wind whips at them.

3 EMPRESS: Just because it says Hunter-Killer in the name doesn't mean we have to kill everyone we hunt.

4 DARLING: Just wanted to put the fear of God in this asshole.

5 DARLING: No one gets me up before dawn without paying some kind of price.

5.3 2 shot of Empress and Darling. Empress is mad, but not ranting. She's looking at a high tech pair of binoculars as if they were broken. Darling is raising his eyebrows like, "whatever."

6 EMPRESS: Well, your fireworks overloaded the thermal. We lost him.

7 DARLING: Bullshit, he's in that parking ramp or whatever. Where else could he be?

5.4 Wide shot of the chopper in silhouette as it climbs toward the top of the parking ramp. Trinh leaps from the chopper unexpectedly.

8 EMPRESS: Set us down on the roof. We'll start a top to bottom-

9 EMPRESS: Trinh!

5.5 Trinh in FG as he leaps toward camera. Darling and Empress in chopper door in XBG. Empress shouts after Trinh.

DARLING (from chopper): Ball hog. Thinks catching this guy single handed is gonna get him bumped up to A-team.

EMPRESS (from chopper): Trinh! Leave your com open, at least!

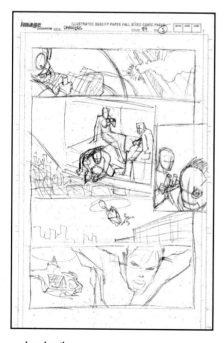

thumbnail   line art

6.1 Just inside the parking ramp's first level. Inside it's dark enough for Jackie to have mustered his armor, but he is still staggering and weak-looking. Behind him Trinh is perched on one of the concrete half-walls like Nightcrawler.

1 CAP: Agent Trinh
Operation Umbra
Mission clock: 5:59:22

2 JACKIE: Wait- ah-

3 JACKIE: Wait a minute-

6.2 Trinh leaps and kicks Jackie square in the back.

4 SFX: Whrok

5 JACKIE: Ungh!

6.3 As Trinh vaults over Jackie (now on his knees) the whips coiled in his forearms snake down and whip around Jackie's torso.

6 SFX: Shwippak!

7 JACKIE: U

6.4 Trinh alights on a high wall, just like Spider-Man, and sends another whip tendril into the FG.

8 TRINH: Easy, easy.

9 SFX: Shrak!

6.5 Shot down along Trinh's arm in FG to Jackie writhing on the floor of the garage as electricity courses through the whips snaking from Trinh's arm and wrapping around Jackie's neck.

10 TRINH: Play some. Play with Trinh.

11 SFX: Zzzzkkkk!

12 JACKIE: G-gggghhh!

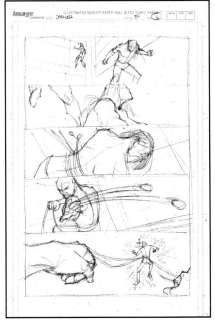

thumbnail

line art

7.1 MCU Trinh as The Foreigner's staff butts him just under the chin from below. EDITORIAL NOTE: For Foreigner ref see issues 76 & 77 (Red Ribbon).

1 SFX: Throk!

7.2 Wide. We see The Foreigner clearly. He stands between Trinh and the helpless Jackie as Trinh lowers himself from the wall to fight, recalling his tendrils.

2 TRINH: Hrrr.

3 TRINH: Now you play with Trinh.

7.3 MCU Foreigner as Trinh's whips wrap around the staff he holds defensively before him.

4 FOREIGNER: Not likely.

5 SFX: Swup!

7.5 Wide, low angle. Almost a diagram of the scene. Foreigner swings the staff, pulling Trinh off his feet and slamming him into a wall.

6 SFX: Throk!

7.6 Medium shot from just behind Foreigner as he swings his staff like a baseball bat, hitting Trinh squarely in the face.

7 SFX: K-Krak!

thumbnail

line art

8.1 Wide, low angle. Trinh is slumped in the middle of the panel in the FG, knocked out and bloody. At panel left is Foreigner standing confidently. At panel right is Jackie just now rising to a crouch.

1 FOREIGNER: Look at you, Estacado. You really are a two steps forward one step back kind of guy.

2 JACKIE: You- you want to kill me? The line forms behind these assholes.

8.2 MCU Foreigner looking calm as he rests the staff against his shoulder like an umbrella.

3 FOREIGNER: Oh, I don't want to kill you, kid. Just pretty sure it will end up that way.

4 FOREIGNER: Unless you become master of The Darkness...

8.3 2 shot past Foreigner to perturbed Jackie.

5 FOREIGNER: Instead of its slave.

6 JACKIE: Yeah, can we save the Yoda shit for another time?

7 JACKIE: Maybe when a helicopter full of bloodthirsty freaks aren't trying to kill me?

8.4 Wide shot. Foreigner now points at Jackie with the staff, like he's fencing with him. Jackie is wary, but in no shape to fight.

8 FOREIGNER: You're making my point, Estacado.

9 FOREIGNER: You're always in the shit and it's always The Darkness that puts you there.

10 FOREIGNER: You don't run it; it runs you.

8.5 CU Foreigner looking truly menacing for the first time.

11 FOREIGNER OP: Last chance, Jackie. Change the game...

12 FOREIGNER OP: Or I end it.

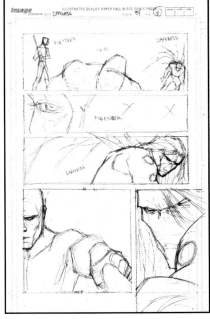

thumbnail   line art

9.1 Wide shot of the roof just after the chopper has landed. Darling and Empress leap out and fan out. Empress barking orders.

1 CAP: Agents Empress, Darling; Pilot Claymoore
Operation Umbra
Mission clock: 6:02:39

2 EMPRESS: The good news is the structure isn't occupied yet. No bystanders.

3 EMPRESS: Let's assume Trinh has him engaged on the first floor.

9.2 Empress in FG as she points, her arm framing Darling as he looks back at her, gun at the ready.

4 EMPRESS: You take the east stairwell and I'll go west, sweep each floor on the way down to be sure.

5 EMPRESS: Keep your com open this time, okay?

6 DARLING: Yeah, but if he slips Trinh he'll just bolt again.

9.3 MCU professional looking Empress. She's cool and collected.

7 EMPRESS: Doubt it. We ran him ragged. Besides, you read his file.

8 EMPRESS: In low light situations he's an off-the-charts Ultra.

9.4 Wide shot of the whole parking ramp. We can see the sun rising behind it.

9 EMPRESS (from int): Dawn's broken, but it's still dark enough in there for him to make his last stand.

9.5 Darling running into the FG ready for action and muttering under his breath. Behind him we see Empress running in the other direction, toward a stairwell access. Remember, no cars yet.

10 DARLING: Brilliant. Last stands.

11 DARLING: My fucking favorite.

thumbnail   line art

ARKNESS #84 PAGE 10

0.1 Back on the first level Jackie has lost his temper with Foreigner's cryptic clues. He jabs his armored finger at Foreigner.

JACKIE: Easy for you to say.

JACKIE: Look at me, man. This thing is in my blood, wrapped around my spine.

JACKIE: I don't know where it ends and I start. Never did.

JACKIE: Until you've lived this you can't know-

0.2 CU calm, collected Foreigner. The staff rests across his shoulders.

FOREIGNER: But I have lived it. I told you last time; I once wielded the Darkness.

FOREIGNER: And I beat it.

FOREIGNER: I willed it out of my body.

0.3 Jackie gets right in Foreigner's face. Make sure that in one or two of these shots we can see Trinh's slumped body.

JACKIE: Bullshit. You're no Darkness wielder, no Estacado.

0 OP FOREIGNER: Son, the only reason you can't find me in the family tree it because you aren't looking deep enough.

1 OP FOREIGNER: I'm at the roots. Deep underground.

0.5 2 shot. Foreigner in FG as he places his hand on Jackie's shoulder in an effort to calm him.

2 FOREIGNER: I did what you're doing for decades before I cast off The Darkness.

3 FOREIGNER: But I studied, meditated, fought it, starved it for almost a century.

0.6 repeat 10.5, but now we can see the Darkness armor begin to recede away from Foreigner's touch. It's like he has a Darkness nullification aura (he does).

4 FOREIGNER: And it did leave me. In fact, it can't even function anywhere near me.

5 FOREIGNER: Remember?

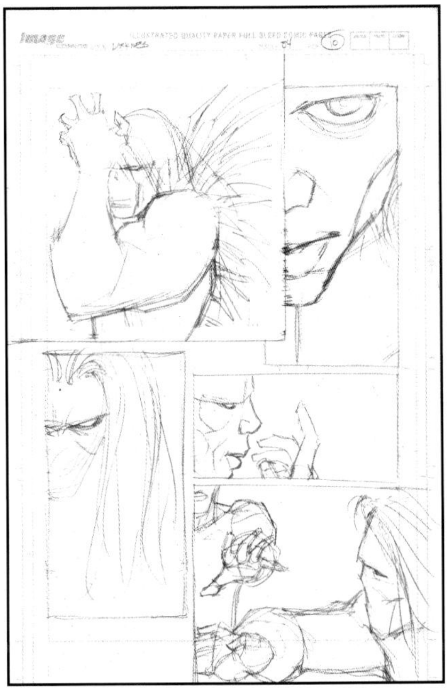

thumbnail

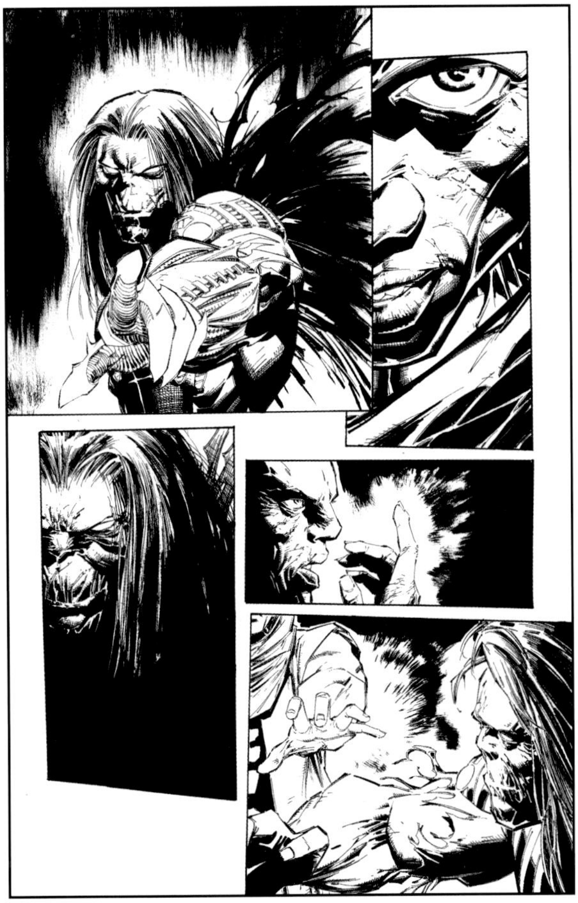

line art

11.1 Jackie brushes Foreigner's hand away and steps back.

1 FOREIGNER: I drove The Darkness out over ten thousand years ago.

2 JACKIE: Ten thou-- So how are you still around?

11.2 CU Foreigner. In the BG we see a flashback image of The Foreigner at some point in the distant past sitting in a lotus position. He's in orange monk robes and sits in the desert.

3 FOREIGNER: That's a whole different story, kid.

4 FOREIGNER: Point is I drove it out, but I learned that was a mistake.

11.3 Repeat 11.2, but the flashback image has changed to The Darkness in the distant past waging war on some Conan-like warriors.

5 FOREIGNER: I had my foot on the head of the serpent, but instead of crushing it I walked away.

6 FOREIGNER: Its venom found purchase in my descendants, continued to plague mankind.

11.4 CU Jackie.

7 OP FOREIGNER: And since that day I've been waiting for someone like you.

11.5 2 shot.

8 FOREIGNER: Someone with the guts to finish the job I couldn't.

9 FOREIGNER: Someone to kill The Darkness.

JACKIE: But-

11.6 Low angle in front of Foreigner. A shaft of light backlights him.

10 FOREIGNER: It's got to be an inside job, you understand? Only you know its strength, suffered its cruelty.

11 FOREIGNER: Only you hate it enough.

12 FOREIGNER: But to get to that point you've got to survive today.

13 FOREIGNER: In your state any one of the agents hunting you is capable of taking you out.

14 FOREIGNER: You posses the most powerful weapon on earth, but your fear makes it no more than a parlor trick.

thumbnail   line art

)ARKNESS #84 PAGE 12

2.1 Full body shot of Jackie looking down at his armor in surprise.

FOREIGNER OP: Your armor, for example. Why does it look that way?

JACKIE: What do you mean? It's always looked this way. It's how it came.

2.2 Foreigner now crouches on the half wall, about to leave.

FOREIGNER: Take some responsibility. It's because you don't have the courage or imagination to change it.

FOREIGNER: You've built autonomous beings before, you've made them look like whatever you want.

FOREIGNER: What you need now is an army, but not of those useless Darklings.

12.3 Foreigner's staff pokes at Jackie from off panel.

OP FOREIGNER: An army of you.

12.4 MCU Foreigner as he looks back over his shoulder at Jackie.

FOREIGNER: All you need to get out of this scrape is an ounce of imagination and a ton of will.

3 FOREIGNER: If you have both we'll talk again. If not, well...

) FOREIGNER: See you in Hell, right?

12.5 Wide. In the FG we can see Jackie (actually it's a facsimile) darting across the panel. In the BG we can see Darling whirling to see him. We're in one of the middle levels of the ramp.

10 CAP: Agent Darling
Operation Umbra
Mission clock: 6:04:11

11 EMPRESS (RADIO): You got anything, Darling?

12 EMPRESS (RADIO): Darling?

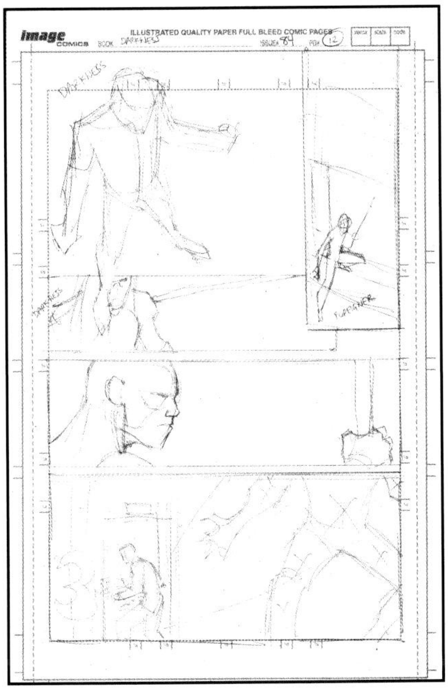
ILLUSTRATED QUALITY PAPER FULL BLEED COMIC PAGES
thumbnail

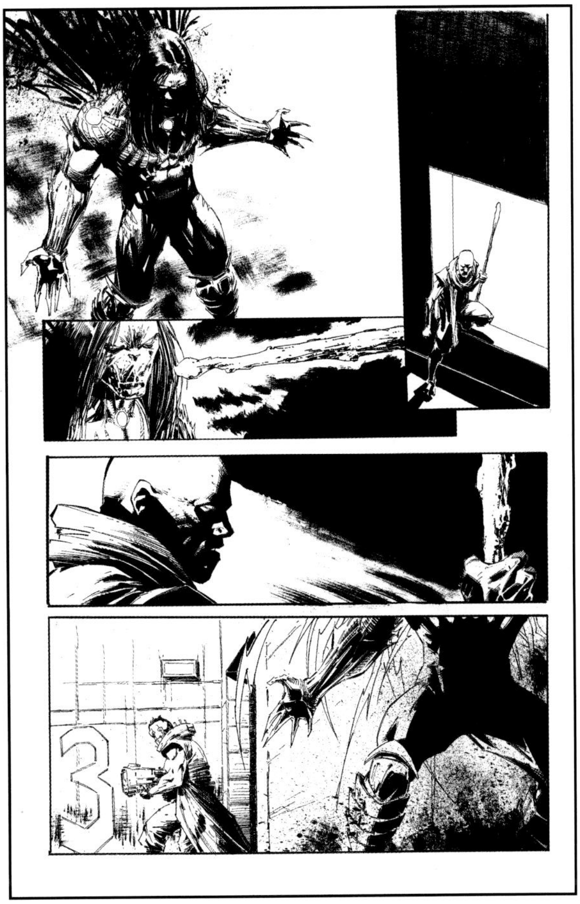
line art

13.1 Reverse 12.5. Darling in XFG from mid torso to mid thigh as he calmly clicks off the radio pack at his belt. In the BG we see Jackie's leg as he scurries behind a concrete barrier.

1 SFX: >klik<

2 DARLING: Nah, Empress.

13.2 Low angle of Darling advancing on Jackie's hiding place.

3 DARLING: Nothing I can't handle myself, anyhow.

4 DARLING: Trinh ain't the only one sick of being stuck on the B-team.

13.3 High angle behind Darling as he approaches a cinderblock utility room with a steel door ("Utility" stenciled on door). It's obvious the Jackie is hiding in here. Room sticks out from larger exterior wall like a 6x6 cube.

5 DARLING: Ha! I see you working there.

6 DARLING: Read your file. I know you get tougher in the dark.

13.4 MCU of Darling balling up his big, ham-like fist. All H/K agents have "tattoos" augmenting their powers and Darling's are around his fists and forearms. If he has gloves no need to see them, but if he doesn't we can see them glow just under his skin. They form a diamond matrix, like chicken wire.

7 DARLING: Too bad you don't know as much about me. See, I can harden up these fists...

13.5 Wide as Darling punches effortlessly through the cinderblock wall of the utility room.

8 DARLING: Punch through nearly anything.

9 SFX: Throk!

13.6 Same, but push in closer.

10 DARLING: That means...

11 SFX: Whok!

13.7 Same, but push in even closer. Darling grinning. Dust flying.

12 DARLING: I can shed a little light on your hideout.

13 SFX: Thrunch!

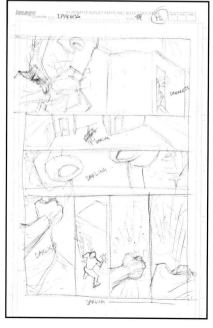

thumbnail   line art

14.1 We're back in the lowest level where Trinh fought Jackie and Foreigner. It looks as if The Foreigner was never there. Trinh is staggering to his feet. In the BG Jackie (another facsimile) is slumped against the wall, seemingly unconscious.

1 CAP: Agent Trinh
Operation Umbra
Mission clock: 6:04:13

2 TRINH: Ah, your friend leaves you alone with Trinh, eh?

3 TRINH: Leaves you alone to play.

14.2 Low angle. Trinh approaches Jackie's prone form eagerly. His whip tendrils snake out prehensile-style toward Jackie. Looks vaguely perverted.

4 TRINH: So... let's play.

5 SFX: Snikk-kkikk-ikk

14.3 Biggish panel. Up one one of the higher levels. Empress is in FG as she fiddles with the radio at her belt, trying to reach Darling. Jackie (another facsimile) leaps at her from the shadows. Jackie is holding what appears to be the severed heads of Darling and Trinh, but that need not be clear yet. In fact, we need to stage this so we can't see that yet.

6 CAP: Agent Empress
Operation Umbra
Mission clock: 6:07:00

7 EMPRESS: Darling? Come in, Darling.

8 JACKIE: You won't take me alive.

14.4 Reverse last shot. Low angle. Empress reflexively backhands Jackie into the FG.

9 EMPRESS: Yaahh!

10 SFX: Shwop!

thumbnail   line art

15.1 Low angle of the two facing off. Empress in FG draws her javelin from her back-holster. Jackie is up against a shadowy wall, avoiding a plane of light falling over it from outside.

1 JACKIE: Nice moves, but it won't help you.

2 EMPRESS OP: What- what are you holding?

15.2 MCU Jackie as he calmly holds the heads up for Empress to see.

3 JACKIE: I told you. I'm not letting you people take me in.

4 JACKIE: I'd rather die. Rather we all die.

15.3 CU Empress looking angry and sad. tears well up.

5 EMPRESS: D- Darling?

15.4 Repeat splash from page 2. Jackie is gesturing toward his heart which makes the Darkness armor recede, exposing his bare chest.

6 JACKIE: Angry, huh? Want to kill me, right?

7 JACKIE: Go ahead, kill me. I'll make it easy for you.

8 JACKIE: Put one right here- the heart.

thumbnail

line art

DARKNESS #84 PAGE 16

6.1 In FG we see Jackie drop the heads. Empress in BG is framed by Jackie's legs in XFG. She holds the javelin, ready to throw.

JACKIE: I know you have orders to bring me in alive.

JACKIE: Ask your buddies how that worked out for them.

6.2 CU Empress trembling. She knows she's supposed to bring him in alive, but the sight of her dead comrades is burning through her resolve.

EMPRESS: You- you-

6.3 CU enraged Empress finally losing it.

EMPRESS: Raaaaaggh!

6.4 Wide. Behind Empress as she throws the javelin right through Jackie's heart, pinning him to the concrete wall.

JACKIE: C'mo-

SFX: Shrakk-k!

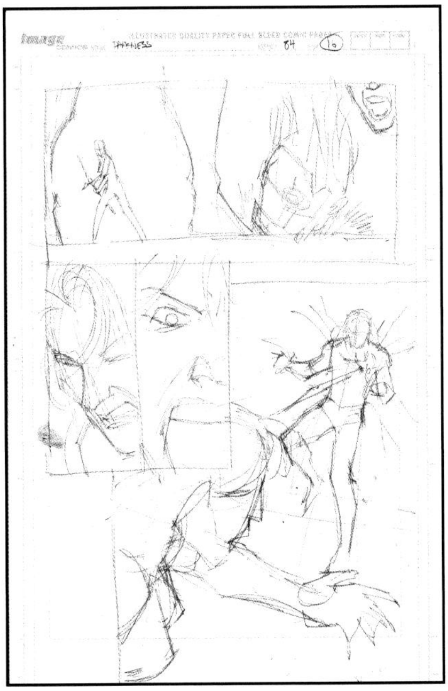

thumbnail

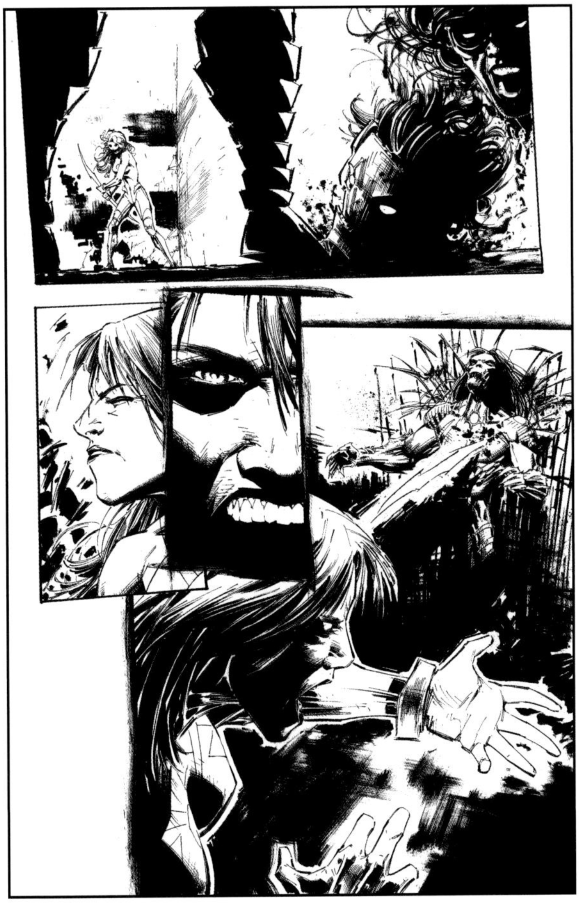

line art

17.1 We're back at the utility room. Darling has punched like six holes through the cinderblock wall and is launching another. High angle establishing shot.

1 CAP: Agent Darling
Operation Umbra
Mission clock: 6:07:45

2 DARLING: Getting kind of bright in there, huh?

17.2 MCU of Darling smashing through wall elbow deep.

3 DARLING: Finding it hard to work your creepy magic, I bet.

4 SFX: Throk! Spluk!

17.3 Repeat 17.2 but Darling comes to a compete stop.

5 DARLING: Uh-Oh.

6 DARLING: That sounded like I hit-

17.4 Repeat 17.3, but Darling pulls a bloody fist (intact- he's fine- he fears he pulped Jackie) from the hole.

7 DARLING: Ugh.

17.5 Inside the dark room as Darling forces the door open a sliver to peek inside.

8 SFX: Rrrnch! Kreeek!

17.6 High angle behind Darling as he stands in front of wide open door. Jackie lies on the door of the small room (like 5x5) with his head smashed. Pipes and ducts running up the wall. NOTE: As the light from the open door hits Jackie's legs they begin to smoke and melt- the light disintegrating darkness constructs.

9 DARLING: So much for bringing him back alive.

10 SFX: Fsssss!

DARLING
HOLES IN WALL
HOLE IN WALL
DARLING BLOODY HAND
DARLING
DARKNESS
DOOR

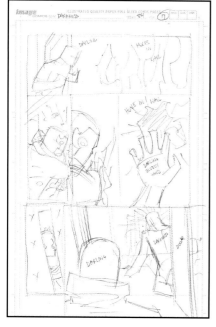

thumbnail

line art

18.1 Low angle in front of Darling as he clicks his radio back on. Smoke trails up in front of him.

1 SFX: >klik<

2 DARLING: Uh, hey, Empress?

3 EMPRESS (RADIO): Darling? Darling is that really you?

18.2 Repeat 17.6, but Darling stands back from the room reacting quizzically to Empress' relief. The Jackie body is really dissolving now.

4 OP DARLING: Sure, why wouldn't it be?

5 OP EMPRESS (RADIO): I- never mind. I have Estacado. Round up Trinh and get back to the LZ.

18.3 CU Darling looking back down at Jackie's dissolved body in bewilderment.

6 DARLING: You have Estacado? But-

7 DARLING: Err, yeah. Be right there.

18.4 Darling dashes away from the ruined utility room, Jackie's body now just a wisp of smoke in the morning light.

8 DARLING: Don't look a gift horse in the mouth, Darling, old boy.

9 DARLING: Might make the A-team yet.

18.5 From behind Darling as he shouts down at Trinh from the level above. You know how from certain angles you can see from one deck of a parking ramp down into the lower one? Like that. We can see Trinh, but we can't see what's just in front of him (important). Trinh stands in a puddle of black murk that could be blood.

10 CAP: Agents Darling, Trinh
Operation Umbra
Mission clock: 6:11:52

11 DARLING: Trinh!

12 DARLING: The hell are you up to down there?

18.6 MCU Darling shouting down to Trinh, maybe some ducts, pipes, etc., between them.

13 DARLING: Quit fucking around. Empress says she caught him.

14 TRINH OP: Caught him?

18.7 Low angle CU of Trinh as he looks at something off panel in front of and above him. Black blood coats his arms.

15 DARLING OP: You heard me. Now get your ass up to the top floor.

16 TRINH: Caught him. Hmmm.

thumbnail

line art

19.1 From behind Trinh as we can finally see what he was looking at. It's Jackie's body completely gutted and hanging from the pipes and struts of the deck above. His black guts are splayed out and against the wall, like Trinh was playing with them, turning them into some kind of sick art. A flat pane of light begins to creep toward it as the sun rises. Where the sun catches the body it begins to smoke (another facsimile).

1 TRINH: Heh. Trinh having a funny day.

19.2 On the roof. Empress is dragging Jackie's body from the shadows toward the chopper. Darling and Trinh now surround her. High angle.

2 CAP: Agents Empress, Darling, Trinh; Pilot Claymoore
Operation Umbra
Mission clock: 6:15:27

3 DARLING: I should have known you'd bag him.

19.3 2 shot of impressed Darling and disappointed Empress.

4 DARLING: What happened to bringing him in alive?

5 EMPRESS: I- I don't know. I kind of lost it, I guess.

19.2 Low angle behind Empress in XFG as she drags the body into the light. It begins to smoke behind her. Darling notices in BG.

6 DARLING: Holy shit. That ain't the only thing you're losing.

DARKNESS
TRIHN
DARLING
EMPRESS

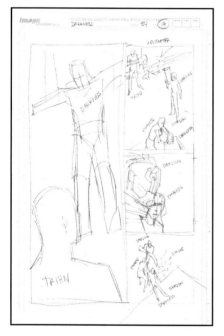

thumbnail

line art

20.1 High angle. The three agents, now in full sunlight, stand around the smoking, almost ghost-like body of Jackie as it dissipates and rises into the sky. All shocked. Big panel.

1 EMPRESS: He- he's gone.

2 DARLING: Yeah, my advice is to get some sleep on the flight back.

3 TRINH: Funny, funny day.

20.2 Low angle. In the XFG we see a final puddle of smoking Darkness matter. Empress stunned in MG. In BG Darling strolls toward the chopper, Trinh loping before him. Darling is like, "Hey, c'est la vie!"

4 DARLING: We're going to be in debrief a looong time.

20.3 Wide. We're back in the one-way mirror room with he two bureaucrats. Make sure it's angled so we can see Empress in the room behind the glass with the MiB's.

5 BUREAUCRAT #2: Our best guess is that Empress actually killed Estacado while Darling and Trinh simply mistook those gremlin-like henchmen he conjures for Estacado himself.

6 BUREAUCRAT #1: What did they call those things in the file?

20.4 Shot past standing Bureaucrat #2 as he looks down at a shocked Bureaucrat #1.

7 BUREAUCRAT #2: Darklings.

8 BUREAUCRAT #1: Jesus, really?

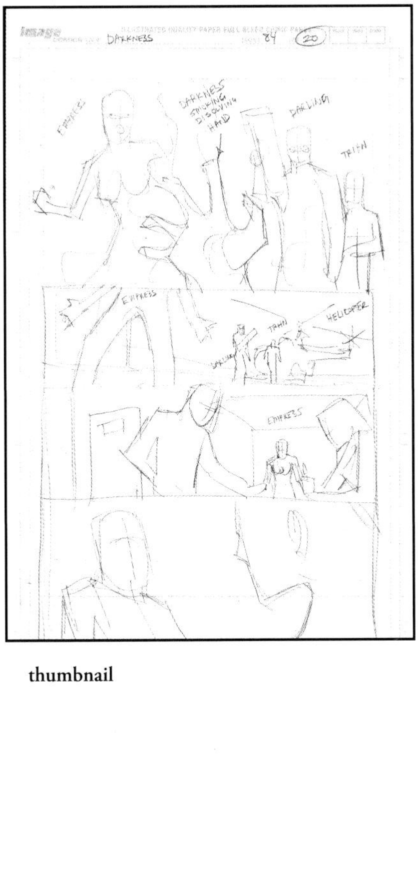
DARKNESS
DARLING
TRINH
EMPRESS
HELICOPTER
EMPRESS

thumbnail

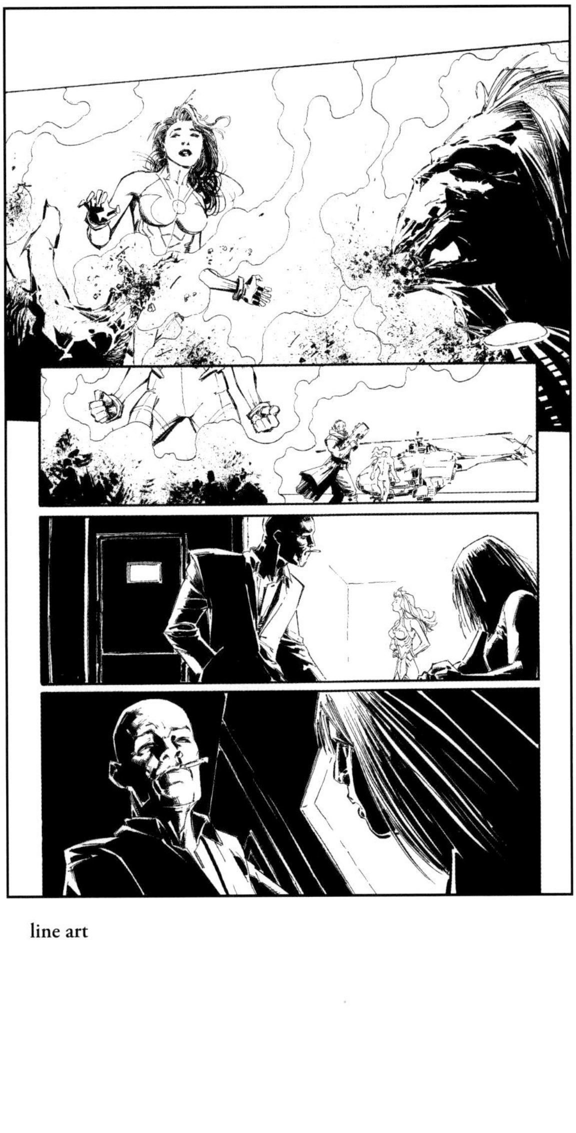

line art

21.1 Begin a voice over sequence. The bureaucrats continue to talk, but our scene has shifted BACK to the parking ramp. The chopper has lifted off and is zooming away from the scene. The sun has risen higher into the sky.

1 BUREAUCRAT #2 VO: Just to be on the safe side they made another sweep of the structure.

21.2 Shot of a really ragged looking homeless woman all bundled in rags and tatters carrying a garbage bag, her loyal dog following, as they emerge from a ground floor side door of the ramp. The tall building casting them in shadow.

2 BUREAUCRAT #2 VO: Only thing they found was a homeless woman and her dog living in the subbasement.

21.3 From just above and behind the woman as she looks back at the camera suspiciously. Light begins to fall on her from the rising sun.

3 BUREAUCRAT #1 VO: A woman? You sure?

4 BUREAUCRAT #2 VO: Yeah, drunk off her ass.

21.4 Worm's eye view of the woman's and dog's feet as they walk away from camera toward the fence of construction area. Little wisps of smoke start to trail from them.

5 BUREAUCRAT #2 VO: Seemed to be in her late fifties, early sixties. Didn't see a thing.

6 SFX: Fssss-

21.5 The feet are now obviously Jackie's, but a few tendrils of smoke still drift from them. The dog is completely gone.

7 BUREAUCRAT #1 VO: So as far as Operation Umbra goes we either killed Estacado, or he just made Houdini look like a rank amateur.

8 SFX: Fssss-

21.6 Repeat 21.3, but instead of an old woman looking back at us, it's Jackie, a few tendrils of Darkness smoke still drifting off of him.

9 BUREAUCRAT #1 VO: Either way we're still completely in the dark.

10 CAP: NEXT: Alkonost

thumbnail

line art

Ready for more? Jump into the Top Cow Universe with more of *The Darkness*!

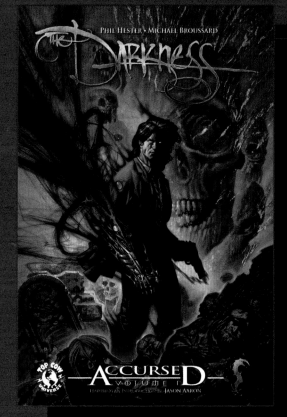

The Darkness
Accursed vol.1

written by:
Phil Hester

pencils by:
Michael Broussard

Mafia hitman Jackie Estacado was both blessed and cursed on his 21st birthday when he became the bearer of The Darkness, an elemental force that allows those who wield it access to an otherwordly dimension and control over the demons who dwell there. Forces for good in the world rise up to face Jackie and the evil his gift represents, but there is one small problem. In this story...they are the bad guys.

Now's your chance to read "Empire," the first storyline by the new creative team of Phil Hester (*Firebreather*, *Green Arrow*) and Michael Broussard (*Unholy Union*) that marked the shocking return of *The Darkness* to the Top Cow Universe!

Book Market Edition
(ISBN: 978-1-58240-958-0) $9.99

The Darkness
Accursed vol.2

written by: Phil Hester

pencils by: Jorge Lucas, Michael Broussard, Joe Benitez, Dale Keown and more!

Collects *The Darkness* volume 3 #7-10 and the double-sized *The Darkness #75* (issue #11 before the Legacy Numbering took effect), plus a cover gallery and behind-the-scenes extras!

(ISBN: 978-1-58240-044-4) $9.99

The Darkness
Accursed vol.3

written by: Phil Hester

pencils by: Michael Broussard, Jorge Lucas, Nelson Blake II and Michael Avon Oeming.

Collects issues #76-79 plus the stand alone Tales of The Darkness story entitled "Lodbrok's Hand." Features art by regular series artist Michael Broussard (*Unholy Union*, *Artifacts*), Nelson Blake II (*Magdalena*, *Broken Trinity: Witchblade*), Jorge Lucas (*Broken Trinity: Aftermath*, *Wolverine*), and Michael Avon Oeming (*Mice Templar*, *Powers*)

(ISBN: 978-1-58240-100-7) $12.99

Enjoy *The Darkness*? Explore the Top Cow Universe with *Witchblade*!

RON MARZ • MIKE CHOI
WITCHBLADE
VOLUME 1
FEATURING AN INTRODUCTION BY
RON MARZ

Witchblade

volume 1 - volume 8

written by:
Ron Marz
art by:
Mike Choi, Stephen Sadowski, Keu Cha, Chris Bachalo, Stjepan Sejic and more!

Get in on the ground floor of Top Cow's flagship title with these affordable trade paperback collections from Ron Marz's series-redefining run on Witchblade! Each volume collects a key story arc in the continuing adventures of Sara Pezzini and the Witchblade, culminating in the epic 'War of the Witchblades' storyline!

Book Market Edition, **volume 1**
collects issues #80-#85
(ISBN: 978-1-58240-906-1) $9.99

RON MARZ • MIKE CHOI • CHRIS BACHALO • KEU CHA
WITCHBLADE
FEATURING AN INTRODUCTION BY
PHIL HESTER

WITCHBLADE
VOLUME 3

RON MARZ • ADRIANA MELO • STJEPAN SEJIC • SAMI BASRI
WITCHBLADE
VOLUME 4

WITCHBLADE
FEATURING AN INTRODUCTION BY
ROBERT KIRKMAN

volume 2
collects issues #86-#92
(ISBN: 978-1-58240-886-6)
U.S.D. $14.99

volume 3
collects issues #93-#100
(ISBN: 978-1-58240-887-3)
U.S.D. $14.99

volume 4
collects issues #101-109
(ISBN: 978-1-58240-898-9)
U.S.D. $17.99

volum
collects issues #110-1
First Born issues #
(ISBN: 978-1-58240-899
U.S.D. $17

WITCHBLADE

RON MARZ • STJEPAN SEJIC
WITCHBLADE
VOLUME 7

WITCHBLADE

volume 6
collects issues #116-#120
(ISBN: 978-1-60706-041-3)
U.S.D. $14.99

volume 7
collects issues #121-#124 &
Witchblade Annual #1
(ISBN: 978-1-60706-058-1)
U.S.D. $14.99

volume 8
collects issues #125-#130
(ISBN: 978-1-60706-102-1)
U.S.D. $14.99

Check out more from DiVide and Top Cow Productions, Inc.!

Berserker
vol.1

written by:
Rick Loverd
art by:
Jeremy Haun

The lives of Aaron and Farris, two young and completely different men, are turned upside down when they discover an animalistic and uncontrollable rage living inside them. Meanwhile, two mysterious organizations seek them out for their newfound strength and power for their own purposes. But what good is strength and power when you can't tell friend from foe?

From screenwriter Rick Loverd and artist Jeremy Haun (*Detective Comics, Leading Man*) featuring cover gallery with works by Haun and Dale Keown.

(ISBN: 978-1-60706-109-0) $14.99

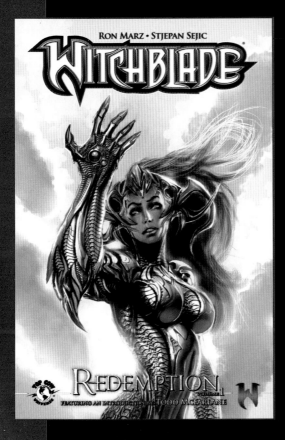

Witchblade
Redemption vol.1

written by:
Ron Marz
art by:
Stjepan Sejic

After the tumultuous events of 'War of the Witchblades,' New York City Police Detective Sara Pezzini is once more the sole bearer of the Witchblade, a mysterious artifact that takes the form of a deadly and powerful gauntlet. Now Sara must try reconcile her darker side while controlling the Witchblade, even as she investigates the city's strangest, most supernatural crimes.

In this first volume of the "Redemption" book series, readers are reintroduced to Sara, her boyfriend and partner, Patrick Gleason, and the strange, supernatural world of the Witchblade. Fans are also reintroduced to Aphrodite IV, the fan favorite emerald-haired cyborg assassin.

This volume collects issues #131-136 by long time writer Ron Marz (*Artifacts*) and artistic partner Stjepan Sejic (*Angelus*) and is a perfect introductory volume for new readers.

Book Market Edition
(ISBN: 978-1-60706-193-9) $9.99

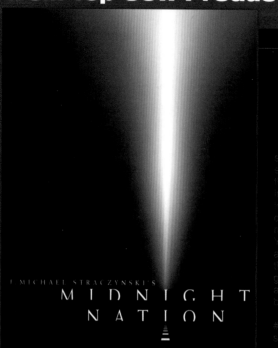